Populism and the Mirror of Democracy

Populism and the Mirror of Democracy

Edited by
FRANCISCO PANIZZA

VERSO
London • New York

First published by Verso 2005
© in the collection, Verso 2005
© in the contributions, the individual contributors 2005

1 3 5 7 9 10 8 6 4 2

Verso
UK: 6 Meard Street, London W1F 0EG
US: 20 Jay Street, Suite 1010, Brooklyn, NY 11201
www.versobooks.com

Verso is the imprint of New Left Books

ISBN 1-85984-489-8 (Paperback)
ISBN 1-85984-523-1 (Hardback)

British Library Cataloguing in Publication Data
Populism and the mirror of democracy. – (Phronesis)
1. Populism 2. Democracy
I. Panizza, Francisco
321.5'13

Library of Congress Cataloging-in-Publication Data
A catalog record for this book is available from the Library of Congress

Typeset in Garamond
Printed in the US

CONTENTS

INTRODUCTION

Populism and the Mirror of Democracy

FRANCISCO PANIZZA

Reading populism

It has become almost a cliché to start writing on populism by lamenting the lack of clarity about the concept and casting doubts about its usefulness for political analysis.[1] Populism is a contested concept and agreements on what it means and who qualifies as a populist are difficult because, unlike other equally contested concepts such as democracy, it has become an analytical attribution rather than a term with which most political actors would willingly identify.[2] But unless we perform a Brechtian gesture and abolish the people, populism is part of the modern political landscape and will remain so in the future. However, while there is no scholarly agreement on the meaning of populism, it is possible to identify an analytical core around which there is a significant degree of academic consensus. This core is both theoretically elegant and, as the contributions to this volume show, provides the basis for rich empirical analysis. After briefly surveying the main approaches to populism, I will present populism's analytical core in terms of three elements: a mode of identification, a process of naming and a dimension of politics. In the following sections, I look at the conditions of emergence of populism and address three key questions necessary for understanding it: Who are the people? Who speaks for the people? How does populist identification take place? I illustrate my arguments with references to cases of populist politics from the contributors to this volume as well as examples taken from studies of populism in Latin America and elsewhere. I conclude this introduction with some reflections on the relations between politics, populism and democracy.

What is Populism?

There is little purpose in attempting to summarise the many studies of populism in the already vast academic literature on the topic. However, as part of the intellectual inquiry leading to the concept's analytical core it is important to distinguish between three ways of approaching populism, which in turn have significant internal variations. The purpose of this overview is not to look in detail at contending theories of populism, but rather to highlight the problems raised by the different approaches, as well as to draw attention to some shared assumptions that will be examined in more detail in the discussion of the concept's analytical core. For this purpose I will divide approaches to populism into three broad categories: a) empirical generalisations; b) historicist accounts; and c) (following Stavrakakis in Chapter 9, this volume) 'symptomatic readings'.

The empiricist approach looks at alleged cases of populism in an attempt to extract a set of positive definitional characteristics that could provide a distinctive group of attributes to characterise the phenomenon. One of the earliest examples of this approach is Peter Wiles' definition of populism that includes twenty-four different features, which unless we are told what their mutual relation is, makes the categorisation meaningless.[3] Other scholars list a more limited number of attributes and blend them together in a loosely descriptive definition, but the results are scarcely more illuminating.[4] Some empiricist studies of populism construct typologies of the concept. But while typologies have a useful role to play in political analysis, if they are not built up around a conceptual core they cannot account for the common element that binds together their otherwise heterogeneous elements. Most observers assume the common element to exist when they use the term populism but, for the most part, they do so implicitly and intuitively rather than explicitly and analytically. Yet such assumptions are by no means self-evidently justifiable.[5]

A second approach consists in linking populism to a certain historical period, social formation, historical process or set of historical circumstances. Typical of the historicist reading is the vast literature on Latin American populism that restricts the term to the golden era of populist politics, spanning from the economic crisis of the 1930s to the demise of the import-substitution-industrialisation (ISI) model of development in the late 1960s. This approach stresses the close association between populist politics – as a class alliance under the leadership of a charismatic leader such as Juan Domingo Perón in Argentina, Getúlio Vargas in Brazil and Lázaro Cárdenas in Mexico – and the ISI development strategy.[6] While the considerable number of populist regimes that were in power in the region over that period needs to be accounted for, this restricted interpretation of populism fails to justify its self-imposed narrow geographical and temporal limits, which exclude earlier and later cases of populism in Latin America and elsewhere.

In contrast with the previous approaches, a symptomatic reading of populism incorporates some of the features that characterise populism according to the empiricist and historicist approaches, but justifies their inclusion in terms of the concept's analytical core, based on the constitution of the people as a political actor.[7] This approach understands populism as an anti-status quo discourse that simplifies the political space by symbolically dividing society between 'the people' (as the 'underdogs') and its 'other'.[8] Needless to say, the identity of both 'the people' and 'the other' are political constructs, symbolically constituted through the relation of antagonism, rather than sociological categories. Antagonism is thus a mode of identification in which the relation between its form (the people as signifier) and its content (the people as signified) is given by the very process of naming – that is, of establishing who the enemies of the people (and therefore the people itself) are. An anti-status quo dimension is essential to populism, as the full constitution of popular identities necessitates the political defeat of 'the other' that is deemed to oppress or exploit the people and therefore to impede its full presence. The specific content of a given populist appeal varies in accordance with the different ways this antagonistic relationship is defined. The *'other'*, in opposition to 'the people', can be presented in political or economic terms or as a combination of both, signifying 'the oligarchy', 'the politicians', a dominant ethnic or religious group, the 'Washington insiders', 'the plutocracy' or any other group that prevents the people achieving plenitude. The antagonism between the *people* and its *other* and the promise of plenitude once the enemy is vanquished is neatly presented in the following popular song, sung in Peru by supporters of Alianza Popular Revolucionaria Americana (APRA), one of Latin America's historic populist parties:

> Aprista forever forward
> Aprista we must fight
> The oligarchy will eventually be defeated
> And there will be happiness in our motherland[9]

Populism is thus a mode of identification available to any political actor operating in a discursive field in which the notion of the sovereignty of the people and its inevitable corollary, the conflict between the powerful and the powerless, are core elements of its political imaginary.[10] As Ross Perot put it, with striking clarity, 'We [the people]'re the owners of this country…', a statement echoed with a more rhetorical flourish by Venezuela's leader Hugo Chávez: 'I declare the people to be the only and the true owners of their sovereignty. I declare the Venezuelan people the true owners of their own history.'[11]

The notion of the *sovereign people* as an actor in an antagonistic relation with the established order, as the core element of populism, has a long tradition in the writings on the topic. Edward Shils claimed that populism involves subscription to two cardinal principles: the notion of the supremacy of the will of the people, and the notion of the direct relationship between people and the government.[12] Elaborating on Shils' insights, Peter Worsley summarised this commonality when he noted that, at its very loosest, the term 'populism' had been used to describe any movement invoking the name of the people.[13] More recently, Margaret Canovan advances a definition of populism that shares with Worsley, Shils and Laclau the claim that the constitution of popular identities is at the heart of the populist appeal, by arguing that populism in modern democratic societies 'is best seen as an appeal to "the people" against both the established structure of power and the dominant ideas and values of society.'[14]

The populists' claim to embody the will of the people is hardly new or original. Notions of 'the people' and of popular sovereignty are at the heart of the narratives of political modernity and, as Canovan notes, are related to key questions about the meaning and nature of democracy. Moreover, in modern politics almost every political speech appeals to the people or claims to speak for the people, which could make it impossible to distinguish populist from non-populist political entities. But if we want to remain within a non-essentialist notion of populism we need to agree that 'the people' has no fixed referent or essential meaning, which amounts to concurring with the Humpty Dumpty-like assertion that the term means what its users choose it to mean.[15] However, to claim that 'the people' has no ultimate meaning or fixed referent is not the same as saying that it has no meaning at all. Rather, it is to argue that its meaning is constituted by the very process of naming or, as Oscar Reyes puts it in Chapter 4, that it is determined by a process of naming that retroactively determines its meaning.

Worsley notes that appeals to the people *embrace and wean from existing attachments* 'workers, peasant/farmers, micro-entrepreneurs, tribesmen; anyone small, threatened, xenophobic [...] offering to all these a new communal transectional identity [...] *the Volk*'.[16] This double process of de-identification and re-identification – Worsley's 'embracing and weaning' – is central for the constitution of collective identities. Chantal Mouffe (Chapter 2) highlights the centrality of antagonism in the process of deconstruction and reconstruction of identities when she claims – against all those who believe that politics can be reduced to individual motivations and is driven by the pursuit of self-interest – the populists are well aware that politics always consists of the creation of an 'Us' versus a 'Them'. In its extreme form, antagonism may include an element of physical violence. In his analysis of Palestinian nationalism Glenn Bowman (Chapter 5) shows how violence plays a constitutive role in the formation of nationalist identities. But antagonism is not necessarily about physical violence or even the threat of violence. Rather, it is a mode of identification. As Ernesto Laclau argues in Chapter 1, the constitution of the political frontier between the underdogs and the powerful requires that the particularities that make up the signifier 'the people' become elements in a chain of equivalences in which they only have in common the relation of antagonism itself. In other words, we can only name the people by naming its *other* because, paraphrasing Bowman, in oppressing all of them, the oppressor simultaneously renders all of them 'the same'.

The constitutive role of antagonism in processes of identification can be illustrated by the events of September 11, 2001. The inhabitants of the US are deeply fragmented by race, class, gender, religion and other markers of identity. Prior to September 11, they were also deeply divided politically, following an election that raised serious questions about the legitimacy of George W. Bush's victory. However, the terrorist attack of September 11 temporarily suspended the web of differences that traverse American society and made the people of the US identify themselves as 'Americans' – that is, as a single people threatened (in this case) by a violent external enemy. It would be wrong, however, to equate the appalling physical violence of the 9/11 attack with the constitution of a relation of antagonism. The attack itself was a material event that only acquired its meaning by being placed within a certain discursive framework in which the relation of antagonism was constituted. It was not the planes crashing into the World Trade Center but President Bush's famous 'Either you are with us, or with the terrorists' that crystallised this antagonism. In his dichotomisation of the political space Bush erased all internal differences among the US people and constituted them into a collective 'Us' against a 'Terrorist Other'. In this formulation, the positive value of the 'Us' derives not so much from the abstract opposition between 'us and them' but from the normative value implicit in the actual naming of the 'them' as the terrorists. Terror, and not any 'them', is the normative constitutive outside of Bush's 'Us'.

The process of naming – Bush's 'Us'– did not create an American people out of a blank canvass, as obviously there was an American identity before September 11. As Sebastián Barros (Chapter 10) puts it, novelty is never completely new but always bears the traces of the relative structurality of the dislocated order, which sets up its conditions of production and reception. While US society was subject to different forms of fragmentation and dislocation prior to September 11 it was nonetheless a society in which social relations structured relatively stable identities. This means that Bush's process of constituting the 'Us' of American identity was partially grounded in existing forms of American patriotism and previous versions of what it is to be American. And yet, Bush's naming was not just the retrieving of an already fully constituted identity. It also redefined what the meaning of being American is. As he put it in his State of the Union address of January 2002, perhaps unaware of the full implications of his remark: '*Yet after America was attacked, it was as if our entire country looked into a mirror and saw our better selves.*' He was, of course, the one holding the mirror for the people to identify with and to make sense of 9/11. And he used the mirror of identification to redefine what it means to be American. Remarkably for a right-wing individualist, Bush's American people embraced collective goals and self-sacrifice in a way reminiscent of Kennedy's phrase, much maligned by the libertarian right, 'Ask not what your country can do for you; ask what you can do for your country.'

> We were reminded that we are citizens, with obligations to each other, to our country, and to history. We began to think less of the goods we can accumulate, and more about the good we can do. For too long our culture has said, 'If it feels good, do it.' Now America is embracing a new ethic and a new creed: 'Let's roll.' In the sacrifice of soldiers, the fierce brotherhood of firefighters, and the bravery and generosity of ordinary citizens, we have glimpsed what a new culture of responsibility could look like. We want to be a nation that serves goals larger than self.[17]

The collective 'Us' named by Bush was pregnant with ambiguity, as it begs the question of whom he was talking about when he divided the political space between 'them and us'. Did the 'Us' refer to the American people? And if so, to all of them or just some of them? Did it include non-American people? And if so, who were these others? The West? Those who share American values? Those who, irrespectively of their values, are against terrorism? Similar questions arise about the terrorist 'them-other'. The ambiguity of the expression overflowed the 'with us or against us' divide with a richness of meaning. However, Bush fixed the significance of the events of September 11 within a certain ideological tradition. By claiming that the event was the work of evil people and an attack against freedom, he crystallised the meaning of 9/11 in terms of a moral absolute that identified America as the incarnation of freedom, the master signifier of America's political discourse.[18] The constitutive force of Bush's signification of 9/11 as an attack on freedom was reinforced rather than diminished by his use of the term 'freedom'.[19] For the American people, traumatised by the attack, it provided a simple answer to the complex question of why the attack and why them.

Does Bush's constitution of a discursive antagonism between 'them and us' make him a populist? A non-essentialist reading of populism mixes awkwardly with attempts at labelling certain parties or politicians as 'populists', although in practice it is hard not to do so. Populism refers to modes of identification rather than to individuals or parties. As Michael Kazin put it, the use of the term 'populist' should be understood not to signify that his subjects *were* populists, in the way they were unionists or socialists, liberal Democrats or conservative Republicans, but rather that all these people employed populism as a flexible mode of persuasion to redefine the people and their adversaries.[20] And to say mode of persuasion is also to say mode of identification, because one is no longer 'the same person' after having been persuaded of a certain proposition.[21]

The 'other' of Bush's war on terrorism refers to a mainly external enemy defined in terms of evilness, rather than as the oppressor of the American people, but, as noted above, its ultimate meaning is never clear. The search for alleged terrorists inside the US, the suspicions aroused by Arab Americans, the calls to the people to be vigilant at home, and the detention without trial of American residents as virtual prisoners of war suggest that there is indeed an enemy within. There may be no traces in Bush's discourse of the conflict between the people and the privileged few, which would mark it as a populist mode of identification. But in his speeches about September 11 there are plenty of appeals to ordinary Americans as a virtuous people, which is part of the country's populist tradition.[22] And while 'the people' may be an empty signifier that has no fixed signified, as Joseph Lowndes puts it in Chapter 6, it always evokes the traces of a certain content shaped by language and history.

The conditions of emergence of populism

Populist practices emerge out of the failure of existing social and political institutions to confine and regulate political subjects into a relatively stable social order. It is the language of politics when there can be no politics as usual: a mode of identification characteristic of times of unsettlement and de-alignment, involving the radical redrawing of social borders along lines other than those that had previously structured society. It is a political appeal that seeks to change the terms of political discourse, articulate new social relations, redefine political frontiers and constitute new identities.

To explore further the process by which populist politics can take hold of a political formation it is necessary to look at Laclau's notion of a 'chain of equivalences' and at Worsley's 'weaning and embracing' identities. Laclau (Chapter 1) argues that the condition leading to a populist rupture is a situation in which a plurality of demands coexists with an increasing inability of the institutional system to absorb them. In this process, a populist identity emerges out of the dislocation of the specific identities of the holders of particularistic demands (neighbours, workers, peasants, the unemployed, women, ethnic groups, etc.) and their reconstitution in the imaginary unity of the people.

The image of a chain of unfulfilled demands implies the notion of politically mobilised actors advancing their demands against a political system that is unwilling or unable to address them. Thus, the notion of unmet demands presupposes an already existing political identity – however precarious and incomplete this may be – upon which the demands can be predicated, as their holders need to know who they are in order to know what they want that cannot be provided by the system. The process that transforms these demands into an antagonistic relation with the established order thus becomes an aggregation of discontents that crystallises in a new popular identity.

It is possible, however, to radicalise Laclau's arguments about the constitutive nature of representation by arguing, as Reyes (Chapter 4) does, that the demands are constructed by the other, by desire and identification. At their most radical, populist practices operate within a social space in which people have grievances, desires, needs and wants that have not yet been constituted as political demands or, to put it in another way, people do not know how to name what they are lacking.[23] In his study of Peronism, Alejandro Groppo cites old Peronist militants' claims that Perón 'awoke the workers' and that Perón awarded the workers some welfare benefits which 'the workers had never even dreamt about'.[24] A superficial reading of these quotes would take them as an example of the paternalistic, top-down nature of populism. And yet, as Groppo points out, it is possible to interpret the workers' words as signifying a political relation in which private wants and needs were transformed into public demands by the leader's action of bringing them into public discourse. As Howard Gardner put it, the leader who will succeed is the one who best senses and delivers what an audience already desires.[25] This rapport is exemplified by Steve Stein when he says that Víctor Raúl Haya de la Torre, the founder and historical leader of Peru's APRA, 'served as supreme interpreter and director [in the words of an Aprista publication] of the vague and imprecise desires of the multitude'.[26]

The metaphor of awakening suggests a dormant identity that was 'already there', but the 'awakening' can be best understood as the constitution of new political identities and the politicisation of issues that had previously not been part of the political agenda. Thus, populism is not just about a crisis of representation in which people are weaned off their old identities and embrace a new 'popular' one. It is also about the beginning of representation, allowing those who have never been represented because of their class, religion, ethnicity or geographical location, to be acknowledged as political actors. Populist leaders appeal to both the never-enfranchised and the newly disenfranchised, but there is no populist leadership unless there is a successful constitution of new identities and of a representative link with those identities. In both cases we are dealing with new relations of representation that become possible because of dislocations of the existing political order.

Traditionally, failures of representation are characteristics of times of political, cultural, social and economic upheaval, as it is at these times that previously relatively stable relations of representation and subordination become unsettled and dealigned, and thus open to new forms of identification. Without seeking to make a comprehensive typology of the conditions of emergence of populist politics, below are some of the circumstances in which relations of representation become dislocated and populism is more likely to become a dominant mode of identification.[27]

The first is a breakdown of social order and the loss of confidence in the political system's ability to restore it. Typical of these situations are economic crises manifested in phenomena such as hyperinflation. Economic crises are always about more than economics. Hyperinflation brought Hitler to power in Weimar Germany, as it did for populist politicians elsewhere, because money is a crucial institution of modern societies, articulating social relations and symbolising national identities. High inflation produces deep social dislocations as it affects notions of social time and disrupts the myriad collective and individual relations that depend on monetary exchanges. Incomes and jobs are obliterated, and the economy becomes de-institutionalised as its mooring in the national currency, the tax system and other public institutions – including the political system – is dangerously loosened.[28] Breakdowns of social order can also be produced by civil wars, ethnic conflicts or natural catastrophes. But crises are often a combination of the economic and the political. These circumstances can be exemplified by the conjuncture in which Alberto Fujimori won the Peruvian election in 1990. At the time of the election, hyperinflation and the activities of the Shining Path guerrilla group produced a breakdown of social order that affected all sectors of Peruvian society. It was in this conjuncture of extreme political and economic instability that the figure of Fujimori emerged. As John Crabtree notes, Fujimori was the product of a desperate situation in which the alternatives appeared so much less attractive. He was not chosen by the electorate because of his political programme – he made few specific promises – but because he presented himself as a complete outsider with no links with the political establishment.[29]

A second situation is the exhaustion of political traditions and the discrediting of political parties. Allegations of corruption, malpractice or, more generally, the control of public life by a non-accountable and self-serving political elite are typical of the situation in which populism takes the form of the 'politics of anti-politics', as politicians and political parties become the 'other' of the people. In these circumstances traditional ideological templates such as left and right lose their power to organise political discourse, and parties that may have been in office for a long time are swept from power. An example of this phenomenon is the dismissal of the *partidocracia* in Venezuela, where the discrediting of Acción Democrática (AD) and Copei, the two political parties that had dominated Venezuelan politics for the second half of the past century, led to their collapse and the electoral victory of former military officer Hugo Chávez in December 1998. In Europe, corruption scandals effectively finished off the Christian Democrat and Socialist parties' political machines in Italy, and allowed the emergence of Silvio Berlusconi; and – as Chantal Mouffe shows in Chapter 2 – the voters' rejection of the Social Democratic and Conservative Parties' colonisation of the Austrian state was behind the rise of Jorg Haider's Freedom Party.

A third circumstance favouring the emergence of populist politics are changes at the level of the economy, culture and society, such as processes of urbanisation and economic modernisation, shifts in the demographic balance between social classes, and between regional and ethnic groups, as well as, more recently, globalisation. Social turmoil and social mobility alter established identities, loosen traditional relations of subordination and open up new forms of identification. Not by chance were the 1930s and 1990s characterised by a flourishing of populist politics in Latin America, since these decades saw radical transformations in the region's models of development. In 1930s Argentina, a new working class composed of migrants from the rural provinces to the new industries in cities such as Buenos Aires and Rosario became the social base of Peronism in the 1940s. A similar process took place in Brazil over the same period. In the 1990s, economic liberalisation went hand in hand with populist politics in a number of Latin American countries, including Argentina, Brazil and Peru. But as Kurt Weyland suggests, in contrast to the 1930s and 1940s, in this case it was the growing urban informal sector rather than the shrinking industrial working class that provided the social bases for the new breed of populist leaders.[30] For instance, Alberto Fujimori's electoral triumph has been linked to the decline in the Lima-based white *criollo* establishment historically represented by Peru's traditional parties, and the emergence of new groups of rural migrants who have adopted urban ways, and a new 'mestizo' middle class.[31]

Finally, populist politics are also linked to the emergence of forms of political representation outside traditional political institutions. The emergence of the radio as a form of mass communication was associated with the first wave of populist leaders in Latin America and elsewhere. In Brazil, Getúlio Vargas used a radio programme, 'A Voz do Brasil', broadcast daily by a national network of radio stations, to appeal to the Brazilian people in a country that had very few means of national integration at that time. The ghost of Citizen Kane in the US and, more recently, Ross Perot's hugely successful 'infomercials' show that the mass media is also a powerful vehicle for populist politics in a country of continental size such as the US. And in Europe the rise of Pim Fortuyn in Holland was linked to his popularity as a TV social commentator.

Who are the people?

The people that is immortal will rebel energetically, drawing from within the all-conquering intelligence and the strong and vengeful arm ... Let the people be, do not obstruct her and do not fear her excesses. The people in its fury is like the Nile, it overflows but then it fertilises.[32]

Political and economic crises do not necessarily lead to populist politics. Other outcomes are possible under conditions of crisis, such as authoritarian governments, military dictatorships or the renewal of political institutions.[33] Populism is more than just a response to a political breakdown: it is an ingrained feature of the way in which politics is conducted, derived from the gap that exists between leaders and the led and the difficulties encountered by political organisations in mediating between them effectively.[34] However, crises of representation open up the possibility of the emergence of modes of identification that seek to bridge the gap between representatives and the represented in the name of the people.

But who *are* the people? And how does a fragmented and divided society become 'one people'? The question has received a variety of answers through history that are at the heart of issues of sovereignty and democracy. Tracing back the imaginary constitution of the people to early political modernity, François-Xavier Guerra notes that in the early nineteenth century the people were imagined as a living entity that 'spoke', 'wanted' or 'acted' in a unanimous way, either through particular spokesmen or by its own actions. These imaginary–real people were seen as oppressed by the powerful and prevented by them from airing their grievances, so that most of the time it remained unheard except when it burst into history, often in a brutal and uncontrolled way.[35]

As a social category the people were identified as *the plebs, el vulgo, the populace*; that is, as the lowest sectors of society defined in terms of their intellectual, cultural and socio-economic inferiority in relation to civilised society. This multitude, akin to *il popolo minuto* of medieval Italian towns, was constituted by the inhabitants of the urban slums, craftsmen, those performing menial jobs, the unemployed and those engaged in petty crime. With no formal education or political rights, this underclass erupted into political life as actors in sporadic uprisings and brutal and often unpredictable riots. Characteristically, these uprisings were perceived as events in which emotions and passions threatened not just public order but also the rationality and manners of civilised society that underpinned order. Thus, in the nineteenth century the dividing line between this dangerous and unpredictable mob and the men of good standing was often construed as the divide between civilisation and barbarism.

With the democratisation of political life there was a fundamental shift in the imagining of the people. Under democracy, the people came to be identified as the holders of sovereignty and the term became coextensive with the citizen. However, traces of the original image of the people as dangerous and irrational plebs still resonate in late modern politics, in an uneasy articulation with that of holders of democratic rights. Thus, the people of the populist imaginary can be both dangerous and noble. As Michelet points out, the people embodies two treasures: 'first is the virtue of sacrifice, and second the instinctual ways of life that are more precious than all the sophisticated knowledge of the so-called cultured men'.[36] Talking about the US populist tradition, Kazin notes that it involves the belief that 'virtue resides in the simple people, who are the overwhelming majority, and in their collective traditions'.[37] In contrast, analyses of populism rooted in theoretical traditions as different as Marxism and modernisation theory have often stressed the lower qualities of the followers of populism. So, for instance, Gino Germani, an exponent of the latter, attributes the rise of Peronism in the 1940s to an expression of the irrationality of the newly mobilised, politically inexperienced and uneducated masses.[38]

Those with first-hand experience of the eruption of the people onto the political scene have often expressed the fears raised within the establishment by the actions of the mobilised people. Referring to the birth of populism in Peru in 1930, during which working-class people staged demonstrations and riots that destroyed the residences of some prominent persons, army general and future president Oscar Benavides wrote: 'Unfortunately it appears as if a streak of ignorance, of madness, has invaded us, wresting from us our innermost feelings of nationality'; while another conservative commentator noted that 'the very bases of civilised life threaten to disappear'.[39]

Both lewd and virtuous, both irrational and an embodiment of the nation's true values, both a threat to democracy and the holders of sovereignty, contested and often mutually contradictory visions of the people determine the political terrain in which populist politics battles with its enemies to define and redefine who are 'the people' and what are their role in society. The social makeup of the people in different populist politics is diverse. The people of populist politics are not necessarily the poor, and have little to do with Marxist notions of class alliances against the economically dominant class. They are those who consider themselves as disenfranchised and excluded from public life.

In the American populist tradition – both in its early progressive version and the later conservative one – the people were identified with the ordinary (white) working man. In Canada, as David Laycock puts it in Chapter 7, they are ordinary, hard-working Canadians who have financed an unfairly re-distributive and freedom-denying regulatory welfare state. In mid-twentieth-century Latin America they were the new industrial working class and national entrepreneurs, and in its late-twentieth-century version, which associated populism with neoliberal economics, they were the unemployed and self-employed of the urban informal sector. In apartheid South Africa the people were the disenfranchised black majority, and in its post-apartheid society they were the alienated whites of Eugene Terreblanche. In Greece, they were those that identified themselves with the orthodox religious tradition (see Stavrakakis Chapter 9), while in contemporary western Europe they are often the same working-class people that voted Communist or socialist in the past.

At the heart of populist identification is an image of the fullness of the people, which is always incomplete, achieved by the exclusion of an outside that can never be fully vanquished. As Ernesto Laclau points out in Chapter 1, populism depends not only on a sense of internal homogeneity, but also on a constitutive outside – a threatening heterogeneity against which the identity is formed. The 'other' of populist identities is as diverse as the identity of the people of which it is the outside: Washington insiders and financier plutocrats epitomised the enemy of the people for America's conservative populism, as much as the threat from the black ghetto and the so-called liberal establishment. The landed elite and foreign interests represented the enemy of the people in classic Latin American populism, and corrupt politicians became its other in its late-twentieth-century version. Special interests, minority groups and rights movements such as feminists and environmentalists are the other of the people in the discourse of the Canadian right. Welfare recipients, immigrants, criminals, asylum seekers and the techno-bureaucracy of the European Union are the constitutive enemies of the people for right-wing European populists.

Political battles between the 'us and them' of populist politics involve struggles to fix and unhinge the divides that constitute populist identities, and set up new political frontiers. These battles are as much against the 'other' of the people that prevents popular identity from achieving complete fullness as they are against the enemy within, which seeks to divide the popular field or set up alternative claims to represent the people. But when the political frontier between the people and their 'other' breaks down, the previous dichotomist division of the political space ceases to operate, and a number of alternatives become possible: a system of differences may develop within which a plurality of identities becomes institutionalised in a renewed pluralist political system; alternatively, a redefinition of the populist antagonism can also emerge along different lines. For instance, in Bolivia, ethnic groups that were subsumed into a unified image of the people identified by a white or *mestizo* political leadership in early versions of Latin American populism have in its later versions used their own cultural and ethnic differences as raw materials for the constitution of new populist identities based on ethnic identification. Finally, the dissolution of populist identities can lead to the atomisation of social identities and a collapse of all relations of representation.[40]

Who speaks for the people?

I am a little of all of you
Hugo Chávez, President of Venezuela[41]

Most studies of populism regard the populist leader as an essential element of the concept. Arguably, populism does not necessarily depend on the existence of a leader. Populist parties have survived the death of their leader, as in the case of the Justicialista (Peronist) party in Argentina. In these circumstances, populism becomes a tradition embedded in the party's myths, institutions and official discourse. However, more than a quarter of a century after his death, the figure of Perón still constitutes the myth that binds the party together, and although we can talk of populist parties, governments and regimes, it is mostly the relation between the leader and his/her followers that gives populist politics its distinct mode of identification.

Populist leaders share with the broader category of *caudillos* and other types of similarly strong, personalist leaders a style of politics based on the prevalence of personal allegiances and top-down representation over party support and institutional debate. In common with *caudillos*, and in contrast with the political forms of liberal democracy based on strong institutions and checks and balances, populist leaders are a disturbing intrusion into the uneasy articulation of liberalism and democracy, and raise the spectre of a tyranny with popular support. As Juan Pablo Litchmajer put it in relation to *caudillismo*, populist leaders establish a relationship with their followers that goes against republican forms of political identification. Whereas the latter allegedly emerge out of a rational identification with the universal institutions of the republic, the former is associated with an irrational, instinctive and spontaneous identification with the strong leader.[42]

The following excerpt from the 1944 manifesto of Ecuador's Liberal party attacking populist leader José Mariá Velasco Ibarra conveys widely shared assumptions about the archaic and backward nature of the *caudillos*:

The times are not made for idolatry. They cannot be because the time for providential men has gone away. The true statesman that embodies principles, personifies collective aspirations and synthesises ideals has replaced the demagogue and the caudillo. The organisation of political parties as orienting forces of political life of nations implies the extinction of old-fashioned personalistic forms of government.[43]

And yet, against the assumptions of political modernisers, populist leaders are not anachronistic figures to be superseded by the political institutions and rational debate of modern democracy. Mouffe's chapter in this volume traces the rise of populism in contemporary Europe and analyses its very modern conditions of emergence. And as Arditi, following Manin, suggests in Chapter 3, in contemporary 'audience democracy' the populist mode of representation becomes more salient due to the personalisation of the link between candidates and voters, rather than being an awkward anachronism. In short, populism is here to stay.[44]

The attribution to the leader of ill-defined charismatic powers is a common feature of the analysis of populism. However, an historical study of some of the most prominent populist leaders would show that most of them were neither particularly charismatic nor necessarily budding tyrants. Rather, the figure of the leader functions as a signifier to which a multiplicity of meanings can be attributed or, as Jason Glynos put it, as an enigma that promises meaning: the promise of a fully reconciled people.[45] In other words, if populism can be redefined as a process of naming that retroactively determines what is the name of 'the people', the name that best fills the symbolic void through which identification takes place is that of the leader himself.

The leader's populist enigma is never more evident than when he is physically absent because of exile or other reasons, as has been the case of many populist leaders, including Velasco Ibarra in Ecuador, Haya de la Torre in Peru, and Perón in Argentina. In the leader's absence, his/her return becomes a longing that crystallises every political demand as the return of the leader carries with it a promise of redemption. In his

absence, the leader's political message becomes a floating signifier as
every utterance, letter or statement becomes open to conflicting interpretations by his followers, while the authority of the absent enunciator
cannot be used to fix its 'true meaning'.

In Ecuador the exiled former President Velasco Ibarra came to be
known as the 'Great Absentee' (*El Gran Ausente*). From exile, he became
the candidate of a broad alliance of political groups with conflicting
ideologies and interests, which was possible because the return of the
exiled Velasco came to embody the solution to all the country's problems. Meanwhile in Perú, Haya de la Torre referred to his long period in
exile in the following terms:

> I waited eight years in persecution, in prison, and in exile. Eight years of
> solitude which were eight years of unflagging determination. Often I
> was alone. Often I knew the tremendous reality *of being misunderstood and
> forgotten*. But I never faltered. The decision to conquer, in spite of all
> obstacles, I never abandoned for a single day.[46]

The physical presence of the leader does not necessarily make
populist discourse less ambiguous or less open to conflicting interpretations. People identify with a leader chiefly through the stories he or
she relates not only with words but, more broadly, by the use of
symbols, including the leader's own body and personal life. As in any
other political narrative, the narrative of populism articulates a variety
of myths, symbols, ideological themes and rational arguments,
telling its audience where the people come from, how to make sense
of their present condition, and offering a path towards a better future.
The ultimate impact of the leader's appeal depends on the particular
story that he/she relates or embodies, and the audience's reception to
the story.

At the heart of populist narratives is populism's relation with the
political. Populism both depoliticises and hyper-politicises social
relations. To this effect, the populist leader often places him/herself
symbolically outside the political realm, by claiming that he/she is not a

politician, or at least that he/she is 'not a politician like the others'. The construction of the leader as an outsider has little to do with his/her political career or institutional position. Jorge Pacheco Areco, president of Uruguay in the late 1960s, addressed the citizens in the following way after several years in office as president:

> *I am not a politician*, at least not in the common sense of the term. *I am a man* who fights with all his force against everything which is not in the national interest.
>
> ...
>
> *Mine* is the conduct of the affairs of the state, *mine* are the decisions which I have been taking – *frequently and alone* – *to defend you* from violence, inflation and the country's international discredit and economic delinquency.
>
> ...
>
> Today I came to tell you that, more than ever, I regard myself as responsible not just for leading the nation towards peace and well-being but also that, *without any intermediary*, I intend with renewed vigour to bring forward the solutions required by the new circumstances.[48]

Through his metaphorical loneliness, Pacheco placed himself discursively outside the political system and in direct relationship (*'without any intermediary'*) with the people. Politics is what traditional politicians do. The politicians, all except him, even politics as such, are not geared towards the fight against 'everything that is not in the national interest'.

The leader's personal qualities straddle the personal/political divide. As a political figure who seeks to be at the same time one of the people and their leader, the populist leader appears as an ordinary person with extraordinary attributes. Successes in business or other private pursuits are used to legitimise the leader's political persona by showing that his or her qualities are both different to and more valuable than those of ordinary politicians. As an outsider who has 'made it', the leader's journey to political leadership is not different to that of ordinary people who, through their efforts and endeavours, made it to the top of society. Ross

Perot's image as a folk billionaire is a case in point. His personal biography embodied the American Dream that any ordinary citizen can improve their lot in life through hard work and determination.[49] In a very different context, in Ecuador, Abdalá Bucaram presented himself as a person from a humble background, who belonged to the people and was discriminated against by the elites because he was the son of Lebanese immigrants. However, Bucaram sought to make clear that even if he was of the people, he was much more than the people. In his books, speeches and interviews Bucaram narrated in detail how his humble social origins had not prevented him from becoming a successful lawyer, politician and businessman, thus presenting himself as proof that ordinary people can achieve wealth and power in spite of the opposition of the establishment.[50]

In populist discourse, politics and political parties are often considered as divisive institutions that should be eliminated, or at least purified of factions and particularistic interests, to allow the people to become united. Institutions, parties and established politicians that pretend to represent the people muffle the voices they claim to represent and betray their followers. In contrast, the leader claims to have a direct rapport with the people that allows him to advance their interests without becoming prisoner to the powerful. Ross Perot highlights this condition as follows:

> The principle that separates me [from other presidential candidates] is that five and one-half million people came together on their own and put me on the ballot. I was not put on the ballot by either of the two parties, by any PAC money, by any foreign lobbyist money, by any special interest money. This is a movement that came from the people. This is the way the framers of the Constitution intended our government to be, a government that comes from the people.[51]

In order to talk politics while denouncing it as a dirty game, the populist leader often substitutes political discourse for the discourse of morals, and uses universal abstractions to contrast the high moral grounding of

his/her message with the corruption and betrayal of the political establishment. Moral divides also disqualify political adversaries, without
leaving room for legitimate dissent. But moral universals acquire a different meaning by their articulation with political signifiers. The populist
appeal of Greece's Archbishop Christodoulos (see Stavrakakis, Chapter
9) was based on his articulation of a religious and a nationalist discourse,
in which religion defines the national identity. But lay politicians likewise
appeal to lofty universals to make political points. Here is Ecuador's
Velasco Ibarra:

> All of you, in this solemn moment of the nation's history, are showing the
> world that the material is only a transitory aspect of the life of man; that
> which is eternal is the striving for moral greatness, for progress and for
> liberty.[52]

Against the corruption of politics, populism offers a promise of eman-
cipation after a journey of sacrifice. For instance, Haya de la Torre's
speeches included themes of agony, martyrdom and regeneration, blood
and purification. Suffering was the source of the spiritual energy that
could transform what was corrupt and of a material nature into a supe-
rior moral being. In Haya's own words:

> We must not forget that the Aprista has to suffer to be strong. We must
> not forget that in the Peruvian case we struggle against barbarism, against
> a caste sick with hatred, envy, old age, and lack of culture that sees with
> disdain the rise of a superior, austere, united, and young force.[53]

Identification, however, is not a process in which the leader interpellates
a passive addressee. As Gardener notes, the audience is not simply a
blank slate waiting for the first, or for the best, story to be etched on its
virginal tablet. The stories of the leader must compete with many other
extant stories and if the new stories are to succeed, they must transplant,
suppress, complement, or in some measures, outweigh the earlier story
as well as contemporary oppositional counterstories.[54]

The populist gaze

The singer [Abdalá Bucaram, a presidential candidate in Ecuador in 1996, who used to sing popular songs in his political rallies] gathered all the filth from the most pestilent sewers to throw them at the face of its audience with no other intention than to perform a spectacle.[55]

It has been claimed that populist leaders manipulate their followers, blinding them to their true interests by a mixture of propaganda and charisma. And yet manipulation and ignorance are often in the eyes of the critic. As was suggested above, the other side of populism's depoliticisation of the political is the hyper-politicisation of social relations. Populism blurs the public–private dividing line and brings into the political realm both individual and collective desires that previously had no place in public life. If the feminist movement shifted the public–private divide by claiming that the personal is political, populism erases it by making the political personal and incorporating into public life issues that were left outside the political realm by the hegemonic discourse: 'The success of Bucaram's electoral style was explained by his politicisation of everyday interactions. Many voted for him to reject the candidate of their bosses. They also voted for a candidate that symbolised plebeian culture and mannerisms.'[56] In some cases of populist politics the erosion of the divide between the personal and the political takes the form of relations of patronage and subordination:

Sánchez Cerro, on the other hand, generally avoided references to recognised occupational or social categories, emphasising instead his one-to-one commitment to each and every Peruvian ... The masses' identification with the cholo candidate [Sánchez Cerro], in turn, helped to convey a fundamental theme of his campaign: potential supporters could approach Sánchez Cerro personally to ask for individual favours.[57]

Relations of patronage are contingent and by no means characteristic of all cases of populism. However, even in those cases in which patronage is part of the populist mode of identification, the relation of exchange between the leader and his/her followers entails more than the subordination of the client to the patron. Personal needs are met by the mediation of the leader rather than as a matter of rights, but patronage exchanges are often invested with an element of social justice. A brief analysis of the testimony of Julio Rocha, an eighty-five-year-old follower of Haya de la Torre, illustrates the articulation of the personal and the political in the populist mode of identification. Asked why he was a follower of Haya, Rocha answered:

> The reason is the affection, the love and the care he has had for all of us. [He is] a gentleman that has shown appreciation for everybody, from the lowest person to the highly placed and from the highly placed to the lowest, from the millionaire to the poor. Not everybody does this. In the public meetings, for instance, at the very least he shook your hand and this showed such kindly affection ... [We follow him] because of this and at the same time because of the struggle he brought to us, to elevate ourselves a little, to make us aware of our human rights, of the rights that we all ought to have.[58]

Notable here is the erosion of the dividing line between the personal and the political, as it is both Haya's personal love and affection *and* his bringing the struggle to the workers to make them aware of their rights that are cited by Rocha as the reasons for his identification with Haya. Personal and political dignity (recognition) are inseparable in Rocha's narrative, as in many other accounts of populist identification. In a context in which the divide between the elite and the lower sectors of society was as deep as in Peru in the 1930s, the rituals of everyday life exchanges between members of the elite and the people reinforced the markers of subordination. Within this context the typical politician's gesture of shaking hands with ordinary people acquired a different dimension from the routine nature of the gesture in more equal societies: it became a marker of political equality and personal recognition. However, Rocha was not a politically naïve person who could be contented with empty gestures. He had been a trade unionist before Haya came to public life. He continued to fight for the rights of the Peruvian people under his leadership, and he stressed the fight for workers' rights that was part of Haya's political campaign.

As noted above, a key element in many accounts of populist identification is the dignity and recognition that the leader brings to his/her followers. As a Brazilian worker wrote to President Vargas of Brazil in 1939, in contrast with his predecessor, who looked down on the workers, Vargas had acknowledged that they were 'worthy people' and 'legitimate sons of Brazil', and he had granted them 'wise and patriotic laws'. In other words, Vargas had for the first time in Brazil's history imbued the workers with personal dignity and political legitimacy, as well as passing legislation to advance their interests.[59] As was said of the relation of Ecuador's Velasco Ibarra to his followers, 'He made them feel important, like participants in charting Ecuador's destinies.'[60]

While material concessions are an important element for the identification of the leader with his followers, the symbolic dimension of the process cannot be separated from its material elements. Slavoj Žižek notes that imaginary identification is identification with the image in which we appear likeable to ourselves. Žižek points out that the trait by which we identify with someone is by no means necessarily a glamorous feature. This trait can also be a certain failure, weakness or even the guilt of the other, so that by pointing out the failure we can unwittingly reinforce the identification.[61] Identification with an apparent failure of the other explains why it is that the more their adversaries demonise the populist leaders, the more it usually reinforces the people's identification with them.

Identification is strengthened by the leader's adoption of cultural elements that are considered markers of inferiority by the dominant culture. In the US, George Wallace purposely mispronounced words to create an image of an uneducated hillbilly, a trait that highlighted both his distance from the centres of power and his proximity to the people (see Chapter 6). From Perón's vindication of the shirtless – los descamisados – in contrast to the suited followers of his country's traditional parties, to the wearing in public space of the traditional *pollera* (clothing associated with indigenous women) by Remedios Loza, a congresswoman for La Paz, Bolivia, populist leaders transform what the dominant culture considers signs of inferiority into symbols of the dignity of the people. In Ecuador, Abdalá Bucaram's lack of manners and unorthodox campaigning style, incorporating profanities and verbal improprieties, was presented by the media as an embarrassment to the country's civility, and proof that he was unfit for high office. However, as Carlos de la Torre notes, by consciously embodying the dress, language, mannerisms and masculinity of the common people, who were despised by elites and their middle-class imitators, Bucaram presented himself as a man of common origins who had ascended through society, and who deserved to be the leader of the nation: 'Bucaram inverted the meaning of accusations that he was "crazy" (*loco*) and unfit for the presidency, transforming himself into the beloved *loquito* (the diminutive of *loco*) Abdalá.'[62]

Populist identification also derives from what Oscar Reyes calls 'the solidarity of the dirty secret'.[63] The populist leader who says what 'we all secretly think but feel guilty about' changes the rules of political discourse, and transforms what the hegemonic discourse regards as the irrational prejudice of uneducated people into part of the political agenda. Wallace's use of racial coding to appeal beyond his traditional southern constituency was an example of this discursive operation, as was Pim Fortuyn's ability to articulate popular concerns about immigrants within the Netherland's liberal hegemonic discourse (we cannot tolerate more Muslim immigrants because they discriminate against women and will destroy our tolerant culture).

However, populism's idealisation of the 'good common people' – an image as far removed from the complexity of popular culture and beliefs as the upper-class denigration of the populace as irrational ignoramuses – also serves to legitimise relations of domination. By turning upside down the traditional view of the southern rednecks as backward bigots, and transforming it into the very essence of what being American was about, Wallace was legitimising a vision of America that consolidated the marginalisation of black people and the acceptance of the racial status quo. And while Fortuyn's political discourse was ideologically much more complex than Wallace's, he nonetheless gave political respectability to prejudices against immigrants.

Populism, politics and democracy

The divide between the people and its 'other' defines the political nature of populism. Antagonism is central to politics, because it is through antagonism that political identities are constituted, and radical alternatives to the existing order can be imagined. As Laclau argues, without the traces of social division we have no politics but administration. But Laclau's argument is vulnerable to the misrepresentation that the only form of politics is the permanent revolution, in which the creation and recreation of an enemy is a necessary condition for political action. However, if populism is politics par excellence (based as it is on relations of antagonism), it also represents the negation of politics. The unified people at one with its leader, as represented in the populist imaginary, defines the end of history as much as liberalism's illusion of pluralism without antagonism, the social order of Hobbes' Leviathan or Marx's classless society. Of course, the final unity of the people is an illusion, as is a classless society. As Laclau reminds us, because it is impossible to erase the traces of the particular from the universal, identification always fails to produce full identities. Rather, it generates a dialectic of aspiration, disappointment, and grievances.[64]

Politics is about challenging the institutional order with the radical language of the excluded, but it is also a dimension of the practices that make institutions operative, and contribute to both their subsistence and erosion through time. As such, it operates in the spaces between the political logic of the permanent revolution and the technocratic logic of the end of history. The fact that rights are legally codified in modern liberal democracy does not mean that their existence is only conceivable in legal or administrative discourse. Democratic demands are as much constitutive of the political in modern societies as is the chain of equivalences that subvert the said order.

This brings us to some final considerations on the relations between populism and democracy, a topic that is addressed by several of the contributors to this volume (see particularly Mouffe and Arditi). Populism has traditionally been regarded as a threat to democracy. The vertical relation between the populist leader and his/her followers; the alleged appeal to the raw passions and basest instincts of the crowd; the disregard for political institutions and the rule of law – all make populism an easy target for those who use it as a term of derision. In most cases of populism, top-down control tends to outweigh the empowerment that may arise from political mobilisation.[65]

However, Canovan raises a disturbing question when she asks why, if notions of popular power and popular decision are central to democracy, are populists not acknowledged as the true democrats they say they are.[66] As Mouffe in this volume reminds us, behind the rise of right-wing populism in contemporary Europe is an attempt to reassert popular sovereignty as the essence of democracy, an aspect that has been substantially underplayed in actually existing liberal democratic regimes.

Populism may expose liberalism's democratic blindspots, but its relation with democracy is also problematic. If democracy is about the enactment of the will of the people, its survival depends on the acknowledgement that the people's will can never be fully enacted, and that the people do not exist except as part of an ever-receding imaginary horizon. In other words, because there could only be contested versions of who the people are, and who has the right to speak on their behalf, we can only have provisional versions of popular sovereignty, and therefore the argument for the toleration of differences is not only a liberal argument but a democratic argument as well. As Claude Lefort reminds us, in a democracy power is an 'empty place' that can only be provisionally occupied.[67] If the uncertainty associated with a place of power which remains 'empty' is negated by a political discourse that claims to speak for the people as its unmediated representative – and which, under the cover of this identification, seeks to appropriate the place of power – it is democracy itself, and not just liberalism, that is being denied. Taken to the extreme populism descends into totalitarianism. Democracy, as a space of contest, hinges on recognising both the constitutive lack at the centre of being and the longings for wholeness that people invest in identification with others; a double recognition that helps to keep open the space of contestation by, in William Connolly's words, 'loosening demands for a generalized way of being'.[68]

This does not mean that populism is necessarily a form of totalitarianism, or that it is always the enemy of democracy. Attempts to enact the will of the people are an intrinsic part of democratic struggles, which have always involved a great deal more than parliamentary procedures. As Worsley puts it:

> There is always a tension in our conception of a just society between the rights of minorities and the rights of the majority. Insofar as populism plumps for the rights of majorities to make sure – by 'intervening' – that they are not ignored (as they commonly are) populism is profoundly compatible with democracy.[69]

Populism reminds us of the totalitarian ghosts that shadow democracy. But it also reminds us that all modern democratic societies are a compromise between democratic and non-democratic logics, and that the checks and balances of modern liberal democracy simultaneously guarantee and limit the popular will (as they were originally intended to do by the constitutionalists). In modern global society, populism raises uncomfortable questions about those who want to appropriate the empty site of power, but also about those who would like to subordinate politics to technocratic reason and the dictates of the market. By raising awkward questions about modern forms of democracy, and often representing the ugly face of the people, populism is neither the highest form of democracy nor its enemy, but a mirror in which democracy can contemplate itself, warts and all, and find out what it is about and what it is lacking. If the reflection is not always a pretty sight, it is because, as the ancient Greeks already knew, democracy has an underside, which they called demagogy, because democratic representation can never live up to its promise, and because even the most democratic political regime is a mixture of elements of democracy with others of a non-democratic nature in which principles of technocratic rationality and guardianship constrain or override the principle of the sovereignty of the people.

1

Populism: What's in a Name?

ERNESTO LACLAU

Any definition presupposes a theoretical grid giving sense to what is defined. This sense – as the very notion of definition asserts – can only be established on the basis of differentiating the defined term from something else that the definition excludes. This, in turn, presupposes a *terrain* within which those differences as such are thinkable. It is this terrain which is not immediately obvious when we call a movement (?), an ideology (?), a political practice (?), populist. In the first two cases – movements or ideologies – to call them populist would involve differentiating that attribute from other characterisations at the same defining level, such as 'fascist', 'liberal', 'communist', etc. This engages us immediately in a complicated and ultimately self-defeating task: finding that ultimate redoubt where we would find 'pure' populism, irreducible to those other alternative characterisations. If we attempt to do so we enter into a game in which any attribution of a social or ideological content to populism is immediately confronted with an avalanche of exceptions. Thus we are forced to conclude that when we use the term some actual meaning is presupposed by our linguistic practices, but that such a meaning is not, however, translatable into any definable sense. Furthermore, we can even less, through that meaning, point to any identifiable referent (which would exhaust that meaning).

What if we move from movements or ideologies as units of analysis, to political practices? Everything depends on how we conceive of that move. If it is governed by the unity of a subject constituted at the level of the ideology or the political movement, we have not, obviously, advanced a single step in the determination of what is specifically populist. The difficulties in determining the populistic character of the subjects of certain practices cannot but reproduce themselves in the analysis of the practices as such, as far as the latter simply *expresses* the inner nature of those subjects. There is, however a second possibility – namely, that the political practices do not *express* the nature of social agents but, instead, *constitute* the latter. In that case the political practice would have some kind of ontological priority over the agent – the latter would merely be the historical precipitate of the former. To put it in slightly different terms: practices would be more primary units of analysis than the group – that is, the group would only be the result of an articulation of social practices. If this approach is correct, we could say that a movement is not populist because in its politics or ideology it presents actual *contents* identifiable as populistic, but because it shows a particular *logic of articulation* of those contents – whatever those contents are.

A last remark is necessary before we enter into the substance of our argument. The category of 'articulation' has had some currency in theoretical language over the last thirty or forty years – especially within the Althusserian school and its area of influence. We should say, however, that the notion of articulation that Althusserianism developed was mainly limited to the *ontic* contents entering into the articulating process (the economic, the political, the ideological). There was some *ontological* theorisation as far as articulation is concerned (the notions of 'determination in the last instance' and of 'relative autonomy'), but as these formal logics appeared as necessarily derived from the ontic content of some categories (for example, the determination in the last instance could *only* correspond to the economy), the possibility of advancing an ontology of the social was strictly limited from the very beginning. Given these limitations, the political logic of populism was unthinkable.

In what follows, I will advance three theoretical propositions: 1) that to think the specificity of populism requires starting the analysis from units smaller than the group (whether at the political or at the ideological level); 2) that populism is an ontological and not an ontic category – i.e. its meaning is not to be found in any political or ideological content entering into the description of the practices of any particular group, but in a particular *mode of articulation* of whatever social, political or ideological contents; 3) that that articulating form, apart from its contents, produces structuring effects which primarily manifest themselves at the level of the modes of representation.

Social demands and social totality

As we have just asserted, our starting point should be the isolation of smaller units than the group and the consideration of the social logics of their articulation. Populism is one of those logics. Let us say, to start with, that our analysis postulates an asymmetry between the community as a whole ('society') and whatever social actor operates within it. That is, there is no social agent whose will coincides with the actual workings of society conceived as a totality. Rousseau was perfectly aware that the constitution of a general will – which was for him the condition of democracy – was increasingly difficult under the conditions of modern societies, where their very dimensions and their heterogeneity make the recourse to mechanisms of representation imperative; Hegel attempted to address the question through the postulation of a division between civil and political society, where the first represented particularism and heterogeneity (the 'system of needs') and the second the moment of totalisation and universality; and Marx reasserted the utopia of an exact overlapping between communitarian space and collective will through the role of a universal class in a reconciled society. The starting point of our discussion is that no attempt to bridge the chasm between political will and communitarian space can ultimately succeed, but that the attempt to construct such a bridge defines the specifically political articulation of social identities.

We should add, to avoid misunderstanding, that this non-overlapping between the community as a totality and the actual and partial wills of social actors does not lead us to adopt any kind of methodologically individualistic approach to the question of agency. The latter presupposes that the individuals are meaningful, self-defined totalities; it is only one step from there to conclude that social interaction should be conceived in terms of negotiations between agents whose identities are constituted around clear-cut interests. Our approach is, on the contrary, entirely holistic, with the only qualification that the promise of fullness contained in the notion of an entirely self-determined social whole is unachievable. So the attempt at building communitarian spaces out of a plurality of collective wills can never adopt the form of a contract – the latter presupposing the notions of interests and self-determined wills that we are putting into question. The communitarian fullness that the social whole cannot provide cannot be transferred either to the individuals. Individuals are not coherent totalities but merely referential identities which have to be split up into a series of localised subject positions. And the articulation between these positions is a social and not an individual affair (the very notion of 'individual' does not make sense in our approach).

So what are these smaller units from which our analysis has to start? Our guiding thread will be the category of 'demand' as the elementary form in the building-up of the social link. The word 'demand' is ambiguous in English: it has, on the one hand, the meaning of *request* and, on the other, the more active meaning of *imposing* a request – a claim – on somebody else (as in 'demanding an explanation'). In other languages, like Spanish, there are different words for the two meanings: the word corresponding to our second meaning would be *reivindicación*. Although when in our analysis we use the term 'demand' we clearly put the stress on the second meaning, the very ambiguity between both is not without its advantages, because the theoretical notion of demand that we will employ implies a certain undecidability between the two meanings – in actual fact, as we will see, they correspond to two different forms of political articulation. Let us also add that there is a common hidden assumption underlying both meanings: namely that the demand is not self-satisfied but has to be addressed to an instance different from that within which the demand was originally formulated.

Let us give the example of a straightforward demand: a group of people living in a certain neighbourhood want a bus route introduced to transport them from their places of residence to the area in which most of them work. Let us suppose that they approach the city hall with that request and that the request is satisfied. We have here the following set of structural features: 1) a social need adopts the form of a *request* – i.e. it is not satisfied through self-management but through the appeal to another instance which has the power of decision; 2) the very fact that a request takes place shows that the decisory power of the higher instance is not put into question at all – so we are fully within out first meaning of the term demand; 3) the demand is a punctual demand, closed in itself – it is not the tip of an iceberg or the symbol of a large variety of unformulated social demands. If we put these three features together we can formulate the following important conclusion: requests of this type, in which demands are punctual or individually satisfied, do not construct any chasm or frontier within the social. On the contrary, social actors are accepting, as a non-verbalised assumption of the whole process, the legitimacy of each of its instances: nobody puts into question either the right to present the request or the right of the decisory instance to take the decision. Each instance is a part (or a differential point) of a highly institutionalised social immanence. Social logics operating according to this institutionalised, differential model, we will call *logics of difference*. They presuppose that there is no social division and that any legitimate demand can be satisfied in a non-antagonistic, administrative way. Examples of social utopias advocating the universal operation of differential logics come easily to mind: the Disraelian notion of 'one nation', the Welfare State, or the Saint-Simonian motto: 'From the government of men to the administration of things'.

Let us now go back to our example. Let us suppose that the request is rejected. A situation of social frustration will, no doubt, derive from that decision. But if it is only *one* demand that is not satisfied, that will not alter the situation substantially. If, however, for whatever reason, the variety of demands that do not find satisfaction is very large, that multiple frustration will trigger social logics of an entirely different kind. If, for instance, the group of people in that area who have been frustrated in their request for better transportation find that their neighbours are equally unsatisfied in their claims at the levels of security, water supply, housing, schooling, and so on, some kind of solidarity will arise between them all: all will share the fact that their demands remain unsatisfied. That is, the demands share a *negative* dimension beyond their positive differential nature.

A social situation in which demands tend to reaggregate themselves on the negative basis that they all remain unsatisfied is the first precondition – but by no means the only one – of that mode of political articulation that we call populism. Let us enumerate those of its structural features that we can detect at this stage of our argument: 1) While the institutional arrangement previously discussed was grounded on the logic of difference, we have here an inverse situation, which can be described as a *logic of equivalence* – i.e. one in which all the demands, in spite of their differential character, tend to reaggregate themselves, forming what we will call an *equivalential chain*. This means that each individual demand is constitutively split: on the one hand it is its own particularised self; on the other it points, through equivalential links, to the totality of the other demands. Returning to our image: each demand is, actually, the tip of an iceberg, because although it only shows itself in its own particularity, it presents its own manifest claim as only one among a larger set of social claims. 2) The subject of the demand is different in our two cases. In the first, the subject of the demand was as punctual as the demand itself. The subject of a demand conceived as differential particularity we will call *democratic subject*. In the other case the subject will be wider, for its subjectivity will result from the equivalential aggregation of a plurality of democratic demands. A subject constituted on the basis of this logic we will call *popular subject*. This shows clearly the conditions for either the emergence or disappearance of a popular subjectivity: the more social demands tend to be differentially absorbed within a successful institutional system, the weaker the equivalential links will be and the more unlikely the constitution of a popular subjectivity; conversely, a situation in which a plurality of unsatisfied demands and an increasing inability of the institutional system to absorb them differentially co-exist, creates the conditions leading to a populist rupture. 3) It is a corollary of the previous analysis that there is no emergence of a popular subjectivity without the creation of an internal frontier. The equivalences are only such in terms of a lack pervading them all, and this requires the identification of the source of social negativity. Equivalential popular discourses divide, in this way, the social into two camps: power and the underdog. This transforms the nature of the demands: they cease to be simple requests and become fighting demands (*reivindicaciones*) – in other words we move to the second meaning of the term 'demand'.

Equivalences, popular subjectivity, dichotomic construction of the social around an internal frontier. We have apparently all the structural features to define populism. Not quite so, however. A crucial dimension is still missing, which we have now to consider.

Empty and floating signifiers

Our discussion so far has led us to recognise two conditions – which structurally require each other – for the emergence of a populist rupture: the dichotomisation of the social space through the creation of an internal frontier, and the construction of an equivalential chain between unfulfilled demands. These, strictly speaking, are not two conditions but two aspects of the same condition, for the internal frontier can only result from the operation of the equivalential chain. What is important, in any case, is to realise that the equivalential chain has an *anti-institutional* character: it subverts the particularistic, differential character of the demands. There is, at some point, a short-circuit in the relation between demands put to the 'system' and the ability of the latter to meet them. What we have to discuss now are the effects of that short-circuit on both the nature of the demands and the system conceived as a totality.

The equivalential demands confront us immediately with the problem of the representation of the specifically equivalential moment. For, obviously, the demands are always particular, while the more universal dimension linked to the equivalence lacks any direct, evident mode of representation. It is our contention that the first precondition for the representation of the equivalential moment is the totalisation (through signification) of the power which is opposed to the ensemble of those demands constituting the popular will. This should be evident: for the equivalential chain to create a frontier within the social it is necessary somehow to represent the other side of the frontier. There is no populism without discursive construction of an enemy: the *ancien régime*, the oligarchy, the Establishment or whatever. We will later return to this aspect. What we will now concentrate on is the transition from democratic subject positions to popular ones on the basis of the frontier effects deriving from the equivalences.

So how does the equivalence *show* itself? As we have asserted, the equivalential moment cannot be found in any positive feature underlying all the demands, for – from the viewpoint of those features – they are entirely different from each other. The equivalence proceeds entirely from the opposition to the power beyond the frontier, which does not satisfy any of the equivalential demands. In that case, however, how can the chain as such be represented? As I have argued elsewhere,[1] that representation is only possible if a particular demand, without entirely abandoning its own particularity, starts also functioning as a signifier representing the chain as a totality (in the same way as gold, without ceasing to be a particular commodity, transforms its own materiality into the universal representation of value). This process by which a particular demand comes to represent an equivalential chain incommensurable with it is, of course, what we have called *hegemony*. The demands of Solidarność, for instance, started by being the demands of a particular working-class group in Gdansk, but as they were formulated in an oppressed society, where many social demands were frustrated, they became the signifiers of the popular camp in a new dichotomic discourse.

Now there is a feature of this process of constructing a universal popular signification which is particularly important for understanding populism. It is the following: the more the chain of equivalences is extended, the weaker will be its connection with the particularistic demands which assume the function of universal representation. This leads us to a conclusion which is crucial for our analysis: the construction of a popular subjectivity is possible only on the basis of discursively producing *tendentially* empty signifiers. The so-called 'poverty' of the populist symbols is the condition of their political efficacy – as their function is to bring to equivalential homogeneity a highly heterogeneous reality, they can only do so on the basis of reducing to a minimum their particularistic content. At the limit, this process reaches a point where the homogenising function is carried out by a pure name: the name of the leader.

There are two other important aspects that, at this point, we should take into consideration. The first concerns the particular kind of distortion that the equivalential logics introduce into the construction of the 'people' and 'power' as antagonistic poles. In the case of the 'people', as we have seen, the equivalential logic is based on an 'emptying' whose consequences are, at the same time, enriching and impoverishing. Enriching: the signifiers unifying an equivalential chain, because they must cover all the links integrating the latter, have a wider reference than a purely differential content which would attach a signifier to just one signified. Impoverishing: precisely because of this wider (potentially universal) reference, its connection with particular contents tends to be drastically reduced. Using a logical distinction, we could say that what it wins in *extension* it loses in *intension*. And the same happens in the construction of the pole of power: that pole does not simply function through the materiality of its differential content, for that content is the *bearer* of the negation of the popular pole (through the frustration of the latter's demands). As a result, there is an essential instability which permeates the various moments that we have isolated in our study. As far as the particular demands are concerned nothing anticipates, in their isolated contents, the way in which they will be differentially or equivalentially articulated – that will depend on the historical context – and nothing anticipates either (in the case of the equivalences) the extension and the composition of the chains in which they participate. And as for the two poles of the people/power dichotomy, their actual identity and structure will be equally open to contestation and redefinition. France had experienced food riots since the Middle Ages but these riots, as a rule, did not identify the monarchy as their enemy. All the complex transformations of the eighteenth century were required to reach a stage in which food demands became part of revolutionary equivalential chains embracing the totality of the political system. And the American populism of farmers, at the end of the nineteenth century, failed because the attempt at creating chains of popular equivalence unifying the demands of the dispossessed groups found a decisive obstacle in a set of structural *differential* limits which proved to be stronger than the populist interpellations: namely, the difficulties in bringing together black and white farmers, the mutual distrust between farmers and urban workers, the deeply entrenched loyalty of Southern farmers to the Democratic Party, and so on.

This leads us to our second consideration. Throughout our previous study, we have been operating under the simplifying assumption of the de facto existence of a frontier separating two antagonistic equivalential chains. This is the assumption that we have now to put into question. Our whole approach leads us, actually, to this questioning, for if there is no a priori reason why a demand should enter into some particular equivalential chains and differential articulations rather than into others, we should expect that antagonistic political strategies would be based on different ways of creating political frontiers, and that the latter would be exposed to destabilisations and transformations.

If this is so, our assumptions must, to some extent, be modified. Each discursive element would be submitted to the structural pressure of contradictory articulating attempts. In our theorisation of the role of the empty signifiers, their very possibility depended on the presence of a chain of equivalences which involves, as we have seen, an internal frontier. The classical forms of populism – most of the Latin American populisms of the 1940s and 1950s, for instance – correspond to this description. The political dynamic of populism depends on this internal frontier being constantly reproduced. Using a simile from linguistics we could say that while an institutionalist political discourse tends to privilege the syntagmatic pole of language – the number of differential locations articulated by relations of combination – the populist discourse tends to privilege the paradigmatic pole, i.e. the relations of substitution between elements (demands, in our case) aggregated around only two syntagmatic positions.

The internal frontier on which the populist discourse is grounded can, however, be subverted. This can happen in two different ways. One is to break the equivalential links between the various particular demands, through the individual satisfaction of the latter. This is the road to the decline of the populist form of politics, to the blurring of the internal frontiers and to the transition to a higher level of integration of the institutional system – a transformist operation, as Gramsci called it. It corresponds, broadly speaking, to Disraeli's project of 'one nation', or to the contemporary attempts by theoreticians of the Third Way and the 'radical centre' at substituting administration for politics.

The second way of subverting the internal frontier is of an entirely different nature. It does not consist in *eliminating* the frontiers but in *changing their political sign*. As we have seen, as the central signifiers of a popular discourse become partially empty, they weaken their former links with some particular contents – those contents become perfectly open to a *variety* of equivalential rearticulations. Now, it is enough that the empty popular signifiers keep their radicalism – that is, their ability to divide society into two camps – while, however, the chain of equivalences that they unify becomes a different one, for the political meaning of the whole populist operation to acquire an opposite political sign. The twentieth century provides countless examples of these reversals. In America, the signifiers of popular radicalism, which at the time of the New Deal had a mainly left-wing connotation, were later reappropriated by the radical Right, from George Wallace to the 'moral majority'. In France the radical 'tribunicial function' of the Communist Party has, to some extent, been absorbed by the National Front. And the whole expansion of fascism during the inter-war period would be unintelligible without making reference to the right-wing rearticulation of themes and demands belonging to the revolutionary tradition.

What is important is to grasp the pattern of this process of rearticulation: it depends on partially keeping in operation the central signifiers of popular radicalism while inscribing in a different chain of equivalences many of the democratic demands. This hegemonic rearticulation is possible because no social demand has ascribed to it, as a 'manifest destiny', any a priori form of inscription – everything depends on a hegemonic contest. Once a demand is submitted to the articulatory attempts of a plurality of antagonistic projects it lives in a no-man's-land vis-à-vis the latter – it acquires a partial and transitory autonomy. To refer to this ambiguity of the popular signifiers and of the demands that they articulate we will speak of *floating signifiers*. The kind of structural relation that constitutes them is different from the one that we have found operating in the empty signifiers: while the latter depend on a fully fledged internal frontier resulting from an equivalential chain, the floating signifiers are the expression of the ambiguity inherent to all frontiers and of the impossibility of the latter acquiring any ultimate stability. The distinction is, however, mainly analytic, for in practice empty and floating signifiers largely overlap: there is no historical situation where society is so consolidated that its internal frontier is not submitted to any subversion or displacement, and no organic crisis so deep that some forms of stability do not put limits on the operativity of the subversive tendencies.

Populism, politics and representation

Let us put together the various threads of our argument so as to formulate a coherent concept of populism. Such a coherence can only be obtained if the different dimensions entering into the elaboration of the concept are not just discrete features brought together through simple enumeration, but part of a theoretically articulated whole. To start with, we only have populism if there is a series of politico-discursive practices constructing a popular subject, and the precondition of the emergence of such a subject is, as we have seen, the building up of an internal frontier dividing the social space into two camps. But the logic of that division is dictated, as we know, by the creation of an equivalential chain between a series of social demands in which the equivalential moment prevails over the differential nature of the demands. Finally, the equivalential chain cannot be the result of a purely fortuitous coincidence, but has to be consolidated through the emergence of an element which gives coherence to the chain by signifying it as a totality. This element is what we have called *empty signifier*.

These are all the structural defining features which enter, in my view, into the category of populism. As can be seen, the concept of populism that I am proposing is a strictly *formal* one, for all its defining features are exclusively related to a specific mode of articulation – the prevalence of the equivalential over the differential logic – independently of the actual *contents* that are articulated. That is the reason why, at the beginning of this essay, I asserted that 'populism' is an ontological and not an ontic category. Most of the attempts at defining populism have tried to locate what is specific to it in a particular ontic content and, as a result, they have ended in a self-defeating exercise whose two predictable alternative results have been either to choose an empirical content which is immediately overflowed by an avalanche of exceptions, or to appeal to an 'intuition' which cannot be translated into any conceptual content.

This displacement of the conceptualisation, from contents to form, has several advantages (apart form the obvious one of avoiding the naïve sociologism which reduces the political forms to the preconstituted unity of the group). In the first place, we have a way of addressing the recurrent problem of dealing with the ubiquity of populism – the fact that it can emerge from different points of the socio-economic structure. If its defining features are found in the prevalence of the logic of equivalence, the production of empty signifiers and the construction of political frontiers through the interpellation of the underdog, we understand immediately that the discourses grounded in this articulatory logic can start from *any* place in the socio-institutional structure: clientelistic political organisations, established political parties, trade unions, the army, revolutionary movements, and so on. 'Populism' does not define the actual politics of these organisations, but is a way of articulating their themes – whatever those themes may be.

Secondly, we can grasp better, in this way, something which is essential for the understanding of the contemporary political scene: the circulation of the signifiers of radical protest between movements of entirely opposite political signs. We have made reference before to this question. To give just one example: the circulation of the signifiers of Mazzinism and Garibaldianism in Italy during the war of liberation (1943–45). These had been the signifiers of radical protest in Italy, going back to the Risorgimento. Both fascists and communists tried to articulate them to their discourses and, as a result, they became partially autonomous vis-à-vis those various forms of political articulation. They retained the dimension of radicalism, but whether that radicalism would move in a right or in a left direction was at the beginning undecided – they were floating signifiers, in the sense that we have discussed. It is obviously an idle exercise to ask oneself what social group expresses itself through those populist symbols: the chains of equivalence that they formed cut across many social sectors, and the radicalism that they signified could be articulated by movements of entirely opposite political signs. This migration of signifiers can be described if populism is conceived as a formal principle of articulation; not if that principle is concealed behind the particular contents that incarnate it in different political conjunctures.

Finally, approaching the question of populism formally makes it possible to address another, otherwise intractable issue. To ask oneself if a movement *is* or *is not* populist is, actually, to start with the wrong question. The question that we should, instead, ask ourselves, is the following: *to what extent* is a movement populist? As we know, this question is identical to this other one: to what extent does the logic of equivalence dominate its discourse? We have presented political practices as operating at diverse points of a continuum whose two *reductio ad absurdum* extremes would be an institutionalist discourse, dominated by a pure logic of difference, and a populist one, in which the logic of equivalence operates unchallenged. These two extremes are actually unreachable: pure difference would mean a society so dominated by administration and by the individualisation of social demands that no struggle around internal frontiers – i.e. no politics – would be possible; and pure equivalence would involve such a dissolution of social links that the very notion of 'social demand' would lose any meaning – this is the image of the 'crowd' as depicted by the nineteenth-century theorists of 'mass psychology' (Taine, Le Bon, Sighele, etc.).

It is important to realise that the impossibility of the two extremes of pure difference or pure equivalence is not an empirical one – it is logical. The subversion of difference by an equivalential logic does not take the form of a total elimination of the former through the latter. A relation of equivalence is not one in which all differences collapse into identity, but one in which differences are still very active. The equivalence eliminates the *separation* between the demands, but not the demands themselves. If a series of demands – transport, housing, employment and so on, to go back to our initial example – are unfulfilled, the equivalence existent between them – and the popular identity resulting from that equivalence – requires very much the persistence of the demands. So equivalence is still definitely a particular way of articulating differences. Thus between equivalence and difference there is a complex dialectic, an unstable compromise. We will have a variety of historical situations which presuppose the *presence* of both, but at the same time, their *tension*. Let us mention some of them:

1) An institutional system becomes less and less able to differentially absorb social demands, and this leads to an internal chasm within society and the construction of two antagonistic chains of equivalences. This is the classic experience of a populist or revolutionary rupture, which results generally from the types of crisis of representation that Gramsci called 'organic crises'.

2) The regime resulting from a populist rupture becomes progressively institutionalised, so that the differential logic starts prevailing again and the equivalential popular identity increasingly becomes an inoperative *langue de bois* governing less and less the actual workings of politics. Peronism, in Argentina, attempted to move from an initial politics of confrontation – whose popular subject was the *descamisado* (the equivalent of the *sans-culotte*) to an increasingly institutionalised

discourse grounded in what was called 'the organised community' (*la comunidad organizada*). We find another variant of this increasing asymmetry between actual demands and equivalential discourse in those cases in which the latter becomes the *langue de bois* of the state. We find in them that the increasing distance between actual social demands and dominant equivalential discourse frequently leads to the repression of the former and the violent imposition of the latter. Many African regimes, after the process of decolonisation, followed this pattern.

3) Some dominant groups attempt to constantly recreate the internal frontiers through an increasingly anti-institutional discourse. These attempts generally fail. Let us just think of the process, in France, leading from Jacobinism to the Directoire and, in China, the various stages in the cycle of the 'cultural revolution'.

A movement or an ideology – or, to put both under their common genus, a discourse – will be more or less populistic depending on the degree to which its contents are articulated by equivalential logics. This means that no political movement will be entirely exempt from populism, because none will fail to interpellate to some extent the 'people' against an enemy, through the construction of a social frontier. That is why its populist credentials will be shown in a particularly clear way at moments of political transition, when the future of the community is in the balance. The degree of 'populism', in that sense, will depend on the depth of the chasm separating political alternatives. This poses a problem, however. If populism consists in postulating a radical alternative within the communitarian space, a choice at the crossroads on which the future of a given society hinges, does not populism become synonymous with politics? The answer can only be affirmative. Populism means putting into question the institutional order by constructing an underdog as an historical agent – i.e. an agent which is an *other* in relation to the way things stand. But this is the same as politics. We only have politics through the gesture which embraces the existing state of affairs as a system and presents an alternative to it (or, conversely, when we defend that system against existing potential alternatives). That is the reason why the end of populism coincides with the end of politics. We have an end of politics when the community conceived as a totality, and the will representing that totality, become indistinguishable from each other. In that case, as I have argued throughout this essay, politics is replaced by administration and the traces of social division disappear. Hobbes' Leviathan as the undivided will of an absolute ruler, or Marx's universal subject of a classless society, represent parallel ways – although, of course, of an opposite sign – of the end of politics. A total, unchallengeable state and the withering away of the state are both ways of cancelling out the traces of social division. But it is easy, in that sense, to see that the conditions of possibility of the political and the conditions of possibility of populism are the same: they both presuppose social division; in both we find an ambiguous *demos* which is, on the one hand, a section within the community (an underdog) and, on the other hand, an agent presenting itself, in an antagonistic way, as *the whole* community.

This conclusion leads us to a last consideration. As far as we have politics (and also, if our argument is correct, its derivative which is populism) we are going to have social division. A corollary of this social division is that a section within the community will present itself as the expression and representation of the community as a whole. This chasm is ineradicable as far as we have a *political* society. This means that the 'people' can only be constituted in the terrain of the relations of representation. We have already explained the representative matrix out of which the 'people' emerges: a certain particularity which assumes a function of universal representation; the distortion of the identity of this particularity through the constitution of equivalential chains; the popular camp resulting from these substitutions presenting itself as representing society as a whole. These considerations have some important consequences. The first is that the 'people', as operating in populist discourses, is never a primary datum but a construct – populist discourse does not simply *express* some kind of original popular identity; it actually *constitutes* the latter. The second is that, as a result, relations of representation are not a secondary level reflecting a primary social reality constituted elsewhere; they are, on the contrary, the primary terrain within which the social is constituted. Any kind of political transformation will, as a result, take place as an internal displacement of the elements entering the representation process. The third consequence is that representation is not a second best, as Rousseau would have had it, resulting from the increasing chasm between the universal communitarian space and the particularism of the actually existing collective wills. On the contrary, the asymmetry between community as a whole and collective wills is the source of that exhilarating game that we call politics, from which we find our limits but also our possibilities. Many important things result from the impossibility of an ultimate universality – among others, the emergence of the 'people'.

2

The 'End of Politics' and the Challenge of Right-wing Populism

CHANTAL MOUFFE

The theme of populism has recently been put at the centre of attention in Europe. The unexpected qualification of Jean-Marie Le Pen for the second round of the presidential elections in France in May 2002 and the excellent results of the Pim Fortuyn List, which came second in the Dutch legislative elections on May 15 – after the murder of their leader – have created a shock which has forced Western democracies to finally take seriously the growth of right-wing populism. To be sure, such parties have already existed for some time, but they were considered marginal and their strong presence in countries like Austria was explained by specific national idiosyncrasies, so it was possible to dismiss them as a ghost from the past, soon to be brushed away by the advances of the process of 'modernisation'

However, the increasing success of right-wing populist parties in most European countries and their increasing popular appeal makes it very difficult to maintain such a thesis. So instead of being seen as an exception, those parties are now presented as the main threat to our democratic institutions. But the fact that they have become a central subject of discussion has not meant that progress has been made in coming to terms with their nature. The reason is that the theoretical framework informing most democratic political thinking precludes grasping the roots of populist politics. Hence the disarray in which all those who proclaimed the end of the adversarial model of politics find themselves. Having announced the dawn of a consensual politics 'beyond left and right', they are suddenly confronted with the emergence of new political frontiers which pose a real challenge to their post-political vision. By constructing an opposition between 'the people' and the 'establishment', not only does right-wing populism shatter the consensual framework, it also brings to the fore the shallowness of the dominant theoretical perspective. Indeed if, as I will argue, the attraction exerted by right-wing populist discourse is the very consequence of the 'end of politics' Zeitgeist which prevails nowadays, we should not be surprised by the incapacity of most theorists to explain what is currently happening.

The thesis that I want to put forward is that, far from being a return of the archaic and irrational forces, an anachronism in times of 'post-conventional' identities, to be fought through more modernisation and 'Third Way' policies, right-wing populism is the consequence of the post-political consensus. Indeed, it is the lack of an effective democratic debate about possible alternatives that has led in many countries to the success of political parties claiming to be the 'voice of the people'.

The shortcomings of the liberal conception

An important part of my argument will be of a theoretical nature because I am convinced that in order to understand the appeal of right-wing populist discourse it is necessary to question the rationalist and individualist tenets which inform the main trends of democratic political theory. The refusal to acknowledge the political in its antagonistic dimension, and the concomitant incapacity to grasp the central role of passions in the constitution of collective identities, are in my view at the root of political theory's failure to come to terms with the phenomenon of populism.

While of course not new, those limitations have been reinforced by the recent evolution of liberal democratic societies and the effects of the prevailing ideological framework. This framework presents two aspects:

free market on one side, human rights on the other. Jointly they provide
the content of what is today generally understood by 'democracy'. What
is striking is that the reference to popular sovereignty – which constitutes
the backbone of the democratic ideal – has been almost erased in the
current definition of liberal democracy. Popular sovereignty is now
usually seen as an obsolete idea, often perceived as an obstacle to the
implementation of human rights.

What we are witnessing, actually, is the triumph of a purely liberal
interpretation of the nature of modern democracy. According to many
liberals, democracy is secondary with respect to liberal principles. As
Charles Larmore, for instance, puts it, 'Liberalism and democracy are
separate values whose relation, it seems to me, consists largely in democratic self-goverment being the best means for protecting the principles
of a liberal political order.'[1]

Although agreeing with Larmore that liberalism and democracy are
separate values, I do not think that the relation that exists between them
could be reduced to an instrumental one of means/ends, as many liberals would have it. While human rights are indeed crucial and constitutive
of the modern form of democracy, they cannot be considered the only
criteria to judge democratic politics. Without effective democratic participation in the decisions concerning the common life, there can be no
democracy.

Different terms have been used to refer to the new type of 'politeia'
(regime) brought about by the democratic revolution: liberal democracy,
constitutional democracy, representative democracy, parliamentary
democracy, pluralist democracy. They all point to the fact that we are
dealing with the articulation between two different traditions: the liberal
tradition (individual liberty and pluralism) and the democratic tradition
(popular sovereignty and equality). This articulation happened during the
nineteenth century, when an alliance was established between liberal and
democratic forces. The result, as C. B. MacPherson indicated[2], was that
liberalism was democratised and democracy was liberalised. This process
took place in a diversity of ways according to existing relations of forces,
and the resulting configurations were therefore different.

Since then the history of liberal democracies has been characterised by the sometimes violent struggle between social forces whose objective was to establish the supremacy of one tradition over the other. This struggle has served as a motor for the political evolution of Western societies, and it has led to temporary forms of stabilisation under the hegemony of one of the contending forces. For a long time this adversarial form of confrontation was considered legitimate, and it is only recently that this model has been declared outdated. For some, the end of the confrontation means the victory of liberalism over its adversary, while for others, the most democratically minded liberals, it means the end of an old antagonism and the reconciliation between liberal and democratic principles. Both groups, however, see the present consensus as a great advance for democracy.

What those liberals fail to grasp is the necessary tension which exists between the logic of liberalism and the logic of democracy, and the impossibility of a final reconciliation. In fact to announce the end of the confrontation signifies accepting the prevailing liberal hegemony, and foreclosing the possibility of envisaging an alternative to the existing order.

The liberal conception also misses the crucial symbolic role played by the democratic conception of popular sovereignty. The legitimacy of modern liberal democracy is grounded on the idea of popular sovereignty, and those who believe that it can be discarded are profoundly mistaken. The democratic deficit that manifests itself in a multiplicity of ways in a growing number of liberal democratic societies is no doubt a consequence of the fact that people feel that no real scope is left for what would be a meaningful participation in important decisions. In several countries this democratic deficit has contributed to the development of right-wing populist parties claiming to represent the people and to defend its rights, which have been confiscated by the political elites. It is worth noting that they are usually the only parties which mobilise the theme of popular sovereignty, viewed with suspicion by traditional democratic parties.

The end of politics?

The effacement of the theme of popular sovereignty in liberal-democratic societies constitutes a first important element for apprehending
the current rise of right-wing populism, and we can already see how it
has to do with the kind of liberal consensus existing today both in political life and in political theory. There is indeed a striking convergence
between the lack of effective alternatives offered to citizens in advanced
industrial societies and the lack of an adequate theoretical grasp of the
complex relationship existing between democracy and liberalism. This
explains in my view why it has become so difficult to challenge the prevailing liberal hegemony. Think for instance of the way in which, in one
form or the other, most social-democratic parties have been converted
to the ideology of the 'Third Way'. Nowadays the key terms of political
discourse are 'good governance' and 'non-partisan democracy'.

Politics in its conflictual dimension is deemed to be something of the
past, and the type of democracy that is commended is a consensual, completely depoliticised democracy. This 'politics without adversary'[3] chimes
with the consensual way in which the discourse of human rights is
utilised. Indeed the subversive potential of human rights is neutralised by
their articulation with the neoliberal dogma. Human rights are reduced to
providing the moral framework that such a politics needs to support its
claims of representing the general interest beyond partisan fractions.

As a consequence of neoliberal hegemony, most crucial decisions
concerning social and economic relations have been removed from the
political terrain. Traditional democratic political parties have become
unable to face societal problems in a political way, and this explains the
increasing role played by the juridical sphere as the realm where social
conflicts can find a form of expression. Today, because of the lack of a
democratic political public sphere where a political confrontation could
take place, it is the legal system which is made responsible for organising
human co-existence and for regulating social relations. This displacement of the political by the legal terrain as the place where conflicts are
resolved has very negative consequences for the workings of democracy.

No doubt this fits with the dominant view that one should look for 'impartial' solutions to social conflicts, but this is precisely where the problem lies. There are no impartial solutions in politics, and it is this illusion that we now live in societies where political antagonisms have been eradicated that makes it impossible for political passions to be channelled through traditional democratic parties.

In my view, it is the incapacity of traditional parties to provide distinctive forms of identifications around possible alternatives that has created the terrain for the flourishing of right-wing populism. Indeed, right-wing populist parties are often the only ones that attempt to mobilise passions and create collective forms of identifications. Against all those who believe that politics can be reduced to individual motivations, and that it is driven by the pursuit of self-interest, they are well aware that politics always consists in the creation of an 'us' versus a 'them' and that it implies the creation of collective identities. Hence the powerful appeal of their discourse, because it provides collective forms of identification around 'the people'.

If we add to that the fact that, under the banner of 'modernisation', social-democratic parties have in most countries identified themselves more or less exclusively with the middle classes, and that they have stopped representing the interests of the popular sectors – whose demands are considered 'archaic' or 'retrograde' – we should not be surprised by the growing alienation of an increasing number of groups who feel excluded from the effective exercise of citizenship by the 'enlightened' elites. In a context where the dominant discourse proclaims that there is no alternative to the current neoliberal form of globalisation, and that we have to accept its laws and submit to its diktats, it is small wonder that more and more workers are keen to listen to those who claim that alternatives do exist, and that they will give back to the people the power to decide. When democratic politics has lost its capacity to shape the discussion about how we should organise our common life, and when it is limited to securing the necessary conditions for the smooth working of the market, the conditions are ripe for talented demagogues to articulate popular frustration.

The current state of liberal-democratic societies is therefore particularly favourable for the development of right-wing populism. The displacement of the idea of popular sovereignty dovetails with the idea that there is no alternative to the present order, and this contributes to the creation of an anti-political climate that is easily exploited to foment popular reactions against the governing elites. We should realise that, to a great extent, the success of right-wing populist parties comes from the fact that they provide people with some form of hope, with the belief that things could be different. Of course this is an illusory hope, founded on false premises and on unacceptable mechanisms of exclusion, where xenophobia usually plays a central role. But when they are the only ones to offer an outlet for political passions, their pretence of offering an alternative is seductive, and their appeal is likely to grow. To be able to envisage an adequate response, it is urgent to grasp the economic, social and political conditions that explain their emergence. And this requires the elaboration of a theoretical approach that does not deny the antagonistic dimension of the political.

Politics in the moral register

I think that it is also crucial to understand that it is not through moral condemnation that those parties can be fought, and this is why most answers have so far been completely inadequate. Of course, a moralistic reaction chimes with the dominant post-political perspective, and it had to be expected. This is why it is worth examining it in some detail since this will bring us important insights into the way political antagonisms manifest themselves today.

As we saw earlier, the dominant discourse announces the end of the adversarial model of politics and the advent of a consensual politics beyond left and right. However, politics always entails an us/them distinction. This is why the consensus advocated by the defenders of the 'non-partisan democracy' cannot exist without drawing a frontier and defining an exterior, a 'them' which assures the identity of the consensus and secures the coherence of the 'us'. To put it in another way, the consensus at the centre, which is supposed to include everybody in our post-political societies, cannot exist without the establishment of a frontier, because no consensus – or no common identity, for that matter – can exist without a frontier. There cannot be an 'us' without a 'them', and the very identity of a group depends on the existence of a 'constitutive outside'. So the 'us of the good democrats' needs to be secured by the determination of a 'them'. Nowadays the 'them' is provided by what is designated as the 'extreme right'. This term is used in a very undefined way to refer to an amalgam of groups and parties whose characteristics and objectives are extremely diverse and it covers a wide spectrum which goes from fringe groups of extremists, skinheads and neo-nazis to the authoritarian right and a variety of right-wing populist parties.

Such a heterogeneous construct is of course useless to grasp the nature and causes of the new forms of right-wing politics. But it is very useful to secure the identity of the 'good democrats' and to procure a positive image of the post-political consensus. It is clear that, since politics has supposedly become 'non-adversarial', the 'them' which is necessary to make possible the 'us' of the good democrats cannot be envisaged as a political adversary, and the frontier has to be drawn in the moral register. So, to draw the frontier between the 'good democrats' and the 'evil extreme-right' is very convenient, since the 'them' can now be considered as a sort of moral disease which needs to be condemned morally, not fought politically. This is why no attempt is made to try to understand the reasons for its existence – an understanding, in any case, made impossible by the amalgam on which the very notion of 'extreme-right' is based. Moreover, attempts at understanding are deemed suspect, and perceived as a move towards condoning something which is morally unacceptable. As a consequence, moral condemnation and the establishment of a cordon sanitaire have become the dominant answers to the rise of right-wing populist movements.

The increasing moralisation of political discourse that we are witnessing goes hand in hand with the dominant post-political perspective. Far from indicating a new stage in the triumphant march of democracy, such a phenomenon represents a very negative development. Let's not misunderstand my point. It is not my intention to defend Realpolitik and to deny that normative concerns should play a role in politics. But there is a big difference between morality and moralism, which limits itself to the denunciation of evil in others. Yet today's good democrats are so confident that they have the truth, and that their mission is to impose it on others, that they refuse to engage in debate with those who disagree. It is no doubt easier to present them as a moral enemy, to be destroyed and eradicated, instead of having to envisage them as adversaries in the political terrain.

In fact what is happening is very different from what the advocates of the post-political model, like Ulrich Beck and Anthony Giddens, would want us to believe. It is not that politics with its old antagonisms has been replaced by moral concerns about 'life issues' and human rights. The political in its antagonistic dimension is very much alive, and political antagonisms are still with us. The main characteristic of our 'end of politics' age is that politics is now played out in the register of morality, and that antagonisms are being framed in a moral vocabulary. Far from having disappeared, frontiers between us and them are constantly drawn, but nowadays they are drawn in moral categories, between 'good' and 'evil', between the 'good democrats' who defend the universal values of liberal democracy and the 'evil extreme right', racist and xenophobic, which must only be 'eradicated'.

What I am suggesting is that what has been presented as the disappearance of antagonism is in fact the generalisation of a different form of its manifestation. To be sure, the moralistic type of rhetoric is not new. It has been used before, and the Americans are particularly fond of it. Remember Reagan's 'evil empire', not to mention the current crusade of George W. Bush against the 'axis of evil'! But this language was usually reserved for international relations, while now it pervades domestic politics. And in that field the consequences are different, because such a rhetoric transforms the very way we envisage the workings of democratic politics.

When politics is played out in the moral register, democracy is endangered. Besides preventing us from adequately grasping the nature and causes of current conflicts, this moralisation of politics leads to the emergence of antagonisms that cannot be managed by the democratic process and redefined in what I propose to call an 'agonistic' way – i.e. as a struggle not between enemies, but between 'adversaries' who respect the legitimate right of their opponents to defend their position.[4] It is clear that when the opponent is defined in moral terms, it can only be envisaged as an enemy, not as an adversary. With the 'evil them' no agonistic debate is possible. This is why moral condemnation replaces political struggle and why the strategy consists in building a cordon sanitaire to quarantine the affected sectors. As far as right-wing populist parties are concerned this strategy is generally counterproductive since, as we have seen, their appeal is often linked to their anti-establishment rhetoric, so their exclusion by the governing elites serves to reinforce their oppositional image.

There is an urgent need to understand that it is the incapacity to artic-ulate proper political alternatives around the confrontation of distinctive socio-economic projects that explains why antagonisms are nowadays articulated in moral terms. Since there is no politics without an us/them discrimination, when the 'them' cannot be envisaged as a political adver-sary it is constructed as 'evil', as a moral enemy. This explains the flourishing of moralistic political discourse in circumstances where the adversarial model of politics has lost its capacity to organise the political system, and when its legitimacy has been undermined by Third Way theorists. The 'extreme right' is therefore very handy for providing the 'evil them' necessary to secure the 'good us'. This of course is not meant to deny the existence of something that should be properly called 'extreme-right', but to insist on the danger of using this category to demonise all the parties who defend positions that are seen as a challenge to the well-meaning centre-establishment.

Right-wing populism in Austria

I have chosen the case of Austria to illustrate my argument because this will give me the opportunity to examine the two aspects of my thesis: the negative consequences of consensus politics, and the inadequacy of the moralistic answer to the challenge of right-wing populism.[5]

To grasp the reasons for the success of the Freiheitliche Partei Österreichs (FPÖ) it is necessary to recall the type of politics that prevailed in Austria since the beginning of the second Austrian Republic. When Austria was reestablished in 1945 the three existing parties – the Socialist Party (SPÖ), the People's Party (ÖVP) and the Communist Party (KPÖ) – decided to govern in coalition in order to avoid the conflicts that had dominated the First Republic, which had exploded into a civil war in 1934. The KPÖ was quickly excluded because of the effects of the Cold War, and the coalition reduced to the SPÖ and the ÖVP. Those parties were the representatives of the Christian-conservative and the Socialist Lagers around which Austrian society was organised after the break-up of the Habsburg monarchy. They devised a form of co-operation through which they managed to establish their control on the life of the country in a variety of fields: political, economic, social and cultural. Thanks to the 'Proporz system' the most important posts in the banks, hospitals, schools and nationalised industries were divided between their respective elites. Furthermore, the development of social and economic partnership secured co-operation between the organisations representing employers and employees in order to reach acceptable compromises, thereby avoiding industrial conflicts and strikes.

To be sure, this kind of consensus politics played an undeniable role in providing the basis of stability for the political system, and when in 1955, after ten years of Allied occupation, Austria won its sovereignty and independence, it had recovered its confidence and prosperity. But the fact that – except for the years between 1966 to 1983 – the SPÖ and the ÖVP formed a Grand Coalition to govern the country led to the blocking of the political system, since very little space was left for any type of contestation not directed against the system itself. Indeed, even when governing alone, the two main parties continued to maintain close contacts through the 'Sozialpartnerschaft'. This created the conditions which were later to allow a gifted demagogue like Jörg Haider to articulate the diverse forms of resentment against the governing coalition and its bureaucratic machine, in the name of 'democracy' and 'liberty'.

When Haider took control of the Freedom Party of Austria (FPÖ) in 1986, the party was facing extinction.[6] The FPÖ, which in 1956 had succeeded the League of Independents (VDU), founded in 1949, was heir to the third component of the Austrian political structure – the German national-liberal Lager which had supported national-socialism and had therefore been marginalised after the war. Since 1960, the FPÖ had tried to redefine itself as a centrist third party under the leadership of a former SS officer, Friederich Peter, by cultivating an image of a progressive, liberal party. But it had been weakened by three years of participation as a junior partner in a coalition with the SPÖ, between 1983 and 1986, and its potential vote was estimated at between 1 and 2 per cent.[7] The situation was therefore critical, and intra-party disputes culminated in 1986 at the Innsbruck conference in the ousting of the party chairman, Norbert Steger. Things changed quickly with the new leadership of Jörg Haider, who drastically transformed the party's orientation, and from then on the FPÖ experienced a dramatic upsurge in electoral support. Notwithstanding temporary setbacks, its share of the vote increased steadily until the November 1999 elections when it became the second party in the country, slightly overtaking the ÖVP with 27 per cent of the vote. Despite lengthy negotiations the ÖVP and the SPÖ were unable to agree on terms for reconvening their coalition, and a new coalition government was established between the ÖVP and the FPÖ in February 2000. This alliance was violently denounced in Austria and abroad, and the other EU members retaliated with a series of measures aimed at isolating the new government. However, the ÖVP/FPÖ coalition managed to withstand this opposition, and when it collapsed in September 2002 it was because of an internal struggle, not external pressure. I will come back to these events when I discuss the response to right-wing populist parties, but we first need to examine the rise of the FPÖ under Haider.

Haider's strategy

As soon as he assumed the leadership, Haider transformed the party into a protest party against the 'Grand Coalition'. He actively mobilised the themes of popular sovereignty and freedom of choice in order to articulate the growing resistance to the bureaucratic and authoritarian way in which the country was governed by the consociational elites. At first his campaigns were directed against the federal government, which he accused of corruption, excessive political patronage, and presented as being responsible for rising unemployment. He advocated the privatisation of state-owned enterprises, lower taxes and a reduction of regulation on business and individuals. From the 1990s onwards, starting with the federal parliamentary campaign in Vienna, the theme of immigration began to play a central role, and the discourse of the party acquired a clearly populist character. It was at that moment that the party, presenting itself as the voice of the 'little man' against the 'establishment', began to appeal to working-class voters disillusioned with the SPÖ.[8]

An important element to take into account in this shift of loyalties was the profound impact of the transition to a post-fordist form of capitalist regulation on the composition and forms of organisation of the working class. Its consequence was the erosion of the traditional links between the workers and the SPÖ. The forms of 'quasi-clientelism' which existed before became eroded, as the workers lost several of the benefits of the consociational system. Since, in the meantime, the Socialist Party under the leadership of Franz Vranitzky, had moved towards the political centre – renaming themselves 'social-democrats' and becoming more middle class in orientation – the terrain was laid for the workers to be attracted by the populist rhetoric of Haider.[9] Besides providing a channel of expression for the increasing disaffection with the political system, the FPÖ also served as an outlet for the growing anxiety and fears induced by the process of globalisation. By articulating all the diverse forms of resentment through a xenophobic discourse, the party could present itself as defending the interests of 'the people' both against the uncaring political establishment and the foreigners, visualised as a threat to the jobs of 'good hard-working Austrians' and their traditional way of life. No doubt the unconditional support given to Haider by the popular daily *Kronen Zeitung*, read by around 3 million Austrians, also contributed greatly to the amazing growth of the FPÖ during those years.

The discursive strategy of Haider[10] consisted in constructing a frontier between an 'us' of all the good Austrians, hard workers and defenders of national values, against a 'them' composed of the parties in power, the trade union bureaucrats, foreigners, and left-wing artists and intellectuals who were, all in their own way, contributing to the stifling of political debate. In his book *Die Freiheit, die ich meine* he declares:

> The ruling political class has got the formation of public opinion in its hands and individual opinion is neglected. A dialectical process of extensive nationalisation of society and socialisation of the state has broken the classic separation of state from society. Ideas and opinions of the citizens cannot be conveyed directly but have been usurped by institutions, interest groups and parties. Between them and the state a power game takes place, leaving little scope for individual freedom and self-determination.[11]

In his view one of the main issues where popular consultation is foreclosed is the question of immigration and multiculturalism. He forcefully argues for the people to be able to decide how many immigrants to allow: 'The question is, Who should decide which path to take? In my opinion: the people. Whoever doubts the role of the people as the highest sovereign, questions the very essence of democracy. People have the right not just to go to the polls every four years but are entitled to have a say in questions which are decisive for the future of their country.'[12]

A debate has been raging in Austria and elsewhere concerning the nature of the FPÖ, many people insisting that it should be described as right-wing extremist, even neo-nazi.[13] There is no doubt that an aspect of the FPÖ's rhetoric was also aimed at rallying the nostalgics of the

Third Reich, and one should not overlook the specificity of the Austrian situation and the complex relationship of many Austrians with their past. Moreover, coming from a nazi family, Haider has a very ambiguous attitude towards the crimes of nazism that he tends to minimise.[14] But it would be a serious mistake to overemphasise this element and to attribute the FPÖ's success to it. Those nostalgic sectors correspond only to a very small fraction of its electorate and, although they cannot be denied, the references to the nazi years do not play an important part in the party's ideology. To claim that Haider and his party are 'neo-nazi' completely misses the specificity of this new form of right-wing politics. It might satisfy the good conscience of those who reject any type of collaboration with them, but it does not help anyone to grasp the causes of their success and their appeal for so many workers and young people.

In fact it can be argued that the strategy of *Ausgrenzung* aimed at permanently excluding the FPÖ from government, thanks to the cordon sanitaire established by the two main parties, contributed to its remarkable rise in the last decades. The refusal of the SPÖ and the ÖVP under the last two legislatures even to consider the possibility of an alliance with the Freedom Party allowed it to be perceived as 'victim' of the political establishment, and reinforced its populist appeal. Indeed it could appear to be like David fighting against Goliath, defending the 'little people' against the elites in power.

It is clear that Austrian politics was trapped in a vicious circle. On one hand, the lack of a real democratic discussion about possible alternatives resulting from consensual politics was at the origin of the success of the FPÖ; on the other, success contributed to the permanence of the coalition, whose main justification had become to stop Haider coming to power. The negative consequences of such a situation were exacerbated by an attempt by the government to arrest the progress of the FPÖ by implementing some of the policies that it was advocating, mainly in the field of security and immigration.[15]

It must be stressed that this strategy to win back voters was accompanied by a strident moral condemnation of Haider's xenophobia, and by his demonization as 'nazi'. Of course, such a hypocritical stance made it impossible to challenge the FPÖ seriously. But the moralistic response to the rise of Haider was very convenient for the governing parties, because it exonerated them from making any autocritique, and from acknowledging their responsibility in his success.

The impasse of moralism

It is always very tempting to claim the moral high ground, but it does not provide a political strategy and it is likely to decrease the appeal of right-wing populist movements. In that respect the case of Austria is very instructive, and it brings us important insights concerning the mistakes to be avoided. Indeed, I believe that the European reactions to the for-mation of the coalition government between the ÖVP and the FPÖ represent the very definition of the wrong strategy. We witnessed an explosion of moral indignation, which led France and Belgium – worried by the possibility of similar alliances at home – to a series of bilateral measures against the new Austrian government. In the name of the defence of European values and the struggle against racism and xenophobia – of course always easier to denounce in others than to fight in your own country – the other fourteen European governments ostracised the new coalition before it had even done anything that could be deemed reprehensible. All the good democrats saw it as their duty to condemn the coming to power of a supposedly 'nazi' party and raised the alarm against a return of the 'brown plague'.

I do not want to deny that there was some cause for concern, or that precautionary measures were legitimate. But this does not justify the near-hysterical outcry that took place. The fourteen could easily have issued a strong warning to the new coalition, announcing that they were going to be under serious observation, and threatened them with sanc-tions in case of any deviation from democratic norms. However, moral condemnation replaced political analysis. No serious attempt was made to scrutinise the nature of the FPÖ, nor the reasons for its success. It was enough to point to the past history of Austria, and to declare that the problem was that it was never properly 'denazified'. People

overlooked the fact that, far from being a specific Austrian phenomenon, right-wing populist parties were already on the rise in many other
European countries: Belgium, France, Italy, Norway, Denmark, the
Netherlands and Switzerland. Led by a militant press, only too happy to
have found a new devil to fight, an incredible campaign of demonisation
was launched, which quickly came to focus on all of the Austrians,
perceived as being collectively responsible for the rebirth of the 'fascist
danger'.[16]

What we witnessed during this episode was a typical case of 'self-
idealisation' – that is, the condemnation of the 'bad Austrians' served to
construct the 'us' of the good democrats, morally beyond reproach. We
are here dealing with a very perverse mechanism, since it allows people
to assert their virtuous nature through an act of rejection. It is also a very
powerful way of mobilising passions and creating unity among people
who feel that their conscience is bolstered by the very act of excluding
others. This is no doubt one of the reasons for the seductiveness of the
moralistic approach, and its increasing role in politics.

A few months later the fourteen European governments realised that
the 'sanctions' were counterproductive, and that they had to find a way
out of the impasse without losing face. Again unable to envisage a political approach, they acted this time on the juridical terrain, deciding to ask
three 'wise men' to scrutinise the nature of the Freedom Party. When
their report concluded that the party, 'despite the presence of extremist
elements', was not 'neo-nazi' but 'right-wing populist', and that it did not
contravene democratic norms, the bilateral sanctions were lifted.[17] Of
course, both sides claimed victory. The FPÖ announced that its legitimacy had been vindicated, while the fourteen declared that, thanks to
their reaction, the new coalition had been kept in check.

Clearly the whole episode had negative consequences for the EU.
For instance, it antagonised small nations like the Danes, who felt that
such treatment would not have been used in the case of a more important country. And, as was demonstrated by the lack of European
reaction to the much more dangerous coalition established by Berlusconi
in Italy with Bossi's Lega Norte and Fini's Allianza Nationale, they were

right. Moreover, this stragegy of moral denunciation did not have the intended effect of arresting the growth of right-wing populist parties. Witness the good results of the Progress Party in Norway in September 2000 (14.6 per cent of the vote), the People's Party in Denmark in November 2001 (12 per cent), the Pim Fortuyn List in Netherlands in May 2002 (26 per cent), not to mention the 18 per cent gained by Le Pen in the second round of the French presidential elections on 5 May 2002.

Particularly interesting for my argument is the case of the Vlaams Blok (VB) whose strong performance in the national Belgian elections of October 2000 should also bring about some rethinking of the effects of the cordon sanitaire. By the way, doubts in this regard had been expressed by Patrick Janssens, the president of the Flemish Socialist Party, one of the very few Belgian politicians to have criticised the measures against the Austrian government. In an interview published in the Belgian daily *Le Soir* on 7 February 2000, he affirmed that in his view the best way to fight the VB was not to establish a 'sacred union' among all the good democrats from right to left, but on the contrary to revive the opposition between left and right, in order to offer the voters real alternatives, instead of leaving to the populist right a monopoly of the opposition to the existing order.

It is important to note the obvious similarities between the Belgian and Austrian cases. As in Austria, where the grand coalition between the SPÖ and the ÖVP allowed the FPÖ to appear as the only real alternative to the 'system', so in Antwerp the centre of VB power (where it reached 33 per cent of the vote in the last elections), a coalition between Socialists and Christian-democrats has monopolised political power for several decades. The effect of the cordon sanitaire was of course to reinforce the image of 'outsider', and therefore the appeal of the VB.[18]

However, the best argument against the strategy of 'Ausgrenzung' is provided by what has been happening in Austria since the establishment of the ÖVP/FPÖ coalition. In the elections that took place in November 2002 the FPÖ's share of the votes was reduced to 10 per cent, after having reached 27 per cent in November 1999. This proves that participation in the Austrian government was fateful for the party. When in opposition it could manage – thanks to a skilful rhetoric combining neoliberal themes with xenophobic ones – to attract groups with opposed interests, but once in power that was no longer possible. As a result it began to lose ground in all local elections: Styria in October 2000, Burgerland in December 2000 and Vienna in March 2001. When Jörg Haider realised that the situation was becoming critical, he attempted to regain the initiative by openly opposing several policies of the government. But his *coup de force* backfired, provoking a split in his party and the resignation of several FPÖ ministers. The outcome was the dissolution of the coalition government and the organisation of elections, which saw the resounding victory of the ÖVP, which with 42.3 per cent of the vote managed to overtake the SPÖ, which lost the leading position that it had long occupied. Reduced to third place and having lost two-thirds of its electorate, the FPÖ was in deep crisis, and its apparently irresistible rise had been stopped. The ÖVP-FPÖ coalition was re-established after the elections of 2002, and the decline of the FPÖ continued. In the European elections of June 2004 they only received 6.3 per cent of the vote, and the very survival of the party is now at stake.

A similar conclusion can be drawn from what happened in the Netherlands, where the centre-right coalition established with the Pim Fortuyn List collapsed after less than 100 days in power because of an internecine power struggle in the party of the murdered politician. Since then the party's popularity has drastically declined. To be sure, this is in part due to the disappearance of their leader, which created disarray in the party, but it is very likely that bringing it into the government – instead of allowing its populist rhetoric to flourish in opposition – accelerated the crisis.

Back to politics!

Let's recall the main points of my thesis. First I want to emphasise that my aim has not been to propose an exhaustive explanation of the phenomenon of right-wing populism, but only to put the accent on one aspect that is generally overlooked in the literature on this topic. It is my contention that a crucial dimension of the recent success of right-wing populist parties in Europe is usually omitted. This is due to the fact that most studies are informed by a rationalistic theoretical framework that prevents them understanding the specificity of the political. They tend to adopt an approach inspired by either an economic or a moral framework, which prevents them from realising the ineradicability of antagonism, as well as the central role played by passions, in the formation of collective political identities. Although this evasion of the political in its antagonistic dimension has always been one of the main shortcomings of the liberal approach, in recent years theories about the end of the adversarial model of politics have amplified this problem. In a political conjuncture in which the move towards the centre by formerly socialist parties has led to the blurring of the frontiers between left and right, this has created a situation in which the cleavage between 'us' and 'them' constitutive of democratic politics can no longer take place within the context of the traditional democratic parties. As I have tried to show, this has created a void which is currently occupied by right-wing populist demagogues who, by articulating a diversity of fears and resentments, have been able to constitute a new form of us/them opposition through a populist discourse in which 'the people' is constituted on the basis of a chain of equivalences between all those who are, in one way or another, presented as being oppressed by the 'power bloc' constituted by the political elites, the bureaucracy and the intelligentsia.

What is problematic is not the reference to 'the people'. Indeed, I have argued that it is necessary to reassert the democratic side of liberal democracy, and this implies reactivating the notion of popular sovereignty. The problem lies in the way in which this 'people' is constructed. What makes this populist discourse right-wing is its strongly xenophobic character, and the fact that in all cases immigrants are presented as a threat to the identity of the people, while multiculturalism is perceived as being imposed by the elites against the popular will. In most cases this populism also contains a strong anti-EU element, European integration being identified with the authoritarian strategy of the elites.[19]

To be able to offer a counter-strategy, it is necessary to acknowledge that, for several decades, important changes have taken place in European countries without real popular consultation and discussion of possible alternatives. It is therefore not surprising that a sense of frustration exists among all those who have not profited from those changes, or who feel that they are jeopardising their present conditions or future prospects. As long as traditional parties refuse to engage with those issues, with the argument that this evolution is a necessary one and that there is no alternative to the neoliberal model of globalisation, it is likely that right-wing populist parties will continue to grow. And it is certainly not moral condemnation that will make them disappear; it might even have the contrary effect.

It is no doubt encouraging to see that the appeal of those parties diminishes once they become part of the government, and that they seem able to strive only when in opposition. This reveals their structural limits. However, without a profound change in the workings of democratic politics, the problems which have led to the emergence of right-wing populism will not disappear. If a serious attempt is not made to address the democratic deficit that characterises the 'post-political' age that neoliberal hegemony has brought about, and to challenge the growing inequalities that it has created, the diverse forms of resentment are bound to persist; and there is even the danger that they will take more violent modes of expression.

But let's not be too pessimistic. At the moment right-wing populism might be on the rise, but there are also some positive signs that things are beginning to change on the left. The recent evolution of the 'anti-globalisation' movement shows that, after a 'negative' phase limited to the critique of institutions like the IMF and the WTO, serious attempts are now being made to construct a positive alternative to the neoliberal order, and this is very promising. The success of the Social Forums reveals that what is at stake in this emerging movement is not, as some would have it, a somewhat futile rejection of a supposedly 'neutral' process of globalisation, but the critique of its neoliberal mode and the struggle for another globalisation, informed by a different political project; a globalisation aiming at a different world order, where inequalities would be drastically reduced, and where the concerns of the most exposed groups would be addressed – instead of an exclusive focus on the welfare of the middle classes. It is by engaging fully with such a project that we will be able to offer an effective political answer to the challenge of right-wing populism.

3

Populism as an Internal Periphery of Democratic Politics

BENJAMIN ARDITI

The verbal smoke surrounding populism

Neopopulism and neocorporatism are regular entries in our political lexicon, yet the meaning assigned to the prefix 'neo' is not as clear in the former as it is in the latter. The rather unambiguous meaning of neocorporatism derives from the conceptual stability of its classical referent in the mainstream literature of political science. In the case of neopopulism, the prefix has not fared so well, partly due to the contested status of populism as such.

One only needs to look at the cluster of meanings associated with the term. The account offered by the sociology of modernisation prevailed throughout the 1960s, at least in the developing world. A classic exponent of this approach is Germani, who sees populist mobilisation as a deviation in the standard path from traditional to modern society.[1] Di Tella proposes a modified yet equally functionalist interpretation. He conceives of populism as the result of the convergence of two anti-status quo forces, the dispossessed masses available for mobilisation and an educated yet impoverished elite that resents its status incongruence – the gap between rising expectations and job satisfaction – and broods on ways of changing the current state of things.[2] Other theoretical interpretations move away from this view of populism as an alternative road to the modernisation of class-divided, traditional societies. Lasch sees it as a response to the crisis of modernity; Laclau, at least in his initial neo-Gramscian approach to populism, conceives of it as a dimension of the popular–democratic imaginary, and argues that its class nature varies in accordance with contending discursive articulations of the concept; Cammack opts for the revival of a Marxist standpoint that associates the phenomenon with resistance to neoliberal capitalism, although he adds a functionalist touch by linking the changing status of neopopulism to the requirements of capitalist reproduction.[3]

Moreover, as Worsley maintains, the term is wide enough to encompass right- and left-wing variants, to appear in advanced countries and in developing ones, in towns and in the countryside, and amongst workers and the middle classes as well as peasants.[4] It includes political phenomena ranging from the Russian *narodnichestvo* of the nineteenth century to William Jennings Bryan and small farmer movements in the US during the 1930s, and Latin American populism of the 1940s and 1950s. The latter, exemplified by Argentina under Perón and Brazil under Getúlio Vargas, had trademark characteristics usually seen as something of a general matrix of classic urban and industrial populism. Among them, strong nationalism; the perception of the state as both a political bounty and the prime mover of economic activity; economic programmes based on subsidies and price controls, import substitution and the protection of local industry; a cavalier allocation of government resources to reward followers and punish opponents, and the use of public spending to build networks of patronage disregarding criteria of fiscal or monetary responsibility; the enfranchisement of the urban underclass of *descamisados* (shirtless) or *cabecitas negras* (dark heads), and their mobilisation against the oligarchy; the creation of mass political parties; the growth of trade union militancy, shadowed by governmental control of organised labour and its use as a reserve army for mass demonstrations in support of the party or the leader; the cult of personality that aggrandises the stature of the leader and turns him or her into a quasi-messianic figure; and the role of leaders as political brokers who bypass formal mechanisms of representation whenever it suits them.

On the political side of the disagreement around populism, those who have focused on the more worrisome traits, like the messianic nature of its leaders or the submission of trade unions to the government, see it as a purely negative phenomenon. Others find it hard to reject many of its avowed goals when these are taken at face value, as they read like a wish-list for a socialist and radical-democratic agenda. For example, the emphasis on welfare policies and employment; the continual appeal to the people, the claim to empower the 'common man' and the capacity to motivate largely un-political individuals to participate; or the professed aim of restoring some dignity to politics, which, instead of representing the aspirations of society, often functions as a pork-barrel business run by corrupt and cynical political impresarios. This, together with the anti-liberal bias that I will discuss below, helps to clarify why in the 1960s and 1970s parts of the Third World intelligentsia – among them, socialist intellectuals who championed nationalist and anti-imperialist demands – saw populism as a positive phenomenon.

Things have changed quite radically in recent years, without dispelling the polemic around the meaning of the term. Populism today seems to have very little in common with its classical urban-industrial referent, except, perhaps, for the self-perception of the leader as a saviour of the nation and the standard – albeit often demagogic – observance of the premise that *'virtue resides in the simple people, who are the overwhelming majority, and in their collective traditions'*.[5] This begs the inevitable questions of who 'the people' are and how the meaning of the term varies from one case to another.[6] Nationalism and economic protectionism are virtually gone, and popular mobilisation tends to be minimised; in its wake, we are left with what some describe as a marriage of convenience between neoliberal economics and neopopulist politics.[7] To talk of a marriage does not settle the question either, for despite the general advocacy of market liberalisation, the differences in the policies they follow once in office remain far too large to allow us to identify this as a common denominator that could function as the genus of the more recent incarnations of the populist experience.

To complicate matters further, the populist drive seems to be virtually indistinguishable from the 'politics of faith' – as Oakeshott calls it – that has characterised a wide range of reform movements throughout modernity.[8] For example, the will to renew politics, the exaltation of the people, and the presumed immediacy of their link with the leader or the party are present in political movements that are not usually branded populist. Besides, one cannot fail to notice that the terms we have been using – populism, modern politics, democracy and reform – do not cease to overdetermine or contaminate one another, and as a result, the conceptual frontiers between them become rather unstable. This puts a limit to any pretension to disambiguate fully the 'as such' of populism vis-à-vis politics. The conceptual contours of the term remain fuzzy, and its theoretically contested status unabated, to the extent that we might want to describe populism as an 'anexact' object. I take this paradoxical expression from Deleuze and Guattari, who in turn borrow it from Husserl's writings on protogeometry or science that studies vagabond or nomadic morphological essences. 'Protogeometry', they say, 'is neither inexact like sensible things nor exact like ideal essences, but *anexact yet rigorous* ("essentially and not accidentally inexact"). The circle is an organic, ideal, fixed essence, but roundness is a vague and fluent essence, distinct both from the circle and things that are round (a vase, a wheel, the sun) … At the limit, all that counts is the constantly shifting borderline'.[9] The interesting thing about this notion is that it falls outside the binary opposition between exact and inexact, for the vagueness of the contours of anexact objects is a requisite condition and cannot be formalised as a clear truth-value. Considering the range of interpretations and positions mentioned above, populism could well be an anexact object, and therefore any precise description faces a real and perhaps insurmountable limit.

This does not mean that the phenomenon is intractable. Worsley puts it quite fittingly when he says that 'since the word *has* been used, the existence of verbal smoke might well indicate a fire somewhere'.[10] Is this fire sufficiently distinct to beget an acceptable descriptive concept? I have some reservations about how precise one can get, although there is a growing awareness that populism might be less of a stand-alone phenomenon than one that intertwines with contemporary politics. Hayward sees it as a response to the failures of elitist democracy in the European polity, whereas for Canovan it emerges in the ever-present gap between the pragmatic and the redemptive faces of democracy.[11] Laclau has taken this idea further, suggesting that we should regard *all* politics as populist to some extent. 'If populism consists in postulating a radical alternative within the communitarian space, a choice in the crossroads on which the future of a given society hinges, does not populism become synonymous with politics? The answer can only be affirmative'.[12] There is some truth to this view, but one needs to say something more in order to avoid a simple and direct conceptual overlap between politics and populism, as well as to account for non-radical instances of the populist appeal.

One possible step in this direction would be to explore the pertinence of situating the phenomenon in its relation to both modern politics and democracy. The evidence for this link is mixed. In the more intuitive use of the term, populism, old and new, is a label applied to crowd-pleasing politicians who are hard to distinguish from demagogues, who will make any kind of promise, no matter how unattainable, as long as it advances their cause, and who will tweak legal procedures and institutional arrangements shamelessly to adjust them to their needs. This, of course, applies to other political movements too. The common-sense use of the term also describes an ambiguous observance of democratic practices and a general dislike of liberal institutional settings. Whether they are in government or in opposition, the populists' impatience with formalised decision-making processes leads them to invoke their trademark distrust of elites as a sweeping device to override institutional constraints on their actions. Perhaps one can attribute this to their inexperience with the intricacies of the legislative and judicial process, for they see themselves, legitimately or not, as political outsiders. Whatever the reason, their disdain for the procedural channels and for the checks and balances of the democratic process reflects a strong anti-establishment ethos that might explain why liberals are not particularly keen on populism. They see populism, especially the urban-industrial one, as a variant of old

Caesarism with a democratic dressing. Yet, even when latter-day populists warp the operational mechanisms of a liberal-democratic framework of politics – representation, partisan competition, accountability and due process of law – they invest considerable energy in defending their democratic credentials and reassuring critics of their observance of that framework. Either as mere posturing or as an actual practice, the democratic vindication is part of the populist imaginary, although the persistence of authoritarian variants is a reminder that one must keep a level head when thinking of its relation to democracy.

Following this lead, I will suggest that populism is a recurrent feature of modern politics, one that iterates itself within both democratic and undemocratic settings, and examine three possible modes of the phenomenon. If one looks at it from the standpoint of the political subsystem, populism appears to be a fellow traveller of contemporary, media-enhanced modes of representation at work in both emerging and well-established democracies. This mode would be fully compatible with the institutional regime form of liberal-democratic politics. A second possibility shifts the focus to the more turbulent modes of participation and political exchange lurking behind the normality of democratic procedures. In this case, the populist mobilisation would be a symptom or paradoxical element capable of both disturbing and renewing the operation of democratic politics: it would function as a mirror where the latter can look at the rougher, less palatable edges that remain veiled by the gentrifying veneer of its liberal format. These two modalities of populism can thrive in a democratic setting, but the third one works as an underside that endangers this setting. It also emerges from within democratic politics, but as a 'misfire' whereby populism can morph all too easily into authoritarianism. This is a reminder that the phenomenon can be something more dangerous than a mode of representation or a disturbance of democracy, as it can also signal an actual interruption of democracy. Taken together, these three possibilities of populism – as a mode of representation, as a politics at the more turbulent edges, and as a threatening underside – will enable us to recast the populist experience as an *internal periphery* of liberal-democratic politics.

Populism as a mode of political representation

The first mode positions the discussion at the level of the political regime: we can regard populism as a mode of representation that has become part of mainstream democratic politics. In specifying this link, it will become clear that the reciprocal applies too. Macpherson's work on liberalism and democracy illustrates this double link very well. He claims that while the expansion of suffrage rights in the second half of the nineteenth century led to the democratisation of liberalism, the permanence of market society and representative government contributed to the liberalisation democracy.[13] This gave birth to the syntagm 'liberal democracy'. Similarly, the presence of a populist mode of representation in liberal democracies is not just an arithmetic addition to that setting; it also brings about a geo-metric dislocation insofar as it permeates the practice of democratic politics itself. Put differently, if populism is a mode of representation compatible with liberal-democratic politics, the latter is not left untouched, as it also incorporates some of the traits of populist representation.

How do we describe a populist mode of representation – warts and all – as part of the territory of democratic politics? One way of approaching this is to draw from authors who have referred to a populist style or mode of persuasion. Knight conceives it as a set of features – rapport with the people, a confrontational mentality, personalism, and mobilization – and claims that style is the basis for a looser model of populism that actually fits better with the phenomenon.[14] 'Fit' might not be the most felicitous term, for despite the avowed instrumentalism and nominalism of his definition of the populist style,[15] it evokes, at least implicitly, the problems associated with a correspondence theory of truth. However, if one leaves this issue aside, the features Knight men-tions, and his emphasis on the relevance of a more flexible view based on the idea of style, open up a productive line of inquiry. It tacitly accepts the impossibility of establishing a Cartesian-style definition of the populist phenomenon, which in turn confirms Oakeshott's well-known claim that the political vocabulary of modernity cannot extricate itself from some degree of ambiguity.[16]

Canovan also speaks of style, which she describes as the ability to communicate in tabloid-like language, offer political analyses that are as simple and direct as the solutions they propose, and a general knack for appearing to be the embodiment of transparency.[17] Similarly, Kazin's study of populism in the US refers to it as a style of political rhetoric or as a mode of persuasion, one whereby speakers use everyday 'expressions, tropes, themes, and images to convince large numbers of Americans to join their side or to endorse their views on particular issues'.[18] In the US, he says, this language has undergone many transformations. The nineteenth-century heritage of *Americanism* and its virtues – the producer ethic constituting 'the people', and an elite that opposes and exploits 'the people' – has drifted into a more conservative territory in the late twentieth century, with the appearance of the moral majority, the criticism of 'Big Government', the scorn for the cultural elite, and so on.[19]

Once again, this seems quite correct. My hesitation here is that a populist persuasion built on the strength of a simple and direct language, which entails a reduction of the complexity of the issues presented to the electorate, also seems to be characteristic of contemporary politics generally. Likewise, the appeal to the people or the interpellation of the common people against the status quo is also a distinctive trait of democracy, or at least of those who mobilize the redemptive side of politics. Perhaps the distinction is a matter of *degree*, in the sense that populism radicalises the appeal to the people, but then there is the problem of measuring the intensity of the appeal. Schmitt faces a similar problem when he invokes the criterion of intensity to define a political opposition. He wants to differentiate friend-enemy oppositions – according to him, the political opposition par excellence – from all others according to the criterion of intensity: political oppositions are the most intense because they are the only ones that can lead to the extreme or decisive case of war.[20] Yet as Derrida has shown, this presupposes a *telos* of intensity. If an opposition becomes more political because it has the possibility of reaching the extreme case of war, then, contrary to what Schmitt claimed, war would become not the limit case but the quintessence of the political.[21] I suppose that a similar problem would plague a distinction between populism and democracy based on the appeal to the people, or the use of a certain rhetoric or mode of persuasion.

I am not saying that we should abandon this argument, as it seems to me that it is quite relevant for the study of populist discourse. I suggest instead that we shift the focus to the field of representation, for this has the double advantage of maintaining a family resemblance with both style and rhetoric, and of connecting populism with mainstream politics. The usual way of dealing with this link is to say that populism arises as the result of a crisis of representation, as a response to either the incapacity or the refusal of elites to respond to people's concerns. There is some evidence to support this view. The populist right often exploits xenophobia to swell its ranks and disqualify (other) professional politicians. For example, they blame establishment politicians for the rise in unemployment among domestic labourers, because they are lax on immigration controls, thus encouraging the influx of foreign workers. A crisis of representation would then constitute a fertile terrain for the emergence of populism. However, the reference to 'crisis' also narrows down the scope of the populist experience to moments when politics fails to address participatory, distributive or other demands. Here we could build on Panizza's advice to distinguish 'populism in the streets' from 'populism in power',[22] and argue that the emphasis on the exception does not allow us to differentiate populist politics in opposition, when the motif of the breakdown of representation is more likely to be salient, from populism in government, when the possibility of such a crisis tends to be dismissed, though a populist mode of representation might remain in place all the same.

Instead of focusing on the moments of crisis, then, we could look at the very idea of representation and see how populism takes it on. Representation means rendering present, bringing into presence through a substitute, 'the making present of something that is nevertheless absent', or, more in tone with the specifically political sense of *acting for* others', representation 'means acting in the interest of the represented, in a manner responsive to them'.[23] This acting for others does not mean that the 'others' are left completely at the mercy of their representatives, for they also act upon them, if only because of their participation in public debates and their capacity to punish or reward elected officials by exercising their suffrage rights. However, 'representation' does have at least three elementary yet important presuppositions. First, the existence of two levels of playing field, that of the represented and that of those who act for them as their representatives. Second, that there is a gap between these levels, which prevents collapsing one into the other and therefore distinguishes representation from self-government. Finally, if the 're-' of representation involves a repetition whereby the people return through a substitute,[24] then that which returns cannot be reduced to an unaltered sameness, to a mere expression of pre-constituted identities and interests. Like any return, which is governed by what Derrida calls the law of iterability or the paradox of a repetition whose sameness incorporates something other,[25] the task of 'rendering present' introduces a differential element that modifies the absent presence of the people, for otherwise, instead of representation we would have the simultaneous presence of the people and their delegates. The main point here is that the presence of 'the people' is at once indirect and constitutively impure. Its presence is at least in part an effect of representation, insofar as the latter involves a drive to configure the identity and interests of the represented by addressing the classical political questions of 'who we are' and 'what we want'.

Populists are notoriously ambiguous about this. On the one hand, they have always claimed to speak in the name of the people and to use their language, to be the voice of those who have no voice and the agency that summons their presence to the political stage. This is often more the expression of a desire than a reality, for, among other things, De Ipola's reminder that the gap between the conditions of production and the conditions of reception of appeals to the people does not guarantee the success of those appeals.[26] On the other hand, populism has also been rather hazy about who the people are, conceiving them variously as the dispossessed, the hard-working middle classes, the burdened tax-payers, the 'common man', the moral majority, and so on. One might say that this is not a relevant point, for the populist rendering-present of the people is still committed to distinguishing between a certain 'us' and 'them' characteristic of political oppositions. That is, populism must make an effort to configure the identity of the people and to specify the disagreement that pitches them against named adversaries – the elites, the oligarchy, Big Government, or what have you. This is correct, but even then, the populist 'us' remains conveniently vague. It is a deliberate vagueness, for it enables it to blur the contours of 'the people' sufficiently to encompass anyone with a grievance structured around a perceived exclusion from a public domain of interaction and decision hegemonised by economic, political or cultural elites.

A similar ambiguity surrounds the gap between the absent presence of the people and the action of representing them. The gap is bridged by a 'presentation' that forgets the iterability at work in the 're-' of representation. First, because of the presumed immediacy of the relation between the people and the leader or his movement, in which case there is no absence but only a joint presence without representation. Second, because populism claims that the trusted leader is a vehicle for the expression of the popular will, which once again dissolves the gap between the represented and the representatives, except that in this case we are only left with the latter by fiat of tacit authorisation. What we have here is a mirror game, an alleged double and simultaneous full presence, of the people and of those who act for them. A representation that pretends not to be such reflects a clear bias for presence. Like Rousseau, populists distrust representation as a corruption of the general will, and see themselves less as representatives than as simple placeholders or spokespeople for the common man, but unlike Rousseau they also distrust autonomous initiatives that empower citizens and encourage them to act by themselves. This ambivalent oscillation between the glorification of the independent action of the people (they are merely their placeholders) and the instrumental appropriation of that action (they incarnate the people and speak in their name) furnishes populist representation with a convenient permanent alibi. Indeed, just as Barthes observed that myth always appears to have an 'elsewhere' at its disposal that allows it to avoid admitting its condition as a second-order semiological system,[27] populism seems to have one too, which it uses to put the spin on its position vis-à-vis representation, participation and mobilisation. This ambivalence explains why some say that populism releases the unadulterated energies of the people, while others claim that it is little more than the shackle that condemns people to a position of subservience to a movement or to its leader. Yet in both readings the leader appears to be a symbolic device. As the presumed incarnation of the popular will, or as a trustee of the people, his (or her) role is to simplify the issues and to disambiguate the identity of the populist camp.

What does this tell us about the populist mode of representation? We have noticed that it revolves around a series of themes: the promise of inclusion and intervention in the public sphere, the ambivalence concerning the 'immediacy' of the relationship of representation, and the role of the leader as a symbolic condensation of the movement. Why is this different from the conventional take on political representation? In order to respond to this question we have to go back to Pitkin's argument. When she discusses political representation, she discards Hobbesian authorisation, for it entails a complete disappearance of the represented: the authorisation that they grant to their representatives is so exhaustive that all the actions and judgments of the latter are valid and binding.[28] She also discards the 'standing for' that defines symbolic representation – when a symbol takes the place of an absent object, as in the case of a flag that stands for the unity of the nation – because this tells us nothing about the *action* of representation proper.[29] Instead, she settles for 'acting for others', for she believes that this formulation deals with the substance of the activity of political representation itself instead of the formal arrangements surrounding the action. Populist representation departs somewhat from this view. This is not because it cancels Pitkin's 'acting for others', but because it is a mode of representation arising from a crossover between the standard 'acting for others' of political representation in

liberal democracies, the re-entry of a Hobbesian authorisation of sorts
under the guise of *trust* for the leader, and a strong symbolic dimension.
The latter presents the leader as the element that articulates diversity and
that seeks to produce an effect of virtual immediacy; that is, an imaginary
identification that suspends the distance between the people and their representatives. My contention is that today the crossover that characterises
populist representation is prevalent within liberal democracy itself.

The work of Manin can provide some clues to construe this relationship between populism and contemporary forms of representative
democracy. Despite the widespread belief in a crisis of representation, he
says, what we are experiencing today is a metamorphosis of representation.[30] He identifies three consecutive forms of political representation in
the West. These are classic English *parliamentarianism*, from 1832 to the
introduction of male universal suffrage in 1867; *party democracy*, an effect
of the entry of the underclass into the political system and the emergence
of mass political parties, which prevailed in Europe and elsewhere since
then and throughout most of the twentieth century; and *audience democracy*,
which started to emerge in the 1970s with the decline of mass parties, the
impact of the mass media on electoral campaigns, and the formation of a
veritable 'stage' for politics. They all share the same principles – the election of representatives, the autonomy of the representatives, the role of
public opinion, and trial by discussion – although these appear differently
in each of these forms of representative government. We are familiar with
the second form, which Kelsen described as *Parteienstaat* or party government,[31] whose demise many continue to mourn as a loss of the *gravitas*
of politics. The old hegemony of fiery leaders and disciplined party
apparatuses is eclipsed in the wake of audience democracy, with its media-
enhanced candidates basking in the cool glow of technopolitical expertise.
The democracy of 'audience', says Manin, is akin to a supply-side politics
that aims to identify the relevant cleavages within the electorate in order
to differentiate the candidate from its adversaries. Media experts replace
party bureaucrats and activists, or at least put an end to their earlier prominence, and electoral discipline weakens due to the volatility of party
loyalties from one election to the next.[32]

For its critics, audience democracy transforms politics into a spectacle run by media and marketing professionals. Former US president Gerald Ford refers to this type of politics in a caustic remark about the dangers of pointless manipulation when he speaks of 'candidates without ideas hiring consultants without convictions to run campaigns without content'.[33] There is some truth to this claim, but it might also be a somewhat unfair rendering of audience democracy. Opinion polls and electoral marketing might replace the serious pondering of party manifestos and electoral promises, says Manin, but they also help voters by reducing the complexity of the issues and lowering the cost of access to information on those issues.[34] More importantly, at least for the purpose of our inquiry, in audience democracy there is a personalisation of the link between candidates and voters. For Manin, today people tend to vote for a person instead of an electoral platform or a party, and while parties do not lose their central role as electoral machines, they tend to become instruments in the service of the leader. He gives two reasons for this, both of which support our claim that populist representation has gone mainstream.

One is that the channels of political communication, mainly radio and television, affect the nature of the representative relationship: candidates can now communicate directly with their constituents without the mediation of party networks.[35] In a way, he says, this entails a return to the face-to-face character of representation in the parliamentarianism of the nineteenth century. This is true, but also imprecise, since mediations have been reconstituted rather than disappeared. We can provide a more rigorous depiction of the phenomenon by arguing that the mass media enable a semblance of immediacy or, better still, that they give rise to a mode of political representation characterised by the 'as if' of *virtual immediacy*. This 'as if' sublimates the representative link by veiling the gap between the people and those who act for them. This virtual immediacy coincides with the populist presumption of enjoying a direct relation with the people. The second reason Manin gives for the personalisation of political options is that the scope of governmental activity has expanded substantially, and elected officials must make decisions on a wide variety of issues that a party platform can neither foresee nor specify in advance. In fact, he says, governmentality requires something analogous to what Locke called 'prerogative' power; that is, a certain discretionary margin whereby elected leaders can 'take decisions in the absence of pre-existing laws', which means that the personal *trust* in the candidate becomes an adequate basis of selection.[36] Manin concludes that 'representatives are thus no longer spokesmen; the personalisation of electoral choice has, to some extent, made them trustees'.[37] Once again, we can see a clear analogy between prerogative power based on trust and the role of populist leaders as trustees of the people and as political brokers.

In many ways, then, audience democracy intertwines with populist representation conceived as a crossover between acting for others, authorisation, and the strong role of symbolic imagery. The election of Arnold Schwarzenegger as governor of California in 2003 is a good illustration of 'trust'. Exit polls conducted on election day 'suggest that for those who voted for Schwarzenegger, his personal qualities mattered far more than the position he had on the issues'.[38] We can also see this at work in the case of Mexico. In 2000, Vicente Fox, the victorious presidential challenger who put an end to the seventy-two-year hegemony of the ruling Partido de la Revolución Institucional (PRI), obtained the nomination of his centre-right Partido Acción Nacional (PAN) not by lobbying the party hierarchy or mobilising the faithful inside the party apparatus. He obtained it thanks to an ad hoc organisation, *Amigos de Fox* ('Friends of Fox'), which mounted an impressive media campaign to present him as a no-nonsense candidate in touch with the feelings of ordinary people. The popularity of Fox rested on his communication skills and the work of the team of advisers that designed his campaign. His success hinged on the way he connected this popularity with the claim for political renewal. People *trusted* Fox and felt they had a direct rapport with him. This allowed him to acquire supra- and extra-partisan legitimacy, which the leadership of his own party did not like but could not stop either; so in the end it had little choice but to follow the lead of public opinion and anoint Fox as its candidate. The PAN and its allies benefited from the pro-Fox electoral tide; they gained more elected positions than they would otherwise have had, although they obtained fewer votes than Fox himself.

Opinion polls and electoral studies conducted in the aftermath of the general elections of 2 July 2000 agree that those who voted for Fox did so less for what he said than for what he symbolised. People saw him as the most credible option for ousting the PRI, says Flores, to the extent that the majority of those who voted for him and his electoral coalition were betting on the idea of change regardless of the specific content of that change.[39] This is similar to what happened with Schwarzenegger in the California elections. In Manin's terminology, Fox's advisers perceived that the central cleavage within Mexican society was one between continuity and change – and not, as the centre-left PRD had calculated, between the sovereign nation and the forces of neoliberalism. If we look at this from the standpoint of discourse theory, or at least of one of its variants,[40] the virtue of Fox's campaign managers was that they correctly identified 'change' as the empty signifier needed to suture the Mexican political field in 2000. More importantly, they succeeded in presenting their candidate rather than his party as the agent capable of effecting a symbolic appropriation of that signifier. Either way, this shows that Fox built his electoral strategy around a typically populist mode of representation – one that welded 'acting for others' and the symbolic 'standing for' with authorisation based on trust – that has become intertwined with contemporary politics. He developed a virtual or media-based face-to-face relation with the electorate, presented himself as the representative of the will of the people, was graced by the trust that people invested in him regardless of the actual platform on which he campaigned, and became the torchbearer of the idea of change.

Populism as a symptom: politics on the edges of democracy

If the former mode of representation defines populism virtually as a phenomenon that coexists with mainstream politics and transforms it, the second modality moves into a different territory, which positions it together with other radical movements in the rougher edges of democratic politics. Here the argument concerning the link between populism and democracy begins to shift from the institutional site of the political regime to the democratic imaginary of modern politics. To put it in a schematic manner, and drawing from psychoanalysis, we could interpret populism as the return of the repressed, or better still, as a symptom of democracy; that is, as an internal element of the democratic system which also reveals the limits of the system and prevents its closure in the pure and simple normality of institutional procedures.

At times Freud thinks of the symptom in the usual medical sense of a sign of illness, but this is not what he wants to highlight in his study of the psychic apparatus. He conceives it mainly as a substitutive formation that stands in for a frustrated desire, or for something amiss in our lives. It shields us from danger by masking a traumatic experience. He mentions the case of a patient with obsessive neurosis. The patient, who was living apart from her husband, was prone to running from one room to another and then calling the servant, but upon her arrival she would forget why she had summoned her, or instruct her to do something trivial. The patient eventually came to realise that her obsessive behaviour both imitated and disguised her husband's behaviour during the wedding night. Affected by impotence, he would go back and forth from his room to his wife's chambers trying – unsuccessfully – to consummate the matrimony, and worrying that the servants would put him to shame if they discovered his failure. The symptom-formation – the compulsive act of going from one room to the other and summoning the servant – was the mechanism whereby the patient's ego attempted to dispel the frustration caused by the husband's sexual failure. It aimed to remove her from a situation of danger. This turns the symptom into something akin to the formation of a compromise between repressed representations and repressing representations. The phenomena of symptom-formation are, then, an expression of the repressed or, to be more precise, they indicate the *return* of the repressed through more or less tortuous paths.[41]

Freud offers us an additional explanation. He says: 'Symptoms are derived from the repressed, they are, as it were, its representatives before the ego; but the repressed is foreign territory to the ego – internal foreign territory – just as reality (if you will forgive the unusual expression) is external foreign territory'.[42] This characterisation of the repressed through the metaphor of the 'internal foreign territory' is ingenious and helpful for our inquiry. On the one hand, the *sui generis* status of the symptom destabilises a clear frontier between inside and outside: it opens up a play or negotiation between *properly* internal phenomena and phenomena that are internal yet somewhat improperly so – they are part of an internal *foreign* territory. On the other hand, it gives us clues for understanding the second modality of populism as an internal foreign territory or internal periphery of democratic politics, as a phenomenon that develops in its edges or more turbulent regions. I want to develop this point through Žižek's social and political reading of the symptom, as he, too, proposes this play between the proper and the improper. In his interpretation – which iterates and hence reformulates Freud's through a reading inspired by Lacan – the symptom is 'a particular element which subverts its own universal foundation, a species subverting its own genus'.[43] In this respect, Marxist critique is symptomatic, for the working of ideology, he says, requires not so much a false consciousness among those who participate in a given social reality but rather that they 'do not know what they are doing'. This misrecognition was already present in the case of the woman with obsessive neurosis mentioned by Freud, in which case a symptom could be defined as '"a formation whose very consistency implies a certain non-knowledge on the part of the subject": the subject can "enjoy his symptom" only in so far as its logic escapes him'.[44]

Žižek illustrates this through an example borrowed from Marx's theory of commodity exchange, or rather from Alfred Sohn-Rethel's reading of it. The universality of the commodity form presupposes that every exchange is always an exchange among equivalents. Yet, this universality happens to be an empty or counterfeited universality; he calls it an ideological universal insofar as the labour force is a special commodity whose use – the actual expenditure of labour – generates surplus value over and above the market value of the labour force itself.[45]

That is why the system gives rise to an equivalent exchange, but also to 'a particular paradoxical exchange – that of the labour force for its wages – which, precisely as an equivalent, functions as the very form of exploitation'.[46] Labour power, he says, is a special commodity, one 'representing the internal negation of the universal principle of equivalent exchange of commodities'. This negation of universal equivalence is internal to equivalent exchange and not merely its violation. Žižek caps this by saying that utopia consists of 'a belief in the possibility of *a universal without a symptom*, without the point of exception functioning as its internal negation',[47] which suggests that the symptom is not an accident but rather a distinctive trait that can be found in the actual working of any system. We can add that if the misrecognition of this fact is required to maintain the semblance of equal exchange, and therefore to enable the effectiveness of commodity exchange, then any effort to unveil the special status of labour power as the site where equivalence breaks down – which is precisely what working-class and socialist movements have been doing since the nineteenth century – introduces a measure of disruption into the system, although this does not necessarily entail its implosion.

Let us connect this with the discussion about the relationship of interiority of populism and democracy. What is the status of this interiority? Earlier we described it as a mode of representation, but the symptom offers us a different angle. As a symptom of democracy, populism functions as a paradoxical element that belongs to democracy by sharing with it the standard traits of participation, mobilisation, informal expression of the popular will, and so on and, at the same, time interrupts its closure as a gentrified or domesticated political order by overlooking standing procedures, institutional relations, comforting rituals. We can illustrate this through an analogy with the discomfort caused by the arrival of a drunken guest at a dinner party. He is bound to disrupt table manners and the tacit rules of sociability by speaking loudly, interrupting the conversations of others, and perhaps flirting with the wives of other guests. The hosts might not be particularly happy with the awkward visitor, but having invited him they probably cannot get rid of him either, so they will do their best to downplay his antics in order to make the rest feel as comfortable as possible. Populism plays the role of the awkward guest; it is a paradoxical element that functions both as an internal moment of liberal democracy and as that which can disrupt the gentrified domain in which politics is enacted. This is because representative politics generally entails the priority of institutional mediations over charisma, the presence of checks and balances to limit the discretionary powers of political leaders, the widespread practice of reaching agreements through negotiations among political elites, and so on. These are the 'table manners' governing democratic politics. Populism disrupts them by mounting its challenge to the redemptive face of democracy, at times in detriment of law and order. As a promise of redemption, the populist mobilisation exerts pressures on the presuppositions of representative democracy, and to some extent warps them through the mobilisation of the people to bypass institutional constraints. Yet even if this mobilisation can be an irritation, one cannot affirm unequivocally that it is *external* to democratic practice as such. The populist 'noise', irritating as it may be, is in fact its internal foreign territory. In principle, its challenge undermines the fullness of any democratic expression of the will of the people, including its own.

How, though, do we distinguish this symptomatic noise from other possible noises? If every disruption of systemic normality – whether it is a demonstration that ends in disturbances or any other non-electoral expression of the popular will – is a symptom of democracy, then the semantic field of the concept of symptom would be stretched so much as to lose its explanatory value. More precisely, it would become useless in accounting for populism in relation to democracy. This poses a real difficulty, but not necessarily an insurmountable one. As mentioned, Macpherson claims that the democratisation of liberalism entailed a liberalisation of democracy. This does not mean that from then on democracy and liberalism became synonymous. We regularly speak of 'democratic liberalism' and use the hyphenated expression 'liberal-democracy', which prevents the closure of democracy in its liberal format of electoral representation or, what amounts to the same thing, is a reminder that the tension between the terms keeps their relationship open. If anything, liberalism managed to hegemonise democracy, not to suppress the alternatives that exceeded electoral representation – demonstrations, sit-ins, takeovers of buildings, and the like. Populism, like many other radical movements, can be democratic or not, but when it is, invoking the participatory supplement of institutional procedures, it puts to the test the obviousness of what passes as a normal democratic order. Following Rancière's reference to the disagreement or polemicisation as that which singularises an operator of difference – 'equality', 'freedom' or what have you – by putting it to the test in order to see in what it is a universal and in what mere power,[48] we are compelled to put the populist disturbance to the test too. That is, we must judge – and confront our judgment with those of others – whether non-electoral manifestations of the popular will are part of normal political exchanges that take place within liberal democracies, if they function as the symptoms of such orders, or if they simply fall outside their scope and become the nemesis of democracy. I must underline the reference to political judgment, first, because there can be no certitude when we speak of politics, and second, because between the norm, the symptom, and that which falls outside the system lies a grey area that prevents any Cartesian reasoning. Hence, the symptomatic character of the populist mobilisation with regard to the acceptable rules of a gentrified democratic order cannot be adjudicated outside of a disagreement.

I borrow the reference to gentrification from Žižek, who in turn uses it to recast Lefort's distinction between politics and the political.[49] In Žižek's reading, politics is the site where the contingency and negativity of the political are gentrified in a political 'normality', forgotten in an order that has the status of one sub-system among others.[50] Gentrification here stands for the domestication of the political, for what Foucault describes as a continuation of war by other means: political normality is the institutional end-result of war.[51] We can think of it either as the self-perception of liberal democracy or as the horizon towards which it aims or, to put it in Žižek-speak, as the means through which citizens enjoy their symptom in liberal democracies. As in the presumed universality of commodity exchange that masks the special case of labour power, it creates a semblance of impersonal institutional virtue that conveniently overlooks the shadier deals concocted regularly among the political and economic elites. Populism functions as the symptom of this gentrified domain by bringing back the disruptive 'noise' of the people; it puts objectivity at stake by announcing the return of the founding negativity of the political. In short, by disrupting gentrification, the populist mobilisation, like all radical challenges, is a reminder of the contingency of political arrangements.

We can also look into this from a perspective closer to political and philosophical language, as is Rancière's conception of politics as the enactment of a disagreement. While he does not speak directly of populism, one could argue that gentrification corresponds to what he calls the order of police or partition of the sensible. These conceive the city as a distribution of parts without remainder, as a hierarchy of parts and their functions that aims to cancel out the polemic nature of politics.[52] Populism disrupts gentrification by summoning the demos, that is, what Rancière would call 'the party of the poor'. But the demos, he says, can only be an *improper* part, for the poor – or in the preferred language of populism, the common people – represent the part of those who have no real part in the polis except for the empty property of their freedom. For him, the impropriety of the demos, which is the scandal of democracy, brings into play the constitutive torsion or disagreement of politics. To the extent that populism mounts its challenge on the strength of its mobilisation of the demos, it prevents any reconciliation of the community, and therefore interrupts the closure of liberal democracy as pure elitism or as detached pragmatism.

Drawing from this discussion, we can say that populism functions in two senses as a symptom of democratic politics. As a promise of redemption and as an index of what Canovan calls the reaction against politics as usual, populism disrupts the gentrified democratic order and expands – or at least claims to expand – the scope of citizen involvement in public affairs. Perhaps it would be appropriate here to speak of populism as a response to 'formal' democracy, as long as we agree that the adjective is not understood in the dismissive sense of a mere travesty of a 'real' or substantive democracy. Following a distinction suggested by Badiou, one could then argue that populism as a symptom recuperates the idea of mass democracy, which he labels 'romantic' and associates with 'collective general assembling, crowded gatherings, riots, and so on', in contrast with the perception of democracy as designating the configuration of the state, which he calls 'formal'.[53] Yet as the awkward guest or element that 'falls out' of the gentrified system, it positions itself in the rougher edges of democratic politics, in a grey area where it is not always easy to distinguish populist mobilisation from mob rule. In this interpretation, populism might not necessarily break loose from a democratic setting, but it becomes something of an unstable and destabilising phenomenon. In the terms suggested earlier, and corroborated by the metaphor of the symptom as a 'internal foreign territory', it becomes part of the internal periphery of the democratic order.

Populism as an underside of democracy

Having said this, the very fact that it has a capacity to disrupt democratic politics compels us to inquire about the darker possibilities that can come along with populism. As a political practice that takes place at its rougher edges, populism can be conceived both as a mirror in which democracy can scrutinise its more unsavoury traits, and as an experience that can become (or not) its underside.

Here we can mention Canovan's depiction of populism as a shadow of democracy. Following Oakeshott, who distinguishes between faith and scepticism as the two styles whose interplay characterises modern politics, Canovan speaks of the two faces of democracy – redemption and pragmatism – that require one another and cohabit as two squabbling Siamese twins.[54] She claims that the populist mobilisation arises in the gap between them, primarily as a way to counteract the pragmatic excesses of established democracies. By locating populism in this gap, Canovan manages to develop a conception of populism that retains a relation of interiority with democratic politics. Populism is not the 'other' of democracy, but rather a shadow that follows it continually.

This is a very good observation, and I would like to take it as a starting point to discuss a supplementary semantic connotation of the metaphor of the shadow, one that is required if one wishes to avoid losing populism in the vastness of democratic politics. For this is the issue: to establish the connection between populism and democracy without overlooking the gap that separates them. What is missing in the metaphor is its additional meaning as a sign of danger or an underside. From horror films to mystery novels, the literary device of the shadow is a topos of something ominous; it functions as a signpost to announce the perils that may lurk ahead. It is no different in this case. Critics have warned against the allure of populism by citing the dangers it poses for democracy. The cult of personality can transform leaders into quasi-messianic figures for whom accountability is not a relevant issue, and the populist disregard for institutional checks and balances can encourage rule by decree and all sorts of authoritarian behaviour while maintaining a democratic façade. In addition, the Manichean distinction between good common people and corrupt elites can become an excuse for using strong-arm tactics against political adversaries, and the continual invocation of the unity of the people can be used as means to dispel pluralism and toleration.

Yet democracy is always exposed to the threat of an underside, populist or otherwise. If democracy, as Lefort describes it, is 'instituted and sustained by the *dissolution of the markers of certainty*', by a process of questioning implicit in social practice, and by a representation of unity dependent upon political discourse bound up with ideological debate,[55] then in limit situations its very functioning may provide the conditions of possibility for the underside. This danger, he says, arises with the exacerbation of conflicts that cannot be resolved symbolically in the political sphere, and when a sense of social fragmentation pervades society. When this happens, there is a real possibility for the 'the development of the fantasy of the People-as-One, the beginnings of a quest for a substantial identity, for a social body that is welded to its head, for an embodying power, for a state free from division'.[56] Lefort associates this with the emergence of totalitarian phenomena, but the fantasy of a unity without fissures is equally present in the populist temptation to confuse the government with the state, which amounts to a perversion of representation.[57] This confusion, of course, refers to populism in government, whose sense of possession rather than occupancy is conducive to a patrimonial use of state resources.

The temptation of a substantial identity will also appear when the internal paradox of the populist mode of representation mentioned earlier is resolved on behalf of the leader – that is, when the leader no longer acts for others because he or she presumes to incarnate those others, and therefore believes him- or herself to be authorised a priori. Oakeshott refers to this as the messianic twist of the politics of faith.[58] There are plenty of examples. In the authoritarian corner one might consider the experience of Peru under Fujimori, and on the more progressive side, at least with regard to his social base and egalitarian discourse, we can illustrate it with Hugo Chávez in Venezuela, a progressive yet often troubling leader imbued with an overriding sense of purpose.[59] Here, the gap that differentiates representatives from the represented – and that sets limits to representation as 'acting for others' – operates haphazardly. Instead of the crossover between acting for others, 'standing for' and authorisation, populist representation gradually slips into the symbolic 'standing for' and ultimately into a Hobbesian authorisation whereby the gap is dissolved de facto in favour of the representative.

Lefort also refers to the populist invocation of social justice,[60] a key element of urban-industrial populism that has sustained its appeal among the dispossessed, as well as among progressive intellectuals. He examines this when he says that populist movements often build their relation with the masses through the mediation of welfare policies, and that this relation might have a negative effect on the health of democratic practice and on the prospects for empowering individuals. While this might sound like a conservative argument against social justice, he is not trying to question equality but to criticise the vertical relation with the people. Social justice and the redistributive policies through which it comes about certainly improve the life of people by satisfying basic needs. Yet populists see this mostly as a top-down process, as a vertical link connecting political leaders and governmental decision-making bodies with grateful masses. The problem with this type of link is that being grateful turns easily into the demand to submit to the dictates of the party, the government or the leader. In Lefort's words:

> [It] instigates what de la Boétie called 'a voluntary servitude'. Being drawn to populism and to the leader, or putting the destiny of all in the hands of the leader, merely highlights this form of servitude. ... What is the point of social justice if all the measures are decided by a government that seeks the obedience of its citizens as repayment for the rewards it offers, and if such a justice does not awaken in the people awareness of their rights, of their sense of endeavour, or of their freedom of association?[61]

What he tells us here is that servitude, voluntary or otherwise, turns citizenship into an empty shell and distributive justice into an instrument of domination. This disempowerment of citizenship – despite verbal reassurances to the contrary – is a reminder that populism can also project a darker shadow on democracy. Just as Canovan could claim that democracy – or at least, and more precisely, modern politics generally – has two faces, redemptive and pragmatic, we may contend that the populist shadow does too, for it follows democratic politics as a promise and as an underside. As a promise, it can contribute to political renewal by harnessing the participatory energy issuing from the redemptive drive of modern politics, but as an underside, populism can turn out to be dangerous. Reiterating Canovan's analogy, the promise and the underside resemble a pair of squabbling Siamese twins. The problem is that while the promise might merely disturb the more gentrified functioning of the democratic process, as in the case of populism as a politics in the rougher edges of democracy, when the underside gets the upper hand, democracy is ready to leave the political stage.

What can we say in summary about the triple characterisation of democracy described here? To begin with, that the contours of populism emerge in the shape of a double bind that describes not the democratic nature of the phenomenon – for we have seen that this cannot be decided by decree, as there can be undemocratic populism too – but the ambiguous and often tense relation of interiority it maintains with the practice of democracy. Populism can flourish as a fellow traveller of democratic reform movements *and* put democracy in jeopardy. This double bind suggests that people like Canovan, but also Worsley and Hayward, are right in proposing that any inquiry about populism is at the same time an inquiry about democratic politics. Yet it also shows that this works as a conceptual strategy only if one stipulates that it can also refer to its more turbulent aspects, to a reflection about politics played at the rougher edges of democracy. More precisely, one could speak of three modalities of populism with regard to modern democratic politics – as a mode of representation, as a symptom, and as an underside. The actual valence it adopts is undecidable, as it can go in any of these three directions. However, determining when the mode of representation and the disruptive edge cross the line and become an underside of democracy is a matter of political judgment, and cannot be settled by conceptual fiat.

That is why I refer to the phenomenon as an internal periphery or 'internal foreign territory' of democracy and of modern politics generally. The expression safeguards the relation of interiority with democracy that I have developed here, but it also conveys the ideas of an edge and a possible underside, and more importantly, the undecidability associated with the term. Like any border or frontier, a periphery is always a hazy territory that indicates simultaneously the outermost limit of an inside and the beginning of the exterior of a system. Populism can remain within the bounds of democracy but also reach the point where both enter into conflict, and perhaps even go their own separate ways. I believe that this internal periphery portrays the paradoxical and contested status of the relationship between populism and democratic politics.

4

Skinhead Conservatism: A Failed Populist Project

OSCAR REYES

Between 1997 and 2001 the British Conservative Party was unable to challenge the political dominance of Tony Blair's Labour Government. The most popular account of this failure blames the Conservatives' unpopular right-wing populism. Instead of emphasising a coherent strategy that dealt with welfare issues like health and education, William Hague drove the party down a series of populist cul-de-sacs – on Europe, crime, asylum and public morality. In June 2001, the inevitable happened and Hague's right-wing bandwagon was washed away by the 'clear blue water' of electoral defeat. Like all good stories, this one works better as a description of what happened in the 1997–2001 period than as an explanation. For if we take seriously the emphasis it places on public service provision, we might be left baffled as to how the Thatcher government ever won while it consistently trailed Labour on these same key issues. This chapter attempts to remedy this deficiency by presenting an account of recent British Conservatism as a failed populist–hegemonic project.

I begin by revisiting Stuart Hall's interpretation of Thatcherism as authoritarian populism, defined as an attempt to forge a reactionary common-sense. Although it is now commonplace among political scientists to see this as a crusade that failed, the opinion poll evidence they present does not account for the distinctive unity of the populist issues it purports to measure. This is crucial, because the explanatory potential of Hall's thesis rests on an interpretation of Thatcherism as an *articulation* and *condensation* of (contradictory) neoliberal and conservative elements into a single hegemonic project.[1] Viewed in this light, the main limitation of the authoritarian populism thesis is that its theorisation is over-descriptive.

As a corrective, I elaborate a series of theoretical conditions for the understanding of populism (authoritarianism temporarily drops out of the picture, as it was never fully operative at this level of abstraction). The notorious indeterminacy of populism's ineliminable core – an opposition between the people and the elite – has driven most commentators to supplement or replace it with something less fuzzy. I argue that we do better if we clarify the theoretical status of these elements. My basic thesis is that *populism is the dimension of the political that constructs and gives meaning to 'the people', which is a name to which no prior concept corresponds.*

At this point my analysis of the failure of recent Conservative populism kicks in. Whereas the standard interpretation of the party's recent history would see the post-election emergence of compassionate Conservatism (1997–1999) thwarted by a resurgent right-wing populism (1999–2001), I argue that the former was always the site of a struggle between moral authoritarian and social liberal elements.[2] The difference between an oxymoronic compassionate Conservatism and a moronic 'skinhead Conservatism' was therefore one of emphasis.[3] The Conservatives retreated from attempts to *redefine* traditional values of family and nation *as compassionate*, and increasingly challenged the very legitimacy of the touchy-feely Blairite model. This did result in a sharpening of antagonism, consistent with a populist politics. But the precedent for this was established at the very outset of Hague's leadership, and built upon the party's early rejection of the euro.

The specifically populist dimension of Hague-era Conservatism is found in its attempt to organise the political terrain in terms of an opposition between the people, or mainstream majority, and the liberal elite. Far from simply 'listening to Britain', the Conservative Party actively attempted to forge a changed understanding of the mainstream, which would embody and define the people in their most reactionary guise. This notion of a mainstream majority is also the fundamental articulating principle of contemporary Conservative discourse – its nodal point, to use Laclau's terms.[4]

At this point, it could be argued that this project altogether failed: 'Hague may have been a brilliant tactician, but he was a poor strategist.'[5] This chapter develops an alternative view, arguing that the Conservatives under Hague *successfully* articulated a series of hard-line stances into a single (though contradictory) political project. My basic method is to show that a loosening of the relationship between various political signifiers (names) and signifieds (concepts) allowed for the transfer of political meaning from one issue to another. This meant, for example, that the ideological substance of Conservative references to 'asylum' became infused with a certain stance on 'crime' or 'sexuality'.

Yet in this successful articulation were sown the seeds of failure, as Labour and the Liberal Democrats managed to neutralise and, more damagingly, to negate Conservative populism. In the case of New Labour, this predominantly took the form of a *transformist* strategy – the absorption of conflictual political demands into a 'consensus of the well-intentioned', to use Marquand's memorable phrase.[6] This did not produce enemies, but it did specify an extreme. Furthermore, the plausibility of the 'extremist' label was inversely proportionate to the clarity of the Conservative message. And that was all but lost on the battlefield of an intra-party dispute over the Thatcher legacy.

In the final analysis, then, I argue that the Conservatives' hard-line stance on Europe, asylum seekers, criminals and Section 28 was successfully naturalised as part of the same populist agenda. But through a combination of internal dissent and opposition pressure, this came to serve as a *metaphor* for the party's extremism and unelectability. The Conservatives' problems were then unwittingly exacerbated, because this successful articulation allowed the 'extremism' of minor issues to transform and give meaning to those higher-salience issues that figured in the same chain of equivalence: tax, Europe and Hague's leadership. The account I have offered thus draws upon and extends Stuart Hall's insight that marginal issues can take on a central political role. And it is with this that I begin.

Authoritarian populism revisited

When populism is evoked in studies of contemporary British politics, the typical move – premised on a misunderstanding of Stuart Hall's work – is to collapse it into authoritarianism, and then identify a series of 'populist issues', which define this condition. Populism in this sense is no more than a descriptive label for an ensemble of Conservative-heartland issues – typically Europe, race, asylum seekers, law and order, the family and sexual morality.

This use of the term has been prevalent since Ivor Crewe 'refuted' the authoritarian populism thesis in his 1988 article 'Has the Electorate become Thatcherite?' In that essay, Crewe abstracts a series of authoritarian populist issues and tests their popularity by means of opinion poll data, which is found to provide overwhelming evidence that the Thatcher government transformed British politics without the need for a cultural counter-revolution in the thinking of ordinary people. The British public remained a body of 'unreconstructed Keynesians'.[7] Authoritarian populism was a mirage. And, we might add, if Thatcherism could not transform the hearts and minds of the voting public, there was no danger that the Tories under Hague could do so.

The main problem with this account is that it presupposes (or simply ignores the issue of) the distinctive unity of the populist issues it purports to measure. This omission is crucial because the very emergence of a Thatcherite hegemony, and the perceived absence of a 'governing alternative', rests on the successful articulation of populist issues around a common nodal point – a knot that binds together and retroactively shapes the elements that inhabit a given ideological field. Just as the crisis of Keynesian social democracy in Britain made possible the rise of authoritarian populism, the coalescence of the latter into a new hegemonic project can only be understood if we attempt to construct theoretically a connection between these issues. In both cases, moreover, the argument draws its explanatory force as much from its theoretical basis as its empirical validity.

In the Gramscian tradition in which Hall works, the emergence of populism is historically linked to an instance of organic crisis, which manifests itself as a proliferation of popular demands that cannot be neutralised by the existing framework of state power. Typically, this coincides with a crisis within the power bloc itself.[8] In the British case, Hall perceived that a movement from above (Thatcherism) intervened to rearticulate a series of popular frustrations from below. *Thatcherism provided a setting for populism, but interrupted its development before it became truly popular.* A symbolic majority of the people were mobilised against the social-democratic consensus, while populist sentiment was simultaneously cut off and transformed into an identification with authority, traditionalism and firm leadership.[9] Hence, the very form of authoritarian populism was contradictory, with its authoritarian moment co-existing with but curtailing its populist appeal.

In Hall's account, the moral panic is the paradigm case of a populist mobilisation. It is therefore afforded a privileged role in undermining the post-war consensus and legitimising Thatcherism. But the experience of Labour's first term has made it amply clear that this way of raising the political temperature need not boil over into a wider hegemonic formation. In the debate on the repeal of Section 28, for example, the emergence of a full-blown moral panic showed few lasting effects, and none at the level of the state, beyond the continued existence of a virulently homophobic statute.[10]

The continuing relevance of Hall's approach, then, lies not so much in the form of the moral panic itself, as in the accompanying insight that seemingly marginal issues can take on a central political role. Thatcherism found the means to translate its social market values into a populist idiom. It offered 'bitter-tasting market economics sweetened and rendered palatable by great creamy dollops of nationalistic custard', washed down with a reactionary social project.[11] Hall offered a prescient and timely account of authoritarian populism, although his concept remained over-descriptive. In order to remedy this deficiency, let us therefore elaborate some theoretical conditions for the understanding of populism, before applying these to the case of contemporary British Conservatism.[12]

Theorising populism

Most scholars define populism as a dimension of political action rather than an ideological position.[13] Yet this is only the beginning of the problem. Although it is widely acknowledged that all populisms refer to a common analogical basis – the people – this is 'so indeterminate an expression that its use, let alone its abuse, obscures almost all political discussions'.[14] In response, numerous efforts have been made to furnish populism with some much-needed conceptual clarity. These generally proceed in one of three directions.

Firstly, there have been attempts to develop a taxonomy of populisms, or even to classify the different variants of 'the people' that occur in actually existing populist formations.[15] While these have sometimes yielded important empirical insights, they do not pay adequate attention to the theoretical and explanatory status of the concept itself, which is effectively dissipated into a series of more refined sub-species (agrarian, national, reactionary, and so on). This plurality of popul*isms* relies on a continued appeal to a singularity – populism – whose unifying force remains hidden behind a smokescreen of descriptive additions.

A second strategy is to untangle populism from 'the people' and suggest an alternative basis for the concept. Taggart, for example, argues that populism's appeal is dependent upon a sense of 'the heartland'. If we accept this move, however, the specificity of populism is altogether lost and it simply collapses into a species of nationalism.[16] Moreover, the indeterminacy of this conception of the heartland reproduces the very problem that it was brought in to solve. What this effort has in common with the first is that both discern the radical insufficiency of populism's core values: 'To say … that all populists are for the people and against the elite is quite true, but not much more helpful than saying that all religious leaders are for holiness and against sin'.[17]

A third route, which I follow here, concentrates on the specificity of populism at a theoretical level. An appeal to the people is a necessary but not a sufficient condition for populism, which also requires that popular interpellations be presented in the form of antagonism.[18] Ernesto Laclau, who is the leading exponent of this view, introduces two distinctive aspects to the study of populism: (i) an insistence that antagonism is constitutive of the political terrain, and therefore ineliminable; and (ii) a recognition that populism does not merely appeal to, but actually attempts to create new political subjects who identify with a particular, decontested conception of the people.[19]

The concept of antagonism is central to Laclau's understanding of populism, although its theoretical status has undergone a number of changes in his subsequent development of a political discourse theory. Laclau's early work treats antagonism as 'a relation of contradiction within discourse', which affords to negation a crucial role in the constitution of political objects.[20] These cannot be taken simply as objective givens, but are constructed and become meaningful in relation to their position within a structure, or system of differences. This line of argument is reinforced in *Hegemony and Socialist Strategy*, which further emphasises the fact that contradiction (in the strict sense) is never fully reducible to a given discursive field, but persists in the form of a negation that permanently holds open the limits of any given structure.[21] This radically negated element, which is incommensurable with the 'inside' of the structure in question, is constitutive of it. The equivalence between particular elements is established by means of their common reference to something external to them, although this can only be expressed *in*directly, in terms of what Laclau would now call an empty signifier.[22]

Let us now add a morsel of political flesh to these dry theoretical bones, and define populism as a particular species of this antagonistic relation that pits 'the people' against 'the elite'. If we take antagonism seriously – that is, if we understand that the meaning of these terms cannot be reduced to a positive set of objectively determinable conditions – then it should be clear that neither term refers simply to a structural position. The theoretical innovation at work here is a simple one: 'the people' can no longer be understood as the analogical basis of the signified (or concept) of populism, but must be treated as a signifier (or name). In fact, populism can be redefined as a process of naming that retroactively determines the meaning of 'the people', or even as a demand for the naming of that to which no prior concept corresponds.[23] This shows us why all attempts to clarify or capture the essence of the concept of populism are futile: *populism is the dimension of the political which constructs and gives meaning to 'the people'.*

A similar thing happens to our definition of 'the elite', which is also indeterminate at a structural level. Indeed, Thatcherism has decisively shown how a populist discourse can be constructed from a structurally elite position. What we are dealing with in the case of populism, by contrast, is the posing of an 'elite' not at a structural but at an imaginary level. In the case of Thatcherism, this led to the demonisation of Reds in the classroom, cultural workers, progressive politicians and intellectuals in general. Under Hague, as I will argue, 'the liberal elite' is similarly castigated.

It is at this level, moreover, that we might reintroduce (in a revised fashion) the question of political subjectivity. Populism is no longer to be understood in terms of interpellation – namely, that instance of (mis)recognition through which the individual comes to see itself as a subject. Whereas the subject (or subject-position) is structurally determinable, the *identification* of which Laclau would now speak inhabits the gap between the individual (agent) and the structure.[24] And where popular interpellation would tend to involve the creation of a new political subject (the people), identification is predicated on the repeated and perpetual failure for this to be the case. Indeed, it is this very failure that makes possible a hegemonic politics.

To summarise, then, it is the very indeterminacy of 'the people' and 'the elite' at a conceptual level that guarantees these terms their articulating function, which is *the* crucial aspect underlying Laclau's theory of populism (and indeed, political discourse theory in general). A successful populist practice would decontest the meaning of 'the people' in the light of its own ideological terms.[25] In the case of Hague-era

Conservatism this would have required an overlap, at the level of common-sense, between signifier ('mainstream majority') and signified (the British people). To understand why this was manifestly not the case, let us now turn our attention to the recent history of the British Conservative Party.

The Conservative Party, 1997–2001

The standard narrative of recent Conservative history can be easily summarised. At the 1997 Conference, William Hague championed an open, tolerant Conservatism, and looked forward to a united and inclusive party.[26] A greater enthusiasm about multiculturalism would help shed the image of a nasty party, as well as opening up the space for a major policy review. The high-water mark for this approach was Peter Lilley's Rab Butler lecture in April 1999, which argued that 'the free market has only a limited role in improving public services like health, education and welfare'.[27] But this spilled over into an internal party row, as senior Tories accused Lilley of repudiating Thatcherism. The case for repositioning was then all but sunk when the Conservatives won the European elections in June 1999 on the basis of an 'In Europe, Not Run by Europe' campaign. Buoyed by this success, Hague dismissed Lilley and steered the party through a series of negative, populist campaigns on Europe, law and order, asylum seekers and Section 28. Long-term strategy was jettisoned in favour of short-term, headline-grabbing tactics.[28] This left the Conservatives with nothing to say about the issues that really matter (health and education). The 2001 election was fought in these same terms, a 'core vote strategy [which] succeeded in reducing the core Tory vote by around one and a half million'.[29]

Putting it bluntly, I will argue that the above account draws the wrong conclusions from a misreading of recent Conservative history. If we now approach the same period by means of a genealogy of contemporary Conservative populism and moral authoritarianism, we will see why.

We can begin by analysing the authoritarian content of modern British Conservatism, which lies at the heart of disputes about the ideological legacy of Thatcherism. The most basic point, for which the evidence is so widespread that I am surprised at having to make it, is that compassionate Conservatism is not and was never a repudiation of Thatcherism.[30] Nor was it simply a foil for social liberalism. In fact, its very purpose was to challenge the reduction of Conservatism to free-market individualism, and place a greater emphasis on voluntary groups, charities, local societies and the family. Far from being cut short, the centrality of these institutions actually increased in the official Conservative discourse of the 'nasty party' period. In the 2000 draft manifesto *Believing in Britain*, for example, 'families, charities, places of worship' become the institutional embodiment of 'the common sense values and ideas of the mainstream majority'.[31]

Let us take the family as our example. In his speech to the Social Market Foundation on 29 January 1998, Hague privileges the family – which he uses as a synonym for marriage – as a core institution, and promises Conservative policies to strengthen it by means of tax incentives (including the Married Couples Allowance). It is against this backdrop, and the 'important signals' that it sends out, that the claim to a 'more tolerant attitude towards homosexuals' should be judged.[32] Hague gestures towards a social liberalism which privileges marriage while tolerating (in a narrow sense) the existence of homosexuality.[33] But his stress on legislative signals simultaneously plays to a moral authoritarian agenda whose definition of tolerance is cast in terms of the majority heterosexual community – as a comparison with the windy rhetoric of Ann Widdecombe would make clear.[34]

Hague's subsequent defence of Section 28, a key symptom of the authoritarian populist approach, places a greater emphasis on this dimension with reference to 'the tolerance demanded by the mainstream majority that its views and values are respected'. But it does not mark a clean break from his earlier stance. Indeed, his 1997 appeal for 'tolerance of people making their own decision about how they lead their lives' can also be interpreted as a defence of traditional family forms and religious organisations, which Labour is said to discriminate against.[35] This might even be said to be its primary meaning, if we pay due attention to the genealogical precedents for Hague's specific type of 'tolerance' within the tradition of Thatcherism.[36]

This picture is reinforced if we pay attention to a second aspect of compassionate Conservatism that is usually missed. In his 1997 Conference speech, Hague already speaks of compassion in terms of 'giving power back ... to real people' to free them from 'welfare dependency'. At the following year's party conference, he repeatedly identifies the party with the British people and their instincts. And by February 1999, this emphasis has developed into a desire to shed the party's 'elitist' image. In fact, it is in opposition to an elite that the party is 'open, inclusive and compassionate'.[37] And it is against this backdrop that the populist antagonism between 'mainstream majority' and 'liberal elite' is established.

An analysis of the *Listening to Britain* exercise, which was conducted during 1998 but published after the 1999 European election, neatly captures this dichotomy. Its ideological preoccupations can be unpacked by looking for signs of over-wording – a proliferation of different words with roughly similar meanings which extend across a wide range of policy fields.[38] Two opposing clusters emerge: the British people on the one hand, and the interfering politicians on the other. This is hardly surprising, given that the whole exercise presumes a deferral of judgment from the political elite to the people. What is more interesting, however, is the meaning given to these terms.

They are far from ideologically neutral. The people are British, taxpayers, married couples (with children), home owners, car owners, (small) business people, farmers, private-sector workers, pensioners and patients. And they are dismayed by red-tape, higher taxes, regulation, bureaucracy, interference, excess paperwork, waste, centralising decisions and political correctness – all of which are imposed upon them by politicians, quangos, government and unelected EU bureaucrats in Brussels.[39] In this formulation, I would argue, we find all the ingredients of what is later dubbed the mainstream majority. With the exception of a few 'cronies', and some scornful references to Whitehall and Islington, it also contains the main components of the liberal (or metropolitan) elite.

It would be easy, I suppose, to dismiss this pattern as no more than a linguistic aberration that belies the true direction of Conservative policy and ideology in the immediate post-election period.[40] But even if it were possible to abstract such realities from the language of Conservatism's populist appeal, we would be left pondering the fact that the most visible manifestation of policy at this time – the 'Keep the Pound' stance – was established from the very beginning of Hague's leadership.[41]

Of course, arguments will persist as to whether or not Europe was *the* defining feature of Hague-era Conservatism. Certainly, there was no necessary development from a hardline on Europe to a hardline on asylum, law and order and sexual morality. Yet I would argue that the increasing prominence of these issues can be traced from this starting point, as can be seen in a speech made by Hague just days after Lilley's ill-fated Rab Butler lecture. Even as Hague affirms the limitations of the free market, he claims that the Conservatives are 'the only party that speaks for the mainstream view of the people of this country. The only party that wants to be in Europe, not run by Europe. … It's our approach to Europe, because it's our approach to everything'.[42]

What this also makes clear is that, far from simply listening to the people, the Conservative appeal to them *actively forges a changed understanding of the mainstream*. In fact, Hague-era Conservatism can be called populist precisely because this notion of the mainstream, and subsequently the 'mainstream majority', functions as its central articulating principle. It can also be called authoritarian, insofar as it advocates a series of interventions in defence of this postulated majority – regulating against the corrosion of British society from within (Whitehall and Islington) and without (the European Union and asylum seekers). But Hague's Conservatism is not 'authoritarian populist' in quite the way Hall understood that category, because authoritarianism and populism operate at different levels of abstraction. Populism refers to an ontological mode of articulation, while authoritarianism specifies an ontic set of ideological contents.[43] Or, to put the point another way, populism opens to question the definition of the people, and specifies the conditions of possibility for the emergence of authoritarianism. But it is only at the level of ideological contents ('mainstream majority') that the people can be articulated in a distinctly Conservative direction. Furthermore, both aspects are vital to my thesis that Hague-era Conservatism sought (and failed!) to displace existing understandings of the majority in an authoritarian direction, and articulate a new common-sense around which the party could reconstruct its electoral support. In the process, the mainstream majority becomes the nodal point (or empty signifier) of Conservative discourse.

The articulation of Conservative populism

At its most basic level, Conservative populism is an opposition between the people and the elite. But this banality is not what I am asserting. For it is only with the successful *articulation* of a series of issues into a coherent (if contradictory) discourse that we can properly speak of populism. For Laclau and Mouffe, articulation is a political practice of linking together elements of an ideological formation so that their identity is modified in the process.[44] I would add that this can be proved (or disproved) in three ways.

Firstly, a successful articulation involves a loosening of the relation between signifier and signified through a process of condensation. This occurs when a single term comes to represent several associative chains at whose point of intersection it is located.[45] A clear example of this can be seen in the reception of Hague's pre-election 'foreign land' speech, which warned of a Labour-run country rife with crime, soaring petrol prices and the euro. This came to be widely interpreted as an anti-immigrant rant.[46] What happened, in effect, was that the signifier 'foreign land' lost its moorings and came to represent the outcome of illegal immigration, which was another conceptual element of the same chain of Conservative populist discourse. Hague's 'foreign land' thereby became a metaphor for his stance towards asylum seekers:

$$\frac{\text{signifier}}{\text{signified}} \qquad \frac{\text{foreign land}}{\text{asylum seekers}}$$

The second proof of a successful articulation requires that each 'moment' of a discourse can, in different contexts, represent the whole. This is essentially a metonymic relationship, which takes the following form:

$$\frac{\text{law-abiding families (... mainstream majority)}}{\text{mainstream majority}}$$

In my example, the part (law-abiding family) is used for the whole (mainstream majority).[47] While I share Laclau's insistence that a nodal point (lately termed an empty signifier) is the articulating principle of any discourse, my presumption that a cluster of ideological meanings will be gathered around this point (over-wording) obviates the need for this signifier to appear in its 'pure' form. In fact, the status of the mainstream majority as a nodal point is proved by the variety of guises in which it appears. With each shake of the Conservative kaleidoscope, it takes on a new look: Britons who take pride in their currency and their country, hard-working people who want lower taxes, law-abiding families who are the victims of crime, parents who do not want Section 28 repealed, pensioners who find their money spent on bogus asylum seekers, and the terrified home-owner (Tony Martin) who acts to protect his home.

The final proof of the Conservative articulation also partly accounts for why the strategy failed. The distinctive unity of the party's populist agenda was recognised by Labour, which was then faced with two logical responses. Either it could accept a limited sub-set of Conservative proposals in an attempt to disarticulate the wider project, or accept the populist articulation as something it negated.[48] New Labour made a characteristically Third Way response, and did both. To take just one example, the Labour government extended a 'son of Section 28' proposal to cover health promotion units, and redoubled its efforts to appear 'entirely conventional' on the family. But it also sought to negate the Conservatives' extreme position, with Blair accusing Hague of doing on Section 28 'exactly the same as he did over the asylum issue ... pandering to prejudice'. The Liberal Democrat leader Charles Kennedy voiced the same accusation with more gusto, as he laid into Hague's knee-jerk 'saloon bar' populism.

Conservative populism was also challenged by New Labour's own attempts to decontest the meaning of 'the people'. This sometimes took the form of a consensual, One Nation Britishness.[49] At other times it involved a top-down appeal to the citizen as consumer: 'In all walks of life people act as consumers not just citizens', as Blair wrote in the government's *Annual Report*.[50] Anthony Barnett has christened this latter tendency 'corporate populism', although in the strict sense of the term it is not populist at all. New Labour has not turned its back upon parliamentarism in favour of a direct appeal to the people. On the whole, it remains complicit with the Thatcherite view that the British people (meaning, in the main, the English) are, by nature, conservative and intolerant.[51] And where the Conservatives sought (and failed) to mobilise a changed understanding of the British people, New Labour seemed content to absorb contradictory demands and decontest 'the people' in its existing guise. In Gramscian terms, this is a transformist strategy par excellence.

Moreover, Blair has sought to heal the wounds that divide the nation and, more recently, the global community. Although New Labour was not without its enemies – the forces of Conservatism, 'wreckers', and Ken Livingstone – the predominant strain was an antagonism-free post-politics. New Labour spoke of 'the people'

> as though it embodies a national consensus – a consensus of the well-intentioned, embracing rich and poor, young and old, suburbs and inner cities, black and white, hunters and animal rights campaigners, successful and unsuccessful. In place of the Thatcherite cold shower, it offers a warm bath, administered by a hegemonic people's party appealing equally to every part of the nation.[52]

The effectiveness of this transformist strategy was compounded by the inconsistency of the Conservatives' own message. When Hague went out of his way to antagonise the liberal elite – 'Great! We've got the whole liberal establishment railing against me' – the impact was felt rather too strongly within the shadow Cabinet. As Michael Portillo was quick to point out: 'I am a liberal. And I am a member of the elite.'[53]

Portillo's private comments speak of a wider, public problem. While opposition MPs (in particular, the Liberal Democrats) *consistently* branded the Conservative agenda 'extreme', the Party's own message was generally lost beneath the noise of its incoherent, or even flatly contradictory pronouncements. This was above all a result of ideological division, rather than a mere lack of focus. The *dis*articulation of Thatcherism's neoliberal and organic Tory elements had bequeathed two opposing legacies, reflected in an ideological rift between 'mods' (social liberals) and 'rockers' (moral authoritarians).[54] This dispute came to a head at the October 2000 conference in a row over drugs policy, when Ann Widdecombe inadvertently displayed her 'zero-tolerance' of almost half the shadow Cabinet.

The same ideological division was reflected in a series of resignations from the party, which were always accompanied by a ritual denunciation of Conservatives' extremity. Ivan Massow puts the point succinctly in an article announcing his defection to Labour: 'Under William [Hague], the Tories have become less compassionate, more intolerant and, frankly, just plain nasty'. The chorus of complaint was then routinely joined by discontented voices from within the party, such as Ian Taylor MP, who claimed: 'We are now defined by who we hate – the euro, the EU, asylum-seekers, gays and criminals. When it comes to voting in a general election, people do not like parties who define their policies only by what they are against.'[55] This combination of internal dissent and opposition pressure proved decisive.

To summarise: the Conservatives' hard-line stance against Europe, asylum seekers, criminals and the repeal of Section 28 – articulated in terms of the mainstream majority – *was* successfully naturalised as part of the same populist agenda. But ideological divisions and incoherence, compounded by an effective Labour transformism, neutralised this threat. The Conservatives' top-down attempts to redefine the mainstream could not connect with any substantial discontent 'from below', but instead came to serve as a metaphor for the party's extremism and unelectability – its skinhead Conservatism.

Skinhead conservatism

Let us now formalise this transition from mainstream majority to skinhead Conservatism. Once again, we can see how the function of metaphor serves to expel the concept of the mainstream majority and replace it with the whole of the sign extremism:

$$\frac{\text{mainstream majority} \; = \; \text{signifier (acoustic image)}}{\text{extremism} \qquad = \qquad \text{signified (concept)}}$$

The clearest manifestations of Conservative extremism were against asylum seekers and gays, though these were never the most salient political factors. Nevertheless, the cementing of a wider populist articulation unleashed the metaphoric content of even these minor policies, and left 'extremism' free to slide under and transform the meaning of higher-salience issues that figured in the same chain of equivalence: tax, Europe and Hague's leadership.

There is also a metonymic dimension to this account. Take, for example, Hague's baldness. It seems risky to ascribe any direct political relevance to this, though Hague can hardly have been helped by the fact that he began to resemble physically the skinheads he seemed to identify with politically. It would also be crass to suggest that the mere fact of baldness has any sociological (and still less a psychological) relevance. I would not even claim that the dominance of the image in modern politics means 'a full head of hair is always going to triumph over a "slaphead".'[56] What I would argue, however, is that Hague's baldness – which really came into its own with the Bruce Willis-style close-crop inflicted at the advice of his personal spin doctor – became a metonymic representation of his political personality. And this, in turn, was a key element of the populist chain of equivalence – a symptom of the contemporary fixation with leadership.[57] The combined effect was that Hague's baldness came to carry an ideological meaning intimately related to the political project of skinhead Conservatism.

It should also be noted that this stress on metonymy involves a slight modification to Laclau's discourse analysis, which deals with 'tendentially empty signifiers'. I have sought to emphasise the *vital importance* of these tendential residues of positive content, which I see as providing the very *substance* of the negative evaluations of the mainstream majority (hate, extremism, moral majority and so on). A specific content – the hatred of asylum seekers and gays – was promulgated as 'typical' of the Conservative Party as a whole. In short, it became too easy to see in the homophobic statements of Tebbit, or the racist Townsend, the out-of-touch 'truth' of modern Conservatism.

My interpretation does not contradict the usual claim that the Conservative obsession with the totems of Europe, asylum seekers and Section 28 cost them dear, but it does offer a different reason as to why that was so. By successfully upgrading the mainstream majority into a symbolic nodal point, and articulating to this a series of issues – Europe, law and order, asylum seekers, the family and sexual morality – which retroactively became 'moments' of the Conservative discourse that it sought to organise, the party inadvertently spread the signification of extremism.

This chapter has also sought to intervene in the debate on recent Conservative history. My genealogy of Hague-era populism has shown that compassionate Conservatism was the site of a dispute over the ideological legacy of Thatcherism, and never merely a repudiation of it. More generally, I have argued that recent Conservatism is a classic example of a populist practice, defined as an antagonistic construction of the people in opposition to an imaginary liberal elite. A kaleidoscope of metonymic representations of the mainstream majority was offered by way of evidence for this.

Finally, this chapter has sought to understand the Conservatives' inability to mount a realistic challenge to the current New Labour (or post-Thatcherite) orthodoxy. Tory factionalism and Labour trans-formism were cited as explanatory factors, though these cannot hope to fill in the whole picture. A comprehensive account of Conservative failure would need to pay more attention to the impact of the ERM crisis, which did untold damage to the party's reputation for economic competence.[58] It would also need to take cognizance of Labour's macro-economic timidity, which largely continued along the neoliberal path of its predecessors, and was only responsible and competent in their terms. Competence, reputation, responsibility: the meaning of these impressions is not economically determined, and even defenders of an economic model agree that 'objective' macroeconomic conditions do not explain the results of the 1992, 1997 or 2001 elections.[59] One direction for further research, therefore, would be to examine the implications of my account of Conservative extremism at the level of the 'subjective economy'.

5

Constitutive Violence and the Nationalist Imaginary: The Making of 'The People' in Palestine and 'Former Yugoslavia'

GLENN BOWMAN

The nationalist imaginary, antagonism and populism

In this chapter I assess the conditions which allowed for the emergence of what I call the 'nationalist imaginary' in the Israeli-Occupied Territories and Palestinian diaspora, as well as in the Socialist Federative Republic of Yugoslavia (particularly the national areas called Serbia, Croatia and Slovenia). I treat the nationalist imaginary as a specific modality of 'imagined community'[1] wherein a group of people comes to conceive of itself as a 'we' through the process of mobilising against an other it is brought to recognize as forbidding it access to national reification as a state. The suffix 'ist' appended to the substantive 'national' indicates agency, thereby connoting a (political) project of bringing a future nation-state into being. The fact that it is a project to be carried out implies that something has impeded its realisation, and it is here my contention that that something – which I, following Laclau and Mouffe,[2] call an 'antagonism' – is precisely what gives shape and substance to the identity it produces and prevents. In analysing the formations of Palestinian nationalist identity and of the various nationalist identities which served to tear apart what we now term 'Former Yugoslavia', I attempt to show the logics of articulation which constituted oppositional nationalist blocs in the two regions.

It is perhaps unsurprising that these logics, and the blocs they produce, are quite similar to those we characterise as 'populist'; the Manichean opposition of 'us' and 'them' evidenced in both the nationalist imaginary and populism is, in both instances, the result of processes by which a number of people are induced to recognise that they share a common antagonist, and to participate in the projects of overcoming of the community of those that enemy antagonises. There are in turn apparent differences; while in populist movements the antagonistic relationship of 'us' and 'them' is played out within the constraints of a single system – with resolution imagined in the ultimate defeat and purging of the antagonist, that relationship in nationalistic movements is seen as resolvable through the separation of peoples and the establishment of distinct territorial domains particular to each. Other chapters in this book will demonstrate the aftermath of populist movements and the forms of identity which surface in the wake of the struggles populism promotes, including the disintegration of the oppositional blocs it has mobilised. The dissolution of the Socialist Federative Republic of Yugoslavia, and the subsequent establishment of (at present) five distinct states, suggests some of the ways in which identities are reformulated after the 'successful' outcome of a nationalist struggle, but also shows that 'the nation' can remain a signifier of unanswered demands and a response to perceived antagonisms, even after the formation of a nation-state. The rapidly changing situation in Palestine, which has in the course of less than a decade moved from the establishment of the Palestine National Authority on 'liberated' territory to the current efforts by the Israeli State to destroy that power and re-establish direct rule, shows the ways in which articulations of identity can recede and re-emerge in the wake of an 'unsuccessful' nationalist movement. I will, in closing, consider these two scenarios and the logics that organise them. It is to be hoped that the inclusion of these two cases of nationalist mobilisation and demobilisation, in the context of a book on populism, will engender further debate as to whether or not nationalism and populism can be treated as analytically distinct.

At the heart of this chapter, however, is the issue of what I term 'constitutive violence' and the role it plays in identity formation. This paper, in observing the emergence of a nationalist imaginary amongst Palestinians as well as amongst Serbs, Croats and Slovenes, will argue that violence is not simply a device nationalists of certain persuasions take up in pursuit of their ends, but that it plays a constitutive role in the formation of all nationalisms. The violence which engenders nationalism is not, however, the violence the imagined community of the future nation turns against its 'enemies', but the violence members of that not-yet-existent nation perceive as inflicted upon them by others they recognise as making it impossible for them to exist in anything other than the embrace of an independent state. The future nation of the nationalist imaginary functions as an antidote to a violence which threatens the survival of persons who did not, prior to its advent, conceive of themselves as members of a distinct community, much less of a nation in waiting. Decisions about what strategies – violent or otherwise – are appropriate to achieving national independence follow from the recognition that such independence is the only guarantor of individual, and collective, survival. Although I will, in the following analyses, demonstrate the ways 'defensive' violence is variously articulated in response to constitutive violence, such strategies are not the focus of this paper. Instead I will concentrate, through investigations of the generation of nationalist movements in the Israeli-Occupied Territories and what is now 'Former Yugoslavia', on the way perceptions of a violence afflicting a diverse range of persons give rise to a concept of a 'national enemy' and, through that concept, to the idea of solidarity with the nation that enemy opposes.

In investigating the way the Palestinian people came into being as a result of the project of nation formation the Zionist movement successfully carried out on the land that the 'Palestinians' had occupied long before they thought of themselves as 'Palestinians', and the way Yugoslavians came to see themselves not as co-nationals within an existent state but as members of opposed national communities unnaturally forced to coexist under the tyranny of an imposed federation, I will emphasise that national identity is an historical construct which emerges from a reformulation of one's relation to a social field, rather than something essential and non-contingent.

Furthermore, by stressing the role played by the perceived violence of an other in formulating that identity, I will criticise the material determinism of nation theorists, such as Benedict Anderson, who argue that the emergence of national consciousness simply reflects developments in systems of communication and exchange (Anderson 1991, 37–46 and *passim*). Mandate Palestine and pre-dissolution Yugoslavia were – in terms of the development of print culture and trans-regional economies – 'modernised' to an extent quite capable of supporting nationalist consciousnesses prior to the articulations of Palestinian, Serbian, Croatian and Slovenian nationalisms. But these national movements did not emerge until antagonisms between groups occupying those territories were interpreted in ways which split the field of sociality into domains of the nation and its enemy. I contend, therefore, that while the development of modes of communication enabling dispersed members of a community to conceive of others sharing with them a common language and a common territory was an essential prerequisite of being able to imagine an extended community, this development was not in itself enough to promulgate nationalist consciousness. Communication might suffice to promote an abstract idea of community, but it was the matter communicated which transformed that abstraction into something with which to identify and for which to struggle. For nationalism to arise it was vital that one had not only to see one's identity as integrally linked with that of the wider community, but also to sense that that community, and the identity it provided to the individual, were at risk. Palestinians, especially after the creation of the state of Israel drove a majority of them into diaspora, rarely (if ever) became Arab nationalists, despite their sharing the Arabic language and Arabic press with other Arabic-reading communities; they became anti-Zionists because they recognised the role of Israel in their own dispossession and that of other 'Palestinians' who suffered from the anti-Palestinian violence central to the Zionist project. Serbs and Croats were not united in an imagined community by their mutual use of Serbo-Croatian and their shared access to a Yugoslav press; despite (and through) that shared medium they came to conceive of each other as blood enemies who had to wage

war for the defence of their respective national identities. In each
instance, it was stories of violence carried through those media which
enabled members of the respective groups to recognise in those scenarios
violence like those they suffered, and enemies like those who tormented
them. Identity, in other words, emerged from identification, and the idea
of the nation was generated as a fantasy of the utopic space to be occupied by all those who suffered 'the same' violence at the hands of the
enemy after that enemy and its violence are extirpated.

The nationalist imaginary is a discursive structure which emerges out
of particular interpretations of violence encountered by those persons
who come to see themselves, in its terms, as members of the future
nation. It serves to articulate most, if not all, of the antagonisms encountered by those diverse persons as manifestations of the violence of a
shared enemy which, in opposing all of them, simultaneously renders all
of them 'the same'. As a consequence it presents the contemporary world
as divided in a Manichean manner between the good, but threatened,
community of 'us' and the evil community of a 'them' which exists solely
to destroy 'us'.[3] Although there tends, in the nationalist articulations
discussed below, to be a utopic future state imagined in which all of
the other's antagonism will have been elided, the chief emphasis of the
nationalist imaginary is on the contemporary struggle to expel or extin-
guish the sources of constitutive violence. It is, in other words, a logic of
mobilisation, and as such gives rise to practices which transform the
worlds of both the imagined community and those it wages nationalist
struggle against. Thus, although the logic which demands an absolute
distinction between the good space of the nation-to-be and the negative
space of its other may be fantastical, it nonetheless constructs a reality
around that opposition.[4]

The articulation of a Palestinian national movement (1881–1994)

In the early years of the twentieth century there were neither
'Palestinians' nor a Palestinian national movement. This was not, as Joan
Peters argued in *From Time Immemorial*, because Arabs only emigrated

into Palestine from surrounding countries after 1920 to take advantage of economic opportunities opened by Zionist settlement,[5] but because the indigenous occupants of the region the British conquered in 1917 and named Palestine had no conception of themselves as a single community. The *millet* system through which the Ottoman Empire had previously administered the region functioned by juridically dividing the population into autonomous religious enclaves that provided their members with legal identity and social support.[6] Such a separation of communities precluded concern for, or even interest in, any people but those of one's own religious community.[7] Among the rural peasantry the tradition of a 1,000-year conflict between *Qais* and *Yemini* provided a categorical opposition allowing communities caught up in local conflicts to articulate their mutual antagonism in terms drawn from the time of Muhammad.[8] In the cities families and clans perceived friends and enemies in terms not only of sectarian affiliation or alliances in long-running feuds, but also of the heated debate between 'Arab nationalists' and 'Ottomanists'.[9] This multiplicity of available categories of identity served to articulate the disparate social and economic interests of relatively autonomous groups, and thereby ensured that the community of 'Palestinians' could not recognise 'itself' as a community.

The development of a sense of a specific land, and of a people whose identity devolved from their residence within its borders, needed a powerful impetus to free itself from the domains of familial, sectarian, regional and economic identities and become amenable to integration within a nationalist discourse. That impetus was provided by the movement of substantial numbers of Jewish immigrants into the region in the period following the escalation of anti-Semitic persecutions of Jews in Russia (1881–82). Jewish immigration changed the face of the land; between 1881 and 1922 the Jewish population more than tripled (rising from 24,000 in 1881 to 84,000 by 1922), and immense tracts of land were bought up by the Jewish colonies, often from absentee Arab landlords.[10] Arab peasants were driven off lands they had long inhabited and cultivated, while others were denied their traditional grazing rights.[11] In 1930 the Hope Simpson Report indicated that 29.4 per cent of the rural population of the Mandated area was landless.[12] Many peasants emigrated to urban slums, where they rarely found opportunities for employment. Throughout the 1920s anti-Jewish rioting frequently broke out in the cities – particularly on occasions when religious festivities generated crowds – and these disturbances would often spread to the countryside where villagers, sparked by rumours of Jewish attacks on Arabs, would take up arms against local Jewish settlements.[13] While there was a general sense among the rural peasantry and urban *lumpenproletariat* of being threatened by 'the Jews', this perception remained inchoate. The disquiet felt by small merchants and craft producers about the incursion of Jewish competitors into *their* economic domains[14] was similarly only voiced among restricted circles of fellow trades-persons, and thus remained un-politicised.

The Palestinian elites, which traditionally provided the political leadership of the region, were unable to forge a vocabulary capable of designating Zionism as a common threat. Even when individual urban notables recognised the need to resist the steady expansion of Zionist settlement and immigration, they nonetheless attempted to articulate that threat in terms of earlier enunciations of identity and antagonism. Such expressions re-sparked antagonism between them and their potential allies across borders already inscribed in the Ottoman period by struggles between 'Ottomanists' and 'Arabists', and in the contemporary period by previous attempts to serve the interests of specific sectarian and family groups by attacking those of others. British diplomacy furthermore convinced most Palestinian politicians 'that the Arabs' position in Palestine was not as severely threatened as they had initially feared, and therefore … [they should] grasp the available levers of power'.[15]

The failure of the urban notables to provide a political vocabulary capable of enunciating the threat Zionist actions seemed to pose to the peasantry forced it to express its fear and its will to resist 'Jewish' violence in terms drawn from the idiom of its own traditions. In 1929, after the political initiatives of the urban leadership had collapsed in a fracas of factionalisms, major rioting broke out in Jerusalem when Jewish militants celebrating the Jewish fast of *Tisha Bav* (the destruction of the Temple) asserted claims to the Wailing Wall on the eve of the Muslim feast of *Mawlad al-Nabi* (the birth of the Prophet Muhammad). The consequent 'Wailing Wall Riots' were legitimated in Islamic terms but, as Nels Johnson points out, Islam provided a banner under which to fight not because of a deep investment of peasant subjectivity in religion, but because religion was the only idiom able to join, a peasantry divided by regional, factional, kin and clan ties join into a united front peasantry:

> There is no doubt that the idea of *national* interests – even the idea of nation itself – were foreign to the Palestinian peasantry. The very name 'Palestine' was new and uncomfortable, as witnessed by the references to 'Southern Syria' as an appellation for the country in this and earlier periods. Ties of faction, clan and religion remained of greatest importance to the mass of Palestinians. Of these, faction, kin and clan ties had no utility as a symbolic armature on which to mold an ideology for mass resistance. If anything, they were a hindrance ... Islam, however, was highly appropriate; faced with a foreign enemy of two different religions who sought domination over the second holiest land of the Faith, Islam provided the cultural categories, in the conceptual field of *jihad* [holy war], to encompass and organise resistance.[16]

Johnson, like Kalkas[17] and Waines,[18] sees the Arab Revolt as a struggle mobilised by the device of religion towards ends which were inarticulately anti-colonial. The identity of the peasantry that rose up in 1929 – and later during the bloody Arab Revolt – was predicated on the antagonism it experienced as a consequence of British and Zionist colonisation. The first widespread manifestation of what later commentators have come to call 'Palestinian nationalism' was thus neither Palestinian nor nationalist; it was purely oppositional. 'Palestinian nationalism was essentially nihilist in the sense that it contained no concept of the shape of future society, but was concerned first and foremost with the destruction of European hegemony.'[19]

The Arab Revolt lacked either a coherent programme or a unified leadership and, although it lasted more than three years, tended to fragment into local skirmishes against perceived enemies who were often

Palestinians on other sides of the *Qays–Yemini* divide. It also faced a well-organised enemy. Widespread mobilisation of the British military throughout Palestine defeated the revolt, inflicting casualties calculated by the Mandate government at 4,007 and by others at 19,792,[20] and destroying rural and urban centres of resistance through aerial bombing, collective demolitions, and 'slum clearance' programmes. Despite this victory, the British – weakened by the six-year attrition of the Second World War and by the subsequent anti-British liberation struggle of Zionist irregulars – pulled out of Palestine in May 1948. A year of war between Arab and Israeli forces followed, resulting, by July of 1949, in the State of Israel occupying 73 per cent of what had been Mandate Palestine (the remaining territory – Gaza and the West Bank – was subsequently commandeered by Egypt and Jordan).[21] Of the 861,000 Palestinian Arabs who had lived on the territory which became Israel, 711,000 (82.6 per cent) were forced into exile outside its borders.[22]

The *nakbah* ('catastrophe' in Palestinian Arabic) initiated nearly a decade's surcease in the elaboration of Palestinian political identity. 'Military defeat and the destruction of the fabric of their society forced Palestinians to adjust either to varying degrees and forms of statelessness or to citizenship in the new Israeli state'.[23] Underlying this was the loss of reference points around which to reconstitute identities. In the refugee camps this experience was perhaps most radical; the loss of lands and properties as well as the dispersal of families and communities left the exiles in a virtual limbo. Rosemary Sayigh, who worked in the Lebanese refugee camps, described the experience of exile from the familiar *habitus*:

> The village – with its special arrangements of houses and orchards, its open meeting places, its burial ground, its collective identity – was built into the personality of each individual villager to a degree that made separation like an obliteration of the self. In describing their first years as refugees, camp Palestinians use metaphors like 'death', 'paralysis', 'burial', 'non-existence', etc.[24]

Palestinians of urban origin sought refuge within a network of well-to-do assimilationist expatriate communities scattered throughout the Middle East, Europe and the Americas.[25] Those who remained in Israel proper experienced radical disruptions of their previous ways of living under the severe regime of military control Israel imposed on its internal enemies.[26] Military authorities strove to enforce upon resident Palestinians even more radical forms of factionalisation than those which had prevailed before the upsurge of anti-colonialist mobilisation.[27] As a result of these diverse experiences communities in the various milieux of Palestinian life began to reconstitute themselves in relation to their settings, rather than with reference to a shared 'Palestinian' identity.[28]

Curiously, it was after the destruction of any shared 'Palestinian' existence that the idea of a Palestinian identity per se came into play. The focus of this identity – the emblem which gave it coherence – was the Palestine Liberation Organisation. This extra-territorial organisation was originally established by the Arab League as a 'gathering of traditional and influential notables'[29] capable of voicing Palestinian interests in the councils of the League. However, the debacle of the 1967 war – during which the rest of what had been Mandate Palestine was lost to Israel, and another 200,000 Palestinians were forced into exile – put paid to the illusion that Palestine could be redeemed by other Arab states, and led to the 'hijacking' of the PLO by Fatah, a political-commando group which had initially come together to resist Israel's occupation of Gaza during the Suez Crisis.[30] As a guerrilla organisation dedicated to military attacks on the State of Israel and its representatives, the PLO was able to stand for Palestinians in exile and under occupation as a representation of their own desires to fight back against the forces which had dispossessed them. For the first time there was an objective correlate to the Palestinians' disparate desires for restitution.

The fundamental reason the PLO was able to serve as an icon of Palestinian identity was that it presented itself as representative of all of the diverse 'Palestinian' constituencies which had been disinherited by the creation of the Israeli state. Its programme was solely that of reinstituting a Palestinian national entity on the territory of Mandate Palestine, and it made no effort to articulate the nature of that future entity save to say that it would be 'Palestinian'. 'Palestinians' were able to recognise themselves as addressed by the oppositional rhetoric of the PLO insofar as that rhetoric did not specify any particular identity to its addressees other than their recognition of themselves as somehow stripped of their rights by the antagonism of the 'Zionist entity'.

The 'Palestine' the PLO promised to redeem was of necessity a place which had never really existed; any accurate evocation of the Palestinian life which had preceded the loss of the national territory was likely to evoke the inter-Palestinian conflicts which had helped to bring about that loss. Palestine as a 'national homeland' could thus only be conjured up through imagining a space in which the Palestinian people *would have* lived as a community if the enemy whose violence had created that community *had not existed*. Palestinian community and Palestinian history were constituted through antagonism to an enemy which had, by stealing the ground on which a nation might have been built, destroyed the possibility of 'Palestine' before it had ever been conceived.

By presenting its programme as the inverse of that of the Zionist state-builders, the PLO provided a space of identification for all those who felt they had lost their identities as a result of Zionism's success. They could see in the PLO's project the negation of the negation which had exposed them to the varied violence that afflicted them. In this national imaginary all Palestinians were 'the same' insofar as all of them – as Palestinians – could recognise their true selves as mutilated and denied by the violence of the Zionist enemy.[31] However, Palestinians in the various locales of their dispossession experienced the impossibility of Palestinian identity in a number of diverse ways, and the particular forms of violence through which Zionism's generalised antagonism was made manifest led Palestinians in various sites to elaborate strategies of survival and resistance specific to that violence.[32] The strategies of the *fedayeen* (guerrillas) of the Middle Eastern refugee camps differed in method and motive as substantially from those of the *samidin* (those who 'stood fast' on the land) of the Occupied Territories as they did from those of the bureaucrats, businessmen and cosmopolitan intellectuals of the urban diaspora. All worked to 'negate' the activities of the enemy and its allies, but the forms of negation (from terroristic 'erasure', through passive resistance, to intellectual and diplomatic revisionism) were formed in response to the specificities of the violence their formulators encountered. The PLO subsidised and supported this diversity of communities and maintained their respective organisations[33] and was thus able to claim a wide range of 'defensive' responses to Zionism as its own. Thus the actions of each community and its representative organisations answered to their respective needs to resist specific antagonisms, while serving, for other communities in different situations, as signs of a generalised Palestinian resistance to the enemies of Palestine. Dispersion meant that the actions each group carried out did not, in any immediate way, interfere with the interests of other groups in other situations.

Concrete moves towards a settlement with Israel, effected by the success of the first *intifada*, shattered that general consensus by bringing into view the possibility of an actual state of Palestine. During the long period of their exile Palestinians had diversely imagined what their nation would be if the antagonisms which prevented it were to disappear. Whatever the specificities of these redemption images, every Palestinian saw a place for himself or herself in a 'reborn' state of Palestine. However, as the project of Palestinian positivity appeared to near fruition, the abstract concept of the 'Palestine' which was lost began to take on discernable form in the shape of a 'statelet' in the rump of what had been Mandate Palestine. PLO negotiations with the Israeli state over which territories would be 'Palestinian' and which permanently surrendered to Israel left many Palestinians from the diaspora and the territories feeling betrayed. Edward Said, one of those Palestinians who watched the PLO accept that his birthplace would never be Palestinian, accused the PLO of betraying 'the diaspora Palestinians, who originally brought Arafat and the PLO to power, kept them there, and are now relegated to permanent exile or refugee status'.[34] Others within the Israeli Occupied Territories who had been crippled by Israeli 'rubber bullets', or had seen friends and family members die fighting for Palestinian freedom, came to believe that they, and the country they suffered to bring into being, had been sold out by their leadership. The authoritarianism and corruption of the 'regime' Arafat imported from Tunis and Yemen, along with the apparent service his 'returning' cadres were performing for the Israeli state in policing the Palestinian population, left many on the 'inside' feeling that, while one set of occupiers had been replaced by another, the occupation, in effect, continued.[35]

When the boundary dividing the antagonist from the objects of its violence breaks down, consensus on identity, discursively structured around that antagonism, loses its coherence. The wide field of Palestinian experience had been 'fixed' by a perceived antagonism which made the various experiences of those who occupied it coherent in nationalist terms. When perceptions of the nature of that antagonism were transformed by the Oslo agreement and the negotiations that followed, various occupants of the formerly 'sutured' field found that former enemies had become allies, while others discovered that former allies now appeared as antagonists. Those in and affiliated with the PNA operated after Oslo as though the antagonism with Israel had ended, and worked, through those operations, a new and differentiated social mechanism they believed would generate a state of Palestine alongside and working with the state of Israel; simultaneously many others, both inside the Occupied Territories and in the Palestinian diaspora, saw those others as traitors to the nation who collaborated with the still virulent antagonist.

The genesis of 'Former Yugoslavia' (1918–92)

In the Palestinian case, we have seen how the violence of an other prompts both the 'invention' of a national identity and the articulation of a national politics capable of promoting that identity; in the case of Former Yugoslavia, we can observe how the politics of an already established state are discursively transformed through the elaboration and promulgation of stories of the violence of 'others' previously perceived as neighbours.

The Socialist Federative Republic of Yugoslavia was an explicitly anti-nationalist state, formed in response to the crises nationalisms had forced on Yugoslavia before and during the Second World War.[36] Between December 1918 and the Nazi invasion of April 1941 an earlier 'Yugoslavia' – known as 'The Kingdom of Serbs, Croats and Slovenes' – had consolidated the diverse national movements of Slovenes, Croats and Serbs within the framework of a single state. This formation had, however, been highly unstable; the representatives of the three *narods* ('nations' or 'peoples') who had joined to create it had different, and in large part incompatible, reasons for uniting. Slovenes wanted a state to guarantee political autonomy to Slovene-speaking peoples formerly under the Austro-Hungarian Empire; Croats wanted self-determination for Croat-speaking Catholics, which entailed independence from that same empire as well as protection from the expansionist nationalism of the Hungarian 'Magyars'; Serbs wanted all Serbs – especially those living outside the borders of the Serbian kingdom established in 1867 after Ottoman dominion was thrown off[37] – to enjoy union under a single state.[38] The kingdom's twenty-three years were scored with assassinations, coups and the violence of nationalist movements fighting to seize the state for their own respective peoples, but it survived until the Nazis broke up Yugoslavia and diversely promoted incompatible national aspirations as a means of dividing and ruling the area.[39] The consequences were dire: the Ustaše operated death camps within which massive numbers of Serbs, Jews, Gypsies and Croat communists and democrats were brutally slaughtered; Ustaše and *četnici* ('Chetniks') respectively carried out whole-sale massacres of Serbian and Muslim civilian populations; and the communist partisans, 'cleaning up' as the war closed, massacred large numbers of 'Chetnik' Serbs, and Ustaše Croats and Slovene 'traitors'. All in all, at least 1,014,000, from a pre-war population of 17,186,000, were killed during the war[40] and, according to Paul Garde, 80 per cent of the deaths were inflicted on Yugoslavs by Yugoslavs.[41] 'During the Second World War the conquerors not only destroyed the state, but they set its components against each other in an unprecedented way, for never before had there been physical conflict among the Yugoslav peoples as such.'[42]

Tito, who had mobilised wartime resistance through a 'National Liberation Anti-Fascist Front of all the peoples of Yugoslavia regardless of party or religion',[43] maintained emphasis on pan-Yugoslav confederation in the post-war period by stressing *bratstvo i jedinstvo* ('brotherhood and unity'). When Tito first used the phrase, in 1942, it was not simply 'brotherhood and unity' but 'armed brotherhood and unity',[44] and throughout his long rule Tito stressed that the space of Yugoslav federation was a good space endangered by an antagonistic outside. That the border between inside and outside was Titoism's essential ideological plank is made clear by the fact that, as in Orwell's *1984*, the external threat continuously shifted its character and its source. From the initial opposition to fascism which gave Tito and the partisans power, Tito oscillated over the years between emphasising 'the Soviet threat'[45] and the threat of 'the capitalist West'. While the interests of the nation – and of the various peoples who constituted it – were always presented as threatened by the conspiracies of a labile set of enemies located outside Yugoslavia's territorial, and ideological, borders,[46] there was no indeterminacy about what threatened Yugoslavia from within. Nationalism, for Tito's Yugoslavia, was a symptom of what the deconstructivists refer to as a 'constitutive outside'[47]; it provided internal evidence of the attempts of external enemies to subvert the integrity of the federal space. Throughout all the discursive transformations of the external enemy nationalism remained firmly fixed as the way external antagonisms were made manifest 'inside' through the perfidy of 'domestic traitors'.

Communist policy did not outlaw national identity but attempted to discursively reformulate it. For Titoism nationalism expressed a politico-economical will to power through which 'one society aspires to dominate, exploit or despoil the others'.[48] The state therefore worked to dissolve the national aspirations through, on the one hand, devolving economic power to the community level, where workers' collectives would cohere around aspirations for mutual economic betterment,[49] and, on the other hand, breaking up the political and economic power blocs of the dominant 'republics' (particularly that of Serbia) through the creation of new nationalities (such as those of the 'Macedonians',

'Montenegrins' and 'Muslims', enshrined in the 1967 constitution)[50] and the devolution of authority to autonomous regions ('Vojvodina' and 'Kosovo' were carved out of Serbia between the early 1960s and 1972). The federal state protected the rights of *narods* (nations) and *narodnosti* (national minorities) and strove, through differential policies of appropriation and distribution of resources, to lift the poorer republics up to the economic level of the wealthier ones. Titoism was founded on the assumption that economic and political homogenisation would lead to the withering away of national differences (and hence of nationalisms) and the enshrinement of a workers' state.

Paul Schoup points out, however, that the system could only work 'as long as the communist system in Yugoslavia retained its revolutionary dynamic, or was perceived to be imperilled from without'.[51] In the 1980s that dynamic collapsed, and the external threat that consolidated the inside came to be interpreted as the threat of the state's policies to the 'good' interior of the nations themselves. The death of Tito and the collapse of the Yugoslav economy challenged the hegemony of Yugoslav ideology. In the popular imagination Tito had been 'a symbol of a Yugoslav style that had less to do with socialism, self-management and non-alignment than with freedom of movement, the advent of the consumer society, and fending for oneself'.[52] His death coincided with the collapse of the debt-ridden economy that had artificially maintained the style of living he represented. In the early 1980s international debts began to be called in, and harsh IMF policies were imposed on Yugoslavia. As a result unemployment had surged by 1984 to 15 per cent, inflation was topping 62 per cent, and the average standard of living had dropped by 30 per cent from its 1980 level.[53] Central state policies began to be seen not as defending the people and their standard of living, but as attacking them; in the early 1980s a wide range of assertions – expressed in idioms ranging from the economic and political to those of art and culture[54] – began to articulate perceptions of the antagonism of *the state* to *the people*.

These expressions did not, however, fall 'naturally' into a nationalist idiom. Tito's anti-nationalist policies, and the modernisation processes which had accompanied them, had to a large extent submerged the idiom of national identity beneath a flood of contending discourses on selfhood. Tito's above-mentioned 'invention' of nationalities had succeeded in dispersing identities across a wider national field than had operated when one was either Slovene, Croat or Serb. The ethnic isolation which had characterised largely rural Yugoslavia prior to the foundation of the communist state had in large part been dispelled by rural migration to the cities and to areas 'outside' Yugoslavia where money could be earned.[55] In the cities a trans-Yugoslav cosmopolitanism had developed around work, education and inter-marriage.[56] The violence of the state was not initially perceived as inflicted upon one's national being; it appeared, in a much less ethnocentric manner, to attack people's abilities to earn and save money, play or listen to rock music, call for greater representation in political forums, and so on. All Yugoslavians were afflicted by the declining standard of living and the clumsy moves of the state to enforce cultural and economic homogeneity during this period. Within the republics the state's antagonism to personal fulfilment struck at all residents, regardless of whether or not they were of the ethnic majority.

The discursive shift to nationalist discourse occurred through the intervention of republican politicians who created 'national' platforms from where they could launch bids to increase their holds on power in a Yugoslav state characterised, after the death of Tito, by a vacuum at the political centre. To gain power they had to consolidate their hold on the dispersed dissatisfactions spawned by the breakdown of Titoist hegemony, and they did so by inventing ethnically defined constituencies to represent. Slobodan Milošević, a banker who became head of the Belgrade city council in 1984, before rising meteorically to the post of president of Serbia in 1987,[57] used Tito's own rhetoric of 'internal enemies' to create a domain of 'Serbian interests' for which he could speak. Through a carefully mediated media campaign, he alerted Serbs within the Serbian republic to the danger posed to their well-being and rights by the presence of Kosovans (ethnic Albanians who made up 90 per cent of the population of the autonomous region of Kosovo) within the borders of Serbia. Kosovo was the poorest region of Yugoslavia, and the substantial financial and political support Kosovans had been granted by the state to raise their standards of living could be cited, after the disappearance of Yugoslavia's wealth, as a 'drain' on the well-being of other republics. Milošević, however, did not limit his attacks on the Kosovans to the domain of the economic, but accused them of being blood enemies of the Serbian people per se. Milošević repeatedly announced an active assault by Kosovans on the 'body' of Serbia: they were said to rape Serbian girls, as well as nuns in the Orthodox monasteries of Kosovo (monasteries which stand in the Serbian imaginary as monuments to a Greater Serbia destroyed by the late-fourteenth-century Ottoman invasion), to raze and desecrate those Orthodox holy places, and to drive Serbs living in Kosovo out of their homes so that they could be taken over as residences for the fast-breeding Kosovan population as well as for the illegal Albanian immigrants they encouraged.[58]

Milošević turned the Titoist rhetoric of internal enemies to nationalist use by suggesting that Albanians 'inside' Serbia would make it impossible for Serbian individuals to live as Serbs on Serbian ground. The threat of Kosovo was not explicitly a threat to the lives of Serbs, but a threat to their ability to manifest their national characteristics. Images of raped women, whether laity or nuns, struck at the heart of a strongly patriarchal society in suggesting that enemies could 'steal' the 'vessels' through which, in the case of lay women, men transmitted their identity to future generations and, in the case of nuns, the wider community of Serbs established kinship links with God by 'marrying' their sisters to Christ.[59] Stories of Serbs driven out of their homes by rapacious Kosovans similarly assaulted the sensed security of a community in which family and family life were central markers of identity, while the 'attacks' by Muslims on Orthodox sanctuaries extended this insecurity to the cherished domain of religion. Through evoking Kosovan violence towards Serbian attempts to inscribe a Serbian identity on Serbia's land, Milošević reconstituted 'Serbia' as a locus of identity and 'Serbian interests' as a focus of concern.

Kosovans were, however, only the internal agents of an external enemy. Their assault against Serbia and Serbians was, according to Milošević, backed by a 'Vatican–Comintern conspiracy'[60] which linked the communist state (which had 'stolen' the Serbian homeland of Kosovo from Serbia) with the Catholic Church (which was said to have sponsored the Ustaše).[61] Milošević and his ideologues effected a further discursive shift whereby the Kosovans – many of whom had, under Ottoman occupation, opportunistically converted to Islam[62] – became *the same as* the 'Muslim Turks'. Kosovo was not only an autonomous region within Serbia, but was also where the defeat of the Serbian armies of Prince Lazar Hrebeljanović by Ottoman forces on 15 June 1389, initiated the collapse of the short-lived Serbian Empire Stephen Dušan had established only forty-three years before.[63] Milošević characterised his struggle to strip Kosovans of their political rights and regional autonomy as yet another 'battle for Kosovo [which] ... we shall win despite the fact that Serbia's enemies outside the country are plotting against it, along with those in the country'.[64] The twentieth-century struggle to suppress Kosovan autonomy thus became a continuation of the struggle against an enemy which, 600 years before, had stripped Serbia of an empire that had once stretched from Bosnia to the Gulf of Corinth. Milošević, by reminding Serbs of the Greater Serbia which had been stolen by the nation's enemies,[65] thus legitimated and popularised his simultaneous drive to strip Montenegro and Macedonia of their republican independence, and to outlaw the autonomy of Vojvodina (these regions, like Kosovo, were parts of the Serbia Tito had dismembered in his anti-nationalism project).[66] Through the evocation of the nation's loss and the people's enemies, Milošević was able to constitute not only a Serbian positivity – a repertoire of Serbian traditions and an agenda of Serbian aspirations grounded in a former wholeness – but also a popular following which saw in its leader's discourse both the 'real' causes of their suffering and the means of expunging them.[67]

Whereas the Titoist programme had been 'supra-national' in its attempt to create a domain of identification that transcended and

encompassed the space of national identification,[68] Milošević's programme was to subsume 'Yugoslavia' within a nationalist discourse.
Milošević had no intention of withdrawing Serbia from Yugoslavia; he
instead intended that Serbia would dominate Yugoslavia so that all the
Serbs scattered throughout the federal state – 42 per cent of Serbs lived
outside of the republic of Serbia[69] – would be united within a single state
serving their interests. Milošević, seventy years after the establishment of
the Kingdom of Serbs, Croats and Slovenes, was attempting once again
to work out the Serbian nationalist agenda of making Yugoslavia over
into a Serbian state.

Milošević's rise to power coincided with the mobilisation, in Slovenia
and Croatia, of 'democratic oppositions' which were to contend for
republican power in the first Yugoslav elections allowing non-communist
participation. Their campaign rhetoric was not grounded on calls for
reforms and changes in the Yugoslav constitution, but on highly nationalistic platforms arguing that the Slovene and Croation peoples were
being destroyed by the communist state. I was in Ljubljana during the
campaigns for the Slovene election, and can remember non-communist
campaign stations bedecked with pictures of caves (*foibe*) filled with the
bones of people killed during the massacres that had taken place at the
close of the Second World War.[70] Although the people the partisans had
killed came from various national groupings and political movements,
the captions on the photographs said simply, 'This is what *They* did to
Us'. The assertion was direct – 'the communists killed Slovenes en masse
as they came to power' – and the implication needed no further elaboration – 'and subsequent policies from the communist state towards the
Slovenes have been a continuation of national genocide by other means'.
This rhetoric called on people *as Slovenes* to recognise that communist
violence towards Slovenes in the past was *the same as* the state's violence
towards them in the present. Antipathy towards communist policies in
the economic and social domain thus became articulated as justifiable
defensive responses to an *external* power motivated by the desire to exter-
minate the Slovene nation. In turn, the Slovene nation was constituted as
a good thing *because* the enemy wished to deny it to the people. Slovenia,

which had never previously moved to constitute itself as an independent nation, committed itself between 1990 and the outbreak of war in 1991 to a programme of nationalist realisation.

In Croatia Franjo Tudjman's Christian Democratic Community Party (the HDZ) also paraded pictures of bone piles, and asserted these were not the skeletons of 'Nazis' or 'quislings' but of 'Croatian victims' of communist brutality. Tudjman, however, in constituting a nationalist position for Croatian identification, drew upon a more salient articulation of the 'us' which opposed the communist 'other'. Croatia had had a recent national positivity, which had been destroyed by the communist state, and Tudjman reclaimed the quisling Ustaše 'Independent State of Croatia' as a 'statement of the historical aspirations of the Croatian people for its own independent state'.[71] Tudjman and the ideologues of the HDZ campaigned for the republican leadership (and later for Croatian independence) with the – not inaccurate – assertion that the Yugoslav state had existed to prevent Croatians from enjoying their nationhood. Tudjman claimed that, since 1945, Titoist policies had served unjustly to 'punish' the Croatian people for attempting to realise themselves as a nation. Equating contemporary Croatian aspirations towards nationhood with those of the Ustaše, Tudjman simultaneously equated the enemies of the Ustaše with the enemies of contemporary Croats. Yugoslavia was, then, not simply a communist state opposed to nationalism, but a state dominated by Serbs who wanted nothing more than to destroy their national enemies, the Croats. To fight back against Serbian 'aggression' against the Croatian people, Tudjman and the HDZ adopted the same anti-Serbian rhetoric and programmes their Ustaše predecessors had utilised to defeat the 'Serbian threat'. Tudjman and the HDZ called for an independent Croatia that would expand to Croatia's 'historical borders' (the borders, encompassing most of Bosnia-Hercegovina, of the 'Independent State of Croatia'), would fly a national flag on which the red star of Yugoslavia would be replaced by the 'chessboard' pattern (šahovnica) which had graced the flag of 'Independent State of Croatia', and would purge the Croatian language of the pollution of 'Serbian' words.

The HDZ's nationalist programme, articulated almost exclusively in anti-Serbian terms, panicked the Serbs of the Krajina, who saw in the post-communist resurgence of all the gestures and policies of the Ustaše a 'return of the repressed' threatening to inflict on them the same genocide they had suffered in the early 1940s. They too had their bone caches.[72] Krajina Serbs invited local and Serbian journalists and photographers into caves where the skeletons of Serbs massacred by Ustaše had been cached. These monuments to the fate of Croatian Serbs under the Ustaše functioned locally to legitimate Croatian Serb resistance to the new Croatian order and attempts to drive out local Croats and constitute a Serbian mini-state within Croatia. They simultaneously served within Serbia itself to substantiate Milošević's claims that the Croats were *the same as* the Ustaše. Denich points out that the consequent ethnic hatred of Croats by Serbs in Serbia was based on this identification rather than on history:

> While the rebellions of Serbian communities in Croatia were motivated by their own memories of the Ustasha [*sic*] regime, now eerily reincarnated in the declarations and symbols of the new nationalist government ... the inhabitants of Serbia itself had not experienced the Ustasha [*sic*] terror, and their wartime suffering had come at the hands of the Germans and other foreign occupiers, rather than Croats. Accordingly, there was little history of overt anti-Croat feeling throughout Serbia.[73]

Serbs in Serbia, already inflamed by tales of the violence inflicted on fellow Serbs within the borders of the Serbian republic, were now offered evidence of what fate awaited Serbs outside the republican borders, at the hands of other ethnic enemies. Milošević's rhetoric about Albanian threats to a Serbian presence in Kosovo made it possible for Serbs to think in terms of a Serbian homeland (albeit one made palpable only through the evocation of its loss); his conjuring up of the 'future holocaust' facing the Serbs in the Croatian Krajina enabled Serbs to imagine a Greater Serbia unifying the 'Serbian people' through the evocation of that people's extermination.[74]

Benedict Anderson, in describing the process of 'imagining commu-nity', posits that one imagines one's own situation (as, for instance, a newspaper reader) reproduced in that of thousands – or millions – of others. Through that imaginative extension, Anderson claims, one is able to conceive of a nation of others 'like oneself'.[75] In the republics of what was Yugoslavia, the imagining of community came about instead through imagining oneself as like others. Audiences – addressed in terms marked as 'ethnic' by diacritics of language, script, cultural and historical reference or site of address – were 'interpellated' into national subject positions by their recognition that it was they who were being addressed.[76] Subsequently the addressee was 'worked on' by a narrative which focused his or her diffuse and often inchoate anxieties upon powerful and graphic images of violence inflicted by the members of other communities on the bodies and properties of fellow 'Serbs', 'Croats' or 'Slovenes'. Here the violence the addressee encountered in his or her life was 'the same' as that which the national enemy inflicted on the bodies of the tormented objects of the discourse. Recognition that one's own apparently minor suffering was in fact a premonition of the greater violence the enemy intended to inflict on all who shared one's national identity impelled the addressee to join defensively in inflicting violence on that other under the inspired leadership of those politicians who had 'recognised' the real nature of that violence, and the implication of the previous order in their infliction.

The rhetoric of violence which carried Yugoslavian politics into the 1990s could only lead to war between the peoples they constituted. The Serb–Croat conflict which began in the Krajina spread to Bosnia-Hercegovina where the Bosnian Muslims became legitimate objects of nationalist violence either because they were the 'historic enemies' of the Serbs or because they impeded the creation of 'Greater Croatia'. Evidence of the violence of the enemy, which proliferates in situations of warfare, fuels the passionate need to extirpate the source of that violence. The ethnic fantasies which sparked the war gave it all the char-acteristics of a millenarian struggle, in which signs of the other[77] had to be fully effaced so that 'real' national identity and territory, which can only be imagined through the absolute absence of the other which prevents it, could be 'reinstituted'. Although the spring of 1992 saw all of the constituent republics of Yugoslavia pronounced and internationally recognised as independent states, vicious inter-*narod* struggles continued wherever a fantasy of national purity remained threatened by the presence of ethnic others. Only Serbia and Slovenia avoided bloodshed on their own territories; Serbia because its fantasy of Serbian sovereignty over subject peoples remained unchallenged (until the eruption of war in Kosovo) and Slovenia because – with a population 90 per cent Slovene[78] – it was already in effect ethnically pure.

The last decade: the recuperation of the nationalist imaginary

Developments over the past ten years in both 'Former Yugoslavia' and 'Palestine' suggest that – in the case of the nationalist imaginary – the empty signifier of the impeded nation achieves a certain monumentality, allowing it to function as a 'site' capable of generating new or rejuvenated articulations of nationalist solidarity against antagonists, even after complete or partial dissolutions of the equivalencies which drew together the originary nationalist bloc.

We have already seen in Former Yugoslavia the way the post-communist national leaderships echoed the Titoist formulation of Yugoslav identity (an interior mobilised against a hostile exteriority, and weakened by the presence of internal traitors allied to that antagonist) in formulating images of post-federal national identity. This echoing suggests the perdurance of something like a 'memory' enabling people who have at one time found themselves identifying with individual and collective images forged by constitutive violence to be interpellated later into new images of identity through being hailed by the familiarity of the underlying structure of identity and antagonism. Certainly, throughout the past ten years in the various republics of Yugoslavia – particularly in Serbia, where I have worked most intensively – every crisis in government, in the economy, in relations with international forums has called onto the streets large demonstrations of people mobilised for the nation and against internal traitors. One such 'nationalist' uprising overthrew the Milošević regime; others have protested against the 'traitor' government which replaced his for allowing his deportation to The Hague to face human rights charges. In each case the 'nation' (and national interests) served as the grounds for mobilising against a perceived antagonism, even when such antagonisms were incommensurate. Even the shape of the nation is unfixed. In the summer of 2000, in Novi Pazar in the south of Serbia, I listened to a man in a bar who, nodding in the direction of an ethnic Serb from nearby Kosovo who had fled as a refugee to Novi Pazar, asked a friend, 'What is that f——— *Shiptar* doing here?' *Shiptar* is a derogatory slur used by Serbs to designate ethnic Kosovar Albanians; this man, by referring to someone of his own *narod* in these terms, was redrawing the borders of the nation and marking ethnic Serbs from 'outside' (although Kosovo remains a province of the new 'Yugoslavia') as *the same as* traditional national enemies. Here the signifier of the nation endures; what it signifies, and the specific antagonisms which invoke it, remain labile. What is significant, however, is that when the name of the nation is evoked in the idiom of the nationalist imaginary,[78] it is always a derivative of an antagonism which is presented as threatening what its enunciators conceive as 'the nation', but which in fact evokes the name of the nation as its negation. Different groups appeal to different formulations of the nation in response to differentially perceived antagonisms; the name remains the same.

In the re-Occupied Territories there is a much clearer consensus over the meaning of 'Palestine'; there the nation remains the *point de capiton*[79] providing an ever-increasing percentage of the Palestinian population with a marker of the place in which the antagonisms that continue to afflict them will have been overcome. As with the post-Yugoslav instances mentioned in the preceding paragraph, the configuration of that yet-to-be-realised homeland is rarely if ever sketched out; what is indisputable is that it is prevented, and that the antagonism which makes a Palestinian identity impossible must be stopped in any way possible. People who had, in the brief period of optimism after Oslo, begun to construct their identities in more nuanced and differential ways[80] have,

since the assassination of Rabin and the formal ascendency of the hard
Israeli right, increasingly adopted an almost millenarian antipathy to
Israeli occupation. What has been demonstrated to the Palestinians by
the massive increase in land expropriations and settlement building –
initiated by Netanyahu, perpetuated by Barak, and accelerated by Sharon
– is that Israel under its current leadership will not only never allow a
Palestinian state, but will do all it can to drive all but the most impoverished and depoliticised Palestinians from historic Palestine. It is this
apparently absolute antagonism – from which the rest of the world's
ineffectuality or indifference offers no respite – that drives increasing
numbers of Palestinians to welcome any blow against the enemy, including suicide bombings against civilian Israeli populations. The recent
attacks on Palestinian cities, towns and villages, instead of reducing
support for militant resistance, offer it substantial reinforcement, not
only by making it brutally palpable that to be Palestinian is to face extinction at the hands of Israeli soldiers and settlers, but also by reinstating
the discredited PNA leadership as national symbols precisely by singling
them out for attack and persecution. The current Israeli government,
whether out of sheer bloody-mindedness or in pursuit of legitimacy for
ethnic cleansing, has massively strengthened the nationalism it claimed
to want to diminish; antagonism produces resistant identity, while
increased antagonism fuels the will to resist by all means possible. That
Palestinians nonetheless perceive the antagonist as the occupation, and
not the Israeli people or Jews per se is demonstrated by the apparently
contradictory information that while, in June 2002, 68.1 per cent of the
Palestinians in the West Bank and Gaza supported the suicide bombings,
63 per cent supported the continuation of peace negotiations with Israel
and 86 per cent backed a peace settlement based on extant UN resolu-
tions.[81] There is, despite appearance, no confusion here. There is a strong
consensus on the need to end the occupation by any means possible; the
confusion will come into play when all of those who are militantly and
unreservedly 'Palestinian' in the face of that occupation are forced, by its
termination, to come to a conclusion about what a Palestinian nation
might actually be.

6

From Founding Violence to Political Hegemony: The Conservative Populism of George Wallace

JOSEPH LOWNDES

Introduction

In the thirty years prior to 1964, populist discourse in the US had been the province of New Deal Democrats. Conservative Republicans, by contrast, were generally considered the politically marginal defenders of privilege.[1] Over the course of the 1960s, however, a conservative populism emerged that set a newly vitalised right on the road to eventual dominance in American politics. This racial, anti-statist populism was pioneered by Alabama governor and segregationist firebrand George Wallace. Wallace's contribution to the rise of the right has been well chronicled in recent years,[2] but more is left to be explained about the nature of that contribution, in content as well as form. Deeper theoretical examination of the Wallace phenomenon can help better explain the success of modern American conservatism, elucidate both the possibilities and limits of populism, and offer insights into the role of discourse and action in the creation of hegemonic political identities.

In the 1964 US presidential election, the pro-civil rights Democratic candidate Lyndon Johnson beat his conservative Republican rival Barry Goldwater in the largest landslide in US history. However, while most white Americans believed in the Democratic rhetoric of inclusion and equality, they were also increasingly hesitant about the changes necessary to raise the economic and social status of African Americans. Liberal

Democratic leaders attempted to manage the increasingly stark racial contradictions of the Democratic regime through broad new policies and initiatives aimed primarily at blacks. But in doing so, they opened the door to the fragmentation of the New Deal coalition, which had excluded blacks from many of its basic benefits.[3] These new political divisions over race also began to tear the Republican Party along the seams of its liberal and conservative wings, leaving even more Americans increasingly unsure about their own partisan and political commitments.

Wallace stepped into this ambivalent political moment as a liminal figure himself – an agitator who migrated between contradictory political positions. Wallace's paradoxes were legion: as the simultaneous embodiment of the 'average citizen' and a self-conscious caricature of a redneck, he was a politician with whom many Americans could identify even as they differentiated themselves from his image. He praised the police and called for stronger law enforcement and more punitive sentencing, yet he was always associated with disruptive violence himself. His national campaign slogan was 'Stand up for America', yet in his regional twang he complained that the South was the victim of national prejudice. He was hailed as a conservative, although he was in some ways more New Deal Democrat than right-wing Republican. And although he always claimed he was not a racist, racial demonisation was fundamental to his success. The advantage of this ambivalent positioning was that Wallace had the latitude to take stances that the established parties would not, and could stake out new territory to delineate new horizons of political discourse.

The fashioning of this new anti-government populism was a moment of founding violence for the new-right, and its power was the result of its opposition to the existing political field as a whole. The Wallace juggernaut was successful to the degree that it was politically disruptive, because creating a new collective political identity involves rending people out of old traditions and political identifications.[4] Wallace did so by combatively cutting new cleavages across the electorate, dissolving old political bonds and forging new ones.

This essay is an analysis of Wallace's impact on American politics, both in language and in action. I will examine both the way he linked heterogeneous themes into a coherent political discourse, and demonstrate how this discourse helped forge a new political identity through active forms of antagonism. While creating a rhetoric that could appeal to broad segments of the American electorate, the Wallace campaigns relied on the public performance of disruption, upheaval and violence to ignite political passions, and distinguish friends and foes. Since this account is about both Wallace and the beginnings of a conservative political regime in the US, I begin with a working theory of populism and hegemony.

Populism and hegemony

Populist discourse assumes a homogeneous notion of *the people*, and that people's right to self-rule. As such, it has greatest purchase as an active political force in moments of crisis, when popular sovereignty, and national identity itself, are open to new interpretations. Political actors who employ populist language de-emphasise differences among the group on whose behalf they claim to speak, depicting group members as wholly equivalent. Moreover, populist leaders claim an immediate identification between themselves and those they represent. This identification is meant to produce a transparency of representation, and the translation of the popular will simply and directly into governance. Populist movements are thus successful to the degree that they can universalise their claims on behalf of the people, and yoke various social groups and discourses into one common identity. The success of this process is what political theorists Ernesto Laclau and Chantal Mouffe, after Gramsci, call hegemony. Reigning political orders, they argue, present themselves as internally coherent, universal forms of truth and representation that transcend politics as such – this, in fact, is the source of their power.[5] But any hegemonic order is actually a highly contingent product of dissimilar elements that get articulated together in political struggle.[6]

In the case of modern conservatism, no overriding principle necessarily merges the positions of federalism, law and order, laissez-faire
economics and Christian morality into one political identity. Federalism,
a call for more authoritarian policing, a belief in the unrestrained economic rights of the individual, and the exhortation to theocratic rule are
all distinct demands. Yet these positions began to be articulated together
by their advocates in the 1960s, and thus their differential struggles
became linked into what Laclau calls *chains of equivalence*.[7] The more the
chain of equivalence was extended, the less enclosed or particular each
element remained. As they were articulated together, each was influenced by the other. This was made possible as they all came to share a
sense of common opposition to the existing political regime *as such*. A
regime is thus more than a ruling coalition of distinct elements; it is,
rather, a shared sense of commonality in a political identity that attempts
to define the very horizon of politics. This horizon is what Laclau refers
to as an *empty signifier* – a universalised political ideal that can never be
fulfilled. Politics are motivated by attempts to fulfil them nonetheless,
and these attempts are the struggle for hegemony. Empty signifiers have
gone under various banners, among them *liberation, democracy, order* and
revolution.[8] In the case of contemporary US conservatism, the empty signifier is *America*, as both an ideal and a promise. For the contemporary
right, *America* now comes to stand for the disparate elements that
Wallace first helped pull together, making its particular political positions
seem universal and, importantly, beyond contest.

In order to develop a common political identity, one political position
or symbolic figure must come to stand for all. Both because the general
identity will be an extrapolation from a distinct one, and because that
distinct one must paper over the differences among the various positions, this identity will always be contingent and unstable. The positions
listed above came together first through Wallace, in the figure of the
white Southerner under attack from the federal government. But as this
symbolic figure was extended it became the more general 'Middle
American', as the embodiment of the signifier *America* – the white
middle-class male from every region who is pushed around by an

invasive federal government, threatened by crime and social disorder, discriminated against by affirmative action and surrounded by increasing moral degradation.[9] This newly constructed identity made the right appear no longer as the defender of privilege, but rather as representative of the whole American people.

Hegemonic identities are always undetermined, but that is not to say that every political identity has an equal chance of filling up a reigning signifier. They are constrained by language and history. Thus the emergence of right-wing populism can be reduced neither to historical determinacy nor to a radical contingency of the political moment. It is the product of both, and continually shaped by both. So both older political identifications and new political events must be studied together in order to understand the way that this given political identity emerged over time. In order to do so, attention must be paid to the context in which a hegemonic movement emerges.

Populism depends not only on a sense of internal homogeneity, but also on a constitutive outside – a threatening heterogeneity against which the identity is formed. Positions outside this universal or homogeneous political identity represent a threat to the very nation itself. Thus, political identity is organised around an absence, an attempt to achieve a communitarian fullness in antagonistic struggle against others who are seen to prevent that achievement.[10] The abstract entity that embodies pure negation for this identity in the case of the right is the state itself, as a metaphor for liberal elites, women, people of colour, the urban poor, and others who claim 'special rights'. Antagonism is key to the Wallace phenomenon, in language, in action, and in the projection of both onto his opponents. Violent antagonism played a particularly strong role in the case of Wallace, the threat, anticipation and performance of which was central to his image and success.[11] As a candidate campaigning against the system, against both parties and against the federal government, Wallace evoked the spectre of unchecked violence that threatened the American people, while threatening violence on behalf of that same people. Through his stand against federal authority, his threats to run over demonstrators if they got in the way of his car, his links to the Ku Klux Klan, and in the fistfights at his rallies, Wallace supporters forged a new sense of *us* and *them*.

Yet although new political orders begin with harsh ruptures, they must 'forget' their founding crimes.[12] Therefore in Wallace's success lay his ultimate failure. He forced more moderate politicians to speak in his language – first Nixon in 1968 and 1972, but soon after that presidential candidates in both the Democratic and Republican parties were drawing on his central themes, while distancing themselves from the man. In 1976 voters elected Jimmy Carter, another conservative Southern Democrat who painted himself as a stranger to Washington, DC, and an enemy of bureaucracy. As the country absorbed Wallace's message, the pugnacious race-baiter himself had to be forgotten. His politics would have to be stripped of disruptive elements in order to be integrated into a new homogenising regime. Like a redneck Moses, Wallace saw the Promised Land but would not get there.

1962: 'You are Southerners too'

Political actors attempt to persuade by exciting anxieties, sparking resentments and providing solace. But the success of these appeals depends on the *readability* of their political narratives – in other words, their ability to provide convincing interpretations of political reality, and their ability to convince people that they have common enemies and therefore common interests.[13] Wallace spoke about the 'average citizen' and 'the common man' in order to claim a majoritarian bloc in the American electorate, and to grant himself authority as a tribune of the people. Yet he claimed that these people were not represented by their political leaders. Rather, he said that his Americans were the outsiders, the scorned, those who were distant from centres of power. The people he attempted to bring together into a common identity were poor white Southerners, working-class urban ethnics, farmers, small business owners, and alienated conservative suburbanites from various regions. The positions he claimed to represent were also heterogeneous: states' rights, law and order, anti-communism, economic libertarianism and Christian values.

In order for Wallace supporters to see themselves as 'average citizens', their enemies had to be cast as the real outsiders; not as people with whom they simply have political disagreements, but as threatening parasites on the national body. In other words, in order to make his outsiders insiders, Wallace had to connect the liberal centre to those he described as unproductive and decadent. Thus as his rhetoric evolved, he fixed bureaucrats, permissive judges, the ultra-wealthy, protesters, rioters, welfare recipients and criminals in a specular gaze that established a fundamental unity among the groups he claimed to represent.

In linking together this new, anti-government populist identity, one particular figure first came to stand for Wallace's national subject – the white Southerner. Both liberals and Southern Democrats at the time generally depicted racial domination as a purely Southern phenomenon.[14] But for Wallace it was not enough merely to say that the South had a unique heritage that had to be protected from Northern intrusion in its affairs. He asserted that the issues he addressed were of paramount importance to the entire nation. His politics were both Southern and national, because he insisted that the South was *the most* American region: that only this region could lead the struggle to safeguard the nation's historic virtues; while liberals claimed that true American identity resided in Gunnar Myrdal's racially inclusive creed, to which the South was an anomaly.[15] Wallace, through an inversion, made the South the guardian of the nation's soul. He understood that America's racial problem was neither a peculiarity of a region nor a relic of the past, but a fundamental aspect of American politics and of white identity.[16]

As black political mobilisation developed in the 1950s and 1960s, what had been relatively stable racial identities became threatened for a great number of whites. Indeed, the threat posed by the black freedom movement was double, and thereby produced a double resentment: not only were whites asked to open up their neighbourhoods, schools, unions and state benefits to African Americans, but the very demand challenged the national self-image of the US as a uniquely democratic and egalitarian nation. Liberals who dismissed racism as merely irrational, regressive and anathema to American ideals missed the fact that, if handled carefully, racism could have enormous political potential.

Wallace first gained national renown as a defender of segregation, but as time went on he rarely spoke openly about race. Rather, he helped create what is often referred to now by critics of the right as 'racial coding'. Generally overlooked, however, is the fact that the very act of coding changes the meaning of that which is being translated. If audiences outside the Deep South required altered language, that could only reflect their ambivalence about racist politics – otherwise, why not simply appeal openly to racial sentiments? In order to make race work for him nationally, Wallace had to convince his audiences that race meant something else – it had to exceed its own boundaries and come to stand for a number of issues. As a key term in an emergent chain of equivalences, race both saturated and was masked by this new anti-government populism.[17]

Wallace was first elected governor of Alabama in 1962 as 'the Fighting Judge' on the campaign slogan 'Stand up for Alabama' and the promise to defy federal orders to desegregate the University of Alabama. This political logic and imagery of violation and resistance was in place when he gained national exposure in his first inaugural address. The oration, penned by former Ku Klux Klan leader Asa Carter,[18] conveyed to white Alabamians and white Southerners generally that Wallace would stand up against a regime that reviled and ridiculed them, and that was now forcing them to alter their way of life. But Wallace also meant for his speech to be heard outside the South. On the steps of the state capitol, 'where Jefferson Davis once stood', Wallace began his inaugural address by invoking long-dead Confederate soldiers to re-commit his white citizens to time-honoured values and practices. Wallace underscored for his audience how appropriate it was, in the very heart of the Great Anglo-Saxon Southland, that

> today we sound the drum for freedom as have our generations of forebears before us ... Let us rise to the call of freedom-loving blood that is in us and send our answer to the tyranny that clanks its chains upon the South ... In the name of the greatest people that have ever trod this

earth, I draw the line in the dust and toss the gauntlet before the feet of tyranny and I say, segregation now, segregation tomorrow, segregation forever![19]

In the speech, the new Governor then specifically referred to the recent fatal clash between white rioters and the military over the integration of the University of Mississippi, asserting that 'the federal troops in Mississippi could be better used guarding the safety of the citizens of Washington, DC, where it is even unsafe to walk or go to a ball game'. In making this claim he was contending that it was whites who needed protection from blacks, not vice versa. In attempting to expose the hypocrisy of his enemies, however, Wallace did not seek to antagonise Northerners. Rather, anticipating more ambitious political goals, he hoped that what he said would resonate with them.[20] Thus he had already begun to link his particular group, pro-segregation white Southerners, to a political universal – the American desire for freedom and democracy. He achieved this by moving beyond segregation to general issues about government intrusion that he claimed affected all Americans. 'It is ... a basically ungodly government', he said, 'and its appeal to the pseudo-intellectual and the politician is to change their status from servant of the people to master of the people'. He went on to say,

> You native sons and daughters of old New England's rock-ribbed patriotism ... and you sturdy natives of the great Midwest, and you descendants of the far west flaming spirit of pioneer freedom, we invite you to come and be with us, for you are of the Southern mind, and the Southern spirit, and the Southern philosophy, you are Southerners too and brothers in our fight.[21]

Like the populists of the late nineteenth century, Wallace aimed to go national to save the local. But while he claimed to be fighting on behalf of the whole nation, it was the South, he asserted, that was best situated to lead the fight, given its distinct history as a champion of states' rights. In other words, his particular figure had to stand for the general.

Wallace went on in the speech to chronicle the trials, humiliation and abuse visited upon white Southerners during and after the Civil War, and related how they stood fast in the face of tyranny. But lest his national audience feel that this suffering had no meaning for them, he reminded them that 'Southerners', including Thomas Jefferson, George Washington, James Madison and Patrick Henry, 'played a most magnificent part in erecting this great divinely inspired system of freedom, and as God is our witness', he told his audience, 'Southerners will save it'.[22] Framed this way, white Southerners were not defending despotism but resisting it, and Wallace, like those before him, was a protector of liberty's heritage. By linking school desegregation to governmental authoritarianism, he allowed working and middle-class whites outside the South to identify with the image of the downtrodden white Southerner. In this move, Wallace used the old Jeffersonian saw of depicting dependants below and elites above as an alliance against the independent, virtuous middle. Wallace knew that the impression of the threatened white man standing up to an arrogant liberalism would have national purchase.[23]

Once in office, Wallace held fast to his bold campaign pledge to block the integration of the University of Alabama. This posturing made state officials worry that there would be a replay of the brutality at the University of Mississippi. But while they fretted, Wallace understood that such a gamble might have an enormous payoff. When the state attorney general expressed his concern about the possibility of riots and federal troop deployment, Wallace enthusiastically replied, 'The first day they bring federal troops into this state, I'm gonna run for President'.[24] A week before the confrontation at the University of Alabama, Wallace ratcheted up the tension by going on *Meet the Press* to defend his plan to personally block the entrance to the University, describing his act as 'a dramatic way to impress upon the American people this omnipotent march of centralised government that is going to destroy the rights and freedom and liberty of the people of this country'.[25]

In the confrontation with assistant US Attorney General Nicholas Katzenbach, Wallace made a speech decrying the 'unwelcomed, unwarranted and force-induced intrusion' by the 'central government', saying that 'millions of Americans will gaze in sorrow upon [this] situation'.[26] The stand-off allowed him to perform his politics before a live national audience. This tension-filled scene that threatened to turn ugly at any moment was carefully orchestrated so as to minimise the possibility of actual violence (he had gotten assurances beforehand from the segregationist Citizen's Councils and the Ku Klux Klan that they would stay away from the University that day), but his willingness to 'make a dramatic impression' by facing down the Kennedy administration, national guardsmen and federal troops immediately elevated his stature to that of a national figure. This racial drama was followed by a second act that evening, when President Kennedy called, in a televised address to the nation, for a comprehensive civil rights bill. In the days that followed, thousands of letters and telegrams poured in from around the country thanking Wallace for his resistance to federally mandated desegregation, and urging him to continue to stand up to Kennedy.[27]

1964: from states' rights to racial anti-statism

Wallace capitalised on his 'stand in the schoolhouse door' by accepting invitations to speak at colleges and political and civic organisations across the country. As he went north with his message, the governor began to move from segregation to new themes, such as anti-communism. 'We have permitted the federal government', he told Northern audiences, 'to lead us dangerously close to a complete rejection of the democratic idea in favor of a form of statism embracing many of the social and economic theories of Marx and Lenin'.[28] This shift to the language of anti-communism would begin to endear him to both traditional conservatives and ultra-rightists. When Wallace entered his first Democratic presidential primary in Wisconsin in 1964, he gave his opening campaign speech in the notoriously anti-communist Senator Joseph McCarthy's hometown of Appleton. There, instead of talking about segregation, he focused on the global Soviet threat, accusing the State Department of treachery, bemoaning Franklin Roosevelt's concessions at Yalta.[29]

On the occasions when he did raise issues of race outside the South, he was careful to attack the federal government for its over-reach of authority, not for integration itself. He claimed that he was not a racist, just that he believed segregation was best for both whites and blacks. Even then, he told Wisconsin audiences:

> I am an Alabama segregationist ... not a Wisconsin segregationist. If Wisconsin believes in integration, that is Wisconsin's business, not mine. That is why I'm here to tell you that Wisconsin has the right to choose the pattern it will follow in race relations, and Alabama has the right to choose the path it will follow ... the central government in Washington has no right to tell either Alabama or Wisconsin what to do.[30]

While still careful to leave race out of his speeches directly, Wallace expanded his opposition to integration to oppose other aspects of the racial liberalism of the Johnson administration. In doing so, he was able to link whites across class lines by claiming that various aspects of the impending federal civil rights legislation would trample freedoms and rights then enjoyed by whites in all classes. When speaking to middle-class suburbanites he decried the destruction of property rights and the federal encroachment on individual market freedoms. When speaking to workers, he speculated that new federal legislation aimed at integrating unions would threaten job security. Going far out of his way to raise the issue of black inclusion without actually mentioning it, Wallace told blue-collar audiences that the civil rights bill would 'tell an employer who he's got to employ'. He went on, 'If a man's got 100 Japanese-Lutherans working for him and there's 100 Chinese-Baptists unemployed, he's got to let some of the Japanese-Lutherans go so he can make room for the Chinese-Baptists ... And of course, what does that do for your seniority rights?', he asked, driving home his point: 'It destroys them!'[31] To both working- and middle-class audiences, he warned that if an open-housing bill got passed, home-owners would be forced to sell to anyone, 'even if it's a man with green eyes and blue teeth'.[32]

In Milwaukee, a city with a sizeable black population, Wallace gave speeches to working-class urban ethnics who were nervous about the changing racial make-up of their jobs and neighbourhoods. At one rally, he was greeted by a packed room that sang 'Dixie' to him in a mixture of English and Polish. Here were Eastern Europeans anxious at the thought that their newly established white racial status and its attendant privileges might be imperiled.[33] Wallace opened that speech by emphasising their citizenship credentials, while affirming their ethnic identity by admonishing the federal government for abandoning the 'proud and gallant Poles who fought so bravely' in World War II. Wallace's relationship to white ethnics was challenged by labour unions and church groups, who accused Wallace of having referred to eastern and southern Europeans as 'lesser breeds'.

Wallace, however, deftly responded to these accusations by actively embracing these groups as part of his expanding political identity. He began demonstrating his commitment by bringing Alabamians of Polish, Greek, Jewish, Italian and German descent with him on his campaign.[34] Prior to Wallace, Southern segregationists contrasted the white South to the rest of the nation by claiming that the region was notable for its pure Anglo-Saxon pedigree.[35] Now Wallace attempted to ensure the descendants of the second great wave of immigration that he, the white Southerner, was defending their social and political status as both ethnics and whites. Speaking as racial victim to racial victim, he drew them into the collective identity he described, articulating their interests as whites who were being betrayed by the federal government and made vulnerable to blacks, who by definition became their political enemies, just as they were his.

While Wallace's 1964 primary campaign brought out many new allies, it also brought out angry progressives enraged by the idea of a Southern segregationist running for the Democratic ticket. But Wallace and his aides understood early on that the protests generated by his rallies, far from being a hindrance, actually helped his cause. They performed the political division that Wallace sought, and could help him and those he represented appear to be the real victims. Bill Jones, the national campaign director in Wallace's 1964 bid, wrote that the Wallace staff booked small venues whenever possible in order to have unruly crowds of opponents outside the door, because, he said:

> We found that having mobs outside, we got a more favorable press than otherwise. Our feelings were that the more pickets who appeared, the greater the favorable reaction for the Governor. They were encouraged every way we knew, short of endorsing what they were doing.[36]

From the stage, Wallace would invite hecklers to shout at him, even egging them on if they were too quiet. But he did not just invite attacks against himself; he incited crowd members against each other. In his rallies he would build up the tension, until clashing became all but inevitable. But through the use of humour, he was generally able to keep fights from erupting outright. For the audience, this provided a cathartic experience, an energetic disavowal of the *other* that deepened their identification with his anti-government racial populism.

However, physical altercations were by no means uncommon at Wallace rallies. There were numerous occasions across the country where fists and folding chairs flew in the audience, or picket signs were wielded as clubs outside venues where he spoke. On more than one occasion, these rallies sparked full-scale riots. On the Eastern Shore of Maryland that year, national guardsmen tear-gassed protesters attempting to march to the site of a Wallace rally, setting off a night of burning and looting.[37] While such events marked Wallace as a polarising figure, they also enhanced his lustre.

Social scientists, looking for a way to explain the new Wallace phenomenon, began referring to it as a racial 'backlash' by white workers who, while liberal on economic matters, were conservative about issues of race and authority.[38] Given that the presiding assumption among scholars like Myrdal, Seymour Martin Lipset, Richard Hofstadter and others was that racism was the irrational response of an uneducated sector of society, it is no wonder that observers of the Wallace campaigns would see it as evidence of a working-class backlash.[39] If racism was the result of ignorance, then his support had to come from a population that was least educated. Detailed electoral analysis of the Wisconsin primary, however, shows that Wallace's votes, reflecting the old base of McCarthy's support, came as much from middle-class suburbanites as from working-class neighbourhoods.[40]

Promulgators of the backlash hypothesis naturalised reaction and thus missed the fundamentally *political* force that race could generate among middle-class whites. In other words, these writers saw Wallace support as an unfortunate behavioural reflex, instead of a new interpretive political framework. Wallace drew on older racial sentiments, to be sure, but he linked them to other political positions by foregrounding racial resentments, fears and desires in a political rhetoric that linked middle-class economic libertarians, poor and middle-class white Southerners, McCarthyite anti-communists, and Northern white ethnics threatened by neighbourhood and job integration. For this reason, Wallace had a surprisingly strong showing in the presidential primaries in these Northern states. However, his political voice was not strong enough to make him a serious contender for the Democratic nomination, and he did not have enough clout to make Barry Goldwater, the Republican presidential nominee, openly embrace him or consider asking him to be his vice-presidential candidate.

1968: Lengthening the chain of equivalence, deepening the antagonism

As the decade wore on, however, two aspects of the political and social climate changed in ways that offered more opportunity for Wallace to expand his political base and exploit new divisions. First, with the passage of the Civil Rights Act of 1964 and the Voting Rights Act of 1965, the Johnson administration intervened in the private and public sectors to protect the rights of African-Americans as never before. Johnson also pushed through a number of pieces of Great Society legislation that targeted poverty on behalf of urban and rural impoverished blacks. Running for president as a third-party candidate for his newly created American Independent Party in 1968, Wallace was able to respond to Johnson by making appeals to business-people on issues of new taxation and federal intervention into real estate and employment, to workers on the basis of union seniority and open housing, and his old white Southern constituency on the basis of racial states' rights.

At the same time, inner-city uprisings and anti-war militancy provided new flames to fan. With the eruption of the black Los Angeles neighbourhood of Watts in 1965, incidents of urban disorder grew increasingly common. A new generation of black activists, such as those in the Student Non-violent Coordinating Committee and the Congress of Racial Equality, moved from the demand for civil rights to 'black power', and organisations such as the Black Panther Party began to promote and practice the principle of armed self-defence. The New Left also became more bellicose in its opposition to the Vietnam War, pushing beyond civil disobedience to direct action, moving from a language of peace to one of revolution. Similarly to his 1964 rhetoric, but now with more stridence, Wallace claimed that American society had descended into dangerous violence and disorder. According to him, street protests, urban uprisings and rising crime rates were all part of the same fundamental problem, and his promise to restore law and order in American society was an increasingly compelling message to white Americans, who had grown increasingly anxious about these issues.[41]

Wallace aggressively addressed these themes when he announced his 1968 candidacy, distinguishing himself from pallid government administrators who were at worst responsible for the growing chaos, and at best powerless to stop it. If elected, he promised, he would 'bring all these briefcase-carrying bureaucrats to Washington and throw their briefcases into the Potomac River'. He pledged that he would 'keep the peace' if it meant putting '30,000 troops standing on the street ... with two-foot-long bayonets'. And linking race to economic conservatism, he pledged to make Congress change 'these so-called civil rights laws', which, he claimed, were 'really an attack on the property rights of this country and on the free enterprise system and local government'. Ever the authoritarian, he recommended that the 'activists, anarchists, revolutionaries and Communists' who were responsible for all the civil unrest in the country 'be thrown under a good jail'.[42]

The emphasis on violence and disorder gave Wallace's antagonism more force, and helped forge a unity out of his various themes. The government was doing nothing to protect the American people from the mounting chaos, the logic went; in fact, disorder was encouraged by government permissiveness. 'President Johnson', Wallace said in one speech, 'wanted a crime commission report to tell him why they were burning cities down. Well I could have told him why they were burning them down like you could', the candidate roared, '"Because you let them burn them down, that's the reason they burn them down!"'[43] However, while it was not doubted who the lawless were in this and other speeches, he was careful, as always, to disclaim any overt racism, even as he evoked powerful racial imagery in his attacks on elites. As he said,

> Well, it's a sad day in this country when you can't talk about law and order unless they want to call you a racist. I tell you that's not true and I resent it and they gonna have to pay attention because all the people in this country [sic], in the great majority, the Supreme Court of our country has made it almost impossible to convict a criminal.[44]

Nevertheless, there was no question that Wallace's lack of obvious reference to blacks constituted an absent presence. And this was not just the charge of his liberal critics – the conservative periodical *Human Events* at the time asked 200 conservative writers, 'Do you believe Mr. Wallace is knowingly conducting a campaign that is calculated to appeal to racial prejudice?' More than two-thirds responded, 'Yes'.[45]

Wallace recognised that he represented a marginal political voice, and that his rallies needed to build political solidarity through emotional impact. In advertisements for his rallies, he was sometimes billed as 'the nation's most exciting political leader.'[46] In that sense, he was as much about spectacle as anything happening in the youth culture at the time. Writer Hunter S. Thompson in fact once described a Wallace rally as being a kind of 'political Janice Joplin concert' in which 'the bastard had somehow levitated himself and was hovering above us'.[47] These 'exciting' Wallace rallies were occasionally fatal, however. For instance, in Omaha, Nebraska, one black youth was killed and dozens injured in unrest set off by a Wallace visit,[48] and at a rally in Berea, Kentucky, there was a shootout involving at least fourteen people, two of whom were killed.[49]

Such clashes were not only the result of the general political polarisation that marked that decade, but also of the fact that the local Wallace campaign chapters were staffed by ultra-right organisations like the John Birch Society and the American Nazi Party, and often violent groups like the Ku Klux Klan and the Minutemen. In some cases, high-level campaign staff leaders were themselves members of these groups, and used their ties to build the Wallace organisation.[50] Wallace's relationship with far-right groups was always kept in delicate balance. If he was seen as being too close to a violent fringe, he would be fully discredited. But had he rebuffed them, he would have given up a fount of on-the-ground support from organisers necessary to bring out voters. When charged with being linked to racist organisations, Wallace would often respond by saying that he could not 'be responsible for everything that someone does who supports me'.[51] He would not repudiate most far-right and white-supremacist groups as much as downplay their importance, however. 'At least a Klansman will fight for his country', he once told *Harper's*. 'But the Klan, it's just innocuous in size and they're just concerned with segregation, not subversiveness'.[52]

In those turbulent years, the Wallace campaigns fed on every new instance of violence and disorder, however tragic. Wallace even used the occasions of the assassinations of Robert Kennedy and Martin Luther King, Jr. to advance his politics. He called Kennedy's assassination 'symptomatic of the lawlessness which has invaded our nation and which threatens to destroy the political system nourished by the freedoms enjoyed by Americans',[53] and King's death 'another example of the breakdown in law and order in this country which must be stopped'.[54] Following the brutality that marred the Democratic Convention in Chicago, Wallace praised the police for using 'the tactics they ought to have used' against both demonstrators and the press.

As the 1968 election drew near, Wallace continued to rise in the polls, at one point gaining favour with 20 per cent of the electorate, which might have robbed any candidate of a majority of Electoral College votes, and hence thrown the election into the House of Representatives to be decided there. Wallace generally drew Republican votes, but he also made substantial inroads into the urban white working-class constituency of the Democratic Party. Wallace continued to define his battle as one of productive members of society against parasitic elites and subversive protesters. He counterposed 'pointy-headed intellectuals', 'bearded bureaucrats', 'anarchists' and 'lawbreakers' to 'this man in the textile mill, this man in the steel mill, this barber, the beautician, the policeman on the beat'.[55] 'I was a pretty good mechanic', he told a reporter in Lubbock, Texas, 'Don't you think I'd make a great President?'[56] Among Northern workers, Wallace tended to attract support from older white ethnic skilled workers who feared black incursions into their neighbourhoods and schools, and from young production workers who were drawn to Wallace's anti-establishment attacks on liberal elites.[57]

Wallace played up this anti-establishment image as a kind of trickster – a mocking figure whose influence is based in his own marginality and ability to lampoon those in authority. The federal government, he would tell audiences, should cease requiring officials of the states to fill out forms 'in triplicate, quadruplicate, or octa-pooplet'. He would also add extra consonants or vowels to words, as in 'stastistics' or 'Electorial College'; or simply mispronounce them, saying 'Latava' for Latvia, or describing demonstrators as 'chomping' in the streets. His aides conceded that use of such language, which they referred to as 'branch-heading', or talking in the style of 'the good folks up the creek' (at the head of the branch), was calculated, or at least easily correctable.[58] In a national context, Wallace's use of branch-heading helped craft an image as an uneducated hillbilly whose authority was derived from his distance from the centres of power – from his very incomprehension of the organisational forms of modern society and his inability to speak in its terms.[59] This strategy, his aides said, made him popular with white working-class and

Southern voters, yet they were unsure whether it would help or hinder his ability to win over better-educated white suburbanites.

Richard Nixon, the Republican candidate in 1968, recognised the potential power of Wallace's message, and adopted a slightly amended version of it, hoping to draw Wallace supporters into his camp. Nixon attempted to win the support of white Southerners by proclaiming his opposition to forced integration and to Wallace constituencies around the nation by making Wallace-like distinctions between law-abiding citizens and rioters. While Wallace did not succeed in throwing the 1968 election into the House, he did come close, receiving over 10 million popular votes. These came mostly from the South, but also from other regions of the country, particularly the Midwest and West. Nixon, the narrow winner of that election, prevailed by using Wallace's rhetoric and pulling together a broad electoral alignment that drew various ethnicities into a white political identity that opposed racial liberalism. This approach was first advocated by Nixon strategist Kevin Phillips two years earlier, and then fully explicated in his book, *The Emerging Republican Majority*.[60] Based both on Wallace's surprising run in 1964 and on Republican gains in the 1966 mid-term elections, Phillips detected a growing conservative, racist populism that could be the basis of a new alignment. 'The emerging Republican majority', wrote Phillips after the election, 'spoke clearly ... for a shift away from the sociological jurisprudence, moral permissiveness, experimental residential, welfare and educational programming and massive federal spending by which the Liberal establishment sought to propagate liberal institutions and ideology'. 'Democrats among these groups', he wrote, 'were principally alienated from their party by its increasing identification with the Northeastern Establishment and ghetto alike'.[61]

1972: 'Always a moderate'

Wallace ran again for president in 1972 as a Democrat, and began changing his rhetoric to come across as a more centrist, and therefore viable, candidate. Early in the race, he announced that he was really 'always a moderate', and that he now no longer believed in segregating schools or public facilities.[62] This altered position did not leave him without a racial fire to stoke, however. Early in 1972 a series of federal court decisions came down to end de facto school segregation by mandating the busing of schoolchildren to other neighbourhoods. Busing was a tailor-made issue for Wallace. He could oppose it without overtly supporting segregation, which allowed him to play to racial anxieties while claiming to do so solely on anti-statist principle. In Florida, where the first primary of the season was held, Democratic voters gave Wallace 42 per cent of the vote, and at the same time voted three-to-one for a non-binding referendum calling for a constitutional amendment prohibiting busing. Two days after the Florida primary, Nixon, who had until then been silent on the issue, called on Congress in a televised national address to impose a moratorium on the federal courts to bar them from ordering any new busing.

Another enormous factor entered into the politics of the 1972 race, as it had not for a generation – economic decline. As recently as the prior presidential election cycle, the strength and continual growth of the American economy was taken for granted by observers across the political spectrum. The boom of the 1960s had convinced most analysts that the US had achieved a permanent state of material abundance. But trends in the global economy long underway were now apparent. The American share of world Gross National Product dropped from 40 per cent in 1950 to 23 per cent in 1970. Imports began pouring into home markets, competing effectively with domestic producers. Inflation was now averaging over 4 per cent annually, productivity rates fell from their peak in 1966, and corporate profits continued a downward slide that had begun in 1965.[63]

In this new climate, Wallace began to employ a slightly altered economic language. Where before he had claimed to 'stand up for the working man', he now presented himself as a champion of the middle class. Just as the shift from segregation to busing helped Wallace move in from the margins of American political acceptability, so did his shift from working-class resenter to tax-burdened bourgeois. He retained the political identity of the white American assaulted by those below and above, but his new target was 'welfare loafers'. He assailed 'liberal give-away programs' that he claimed encouraged people not to work. At the same time he attacked tax loopholes for the very rich. This emphasis on taxes extended to attacks on tax-free foundations, which he saw as underwriting lawlessness and disorder. Through this new tax rhetoric he linked the ultra-wealthy, federal bureaucrats, protesters and criminals. Speaking that year before the National Press Club, Wallace said that 'Middle America is caught in a tax squeeze between those who throw bombs in the streets and engage in disruptive and destructive protest while refusing to work on the one hand, and the silk-stocking crowd with their privately controlled tax-free foundations on the other hand.'[64] In other words, the very rich fund the crime, insurrection and laziness of the very poor, and in the middle is the average citizen, who is powerless, unfairly taxed, and continually threatened by violence.

By focusing on welfare recipients, Wallace could make distinctions between the working poor and the 'undeserving poor', a distinction that would become a staple of Republican rhetoric in the following decades. Hoping to cut into Democrat constituencies, Wallace did not so much abandon 'the working man' as attempt to absorb this identity into a broad middle. Similarly, as he angled for Republican support, he opposed loopholes for the very rich but was not anti-business. Thus Wallace blamed the main economic issue not on business or labour, but on the state itself. Inflation, and the growing recession, he said, was caused by giving foreign aid to Third World governments who 'spit in our face', and hence, somehow, by busing. As he said on *Meet the Press*,

The Democrats sometimes blame big business, and the Republicans sometimes blame labour ... but the blame for inflation is on the Government of the United States. They have brought about inflation running these multi-billion dollar deficits, putting this money into circulation that devalues the dollar in a man's wallet, giving this money overseas by the billions and billions of dollars, and the day of reckoning is here. I think that what they ought to do is cut down on federal spending, and one way you can start is cutting [health, education and welfare]. All these bureaucrats that go around and draw up these busing decrees.[65]

Wallace's attempt to leave his extremist image behind and embrace a larger constituency was also reflected in his campaign literature. In preparation for the 1972 run, his staff began to publish the *Wallace Stand*, a slick-paper publication that was produced in various editions, including a labour edition for workers, and versions produced in Polish, Yiddish, German, Spanish and Chinese. These new tactics – embracing a larger middle and focusing on shared economic concerns while hammering away at busing, taxation, welfare and crime – allowed Wallace to appear non-racist while continuing to appeal to racial sentiments. It began proving effective. After he came in second to McGovern in the Wisconsin primary, other Democratic candidates became increasingly circumspect about the Southern contender. Many Wallace supporters said that McGovern was their second choice, and McGovern claimed to be listening attentively to the frustrations of Wallace voters. Other candidates began to pick up on his themes of tax reform, urban decay and disorder, and alienation from government. After winning the Alabama primary, Wallace came in second in both Indiana and Pennsylvania, and in both states received the majority of the popular vote.

In his quest for mainstream acceptance, Wallace also no longer courted disorder at his rallies. He was now in fact rueful about it. Recalling the mayhem of 'those big crowds' of his 1968 campaign he explained, 'Here's a little girl listening to me, and some extremist is shouting foul language over her head, and her daddy can't stand it any longer, and he picks up a chair, and so that's what the news media tell about, not what I said.'[66] Some former Wallace supporters seemed to feel the same way. As one said, 'You go to the same bar every Saturday night ... You see the same fight. After a while, it's not very entertaining.'[67] Only one event was marked by violence at a Wallace rally that year. The day before the Michigan and Maryland primaries, where Wallace was the frontrunner, he gave a speech in the parking lot of a Maryland strip mall. Afterwards he went into the crowd to shake hands with supporters, and was shot five times at close range by Arthur Bremer, a severely troubled man with no discernable political agenda. Wallace won both primaries, but the shooting left him hospitalised for months and permanently paralysed from the waist down, bringing his campaign to an end.

1976: 'Trust the people'

Wallace's brief and final presidential bid in 1976 demonstrated that the key to his success also opened the door to his failure. In 1975, the Wallace people expressed interest in a possible independent ticket with Ronald Reagan, and the June issue of the *Wallace Stand* had a front-page picture of the two of them together at a meeting in Alabama under the headline 'Anything is Possible'. Reagan never raised the possibility himself, however, and Wallace decided finally to run as a Democrat. If in 1972 Wallace meant to 'send a message' to both parties, by 1976 it was clear that the message had been received – his 1976 campaign slogan 'Trust the People' could have come as easily from Jimmy Carter as from Reagan.

In the attempt to become a serious contender, Wallace now actively tried to cleanse racism from his image, while maintaining the expanding chain of equivalence. He continued to contend publicly that he was a moderate, began appearing publicly with African Americans, and even crowned a black homecoming queen at the University of Alabama. His 1976 campaign promotional film 'A New Day for America' demonstrates this new strategy. The film opens with the announcement of Wallace's candidacy as a 'people's campaign', on behalf of 'average citizens'. Accompanying images are shots of working- and middle-class people on the job or at home; black welders, white cowboys and Asian shop owners. 'Wallace', the film announces, 'touches people of every race, creed, colour and national origin'. These people are 'the great middle class', who are 'the most oppressed class in America'. As in 1972, the enemies of this class are tax-dodging multi-millionaires, welfare recipients, criminals and an irresponsible state that supports and encourages all of these groups.

The film goes on to give a short biography of Wallace, discussing his boyhood under God-fearing parents, his distinguished service during the Second World War, and his time as an Alabama judge. The biography then jumps to his promising run as a Democratic presidential contender in 1972, and the assassination attempt that cut it short. Markedly absent are references to the most important events of Wallace's career: his rise to fame as a fiercely segregationist governor, and his polarising independent bid for president in 1968. In other words, in order to be viable the Wallace people decided that the candidate would have to play down the very thing that had brought him national recognition.

When Wallace directly addresses the audience in the film, it is without his former fury. Speaking from behind his desk in the governor's office, he looks stiff and restrained – more like the image of the bureaucrats he used to skewer than the firebrand who did the skewering. Such a muted presence and delivery may have been more a function of his disability or the medication needed to stay the excruciating pain to which he was now continually subject; but it may also have been an attempt to project presidential gravitas – an awkward look for him indeed.

There are no reports of serious disruption at Wallace rallies or speeches in 1976. This may reflect the fact that Wallace could no longer whip up his audiences by pacing the stage and punching his fists into the air. It may also have expressed Wallace's ambivalence about his own episode with violence. During a moment of indecision prior to the 1976 race, Gerald Wallace, his brother and campaign adviser, exhorted him to run this one last race. In response Wallace replied, 'Gerald, why don't you get your ass shot at, get bricks thrown at you, with you at one end of the country and your wife at the other.'[68] But the absence of a turbulent atmosphere also reflected that the country itself no longer convulsed with the uproar that had marked the 1960s. The Vietnam War was at an end, and the New Left and black power movements had long since gone into decline. There were only traces of this earlier time, now transformed at most into macabre street theatre, as when Wallace was greeted at a Wisconsin rally by protesters wearing Arthur Bremer masks, pushing wheelchairs.[69] Although he remained a candidate until just before the Democratic Convention, Wallace did not garner nearly the support he had had in 1972. Democratic voters backed another Southerner who campaigned against government red tape and the alienation of the people. At the Convention, Wallace attempted to persuade his delegates to throw their support to Carter.

Conclusion: The limits of populism

The rise and fall of Wallace demonstrates that populist movements are ultimately unsustainable in a liberal democracy. Like the People's Party of the late nineteenth century, homogeneous notions of *the people* and the transparency of representation between the people and its leaders in a large, diverse and modern society is no more than a fantasy of wholeness. Fantasies can also be enabling, however, and populist movements can thus produce political identities that fundamentally shape broader hegemonies. But if populism is an illusion, and if the heterogeneous array of political positions it pulls together is always contingent and unstable, why did a conservative populism prevail in the 1960s over liberal and left variants?

In Michael Kazin's otherwise excellent book *The Populist Persuasion*, he argues that conservative populism triumphed in large measure because 'the need to build a new interracial majority was largely ignored' by both liberal Democrats and the New Left, who instead focused entirely on the desires of the civil rights and black power movements.[70] Other versions of this argument proliferate in the work of liberal and former New Left writers seeking to explain both the failure of Democratic liberalism and the emergence of Reaganism. In all of these accounts the aggressive excesses of black power, militancy against the war in Vietnam, and narrowly conceived identity politics sabotaged what could and should have been a hegemonic, interracial social-democratic political bloc. The majority of white working- and middle-class Americans thus became alienated from the left, the story goes, and the populist project was ceded to the right.[71] However, just as liberal social scientists in the 1960s saw the popularity of Wallace as a reflexive backlash against civil rights advancements, so do these contemporary writers see as inevitable what was once merely a hopeful political strategy by the Right.

The idea that the Left was too fragmented, menacing and ideologically extreme to appeal at all to Americans in the 1960s is a retroactive construction that in fact defines the hegemonic project of modern conservatism.[72] In psychoanalytic theorist Jacques Lacan's mirror stage, the fantasy of bodily integrity is not produced in response to an actually dispersed, fragmented body. Rather, it is the idea of a prior uncontrollable body-in-pieces that produces the fantasy of an existing homogeneous identity. Similarly, to the degree that liberals and progressives blame the rise of the Right on leftist excesses and fragmentation, they succumb to the Right's assertion that the nation actually *was* threatened by liberal elites from above, welfare dependants and rioters from below, and by radical dissent from the Left. Indeed as the Wallace case shows, political excess, violence and ideological positioning outside the mainstream of American political culture were by no means the sole province of the anti-war movement, black militancy and identity politics – any more than the Johnson administration's attempts to overcome the New Deal's racial contradictions were necessarily a threat to the basic political commitments that define American national identity.

Given the history of racial domination in the US, populism is easier to exploit in the service of a white majority than an interracial one. Seen this way, the failure of liberals and the Left in the 1960s to produce a workable populist vision was not the result of too much emphasis on race. Rather, the history of white majoritarianism in the US, and in particular the racial exclusions in the New Deal, already shaped the political identity and interests of white Democrats. This made an anti-statist populism attractive when race became the key issue to be managed by the liberal state. Populism has an egalitarian as well as an intolerant legacy, but even populist movements driven by democratic impulses have ultimately foundered on their excessive concern for homogeneity. Hegemonic movements all require some illusion of complete commonality – a particularity that comes to stand for the general – as well as foes .

against which to forge this commonality. But it should be possible to build a democratic, egalitarian movement with hegemonic aspirations that does not require recourse to romantic notions of *the people* or to simplistic majoritarianism. In any case, lamenting the loss of a populist vision in the 1960s only masks its constitutive exclusions, and keeps us in Wallace's long shadow.

7

Populism and the New Right in English Canada

DAVID LAYCOCK

Introduction

In this chapter I portray populism as an ideological phenomenon central to the politics of both the Left and the Right in English Canada over the past century. In focusing on the ideological dimensions of Canadian populism, I follow Ernesto Laclau's recommendation that we attend to the ways in which populist appeals extend across class boundaries to construct politically powerful discursive antagonisms between 'the people' and a 'power bloc.'[1] The Canadian experience illustrates that these political appeals have no necessary ideological sign or class allegiance. Populist appeals have been employed by political and social movement actors, and economic and media elites, at different places and in different historical contexts.

All Canadian populisms have aimed at a system or logic of power, backed by 'special interests' and their political agents, and protected by institutions portrayed as insensitive to the appeal and interests of 'the people'. These populisms rhetorically construct political and ideological projects to take aim at current broad configurations of political, social and economic power. Understanding the character, appeal, and success of any particular Canadian populism requires us to look at its rhetorical construction of the logic of power that pervades interrelations among political and economic structures, 'special interests', 'the people' and 'real democracy'.

Canadian populisms all develop a critique of 'actually existing democracy'. They express distinctive accounts of how democracy in general, and democratic representation in particular, has favoured 'special interests' over 'the people'. Populist discourses find democracy wanting by focusing on the channels, institutions and background conditions of representation. In some cases, the critique of representation moves well beyond the sphere of parliamentary politics, and incorporates demands for inclusion of various elements of 'the people' in a more extensively politicised and democratised economy and society.[2]

Populist intuitions and arguments regarding democratic deficits resonate with a central legitimating logic of Western polities. Their legitimacy relies on broad public acceptance of the idea that political representation allows expression of 'the people's' interests and their sovereign will and authority.[3] These interests and this authority must be not just acknowledged, but constitutive of democratic public life and policy. Typically, a populist political discourse appeals to the belief that, in some manner, these democratic promises to 'the people' are sabotaged by 'special interests', and that the people's properly sovereign authority and interests are thus undermined.

In this sense, populisms invoke what we might call a generic 'democratic morality', according to which the stifling of the people's will inside or alongside mediated experiences of political representation is a normatively unacceptable political practice. To understand how people with widely different interests and experiences can find populist appeals attractive, we need to consider how deployment of rhetorically compelling democratic moralities can legitimise policy programmes that often pay only lip-service to popular democracy.

In this chapter, I argue that a successful harnessing of a populist democratic morality to a new-right policy agenda has done much for the success of new-right parties in Canada since the early 1990s. These parties' economic and social policies are certainly not irrelevant – some voters for these parties are largely indifferent to their democratic reformist appeal, as are most of their big financial supporters. But we need to understand why voters whose interests can easily appear inconsistent with new-right policy agendas still find them attractive. So we need to ask how new-right populisms successfully raise questions of democratic legitimacy, representation and inclusion/exclusion in public life, and now do so more successfully than left-populist discourses.

Finally, a word on my non-coverage of populism in Québec. Québecois populisms are largely intertwined with Québecois nationalism, and hence quite specific to Québec's unique ideological, linguistic and party-competition dynamics.[4] The major new populist force in English Canada over the past generation, the Reform/Alliance party, has virtually no following in Québec.[5] I have thus opted to focus on the English Canadian experience, with which I am most familiar.

Populism in English Canada: historical dynamics

In twentieth-century English Canada, populism emerged among groups for whom the cosy accommodations of two-party politics and the corporate elite of 'central Canada' seemed a matter of basic class injustice and the subversion of democracy. Populism initially formed a key element of anti-establishment politics in nineteenth-century Ontario, where rural and working-class political activists were influenced by the discourses of American populist radicals. Especially influential were those populisms that had attempted to forge broad farmer–labour coalitions in the mid-western and great plains states in the 1880s and 1890s.

At this time, Canadian politics were dominated by two parties, the Liberals and the Conservatives. The Liberals had managed by the 1890s to build a coalition between Anglophone and Francophone elites, Protestants and Catholics, urban and rural voters, and voters in 'the centre' (Ontario and Québec) and in the eastern Atlantic and western prairie and coastal hinterlands. The Conservatives tended to be a party of propertied and Anglophone Protestant businessmen, though they had attracted some Catholic elites in Québec during the latter part of the nineteenth century. Finally, the Conservatives were a protectionist, anti-free trade party, while the Liberals, following their counterparts in

Britain, were ideologically committed to free or at least freer trade, especially across the US border.

Both parties attempted to act as 'brokerage' parties, fostering regional cadres and constituencies in both the metropolitan and hinterland regions of a rapidly changing country. Their challenge in the 'regions' was to convince farmers, fishermen, miners and loggers in the resource-extracting hinterlands that their interests were advanced by a party that was funded, organised and inclined to produce economic policy that favoured Ontario and Québec industrial, commercial and financial capital over most hinterland producers. The Liberals excelled at this from the middle 1890s through most of the twentieth century. But after the end of World War I, dissatisfaction with the anti-union, anti-free trade, pro-central Canadian business policies of a wartime Conservative–Liberal coalition government triggered a wave of third-party and democratic reform energies across most of English Canada. As the Canadian west was rapidly settled by British, American and European immigrants seeking new lives and often interested in unconventional politics between 1890 and 1920, this energy was especially concentrated in the western prairie provinces and British Columbia.[6]

Populism found its fullest expression in a variety of organised farmer, farmer–labour coalition, and third-party politics in the western prairie provinces between the two world wars. Many immigrants who became prairie political activists had experience in either British labour politics or American agrarian populist organisations, and had difficulty accepting the imposition of 'old party politics' from Ontario and Québec on their new communities. The policies of national development shared by the Liberal and Conservative parties since 1880 had essentially treated the prairie hinterland as a source of cheap grain exports, and a captive market for central Canadian corporate profits in the financial, transportation and consumer goods sectors.[7] This pattern of policies spurred westerners' rejection of these parties, as did tough economic times for grain farmers in the immediate postwar period and during the 1930s Depression.

The small urban labour groups in western Canada were radicalised in two waves, first in the immediate aftermath of World War I, and then from 1929 to 1939. By the early 1930s labour activists in the prairie provinces were seeking common political cause with the much larger western population of grain farmers in an expansive left-populist party, the Co-operative Commonwealth Federation (CCF).

The CCF's social democratic populism was one of four distinct populist discourses in the interwar period.[8] It was more statist than other agrarian populist discourses, more distinctly anti-capitalist, and more inclined to see greater similarity than difference in the difficulties presented to farmers and urban labour by Canadian capitalism.

The 'crypto-Liberalism' of the short-lived Progressive Party was the first prairie populism to develop, and the least radical. It aimed primarily at ending the protectionist national policy of Liberal and Conservative governments, but was only a small ideological and political distance from the federal Liberal party.[9]

Prairie farmers' organisations such as the United Farmers of Alberta, the United Farmers of Saskatchewan, and the prairie 'wheat pool' co-operatives had many 'crypto-Liberal' leaders and activists. But they also contained many activists who were willing to employ a more demanding and critical discourse than the Progressives. What I have called 'radical-democratic populists' were more committed to a broader programme of popular democracy, more interested in active state intervention on behalf of farmers and labour, and more convinced that their political organisations had to steer completely clear of the 'old-party/special interests' nexus that had generated the people's plight over the past half-century.[10] Radical-democratic populism included support for quasi-syndicalist schemes of functional representation, which rejected party-dominated parliamentary representation in favour of delegate democracy and a 'group government' scheme. The most sustained expression of this populism was offered by activists in the United Farmers of Alberta, which governed Alberta from 1921 to 1935.

A fourth populist discourse in the inter-war prairies was what I have called 'plebiscitarian populism'. It arose in 1934 when charismatic evangelical radio preacher and school principal William Aberhart founded the Social Credit League of Alberta. Aberhart was a recent convert to 'Social

Credit', a technocratic analysis of under-consumption developed by the British engineer and amateur economist C. H. Douglas. Compared to both radical-democratic and social-democratic populist discourses, Aberhart's Social Credit League was authoritarian and offered a simplistic political and economic critique, which centred on a financial system-vilifying analysis of 'the people's' problems.[11] The Social Credit League swept to power in Alberta in 1935, and governed the province until 1968.

By the late 1930s Aberhart realised that his simple financial reform panaceas could not be implemented provincially. He switched to identifying prospective welfare state programmes and centralising 'state socialism' as the people's real enemies. His successor, Ernest Manning, directed a Social Credit government in Alberta from 1943 to 1968. Manning's technocratic right-populism maintained an anti-centralist ideological critique of the federal government's role in Canada's emerging welfare state.

Though Social Credit's right-populism dominated Alberta politics between 1935 and 1968, the CCF's left-populism restructured party system dynamics in the other three western provinces of British Columbia, Saskatchewan and Manitoba. It became the major opposition party in both British Columbia and Manitoba, while in Saskatchewan the CCF swept to power in 1944, and stayed there for two decades.

The CCF's left-populism also had more of an impact than Social Credit's right-populism on the competitive and ideological dynamics of the federal party system from the mid-1930s until the late 1980s. The CCF and its successor, the union-affiliated New Democratic Party (1961), became a perennial 'third party'. While tame by some European standards, CCF-NDP social democracy articulated a populist anti-capitalism that was notably lacking in US party competition. With the CCF-NDP presence in federal and provincial political competition in English Canada, it was possible to be a socialist in Canadian public life without being widely seen as anti-Canadian. The CCF-NDP's role in English Canadian party competitions was one key reason why the trajectory of Canadian welfare state development was closer to the European than the US norm.

Right-populism in English Canada since 1987

Canada's recent political scene has been dramatically altered by the success of the Reform Party, a vehicle for new-right and right-populist policy nostrums and political discourse from 1987 through 2000. The Reform Party's early western Canadian regionalist appeal, while crucial to its entry into the Canadian federal party system, disguised the extent to which its agenda was typical of post-1980 new-right parties and political discourse throughout the Western world.[12]

The Reform Party was created in 1987, and then dominated until 2000 by Preston Manning, an Alberta business consultant and son of the Social Credit party premier of Alberta from 1943 to 1968. Both Mannings had been interested in creating a new party on the right since the 1960s.[13] Preston Manning had waited patiently for almost two decades for right-wing western Canadians to become thoroughly disillusioned with their long-time federal Progressive Conservative Party home.[14] Conservatives in the United States and the United Kingdom had shifted decisively to the right by the late 1970s, foreshadowing major changes in the opportunity structures of Canada's national party system well before Preston Manning attempted to 'catch the wave'.

After 1988, Reform's appeal to historic western grievances in the federal system was easy to make and eagerly consumed. A federal Progressive Conservative government with substantial western representation had failed over two terms (1984 to 1993) to show the same concern for western industrial development interests that it did for those in Ontario and Québec. This government also failed to satisfy right-wing conservatives' desires for major tax and social spending cuts, and for traditional Christian approaches to social and moral issues.

Manning's new party fortunes owed much to the transformation of the federal Progressive Conservative Party under Brian Mulroney, which won federal elections in 1984 and 1988 due to a modus vivendi between centrist Québecois nationalists and right-wing western conservatives. The incompatible 'nation-building' visions of the Québec and western coalition partners were revealed in two failed attempts at constitutional reform, in 1987–90 and 1992, both aimed primarily at getting the Québec government to accept and legitimise the major Canadian constitutional overhaul that had taken place in 1981. Following the failure of the first attempt, Québec nationalist MPs abandoned the Progressive Conservative Party to form the Bloc Québecois.

Reform Party support among western regionalists and disaffected Progressive Conservative Party supporters was given a major boost by Reform's decision to oppose the 1992 'Charlottetown Accord' proposal for constitutional change. Reform opposed the Accord in a national referendum campaign on the grounds that it had been constructed behind closed doors by unaccountable political elites, and would have given enhanced rights and increased power to native peoples, Québecois nationalists, and 'special interests' such as feminists.

Reform's standing as a party of the people was enhanced because they were the only major party in English Canada to oppose the Accord, which was defeated in the referendum vote. The Progressive Conservative Party meltdown accelerated following this referendum, and freed right-wing conservatives in the west to find a less compromised, more congenial home in the Reform Party fold.

The 1993 federal election was the Reform Party's watershed event. Reform gained fifty-two parliamentary seats and the second-largest proportion of the national popular vote, 17 per cent. Voter defections to Reform in the west, to the Bloc in Québec and to the Liberals in Ontario decimated the Progressive Conservative Party. It dropped from majority government to two federal seats, and has not grown beyond twenty seats since. The Progressive Conservative Party's continued weakness since 1993 opened up considerable space in which a new party of the right could experiment and grow.

In the 1997 federal election the Reform Party came close to doubling the NDP's popular vote, and won three times as many seats, as well as Official Opposition standing in Parliament. After just three federal elections, the Reform Party had clearly displaced the CCF-NDP as an influential third party nationally. Promoting an agenda of major cuts to taxes, and social programmes and business deregulation as favoured by political, economic and media elites in North America and Britain, Reform attained strategic and ideological significance well beyond its western Canadian stronghold. Reform played a major role in pushing the post-1993 federal Liberal government in budget-cutting, tax-reducing directions that would have seemed unthinkable one decade before. And it did this with a clever combination of new-right policy and right-populist appeals.

Reform emphasised further decentralisation of power to the provinces, fiscal belt-tightening through major social and regional development programme cuts, replacement of many social service programmes by private charity work, 'workfare' as an alternative to welfare, elimination of state support for multicultural and other advocacy groups, and elimination of pay equity programmes. It promoted harsher treatment of criminals, juvenile offenders and welfare mothers, provisions for direct democratic accountability for MPs, and a promise that national citizens' initiatives would be used to settle contentious issues of public policy. All told, the Reform Party proposed a dramatic reduction in the Canadian welfare state, and in the scope of organised group participation in public policy development.[15]

The new-right core of Reform policy became clearer once the party reconstituted itself as the Canadian Reform and Conservative Alliance (Canadian Alliance) Party in 2000. This partisan metamorphosis aimed to broaden support beyond the western provinces to include centre-right voters in Ontario. It led to a reduced emphasis on direct democracy and other populist appeals, especially those tied to historical western grievances concerning central Canadian domination of federal political parties and policy agendas. A later metamorphosis in the fall of 2003, involving a merger of the federal Canadian Alliance and Progressive Conservative parties, underscored this move away from populist principles and practices even more. This most recent marginalisation of the populist impulse within the politics of the Canadian new-right will be examined briefly in a later section.

Who supported Reform?

Significant parts of the Reform Party mixture of populist appeals and new-right policy nostrums have appealed broadly in English Canada west of Québec, especially in Alberta and British Columbia, since 1987. In the 1993 and 1997 federal elections, Reform made major inroads into hinterland working-class, farmer, small business and urban middle-class constituencies in the western provinces. By 2000, Canadian Alliance candidates had won over 60 per cent of the popular vote in Alberta's federal ridings, and just under 50 per cent of the popular vote in British Columbia, netting them fifty of the sixty parliamentary seats from these two provinces.

Beginning in 1993 the Reform Party attracted – and the Canadian Alliance from 2000 to 2003 retained – many previous NDP supporters, including at least one-quarter of English-Canadian trade unionists, and roughly one-third of low-income voters.[16] The NDP's moderate 'left-populist' and broadly anti-corporate appeal has experienced a precipitous drop within its two most likely constituencies, which were the backbone of its 15 to 20 per cent of the national popular vote in federal elections between 1961 and 1988.

What can explain this? To begin with, among English Canadian political parties, Reform was the major beneficiary of increasing anti-party resentment during the 1980s and 1990s.[17] Like European parties such as Austria's FPO, the Reform Party managed to attract support from voters disaffected by rapid cultural change, social and economic dislocation, and governing parties' inability to provide security or democratic responsiveness in the face of such change. Clearly, trade unionists and low-income Canadians are well represented in the legions of 'anti-party' voters who saw first the Reform Party and then the Canadian Alliance as the most effective electoral medium for an anti-party message. West of Ontario, many union and low-income voters were attracted to the regionalist, anti-central government discourse of Reform and the Alliance. The federal NDP's support for the two elite-manufactured constitutional proposals of 1987 and 1992 seriously undermined its credentials as a party that would 'stand up to Ottawa.'[18] Finally, some union and even low-income voters have been attracted to Reform/Alliance proposals for deep cuts to taxes and social services.

As Hanspeter Kriesi has pointed out, explaining the mobilisation of working-class and low-income voters by new parties of the right requires us to focus on these voters' relatively low levels of education, their insecurity in 'post-industrial' economies, and their self-perception as losers in processes of economic 'modernisation' sweeping western societies.[19] New right-wing parties have recruited lower-income and working-class voters with 'welfare state chauvinism', which involves rejecting immigrants' – and occasionaly aboriginal citizens' – eligibility for social programme coverage. Such parties have also argued that mainstream parties and state bureaucrats favour immigrants, native peoples, other national minorities (in Canada, francophone Québecois), criminals, and special-privilege-seeking women's groups and gays, over 'ordinary working people' in the distribution of state resources.

This is a large part of the Reform and Alliance party articulation of the classic populist 'people/power-bloc' antagonism. Reform's 'get tough on criminals' message has resonated strongly among less educated voters in Ontario and the west. So has its claim that federal governments have given special rights and increased political power to native peoples, immigrants, Québecois nationalists, and other 'special interests' such as feminists and gays.

Finally, many English-Canadian voters alienated from a political system that has failed to protect them against forces of economy-rationalising globalisation are susceptible to the 'anti-system' appeals characteristic of populist discourses. English Canadians are very enthusiastic about 'direct democracy' mechanisms such as referenda and recall,[20] as sticks with which to beat unrepresentative political elites, with the highest enthusiasm for these devices among voters with less education.

Many western Canadians voted for Reform primarily because they saw it as 'their own' regionally based party, and because none of the other federal parties appeared to be crucially influenced by westerners.

Still, Kriesi's 'losers in modernisation' hypotheses help to explain why voters who would suffer from welfare-state-gutting agendas have nonetheless found Reform/Alliance right-populist appeals attractive, especially when such appeals have included heavy doses of party politician- and political system-bashing.

Reform's legitimacy as a partisan political alternative, and the attraction of key parts of its message across broad swaths of the population, was greatly boosted by coverage given to the party in major daily newspapers across English Canada. Media support for Reform began in the far-right, fundamentalist Christian *Alberta Report* and *BC Report* magazines. Support soon came from the overwhelming majority of weekly 'community newspapers' in small-town British Columbia and Alberta, and then from the daily press across much of urban English Canada. Since Reform's creation, most of the dailies and weeklies have been owned and actively controlled by a succession of right-wing English-Canadian press conglomerates. While few of the dailies endorsed Reform's social conservatism, since 1993 they have consistently supported the Reform/Alliance anti-statist fiscal and economic agenda. Since the late 1990s, a nationally distributed daily, the *National Post*, has offered political commentary that often amounted to little more than cheerleading for the Reform and Alliance parties. The *Post* has continuously advocated a merger between the Reform/Alliance and Progressive Conservative parties, to end what it saw as the disastrous vote-splitting between these two parties.

By 1993, most moral conservatives in the western provinces, and many in Ontario, had found a political home in the Reform Party. Preston Manning is a lay fundamentalist Christian preacher like his father. Stockwell Day became the Alliance Party leader in 2000, after having been everything from rural auctioneer, to small-town Bible college administrator, to Minister of Finance in Alberta. His successful bid for the Alliance Party leadership owed much to his team's recruitment of religious fundamentalists, especially in 'pro-life' movement organisations. Stephen Harper, the Alliance Party's leader from mid-2002 until its merger with the Progressive Conservatives, has emphasised his party's anti-statist, pro-market message far more than its social conservativism, but found himself unable to keep the latter hidden when the federal Liberal government proposed extending marriage rights to same-sex couples in late 2003.

Following the quasi-populist religious right south of the border,[21] Manning's Reform Party promised a referendum on capital punishment, a referendum to re-criminalise abortions, and an active campaign on behalf of traditional family values against the threats posed by gays and feminists. Reform appealed to those disturbed by government officials' unethical behaviour, by non-white immigration, by the secular decline of traditional Christian values, and by intrusive social programmes that reduce 'personal responsibility' and threaten traditional family authority structures. The Alliance Party continued these appeals, though they played a smaller role in the 2000 election campaign – especially in urban Ontario – than they did during the life of the Reform Party.

Reform also appealed to English Canadians who have lost patience with federal governments' efforts to 'satisfy Québec' with enhanced provincial powers, national official bilingualism, and disproportionate shares of industrial development and other grants. Among 'anti-party' voters, Reform voters overwhelmingly believed that the governing Liberals would continue to favour Québec over the west.[22]

'Anti-party' voters in 1997 were three times as likely to support Reform as other parties.[23] Many Reform or Alliance votes have been cast primarily against national 'politics as usual' in Canada, in which national Liberal or Conservative governments typically placed Ontario or Québec interests ahead of western Canada's.

The Reform/Alliance appeal to fiscal and economic conservatives has also been clear. By 2000, the Ontario business community had joined western Canadians in funding the Alliance, and financed the most expensive party election campaign in Canadian history. Most of these backers abandoned the Alliance ship after it failed to win significant numbers of seats in Ontario, and are now slowly returning with the merger of the two parties of the right.

Many Reform supporters felt frustrated with what they saw as the federal system's willingness to accommodate aboriginal demands for financial compensation and self-government.[24] Opposition to aboriginal self-government initiatives in Canada during the 1990s was spearheaded by the Reform Party federally, and was especially evident in 1999–2000 parliamentary debates on a treaty negotiated by the federal and BC governments.[25] Party leader Manning condemned the Nisga'a Treaty's provisions for communal forms of property ownership as 'socialistic', and rejected 'special rights' for aboriginals as an affront to the basic democratic principle of equal rights for all citizens.

Finally, we can list, without elaborating on them, psychic facilitating conditions for the Reform/Alliance brand of democratic politics, recognisable as mainstays of right-populist politics throughout the western world.[26] They include alienation from conventional modes of political life; frustration with and pessimism over the possibility of accountable representation; anger towards emerging minority group elites and political establishments that have allowed their emergence; various senses of powerlessness; anomie and often resentment in the face of massive social and cultural transformation; and a feeling of minimal efficacy in complex systems of democratic representation.

When mixed with psychological insecurities and experiences of declining expectations, rigid political systems incubate populist challenges to existing democratic polities. To political actors keen on rapidly dismantling the multi-level Canadian welfare state, Canada's federal system seems particularly rigid, just as the corporatist foundations of Scandinavian and Austrian welfare states have presented a convenient political target for their Progress, New Democracy and Freedom parties.

Constructing 'the people' and its enemies

Some account of essential social antagonisms between elites and 'the people' is central to all forms of populism. For Alberta's Social Credit premiers, the people's adversaries were initially financiers and their political protectors, but were soon re-identified as government planners, bureaucrats, and promoters of social welfare programmes. Reform's updated portrayal of the people's enemies included 'special interests', and bureaucrats whose jobs depend on administering and expanding programmes to meet special interests' demands. They have also portrayed unaccountable, 'old-line' parties, particularly those with leaders from Québec, as the people's political nemesis.

Reform and Alliance party elites present the market as a neutral distributor of economic and social values, and argue for a corresponding minimisation of the state's role in this regard. In this view, the costs of state-directed redistributive policies are borne disproportionately by individual property-holders through confiscatory taxation. The benefits of such regimes are seen to flow to powerful 'special interests', and to government bureaucrats who manage programmes that pander to such special interests. Remedying this political pathology requires the drastic reduction of special-interest and bureaucratic roles in public life, and the return of the power of political decision-making directly to taxpayers.

The political purpose of Reform Party elites' definition of 'special interests' was to identify and dramatically curtail relationships between various groups and an unfairly redistributive state. In this account, special interests are actors and groups that promote state intervention in the market distribution of social and economic goods, thereby fostering the pathology outlined above. Feminist lobby groups, native organisations, private and public sector unions, anti-poverty organisations, Third World solidarity groups, minority cultural and ethnic groups, crown corporations, and managers of state agencies all fall within this category.

The language that Reform leader Manning used to construct the people and its enemies is both classically populist and distinctly modern, in the sense that it carries the imprint of post-1970s new-right rhetoric found in most Western polities. In the 1993 federal election, a widely distributed Reform Party pamphlet led off with the claim that 'in Ottawa, every special group counts except one: Canadians'. Reform's task was to represent Canadians unrepresented by special interests in the halls of power. According to Manning, the history of modern Canada was one of a 'tyranny of modern "Family Compacts" of bureaucrats, politicians and "special interests" that exercise the tyranny of a minority over democratic majorities'.[27]

As in other new-right populisms, from Australia[28] to Austria, the demonology of Canadian right-populism is heavily populated by the 'who's who' of the groups that contemporary new social movement activists see as victims of our political economy. This 'mirror-imaging'[29] of right-populisms' people/power elite constructions, in relation to those of the left, is a powerful reminder of a basic left/right discursive battleground in Canadian politics.[30]

Like American right-populists since the 1940s,[31] the Reform Party did not designate large business interests, right-wing corporate media or corporate lobbyists as 'special interests'. From its inception, the Reform Party was closely associated with big business-sponsored right-wing organisations such as the Fraser Institute, the Canadian Taxpayers' Federation, and the National Citizens' Coalition. In the Reform perspective, lobbyists, think-tanks and business organisations advocating new-right policy solutions were not just more legitimate public actors than the special interests; their opposition to special interest 'interventionist' agendas made them allies of 'the people'. For Reform, such new-right actors support the people's fundamental interest in reducing taxes, business regulation, and participation by special interest advocates in policy development processes. By contrast, including those whom the right now designates as special interest advocates in policy deliberations has not only generated unfair special treatment for these groups; it has also undermined legitimate business success, honest hard work, and market efficiency.

Like right-populist parties elsewhere, Reform and the Alliance have blamed unemployment and poverty on high taxes and state intervention in the entrepreneurial private economy. Reform's 1997 election platform called for 'a country defined and built by its citizens, rather than by its government'. 'Social justice' would consist in Canadians 'working for themselves and their families, instead of for the government', and in devolving previously public obligations to private individuals, families, and unspecified 'communities'.

Governments beholden to special interests and sustained by party discipline are unable to hear or implement the 'common sense of the common people'.[32] To remedy this, Reform proposed an 'accountability guarantee' for all their candidates, and relaxed parliamentary party discipline to allow their MPs to speak for constituents and not the party elite. They also proposed plebiscitary uses of recall, referenda and citizens' initiatives instruments. Reformers promised that power stripped from the bureaucratic elite and their special interest constituencies would go to 'the people' – that is, to citizens who are neither members of nor represented by the special interests.

Right-populism and democratic reform

In a marked departure from earlier populist politics in English Canada, during the 1990s Reform successfully cornered the market on public advocacy of 'democratic reforms' to federal institutions and political practices. Through most of the twentieth century, democratic reform proposals in Canada were almost the exclusive work of farmer and labour movements, or of socialist and social-democratic parties.

By the 1960s, the electorally viable Canadian political Left – that is, the New Democratic Party – had ceased to devote substantial public attention to political institutional reform. Not wanting to hobble the policy-innovating power of federal or provincial governments, the national NDP and most other forces on the Canadian Left focused on pressuring governments to extend the reach of the federal welfare state. As citizen alienation from the bureaucratic state, and from largely technocratic mainstream politics, rose steadily through the 1970s and 1980s, Canadian social-democrats unwittingly ceded the job of political innovation for 'the people' to whichever political force could put together a coherent story about why 'the people' had been disregarded and taken for granted by the political establishment.

A combination of factors created a superb opportunity for Preston Manning's Reform Party to take up the role of populist institutional innovator in Canadian politics. Most notable were the right-wing winds of ideological change sweeping in from the south, western Canadian dissatisfaction with the Mulroney Conservative government, and the uniform support by all major political parties and elites for the two unpopular constitutional reform packages discussed earlier.

Reform offered an elected and 'equal' Senate (on the American model, with equal numbers of senators from all provinces, irrespective of population). This had special appeal to westerners, who saw no other way of creating a contra-majoritarian force in a federal Parliament dominated by Québec and Ontario. Reform also advocated reduced party discipline in Parliament, to allow MPs to reflect their constituents' views rather than merely toe the 'party line'. Finally, Reform promoted direct democracy – the initiative, referendum and recall – as the people's tool-kit for trumping the power of unaccountable political parties, self-aggrandising bureaucracies, and state-protected special interests in the public policy process.

While direct democracy is promoted by some parties of the new right in Europe, the Reform Party has gone further than most in merging its support for direct democracy with its critique of both the party system and the welfare state.[33] To leader Preston Manning and many party activists, direct democracy was to facilitate the circumvention or counteracting of successful special interest interventions in public life. 'Citizens' initiatives' in particular could operate as 'end runs' around overly mediated and institutionalised policy processes.

Such end runs look attractive to 'anti-political' citizens frustrated by the distant and unaccountable character of conventional modes of representation. To corporate interests wishing to reduce taxes and deregulate business activity in the western United States, citizens' initiatives facilitated the circumvention of legislatures and public debate in achieving corporate objectives. And for insecure middle-class majorities in some western states disturbed by the influx of large linguistic and ethnic minorities, or by the campaigns of gays for equal rights, such initiatives have provided symbolic opportunities to register dissatisfaction with the pace of social and cultural change.

Darin Barney and I have argued elsewhere that Reform's advocacy of direct democracy is best understood in light of the party's challenges to the welfare state and to a public sphere which, in Canada as elsewhere, features the multidimensional representation of organised interests.[34] As promoted by Reform, the instruments of direct democracy were well suited to a down-sized public life, would easily elide the identities of 'citizen', 'taxpayer' and 'consumer', and tended to reduce political decision-making to privatised exercises in 'consumer sovereignty'.

Direct democracy became a defining element of Reform's 'plebiscitarian' critique of democratic representation dominated by 'old-line' parties and special-interest machinations. The party even conducted several internal experiments in the mid-1990s with electronic referenda and 'electronic town halls',[35] to prove its commitment to the sovereign authority of the people as against a corrupt political system.[36]

Reform's case for direct democracy was central to its appeal among less educated low- and middle-income English Canadians experiencing civic alienation and social powerlessness. Reform offered to enable the use of direct democratic weapons like citizens' initiatives (allowing somewhere between 5 and 10 per cent of voters to propose legislation, which is then voted on in a referendum) and recall (allowing anti-MP campaigns initiated by some pre-designated percentage of voters to lead to general votes on retaining or removing the MP). The party promised that, when used properly, these weapons could humble unaccountable political elites on issues whose resolution had been stolen from the people by party elites and their special-interest allies, including the federal Supreme Court, in its 'activist' interpretation of the Canadian constitution's Charter of Rights and Freedoms. According to Reform, these issues included taxation, budget deficits, MPs' pensions, immigration, multiculturalism, affirmative action for women and visible minorities, capital punishment, gun control, abortion and aboriginal self-government. Just prior to its merger with the Progressive Conservative Party, the Alliance added gay rights to legal marriage to the list of issues on which the people's will had supposedly been overriden by unaccountable elites.

It would be a mistake to deny that direct democracy can have any positive democratic impact, or that it is appealing because political elites are largely unaccountable. But close analysis of Reform's advocacy of direct-democratic methods, and its virtual inattention to reasonable procedural requirements in conjunction with use of initiatives and recall (especially concerning limits on organised interest spending during initiative or recall campaigns), show that Reform's version of direct democracy would dramatically reduce, not enhance, social and political equality. The same conclusion is reached when one reflects on what Reform meant in claiming that a 'special-interests-free zone' is a condition of effective democracy. The 'special interests' they wished to exclude were all 'equality seekers', while the groups they wished to politically enable were against state intervention, in favour of social programme reduction, and opposed to a meaningfully inclusive and diverse public sphere. The 'market model' of political competition and social decision-making embedded in Reform's plebiscitarian advocacy of direct democracy is inconsistent with a plausible account of egalitarian social relations or effective popular democracy.[37]

The market model advocated by the Reform Party, along with most parties of the new right, rules out most aspects of inter-group decision-making that disadvantaged groups and classes have used since the Second World War – through labour, women's, ethnic minority, gay and disabled peoples' organisations – to enhance their voice and impact in public policy development, and to counter the power of organised capital in shaping state policy. The market model tends to see political mobilisation of groups and classes as anathema to the market's proper functioning. Such mobilisation is alleged not just to reduce state efficiency, but also (accurately) to increase pressures on the state for the regulation of business and redistribution of resources among social classes, groups and – in the case of environmental regulation – between generations. In these senses, then, the new-right market model is starkly inconsistent with the redistributive and participatory preconditions and practices of 'popular democracy', as conceived by all but new-right theorists and politicians.

Finally, it is worth noting that despite the good ideological fit between Reform's promotion of direct democracy and its attack on the welfare state with its special-interest beneficiaries, direct democracy was rapidly edged out of the Alliance's spotlight by other themes. This happened under pressure from Ontario business backers of the Alliance (and of its merger with the Progressive Conservatives), who saw appeals to direct democracy as annoying distractions from the proper work of a party of the Right. This proper work is to press for and implement cuts to taxes, social programme expenditures, the public sector, trade union power, and to the regulation of business activities.

Drifting to the right in the 1990s

In the two wealthiest Canadian provinces, Alberta and Ontario, Conservative Party premiers Ralph Klein (1993–2004) and Michael Harris (1995–2003) have governed with an emphasis on tax-cutting, social-programme slashing, union-bashing, and the reduction of employment equity programmes for women and visible minorities. Neither leader has seen any electoral advantage in much of the social conservative side of the Reform/Alliance agenda. But their approaches to fiscal, economic and much provincially controlled social policy, along with their rhetorical attacks on bureaucratic, federal government, trade union and new social movement actors and agendas, have done much to legitimise 'Reform-style' politics in English Canadian political life.

These premiers have consistently portrayed opponents of their essentially corporate agendas as 'enemies of the province'.[38] This bolstered the Reform Party's insistence that the Ontario 'Common Sense Revolution'[39] was also the people's, and that its opponents are special-interest enemies of the people. To Canadians familiar with recent US politics, Manning's, Klein's and Harris's rhetorical constructions often appeared heavily plagiarised from the right-populist discourses of Ronald Reagan, Newt Gingrich and eventually George W. Bush.

Manning clearly thought that Harris's two election victories on Reform-style platforms in Ontario indicated that a de-regionalised version of the Reform Party could capture numerous federal seats in Ontario. Faced with the alternative of remaining merely a regionalist party, a majority of Reform Party activists accepted Manning's campaign to transform their party into the Canadian Reform and Conservative Alliance Party just before the 2000 federal election.

Preston Manning lost the new party's leadership race to Stockwell Day, a telegenic cabinet minister from Alberta. The Alliance improved slightly on Reform's 1997 popular vote and seat totals in the 2000 election. Day's inability to forge an electoral breakthrough in Ontario, and clear leadership shortcomings, led to his replacement in early 2003 by Stephen Harper. Harper was an Alberta Reform MP from 1993–97, and is one of Canada's most astute new-right politicians. Ontario conservatives and business elites continued to lobby behind the scenes for a merger of the two federal parties of the Right, and to hope that such a party would be led by an Ontarian so as to maximise its vote-harvesting capacity.

By the fall of 2003, and in spite of their electing a new leader, the Alliance's share of the national popular vote had dropped from just over 24 per cent to barely 10 per cent, in a succession of opinion polls. Even the federal New Democratic Party, on the social-democratic Left, was registering more popular support. By October 2003, complicated and secretive back-room negotiations between the Alliance and Progressive Conservative parties had produced a proposal for a merger into a new party, the Conservative Party of Canada. Many long-time Progressive Conservative activists and leaders contended that the proposal was essentially a hostile takeover of their party by the social conservatives and hard-right in the Alliance. Nonetheless, both Alliance and Progressive Conservative party members voted overwhelmingly in favour of the merger in December 2003.

It is too early to specify the character of this new Canadian party of the Right. But all indications to date suggest that the glue that once held new-right policy agendas and anti-statist, anti-politician populism together in the Reform and Alliance parties will come unstuck in this new party. With most of its political and intellectual energy being supplied by the new-right economic conservativism favoured by leader Stephen Harper and his advisers, the Conservative Party seems on the

verge of dropping the Reform Party's regionalist antagonism towards
central Canadian dominance, and of marginalising Reform-style populist
appeals to traditional moral values and direct democracy.

In the party merger 'agreement in principle' of October 2003, neither
moral traditionalism nor direct democracy receive explicit support in a list
of nineteen 'founding principles'. However, the longest principle endorses
the 'belief that the best guarantors of the prosperity and well-being of the
people of Canada are: the freedom of individual Canadians to pursue their
enlightened and legitimate self-interest within a competitive economy; the
freedom of individual Canadians to enjoy the fruits of their labour to the
greatest possible extent; and, the right to own property'.[40]

The Conservative Party's efforts in the summer 2004 federal election
campaign focused on staying 'on message', with an emphasis on tax cuts
and government accountability, while trying to avoid contentious issues
like gay rights to marriage or abortion rights. At least for purposes of
vote harvesting, the new Conservative Party leadership has abandoned
many earlier Reform Party enthusiasms for a message of conventional
new-right economic orthodoxy. But many of its activists refuse to side-
line their vocal social conservatism. Thus even though Conservatives led
the wounded, incumbent Liberal Party in the polls through much of the
June 2004 election campaign, the Conservatives lost the election after a
disastrous final week in which the leader was on the defensive for off-
message remarks by various socially conservative MPs. Following a
disappointing election result – 100 of 308 seats, and 29.6 per cent of the
national vote – Conservative leader Stephen Harper froze the undisci-
plined social conservatives out of his shadow Cabinet, and re-dedicated
the party to a narrowly economic message.

Making economic conservatism the focus of the new party's appeal is
also the preference of the Ontario business establishment and much
of the print media elite in English Canada. But the risk entailed by
such a transformation is that shedding this populist baggage may eventually trigger the creation of another western party of the right with
populist bona fides. Such a development might occur should the sidelin-
ing of western regionalism and social conservatism continue while the

Conservatives lose the next federal election. This would perpetuate the problem generated by the Reform Party's creation. Between 1993 and 2003 the federal partisan Right had been electorally divided, and thus guaranteed a Liberal Party stranglehold on federal power.

The risk of a 'retro-Reform' party arising is real, because Reform did tap deep veins of western Canadian discontent with politics as usual, and with central Canadian control of federal institutions. Reform gave voice and organisational form to this discontent for over a decade, and gave many who felt it a strong sense that a regional party can have an impact on national policy debates. This discontent will not disappear just because its articulation is inconvenient to Ontario business elites, or because attention to anti-system political antagonisms is inconvenient to the new Conservative Party's attempt to become a plausible governing alternative to the federal Liberal Party. It also seems unlikely that right-populist discontent can be politically contained simply by Conservative Party attacks on the special interests that Reform and Alliance parties vilified in their efforts to harness the high levels of alienation from politics and public life that Canadians share with most western polities' populations.

The future of populism in Canada

For the foreseeable future, right-populist forces within and sympathetic to the new Conservative Party will dominate populist discourse as it relates to partisan politics and most policy options in English Canada. After three dismal federal election performances by the NDP, and its marginalisation in several provinces where it had held office during some or all of the 1990s,[41] a revival of broad popular support for left-populist appeals in Canadian party politics seems unlikely. The NDP has a new and relatively dynamic national leader, but the party's social-democratic/left-populist appeals receive virtually no support in Canada's popular electronic or print media, unlike those of right-populist parties and discourses.

Perhaps more important, left-populists have done little to refashion their appeals or programmes with innovative responses to democratic and representational deficits. However unlikely Reform/Alliance support for direct democracy was to give meaningful power to the people,[42] this support did at least speak to a problem of increasing democratic hopelessness felt by many citizens. Vague suggestions for a participatory, community-based politics contained in a recent 'New Politics Initiative', aimed at giving anti-globalisation and environmentalist movements more clout within a restructured federal NDP,[43] do not add up to much for all but a tiny fraction of 'the people' (the electorate) in Canada today.

Since the mid-1980s, most innovative left-populist politics in English Canada have occurred outside party politics. They began with a broad coalition of social groups, and union and feminist organisations opposed to what became the 1989 Canada–US Free Trade Agreement.[44] This coalition has re-formed, obtained some organisational permanence (most notably in the 'Council of Canadians'), and broadened its initially anti-'continentalist' focus to sponsor many public campaigns opposed to neoliberal deregulation and social-programme cuts by federal and provincial governments. It has set its sights on the prevention of hemispheric free-trade agreements, and the diminution of the power of the World Trade Organisation vis-à-vis Canadian governments.

This activity and discourse has elements of 'left-populism', but does it qualify as a coherent and distinctive Left-populist movement? Over the past two decades, the Canadian Left has identified corporate globalisation as 'the major adversary of the people'. So to the degree that the recent left activists' discourse partakes of populism, it has been what we might call a form of 'left-nationalist populism'. The cultural, economic and political power of the US over Canadian sovereignty is the unavoidable frame of reference for most on the Canadian Left, who value higher levels of popular democracy, political self-determination and social-programme support for Canadians.

Many left activists in English Canada outside the NDP also address the concerns of third-wave 'difference feminism', the 'politics of recognition' conducted by various immigrant and cultural minority groups, and native peoples' struggles for self-determination and economic security. Through the 1990s the federal NDP attempted to combine all of these discourses with its more traditional social-democratic emphasis on reduction of class inequality. But even though this combination is supported by the majority of NDP activists,[45] such appeals do not resonate broadly among the non-feminist, non-ethnic minority and non-native elements of lower-income, working-class and less educated 'ordinary Canadians'.Left-nationalist populist discourse has not been strong enough to shape a left-populist audience that identifies a common political project among the various class- and non-class-based oppositions to the post-1980s drift to fiscal conservatism and social-programme reduction, by provincial and federal governments alike.

Fear of cultural and economic assimilation to US society, and opposition to heavy-handed US influence on Canadian public life and foreign policy, have been elements of English Canadian 'popular-democratic' traditions since the late nineteenth century. These traditions have been central to the NDP's perspective on public policy since the mid-1960s. And they have been strategically incorporated into the centrist federal Liberal Party's successful post-1960s efforts to distinguish itself first from the Progressive Conservative Party,[46] and more recently from the Alliance Party. These traditions also form the ideological and cultural backbone of the recent anti-free trade, anti-globalisation movement in Canada, and arguably also provide ideological support for the Canadian government's decision not to join the US-led 'coalition of the willing' in its war on Iraq.

As noted at the outset, populisms appeal to the idea that the legitimate source and agent of sovereign authority, the people, has been denied the ability to exercise this legitimate democratic authority. The recent Canadian Left, in both its partisan and non-partisan incarnations, has claimed that free trade and/or corporate globalisation substantially constrain whatever domestic institutions Canadians possess, or might construct, to exercise sovereign power over their political, economic, and cultural life. Their references to a 'sovereignty in decline' give anti-globalisation efforts deep historical and cultural roots, and make contact with basic English Canadian popular-democratic traditions, which are crucially lacking in most left-wing campaigns on gender and gay issues, native questions, and ethnic-minority rights. In short, for left-populist discourse in Canada to have any potential for broad social appeal, it can't avoid articulating nationalist and 'democratic sovereigntist' themes and concerns.

Environmental and anti-globalisation movements are closely linked in Canada, and are the preferred venues for political action by young Canadians of a left-wing orientation. To the extent that left-populism retains a place in popular politics, it often does so through the organisational channels of these movements. At the level of communication and social network development, this has increasingly involved creative use of the Internet,[47] which connects Canadian environmentalists and anti-globalisers to each other, to sympathetic feminist and union groups, and to cognate organisations abroad.

One need not become a full-blown 'transnational civil society' romantic to appreciate that, compared to the activities of political parties and conventional organised interests, the motivation and sense of global purpose afforded by such networking is crucial to youthful left-populism. And the broad anti-capitalism shared by many of these social movement organisations bears some comparison to the cross-class, anti-capitalist and anti-old-party alliances that fostered Canadian left-populism between the two world wars. Both old and new social movement alliances have expressed alienation from 'politics as usual', and opposition to prevailing corporate hegemonies.

Of course, what separates the old social movement alliances from the new is the degree to which cultural and economic globalisation set the agendas for their respective left-populist campaigns, and the faded sense of 'democratic promise' in the new compared to the old alliances. For the interwar left populists, the relevant politics were essentially Canadian in scope and causal structure; for anti-globalisation and environmental activists, Canada is a thoroughly international political space. To act locally, as the saying goes, one must think globally. The 'power bloc' confronted by the people has a global identity, even if it has local representatives. And 'the people' itself, in this post-modern left-populism, is often conceived as much in international as national terms.

The contrast here with contemporary right-populist conceptions of the people and the special interests is striking, and decisive for the strength of right over left populism in Canada. Right-populism in the Reform, Alliance, and some provincial Progressive Conservative and Liberal parties, identifies the people in much more local and recognisable terms: they are ordinary, hard-working Canadians who have financed an unfairly redistributive and freedom-denying regulatory welfare state. The people have not benefited from these social programmes and regulations, because they are hard-working and law-abiding, because they have been over-taxed, and because they are not members of the special interests.

In the account offered over the past fifteen years by Canada's right-wing populists,[48] special interests are right here at home. They lobby mainstream parties and governments to reward them with special benefits and programmes; they distort public discussion and Supreme Court rulings with self-serving 'rights talk'; and they join bureaucrats and over-educated political elites in standing between the people and their common-sense majority decisions in an overly mediated public policy process, then in imposing self-serving policy solutions to problems of their own choosing. To add insult to injury, special interests and their political allies do this without attempting to incorporate ordinary people into either the identification or solution of problems.

This characterisation of the people and its antagonists is far easier to contemplate, and far easier to imagine direct-democratic and state-shrinking remedies for, than the left-populist alternative. It is supported by the corporate media, the tabloid press, the heroic individualist story-line of much television drama, and by the most successful new party incursions in western political orders. This portrayal of the people speaks directly to the alienation of working-class and lower-income citizens from politics and public life, and promises a future in which those who work hard will be rewarded.[49]

Perhaps most important to the success of right-populist appeal is that it continually reminds these 'ordinary people' of a basic truth about their political experience: they have been left out of both the processes of the identification and solution of problems, by most social-democratic, centrist and conventional right-wing political elites. Consequently, the right-populist critique of technocratic, special-interest-favouring statism makes direct contact with what Michael Kazin calls the historical populist insight that 'no major problem can be seriously addressed, much less nudged on a path towards solution, unless ... the "productive and burden-bearing classes" participate in the task.'[50] Anti-globalising left-populists try occasionally to speak convincingly in the name of the people, but often show few signs that they trust them to oppose multinational corporate special interests, or to participate in solving the people's problems.

Right-populists talk regularly about trusting the people, and leaving them to make their own honest way on the market's level playing field, free from the meddling of untrustworthy political actors and institutions. Left-wing activists seldom indicate that they appreciate why the currency of North American politics is so devalued that modelling political life on market relations can have a broad appeal to people who experience few of the successes offered by such relations.

For left political activists to draw anywhere near right-populists in the competition for the people's favour, they will have to find effective ways of directly engaging citizens in their alternative political projects, and of demonstrating that their often unconventional identities are not threatening. Creating a viable left-populist discourse will involve convincing people who do not identify with minority groups, feminists, environmentalists or the marginalised poor, that these groups are part of the people, not definitive of the special interests opposed to them. A more successful left-populism will discover ways of responding to the powerful new-right allegation that special rights for such groups are incompatible with the well-being of 'ordinary Canadians', while addressing their experience of social and cultural insecurity.

In doing so, left-populists will have to understand why 'ordinary Canadians' recruited by right-populist appeals feel unrepresented in and excluded from public life, just as the groups left-populists work with and for feel excluded and unrepresented. This must all be woven together with a democratic morality that offers a compelling alternative to the new-right's democratic morality. New-right populism has deployed a democratic morality that demonises special interests, marginalises all but business winners within civil society, exalts the freedom to accumulate, and reduces equality to competitive consumption in the marketplace. To be effective in this very serious contest over populist and hence democratic legitimacy, a left-populist democratic morality will have to focus on a clear and integrated vision of freedom, equality and respect in difference, much of which is already more broadly supported among average citizens than the NDP's recent electoral fortunes would suggest.

There is a lot of work to do on this front. It is by no means the sole task of left-populists, but given the importance of populist discourse to Canadian political life, leaving the field of innovation in populist appeals and political mobilisation to the political Right is a mistake that progressive Canadians cannot afford to continue making.

8

Populism or Popular Democracy? The UDF, Workerism and the Struggle for Radical Democracy in South Africa

DAVID HOWARTH

The term 'populism' has been applied to various political movements and ideologies in the South African context. In the post-Sharpeville period, two cases stand out. These are the United Democratic Front (UDF), which was formed in August 1983 and spearheaded the internal mass protest against the apartheid regime in the mid-1980s, and Chief Gatsha Buthelezi's Inkatha movement, which emerged in the early 1970s and came to play a much more ambiguous role in the politics of liberation during the 1980s and 1990s.[1] The latter movement has been carefully documented by Gerhard Maré and Georgina Hamilton, who describe its ideology and political style as 'the populism of the dominant classes demanding a reordering of the alliances of capitalism rather than a populism directed against capitalism itself'.[2] The UDF, for its part, has also been described as populist, both in recent academic accounts,[3] and by protagonists and ideological opponents of the movement. However, its alleged populism is raised with respect to issues of national liberation and socialist transformation, and not 'the populism of the dominant classes', when they were firmly placed on the political agenda in South Africa during the mid-1980s.

In this chapter, I want to focus on the debates about the appropriate strategies and goals of popular struggle that surfaced in the aftermath of the UDF's formation, concentrating especially on a series of exchanges between its supporters, who came to be known as Charterists because of their shared allegiances to the principles and programmes of the Freedom Charter, and those of the democratic trade union movement, who were deemed by their ideological opponents to be workerists. The trade union movement, which had developed since the early 1970s, represented a different strand of resistance discourse and practice than that articulated by the Charterists, and many of its leaders and strategists voiced powerful reservations about the populist character of the UDF. Apart from documenting an important – perhaps even decisive – aspect of post-Sharpeville popular resistance to the apartheid regime, my goal in revisiting these debates is to use our now available historical hindsight to evaluate these debates in the light of post-apartheid developments. I shall thus begin with a short theoretical discussion of the way in which I employ the concept of populism, after which I examine the theoretical and strategic debates of the mid-1980s, before evaluating these debates in the context of the post-apartheid experience. In all these respects, I will put forward and defend a discourse-theoretical approach to populism and populist politics in South Africa, which draws inspiration from a post-Marxist and post-structuralist conception of politics.[4]

The concept of populism

As most commentators on populism note, usually with regret, a comprehensive and universal theory of populism has proved elusive.[5] What are termed populist movements and ideologies have only provoked a number of failed attempts to construct a theoretical synthesis that can squeeze its irregular shapes and sizes into neat and rigid frames. This chapter does not, therefore, begin by proposing a general theory that subsumes the case study considered. Instead, I propose what might be called a 'picture' of populism – a loose set of features that permits a range of 'family resemblance' phenomena to be connected or derived – which might be said to underpin, but in no way determines or exhausts, the populist experience. Its function is primarily heuristic rather than strictly explanatory, in that it facilitates the categorisation and description of phenomena brought within its orbit.[6]

This picture of populist discourse consists of three basic features. In the first instance, populist discourses appeal to 'the people' as the privileged subject of interpellation. In other words, to use Michael Freeden's[7] terms, populist discourses and movements endeavour to 'decontest' the meaning of 'the people', using such appeals as the principal means to constitute political identities and recruit subjects. Secondly, populist discourses are grounded on the construction of an underdog/establishment frontier which, if successful, opposes the people to its political enemy – say the elite or the power holders. Thirdly, in order to constitute this political frontier dividing the people from the establishment – the production of equivalential effects amongst the particularities that make up the people – populist discourses are necessarily predicated on a certain passage through the universal. There is, in other words, an appeal to *all* the people within a delimited sphere or domain, and the elaboration of ideologies and symbols designed to realise these goals.

Alongside these three features, I introduce a further theoretical assumption in order to analyse and evaluate the content of any concrete populist discourse. This is that the political orientation and character of a populist movement depends upon the kinds of hegemonic articulation available and practised within a given historical context. This assumption builds upon Ernesto Laclau's argument that the content of a political discourse such as populism is not derived from an a priori consideration of its ideological elements, but from the way in which their meanings are conferred by the hegemonic projects that articulate them.[8] In his earlier writings on populism, this 'non-class belonging' of elements is restricted to certain types of discourse (nationalism, fascism, and so on), and the content is ultimately shaped by the actions of fundamental social classes rooted in economic relations. However, in his later writings Laclau extends the logic of 'non-class belonging' or contingency to all political discourses, as there are no privileged social classes that ultimately determine the meaning and form of discourses.[9] Instead, if a political force wishes to articulate and pursue its demands democratically, it must inscribe them into a broader discourse, and help to build organisational forms and levels of accountability, which can ensure that its interests are represented and pursued in political ideologies and public policies.

This theoretical assumption enables the construction of a typology of populist discourses, ranging from authoritarian to democratic modalities. That is to say, populist politics admit of more than one political form, depending on the ideological elements they comprise and the way in which they are socially constructed. Both these aspects depend to varying degrees on the social and cultural context in which populist movements operate, which means that populist movements can take on authoritarian, nationalist, civic or popular-democratic forms, while still exhibiting a distinctively populist style and language of politics. These theoretical remarks will be given greater specificity as we turn to the South African case, more specifically to the formation of the United Democratic Front and the reactions it evinced.

The emergence and formation of the United Democratic Front

Let us begin with two critical events and the processes they connect. On 23 January 1983, during the first conference of the Transvaal Anti-SAIC (South African Indian Council) Committee, Dr Allan Boesak called for a united front of democratic organisations to co-ordinate action against the South African government's reform proposals which, he argued, were designed to perpetuate apartheid domination.[10] As Boesak enjoined:

> Our response to this crisis facing us is a dialectical one. It is the politics of refusal, which has within it both the *Yes* and the *No*. We must continue to struggle for liberation, freedom, and human dignity of all people in South Africa; and so while we say *Yes* to this struggle, we say *No* to apartheid, racial segregation and economic exploitation of the oppressed masses in South Africa ... In order to do this we need a united front ... There is no reason why churches, civic associations, trade unions, students' organisations, and sports bodies, should not unite on this issue,

pool our resources, inform the people of the fraud which is about to be perpetrated in their name, and on the day of the election expose these plans for what they are.[11]

On 8 August of the same year, within a month of the formation of the UDF, about 12,000 people from all parts of South Africa, representing over 400 organisations and associations of all ethnic and racial groups, as well as different social classes, attended its launch in Cape Town.[12] The heady speeches, slogans, flags, chants and charismatic figures which graced the event, consciously harked back to, and echoed, the Congress style of politics of the 1950s. Though the nascent political movement emerged to challenge the National Party's proposed reform programme, and in this spirit refused to be identified with any single strain of resistance politics, thirteen of its twenty patrons had strong historical associations with the Congress movement (nine of whom, including Nelson Mandela and Walter Sisulu, were serving long-term prison sentences), while the three Presidents – Archie Gumede, Oscar Mpetha and Albertina Sisulu – were veteran ANC politicians, and the language and demands of the Freedom Charter assumed centre-stage.[13] More substantively, the character of the emerging discourse was strongly marked by the principles, ideas, strategies and organisational forms of the former African National Congress and its allies.[14]

In order to get a flavour of the practices conducted in the name of the UDF during the 1980s, but without embarking upon a comprehensive analysis, it is enough to draw attention to the movement's major campaigns. The UDF's primary political campaign was the disruption and undermining of the government's constitutional reform proposals. Despite some doubts about the extent to which the UDF's anti-election campaign contributed to the low electoral turnout by Indian and coloured voters for their separately elected assemblies,[15] it definitely managed to raise the profile of the emergent resistance forces, thus providing the movement with a solid platform to establish its national political presence. In tandem with its desire to stop the state's strategy in its tracks were efforts to deepen and expand its organisational presence in the country. The UDF's call for a 'People's Weekend' on 29 and 30 October 1983 – attended by about 30,000 people – aimed to divert attention away from the whites-only referendum on the government's constitutional proposals, while involving masses of South Africans in the activities of the front.[16] Similarly, the 'Million Signature Campaign', which was designed to mobilise mass opinion against the state's constitutional reforms, also demonstrated the UDF's willingness to oppose attempts by the state to legitimise its local government structures, while working side by side with specific communities.[17]

Rosa Luxemburg has argued that the production of a generalised climate of opposition makes possible a situation in which any concrete demand can assume the form of a generalised – or 'overdetermined' – opposition to the entire framework of oppression.[18] In this regard, the emergence and operation of the UDF served as a vehicle for the unification and symbolic condensation of a number of disparate struggles. Thus, despite the uneven success of the campaigns leading up to and including the boycott of the 'tri-cameral' elections in August 1984, the UDF's symbolic significance stretched further than its more narrow organisational profile suggested.[19] This was evident in the greatest political impact the UDF was able to effect – the eruption of the African townships into open political rebellion between 1984 and 1986.[20]

In the period between September 1984 and July 1985 the UDF, in conjunction with militant trade union organisations, fused together a number of antagonistic relations into a more global attack on the apartheid system as a whole. These antagonisms included students protesting against Bantu Education; township dwellers (mostly workers) opposed to the increased cost of living and continued rule by unaccountable and illegitimate representatives and state structures; workers galvanised by growing economic difficulties; women opposed to the increasing costs of transport and housing; and the unemployed, dissatisfied with the absence of meaningful prospects.[21] Although it would be inaccurate to argue that the UDF had co-ordinated and directed the explosion of mass resistance against the state in its various manifestations – this much was acknowledged by the UDF leadership themselves[22]

– the existence of such a political force, especially given the national prominence it had achieved in opposing the government's reform programme, undoubtedly fuelled and accelerated mass protest.[23] In this sense, the various organisations which the UDF had been able to draw together, along with its representation as a more universal anti-status quo signifier, allowed the movement to function as the very form of discontent and resistance against the oppressive order.

By the middle of 1985 the township conflagration had assumed a seemingly unstoppable momentum, with a continuous cycle of state repression and popular resistance.[24] By July of that year – when the official death toll in the conflict had risen to 517, and it was estimated that 109 councillors had been attacked, sixty-six of their homes, shops and property torched, and when the homes of vigilantes and state sympathisers were being regularly petrol-bombed – the state declared a partial state of emergency.[25] Paradoxically, perhaps, in the year that followed, the popular revolt gathered momentum both in its intensity and scope, and as the protest gathered pace and intensity, new strategies, tactics and forms were articulated. Amongst the latter were the UDF's turn to consumer boycotts, and its endeavour to create 'area' and 'street' committees in the black townships, so as to defend popular organisations against state repression, and to facilitate the dissemination of ideas and strategies.[26] More proactive responses were also evident in the putting forward of plans for a 'people's education', in preference to the state's system of Bantu Education, which lay in tatters after years of boycotts and conflict.[27]

Populists versus workerists in the South African liberation struggle

Even though the impact of the UDF was geographically, sectorally and socially uneven, the movement played an undoubtedly important role in stimulating and channelling protest against the apartheid state in the 1980s.[28] However, it also sparked off powerful political, theoretical and strategic debates within the broad resistance movement. Such exchanges closely paralleled the different strands of resistance politics that had

developed since the early 1970s in South Africa. Schematically, these discourses crystallised around the three main internal forces which arose in
the period between 1973, when workers engaged in a series of wildcat
strikes in various parts of South Africa, and 1990, following F. W. de
Klerk's decision to release Nelson Mandela and initiate the negotiations
that eventually ended apartheid rule. They comprised a trade union
movement organised, at least initially, for principled, strategic and tactical reasons, around narrow shopfloor demands and issues; a students'
and cultural movement initially bound together around the ideology of
Black Consciousness, which later mutated into The Azanian People's
Organisation (AZAPO), and then became allied to the Pan African
Congress (PAC); and finally the Charterist approach to political struggle,
which informed the UDF. Before turning to the substance of the debate
between the trade unionists and the Charterists, I will begin by quickly
sketching out the emergence and character of the former.

The independent trade union movement encompassed a number of
currents of progressive, anti-apartheid worker organisations with divergent political and ideological affiliations. The dominant element was the
non-racial and democratic Federation of South African Trade Unions
(FOSATU), which emerged and flourished in the repressive conditions
of the 1970s by developing an ideology and strategy that focused heavily
on the creation of factory- and industry-based unions with strong democratic accountability and 'worker leadership'.[29] In trying to ensure
worker participation at the factory floor level, and borrowing heavily on
a somewhat idealised version of British trade unionism earlier in the
century, elected shop-stewards were given a central role in the structure
and operation of the unions.[30] Probably the best expression of
FOSATU's emergent political position is Joe Foster's speech to the
Federation's 1982 national conference. Calling for the further development and consolidation of factory-floor structures so as to facilitate the
production of 'worker leadership' and a distinctive 'working-class identity', and cautioning against reckless political alliances with popular
resistance forces, Foster argued that

all the great and successful popular movements have had as their aim the
overthrow of oppressive – most often colonial – regimes. But these movements cannot and have not in themselves been able to deal with the
particular and fundamental problem of workers. Their task is to remove
regimes that are regarded as illegitimate and unacceptable by the majority.
It is, therefore, essential that workers must strive to build their own
powerful and effective organisation even whilst they are part of the wider
popular struggle. This organisation is necessary to protect and further
worker interests and to ensure that the popular movement is not hijacked
by elements who will in the end have no option but to turn against their
worker supporters.[31]

A reiteration of this style of argumentation is evident in Alec Erwin's
later distinction between 'liberation politics' – the political overthrow
of illegitimate regimes – and 'transformation politics' – that is, a type
of political strategy in which only the organised working-class at the
point of production has an objective interest, as well as the structural
capacity, to engineer an authentic transformation of capitalist relations
of production.[32] This requires a double logic of, on the one hand, elaborating militant and democratically organised working-class institutions,
while on the other hand setting out a political programme for the
restructuring of the economic base. While, he argues, this political strategy has been rooted historically in the trade union movement, and
concerned specifically with production relations, its logic can be generalised to different fronts, including health, education, engineering and
cultural activities.[33]

As resistance against the regime intensified during the early and mid-
1980s there were growing pressures among political leaders and their
constituencies for the relatively autonomous political forces to unite
around a common programme of action. It was in this context that debate
about the precise form of unity between the more narrowly defined
working-class movement and the wider national popular movement began
to emerge. The debates were registered in the intense theoretical, strategic and ideological contests that occurred in the post-Soweto period,

especially during the early and mid-1980s. Articles and statements in popular journals and community newspapers such as *Grassroots*, *SASPU National*, *South African Labour Bulletin*, *Social Review*, *Transformation* and *Work in Progress* tackled issues that ranged from tactical and strategic questions to deeper theoretical and political problems.[34] In general terms, they concerned the overall objectives of the liberation movement; the structure of the SA social formation; the role of the working class in relation to other political forces engaged in the anti-apartheid struggle; and the democratic character of the liberation movement.

The workerist critique of the Charterists was structured around what they argued were three main deficiencies in the latter's strategy.[35] Firstly, they argued that Charterists valorised struggles for national liberation (including all those who are nationally oppressed or who support the anti-apartheid struggle) over and above the more fundamental question of socialist transformation. They also claimed that Charterism underplayed the specific role of working-class politics – by which they meant democratically constituted working-class organisations characteristic of the trade union movement – as the only force guaranteeing a socialist content for national liberation. Finally, they believed that Charterists provided an inadequate and potentially authoritarian conception of democracy and socialism. With respect to the latter, two major implications of Charterist strategy were focused upon. Firstly, there was the possibility of separating democratic and socialist objectives, with the consequence that the struggle for national liberation would aim simply at a formal bourgeois democracy without the full democratisation of social relations, especially the relations of production. Secondly, they argued that even in the event of a successful socialist seizure of power by the ANC/South Africa Communist Party (SACP) alliance, there was still a strong possibility of an authoritarian statist form of socialism, which would result in the subsumption of the autonomous and historically constituted working-class movement – basically the trade unions – and the undermining of its democratic socialist demands and discourses. By contrast, workerists argued for the extension of democratic socialist demands to other levels of society, under the hegemony of the organised working class. In short, the anti-apartheid struggle should not be aimed at superficial changes in which 'black bosses ... replace white bosses, while the machinery of state and capital remained intact',[36] but should result in the radical transformation of society as a whole.

In defending their position, Charterists made three counter-arguments.[37] Firstly, they argued that the struggles for national liberation and socialist transformation were not necessarily opposed and separate but could, given the correct correlation of class forces, be mutually reinforcing. Indeed, the failure to hegemonise non-working-class sectors of the nationally oppressed would unnecessarily weaken the impetus for national liberation by excluding possible allies in the struggle, leaving them open to hegemonisation by state forces. Secondly, they believed that working-class subjectivity should be seen as 'a real social force' that is historically and politically constituted, which means that its interests and objectives could not be derived from its structural location in the relations of production. Instead, the role of the working class, if it were to succeed in inscribing its interests in the national liberation struggle, would be to intervene actively on a more global political terrain. To do this, socialists and communists in the Charterist tradition proposed a strategy of class alliances in which the working class would assume political leadership in an alliance of different class forces. Finally, with regard to questions concerning democracy and socialism, Charterists accepted the need to democratise their organisational structures, and sought to internalise some of the practices articulated by the trade union movement. Their criticism of the workerists hinged around the economism or syndicalism of their position – that is, their restriction of democratic politics to a narrowly defined constituency and a restricted set of issues and demands. Charterists argued that a necessary condition for socialist transformation was a widespread democratisation of all spheres of the social. Within this democratisation process, working-class leadership and the project for socialism could be built. This conceptualisation constituted what has been called the 'two-stage' theory of socialist revolution.

What are we to make of this exchange? Indeed, given our post-1989 political universe, how are we to approach such a series of issues that possess a quaint, almost anachronistic, character? I shall proceed in two ways. Initially, I shall problematise the exchange by projecting the onto-political assumptions of discourse theory into the existing structure of the debates, so as to disturb and rethink the conventional interpretations.[38] The aim here is not merely to clarify the underlying presuppositions of the South African debate, but also to disclose ways of thinking that might tackle a range of issues in any politics seeking to reconcile values of autonomy and solidarity, freedom and equality, not to mention the strategic and ethical questions that arise in building coalitions to advance political goals. Thereafter, I shall seek to evaluate these debates in light of the post-1990 events in South Africa itself, by concentrating on the choices and politics that have characterised this conjuncture.

Deconstructing and rethinking the theoretical terrain

With respect to the issues raised above, it is clear that both workerists and Charterists made pertinent criticisms of each others' positions. Workerists correctly objected to the possible separation of democratic and socialist demands in Charterist discourse, and trenchantly opposed the stagist conception of history inherent in Charterist theory. For their part, Charterists were right to be wary of the workerists' construction of binary oppositions between transformation and liberation, and between the working class and other political forces, as well as of the restricted scope of a democratic socialism. Instead, they were concerned to artic-ulate these moments into a common discourse and political strategy. However, rather than attempting an exhaustive pair-wise comparison of the different dimensions of the debate – a largely futile exercise in retro-spective point-scoring – it is more useful to excavate the underlying assumptions of the two positions, and then seek to deconstruct their essentialist and deterministic natures. This can be done by considering three central issues: the way they understand the relationship between national liberation and socialist transformation; the question of political subjectivity; and the adumbration of alternative political imaginaries with which to replace the apartheid order.

At the outset, it is important to emphasise that Charterists and work-erists shared a number of objectivist and essentialist presuppositions with respect to the relationship between national liberation and socialist transformation. Thus, while Charterists were correct to argue that the relationship between liberation and transformation politics may be mutually reinforcing, they themselves accepted the stagist imaginary within which the relationship is thought. In other words, though they moved to modify the two-stage theory of political change by talking about 'historically distinct moments' and 'an uninterrupted transition from national liberation to socialist transformation', they retained the idea of a linear progression from one struggle to the next. This common presupposition raises three important theoretical problems. Firstly, both positions posit an objective conception of society in which the social has a rational and knowable underlying structure. Secondly, both positions assume that the different historical stages are fundamentally distinct and self-contained; that is, 'liberation' and 'transformation' politics each have a precise content correlating to a particular phase of struggle. Thirdly, both perspectives reduce the role of distinctively political logics to pre-constituted historical narratives.

How would discourse theory address these problems? It would begin by rethinking the assumptions of the prevailing objectivist conception of history by stressing the moment of politics as a process of hegemonic articulation. Such an approach would refuse the a priori separation of historical stages corresponding to neatly defined social and political demands. Instead, particular tasks and interests are the result of political constructions and practices, and not the product of some underlying social necessity. Moreover, this approach would reject the notion of some final liberatory moment – in workerist and Charterist discourse, the emergence of a socialist society – which would definitively signify the end of political contestation. By contrast, discourse theory stresses the proliferation of political tasks – an expansion of 'liberations' and 'trans-formations' to use Charterists' language – and recognises the possibility that 'gains' might be reversed, as well as the impossibility of any ultimate democratic or socialist resolution.[39] This is not to say that such an approach dispenses altogether with the goals towards which political struggle ought to be directed; it does, however, put into question the idea of a utopian goal that aims at an ultimate transcendence of society's inequalities, social divisions and antagonistic relations.

The second underlying assumption in Charterist and workerist arguments pertains to their theorisation of the subject of political transformation. While both positions tried to conceptualise and articulate a relation between the working class and other political forces, the form of this rethinking – working-class leadership of a class alliance in Charterism for instance – retained the 'ontological' centrality of the working class. By radicalising another strand of Charterist discourse – the idea of the working class as 'a real social force' – the approach developed here suggests an alternative way of thinking about political subjectivity in the South African context.

This involves two moves. Firstly, it requires us to historicise and contextualise the formation of political subjectivity by stressing the different ways subjectivities are socially constructed, rather than deriving their identities from objective positions in the social structure. Hence the emphasis is on the multiplicity of points with which subjects can identify, as opposed to a reduction of these points to a single essence of the social. Secondly, discourse theory emphasises the plural and potentially overdetermined nature of political subjectivity, such that its identity can weld together different identities and interests. In this respect, it is possible to envisage an overdetermination of subjectivities in a broader – one might say 'quasi-transcendental' – political identity, which does not refer back to one essential point of identification (the 'nation', the 'people' or the working class), but incorporates these aspects in a new form of subjectivity.

The last aporia common to workerist and Charterist discourses concerns the political projects – or alternative social imaginaries – around which their objectives for a post-apartheid order are structured. The most important aspect of this discussion is the proposed relationship between democracy and socialism. For workerists, democracy and socialism were conceived of in complementary terms: the struggle for socialist demands required democratic forms of organisation and representation, and vice versa. However, democracy tended either to be restricted to organisational accountability within the trade union movement, or seen as a means of constraining a populist politics that had lost touch with the interests of its constituents.

Within Charterist discourse, by contrast, democratisation was presented as a pre-condition for the transition to socialism, and all social relations – not just productive relations – had in principle to be democratised. However, while discourse theorists view the democratisation of all levels of society as an important aspect of socialism – or, better, an internal moment of the democratic imaginary – a number of problems emerge in the Charterist formulation. Firstly, as workerists insist, there is always the possibility of separating democratic and socialist demands, which is implicit in the two-stage theory of social transformation. Secondly, Charterists retain a classist and instrumental conception of socialism and democracy, in which democracy is ultimately measured in terms of advancing the socialist project. Thirdly, the Charterist discourse maintains the essentialist role of the working class in bringing about socialist transformation, albeit by relying upon an epistemologically privileged agent – the SACP as the universal incarnation of the proleteriat – to bring about this transformation. In short, Charterist proposals make possible two post-apartheid scenarios: the deferment of meaningful social transformations, and the emergence of an authoritarian statist form in the guise of a socialist order.

Populism and workerism in the light of the post-apartheid state

Thus far, I have sought to isolate and contest the theoretical and political assumptions underlying Charterist and workerist discourses, while disclosing different possibilities from a discourse-theoretical point of view. In order to evaluate further these discourses and their consequences, I shall now shift my focus away from the late 1970s and 1980s and consider their proposals and arguments from the privileged vantage point of the present. In order to do so, I propose that we evaluate these two sets of discursive practices along three axes; namely, the logic of democratic transition; the political and constitutional outcome of the transition process; and the degree of social transformation evident in the transition process.

It is evident that a good deal of the 1980s debate concerned the most efficient way to achieve the ending of white settler rule, and its replacement with some form of popular sovereignty. How are we to assess the various debates and proposals on this strategic plane? The balance-sheet is, I think, mixed. On the one hand, Charterist strategy was vindicated to the extent that an essential factor in the demise of apartheid was the extensive and intensive mass protest in the African townships from 1984 onwards.[40] The popular rebellion in the townships, at times rendering them practically ungovernable, provided a critical backdrop to all the other factors – international sanctions, military campaigns, changes in the ruling bloc, and so forth – which eventually coalesced to force the regime into negotiating its own demise. These struggles highlighted the importance of linking a diverse range of constituencies and subjectivities (including dissident whites) in a popular coalition against apartheid. The pitting of the people against the apartheid state – captured in the UDF's slogan 'UDF Unites, Apartheid Divides' – was largely responsible for creating a climate of crisis from which the power bloc never recovered.

On the other hand, the trade union movement, so carefully and meticulously assembled over the previous two decades, displayed the necessary resilience to continue populist forms of politics, especially after the massive state repression took its toll on the resistance forces toward the end of the 1980s. The formation of COSATU in 1985, the development of 'social movement unionism'[41] and its role in constituting the Mass Democratic Movement following the UDF's banning in 1988, catapulted the trade union movement into the forefront of the anti-apartheid struggle in the vital 1987–94 conjuncture. Without these manifestations of popular pressure, it is unlikely that President F. W. de Klerk and the National Party would have agreed so quickly to a democratic and non-racial resolution of the conflict. So, in terms of the transition process the record shows that the populist strategy was necessary to achieve national liberation; however, in executing such a strategy solid organisational structures were needed to sustain protest, and in this regard the union movement was crucial.

If we turn next to the political and constitutional forms that emerged from the transition process, then it seems that the fears of the workerists about the possibility of an authoritarian statist resolution of the national liberation struggle, whether socialist or capitalist, have to some extent been misplaced. Workerist fears about the subsumption of worker demands and representative forms, the 'closure' of civil society under the imperative of a centralising ANC government, and the erosion of worker rights, have not been evident in the post-apartheid regime (at least until the present). Although the interim (1993) and final (1996) constitutions were a result of intense horse-trading among the major political elites that were party to the negotiations, and were thus attacked by forces perceived to be excluded and disadvantaged by their major provisions, the agreed rules of the game generally meet the standards of a well-ordered constitutional democracy. That is to say, the constitution provides for majority government by freely given consent, and is limited by a large number of legally protected individual rights. The different interests reflected in the constitutional negotiations resulted in the prohibition of unfair discrimination on the grounds of ethnicity, gender and sexual orientation, while allowing affirmative action, the protection of workers' rights and guaranteed entitlements to reasonable standards of housing, education, health care and social security.[42]

One issue that needs further consideration in this regard concerns the relationship between state and civil society. Most commentators on democratic transition and consolidation emphasise the importance of a vibrant and active civil society, which can act as a bulwark against over-centralising, bureaucratic and authoritarian forms of government.[43] In this respect the construction of community organisations, civic associations, trade unions, social movements and political parties during the 1970s and 1980s, and their accompanying democratic and participatory ethos, can be seen as an important resource in making possible and sustaining democratic rule in post-apartheid South Africa. One fear expressed in the workerist critique of populism, however, was that for some quarters of the national liberation movement the encouragement of civil society was little more than an instrumental tactic designed to attain the goal of political power; once achieved, it would be subsumed under state institutions. While these arguments do have some resonance in the subsumption of the UDF and the Mass Democratic Movement (MDM) under the ANC/SACP alliance, and though many activists and participants involved in civil society have been drawn ineluctably into governmental structures, the active state regulation and control of civil society for directly political goals has not (thus far) proved to be a major imperative of the new administration. In short, while it is the case that civil society has all too easily been equated with a narrowly defined logic of political economy, the existence of a free press, powerful trade unions and flourishing voluntary associations suggests that the democratic ethos linked to the popular struggles of the 1980s is still intact.[44]

Finally, we turn to what is perhaps the most important issue for the workerist critique of populism – namely, the level of economic redistribution and socialist transformation evident in the first decade of post-apartheid political rule. Here, the answer appears unequivocally in favour of the workerist arguments, against the populism of the UDF and the ANC (which has assumed the mantle of the populist politics of the 1980s and early 1990s). The clearest evidence rests on the strange fate of the COSATU-advocated 'Reconstruction and Development Programme' (RDP). Initially, there were high expectations that the RDP would address issues of poverty, economic redistribution, housing and health provision, and land reform. For instance, the introduction to the programme boldly asserts that 'Minority control and privilege in every aspect of our society are the main obstructions to developing an integrated programme that unleashes all the resources of our country', arguing instead for a 'thoroughgoing democratisation of our society'. It goes on to claim that the 'RDP integrates growth, development, reconstruction and redistribution into a unified programme' based on 'an infrastructural programme that will provide access to modern and effective services like electricity, water, telecommunications, transport,

health, education and training for all our people'. In short, the programme aimed to 'meet basic needs and open up previously suppressed
economic and human potential in urban and rural areas', which would
'lead to an increased output in all sectors of the economy', as well as a
'modernising [of South Africa's] infrastructure and human resource
development'.[45]

However, the ANC government was quick to dash the hopes and
expectations raised by the RDP by adopting neo-liberal economic policies and development strategies. This was evident in June 1996, when the
Finance Minister Trevor Manuel rushed out the government's macroeconomic strategy, called 'Growth, Employment and Redistribution'
(GEAR). Although its rhetoric suggested continuity with the RDP, the
policies represented an important change of tack, towards what the
SACP and COSATU were to label 'conservative fiscal policies' and
'free market dogmatism'.[46] As numerous commentators suggest, its
conservative fiscal and monetary policies, trade liberalisation, and the
privatisation of the state's electricity, telecommunications and transport
networks, belie the movement's radical ideology and commitments of
the past, and have provoked widespread anger as well as increased union
protest. On 30 August 2001 the simmering tensions between the tri-
partite anti-apartheid alliance of COSATU, the ANC and the SACP
came to a head, with a two-day general strike against privatisation.
Thousands of workers and students marched through the centre of
Johannesburg and other cities in opposition to the sell-off of public
assets which unions fear will cost many jobs in a country where approx-
imately 30 per cent of the workforce is unemployed.[47] While this was the
ostensible reason for the two-day protest action, it was indicative of a
growing series of struggles between workers and the post-apartheid
state.[48]

These developments have to be tempered by the fact that there has
been a significant degree of redistribution in the post-apartheid period,
as the ANC government has moved to implement its agenda of socially
progressive concerns, and has targeted expenditures to poor and marginalised communities. Moreover, even if it is acknowledged that there has

been a turn to neoliberal economic policies and spending priorities, the main question is whether the abandonment of its radical agenda and socialist demands is a consequence of the populist style of politics associated with the UDF and its allies. This is a complicated issue to address, as a number of pertinent factors specific to the new conjuncture must be factored in. These include the role of the returning ANC elites, who effectively displaced the more democratically accountable UDF leadership,[49] as well as the new post-1989 global context, which has been marked by the definitive failure of state socialism, and a paucity of legitimate and feasible alternatives to the neoliberal economic hegemony. Nevertheless, the capitulation of the ANC elite to a liberal ideology of globalisation and free trade, and its commitment to 'roll back the state' in the name of freeing up the economy, confirms the workerist image of an aspirant petty-bourgeoisie transforming itself into a new ruling class at the expense of previously held ideological beliefs and commitments.

Conclusion

This chapter has examined the theoretical and strategic debates surrounding populist politics in South Africa during the 1980s, and has evaluated them in the light of changes brought about in the immediate post-apartheid period. While many academic and organic intellectuals involved in the resistance struggles at the time described the UDF as populist, this chapter suggests a different interpretation. On a theoretical level, I argue that it is problematic to seek to determine the essence of populism, which can then be mechanically applied to movements and ideologies. Instead, my contention is that those political forces which construct discourses, and the subjects who are constituted by them, ultimately determine the meaning of ideological elements and styles. This process of construction and reception is relative to the historical contexts and conjunctures in which they occur.

These theoretical remarks result in a more complex interpretation of populist discourses in South Africa during the 1980s. That is to say, while movements and ideologies as different as Inkatha and the UDF all represent a populist *form* of politics, in that their appeal to the people aims to divide social space into two camps by constructing political frontiers between the popular and the state/power bloc poles, they can have very different connotations and consequences at the level of their ideological *content*. More concretely, I have argued that the discourse of the UDF, in terms of both its theoretical and political assumptions – crystallised most clearly in the workerist/populist debates of the mid-1980s – and its impact on the transition and consolidation of democracy, is best understood as a popular–democratic force. Not only did it advance democratic and socialist demands, it also sought to develop a radical democratic ethos, even though its political practices sometimes belied this goal. The UDF also played a highly significant role in ending apartheid, as well as laying the foundations for a non-racial and democratic alternative. The success of the UDF in mobilising and recruiting a diverse range of subjectivities and interests was partly a result of its indeterminate and open-textured ideology and political programme, evident most vividly in its advocacy of the Freedom Charter. To the extent that the UDF was able to conceal its own internal contradictions and tensions, it could weld together the widest possible coalition against the apartheid state and its allies.

However, this is not to say that the non-racial democratic ideology articulated by the UDF, which has in turn (partly) bequeathed the current constitutional democracy to South Africa, cannot also spawn a more authoritarian, exclusivistic and top-down populism (*à la* Inkatha of the 1970s and 1980s). Nor is it to say that the self-same ideological elements advanced by the UDF in the 1980s cannot be articulated in a pro-capitalist fashion in the present. Instead, these possibilities highlight the fact that the ideological indeterminacy of populist discourse can be constituted or hegemonised by very different political forces for different political ends. Hence, to conclude, the irony in a recently leaked confidential document drawn up by the ANC's national executive committee, which warned of a 'systematic assault' from 'ultra-leftists' within its trade union allies, and went on to state that the ANC must learn from other countries, such as Chile, Grenada and elsewhere, if we want to avoid self-destruction of the national democratic revolution through carelessness, *populism* and the excitement of ultra-leftism that believes the task in our country today is to wage a class struggle against capitalists in the ANC.[50]

9

Religion and Populism in Contemporary Greece

YANNIS STAVRAKAKIS

Introduction

In April 2000, after his second consecutive victory in the general elec-tions,[1] Prime Minister Costas Simitis[2] appointed his new government. In an interview on 6 May 2000, the newly appointed Minister of Justice, Michalis Stathopoulos, aired a series of reforms aimed at modernising the Greek legal apparatus in relation to issues of religious belief. He singled out, among other things, the exclusion of religion from identity cards.[3] For Stathopoulos, a professor of law, as well as for other academ-ics and commentators, this was a necessary measure in order to ensure respect for human rights and, in particular, to prevent discrimination against non-Orthodox Greek citizens. Needless to say, this was a view not shared by Archbishop Christodoulos – the head of the Holy Synod of the autocephalous Church of Greece and religious leader of the Greek Orthodox majority of the population. Setting the tone of what was to follow, he responded that on this issue 'only one factor exists and this is *the people*, that cannot and should not be ignored'.[4]

At first no one thought that this dogfight would have any serious political consequences, given that most attempts of the government to intervene in issues related to religion during the 1980s and 1990s have ended in compromise for fear of alienating practising Orthodox voters. Everything changed, however, when the newly instituted – and up to that time generally unknown – independent Hellenic Data Protection Authority convened on the 15 May to discuss the issue. Its unanimous decision was that religious belief, among a set of other sensitive personal data, should be excluded from identity cards. A few days later, on 24 May, during prime minister's questions in Parliament, the prime minister confirmed that his government would stand by and implement the decision to exclude religion from identity cards.

These developments triggered an extraordinary reaction on behalf of the Greek Church, a reaction that has polarised Greek society, and that dominated political life and media coverage for most of 2000 and 2001. Archbishop Christodoulos[5] led a campaign to oppose the decision, articulating a discourse that was marked by a clear political profile. Starting from the premise that an identity card is not a mere administrative document but 'a proof of my personality',[6] he characterised the exclusion (off the record) as a *coup d'état*, and started a struggle to overturn it. This struggle included mass rallies in Thessaloniki and Athens, rallies that were attended by hundreds of thousands of people, interventions in the media – which started following him day in and day out in order to transmit his latest attack on the government – and a campaign to gather as many signatures as possible calling for a referendum on the issue, although such a procedure was not prescribed by the Constitution. The polarisation was also reflected within the political and party systems: New Democracy, the largest opposition centre-right party, supported the Archbishop, almost unconditionally in what many journalists were quick to call his 'holy war' – with many of its MPs attending the rallies, and most of them, including its leader, Costas Karamanlis, signing the petition for a referendum.

On 28 August 2001, it was announced that the Church had managed to gather 3,008,901 signatures asking for a referendum on the *optional* inclusion of religion on Greek identity cards.[7] There is no doubt that, by all standards, the number of signatures was impressive. At around the same time (27 June 2001) the appeal of a group of theology professors and laymen against the exclusion of religion from identity cards was, however, rejected by the Constitutional Court, which decided that any mention of religion (either obligatory or optional) is unconstitutional. At any rate a deep division was established in Greek public life, and no obvious solution was visible since both the government and the church were holding firm to their positions. On 29 August, though, the church received another, this time unexpected and much more politically significant blow, a blow that led to a suspension of most politicised activities on its behalf. After receiving the archbishop and a representation of the Holy Synod that was supposed to inform him of the number of signatures collected for the church petition, the president of the republic, Constantine Stephanopoulos – a former conservative politician – issued a statement that included the following lines: 'The conditions for the calling of a referendum on the issue of identity cards have not been met. Everybody is obliged to abide by the rules of the current Law and the signatures which were collected with a procedure that falls outside legally instituted procedures, cannot overturn the provisions of the Constitution'.[8] This statement was even more damaging because it was coming from someone whose institutional position, huge popularity – higher than the archbishop's – and conservative credentials left no obvious strategy for the Church hierarchy to continue its struggle at the same level of intensity.

How can we make sense, as political and social theorists, of these events? The first conclusion shared by most commentators was that all these developments marked a 'politicisation' of the discourse of the Church. Indeed, this politicisation is so open in the archbishop's discourse that, by now, everyone in Greece is more or less used to it. Take for example his most well-known book, comprising a series of articles published in the 1990s. The titles of some of the articles are suggestive: 'Nation and Orthodoxy: The Unbreakable Bond',[9] 'The Volcano of Islamism: the Lava that "Burns" the Balkans',[10] 'Lost Chances for an "Orthodox Axis" in the Balkans'.[11] Here, instead of discussing strictly religious, theological or even moral issues, it is clear that he is mostly interested in what he calls the 'great' national issues, especially those 'related to the great horizons of our race [*genos*],[12] our identity and our continuity'.[13] He singles out the challenges posed by globalisation and membership of the European Union, Islamic fundamentalism, and so on. It is also clear that these texts are marked by a feeling of eschatological urgency; they are written as a warning and propose a set of measures to avoid 'tragic consequences for Hellenism and Orthodoxy'[14] – two terms that are inextricably linked for the Archbishop. In his pages, the Church is clearly presented as *the* institution that can offer a way to combat what threatens Greece and Hellenism with 'elimination'.[15]

Moreover, although sometimes the Church denies vehemently that its discourse is politicised, the archbishop himself has actually conceded this point. While in the past his view was that if orthodoxy were to become politicised that 'would entail its spiritual alienation',[16] in the Athens rally he stated explicitly: 'They accuse us that we speak politically, that our discourse is political. We reply, *yes our discourse is political,* only in the ancient Greek sense of the term; it was never associated with party politics'.[17] He reiterates this view in a lengthy interview given to the newspaper *To Vima*, and published on 11 February 2001, stating that 'all our actions are political'.[18] In that sense, the 'politicised' nature of his discourse is not in dispute; it is not even denied by the archbishop himself. It is also the case that even a quick glance through some of his speeches reveals not only that are they political, but also that his discourse is *primarily* a political discourse. Furthermore, this 'politicisation' seems to be premised on a particular understanding of the role of the Church within Greek society. The state is deemed by and large incompetent in performing its duty vis-à-vis Hellenism and thus the Church – previously helping the state to fulfil this role – is left alone to accomplish the task. For the archbishop it is clear that, with the strengthening of the European Union and Greece's full participation in it, 'the state has ceased to be the obvious guarantor of national identity'. As a result: 'The salvation of Hellenism can only be the task and accomplishment of the Church'.[19]

This recent 'politicisation' of religious discourse in Greece should not, however, come as a sudden surprise. The heritage of the official Church in Greece is a heritage of political Orthodoxy[20] going back to the Byzantine and the Ottoman past, and given a new lease of life under the auspices of Greek nationalism and the direct control of the Greek state following Greek independence (1830). In fact, the Church of Greece has been invested from its creation as an independent institution with a political role. The conversion of the Church of Greece to the secular values of Greek nationalism, its transformation into 'a secular doctrine and certainly one at odds with its own deposit of faith',[21] was so deep that 'the Church of Greece spearheaded all nationalist initiatives in the latter part of the nineteenth and throughout the twentieth century'.[22] In the twentieth century the open politicisation of the Church took a variety of new forms: it sided with the king against the reformer Prime Minister Venizelos, who was excommunicated and anathematised by the Archbishop in 1916; it played an active role in the ideological aspect of the struggle against communism during the Civil War (1947–49); and was largely obedient to the quasi-religious ideology ('a Greece of Christian Greeks') introduced by the dictatorship (1967–74).[23]

Granted, then, the political legacy of the Greek Church, and granted the political character of the archbishop's discourse and the *primarily political role* that the church – or some sectors within it – envisages for itself. The crucial questions now become: *What type of politics is put forward here? How is this role communicated and established? What is the discursive mode through which it addresses itself to its audience?* In fact, the discourse of the archbishop has been the object of numerous analyses; it has been praised and celebrated as patriotic and faithful to tradition, but also criticised along many lines: as nationalist, anti-democratic, fundamentalist, traditionalist, even reactionary, and, last but not least, as *populist*.[24] It seems to me, however, that it is this last dimension that might be able to illuminate the aforementioned questions, not only in terms of the discourse's concrete content but also of the discursive logics that structure it, and the way it communicates its message to its target – that is, to *the people*.

In this text, then, I aim to explore some of the particular characteristics and tropes of the 'politicised' discourse articulated by the Greek Church. Taking into account the theoretical insights of Ernesto Laclau and others, I will argue that it constitutes a populist discourse par excellence. It is not the first time that the politicisation of religious discourse has been described as 'populist' – liberation theology in Latin America has been given this characterisation by certain analysts,[25] while others have noted the 'semi-theological' language of classical American populism, and its relationship with religion.[26] The Greek case is, however, almost unique in its clear-cut picture, historical context and socio-political significance. It must be made clear from the outset that the term 'populist' is not used here in its *polemical* sense, as is usually the case, but primarily as a tool of *discourse analysis*. In fact, before embarking on our analysis we need to clarify what exactly we mean by populism, since this concept has often been attacked for its vagueness and (lack of) analytical effectiveness. Besides, the nature of this text is envisaged as not only empirical but also theoretical. This theoretical clarification (a task occupying the next section of this chapter) will help us develop a set of criteria in order to examine in detail the discourse articulated by Archbishop Christodoulos (occupying the middle section). In the concluding section we will deal briefly with the relation between populism and nationalism, and the conditions of emergence of populist Church discourse in contemporary Greece.

The concept of populism

Almost all publications on populism, books and articles alike, share a rather pessimistic starting point stressing the essential contestability of the concept, the stark differences in the existing approaches to populism,[27] the difficulties in arriving at a commonly acceptable and operational definition of populism, and so on. As Margaret Canovan points out, although the term is frequently used, it remains exceptionally vague 'and refers in different contexts to a bewildering variety of phenomena'.[28] In fact, she even goes on to admit that it can be 'doubted whether it could be said to mean anything at all'.[29] Laclau, to cite the second standard reference in discussions of populism, also describes populism as both elusive and recurrent: 'Few terms have been so widely used in contemporary political analysis, although few have been defined with less precision', he concludes.[30] This is not a conclusion confined to the 1970s or 1980s; it is still the dominant view as a recent Open University textbook on the concept of populism reveals: 'Populism is a difficult, slippery concept'.[31]

Can this be true? Three decades of theorisation have left no impact? Haven't they helped at all in clarifying the status of the concept and its operational value for the social sciences? Certainly Canovan seems to be posing a legitimate question: Is there something in common in all populist phenomena? 'If we dig deep enough, can we find some central core, some esoteric essence uniting them?'[32] In an age of anti-essentialism one could question the phrasing of Canovan's question. No doubt, her answer comes as no surprise: it is impossible 'to find a single essence behind all established uses of the term'.[33] Unable to locate such an essence Canovan embarks on a classificatory exercise of very limited use, which seems to leave even her unsatisfied.[34] Thus pessimism and frustration persist. What if, however, it is not necessary to dig deep; what if we can start from the premise that deep essences are nowhere to be found as such? What if we can start from a simple *symptomal* reading of discursive structure (by registering, for example, the status of 'the people' as a signifier) and then proceed to explore the modalities of discourse with which populism could be associated?[35] In fact, the pessimist view seems to ignore a slow movement which tends, more or less, to vindicate and develop further one of the approaches to populism which dominated the discussion in the 1970s and 1980s. I am referring to the theory of populism introduced by Ernesto Laclau in his texts 'Towards a Theory of Populism'[36] and 'Populist Rupture and Discourse'.[37]

Besides its Marxist overtones,[38] which are somewhat outdated, the kernel of Laclau's theory still sounds essentially valid. What is Laclau arguing? First of all one has to take into account the political subject addressed and invoked in a given discourse: Is it a nation, the *nodal point* of nationalism? Is it a particular class or section of the population? Or is it 'the people'? According to Laclau, 'Despite the wide diversity in the uses of the term, we find in all of them the common reference to an analogical basis which is *the people* ... it is certainly true that reference to "the people" occupies a central place in populism'.[39] However, the central place of a signifier like 'the people' does not seem enough to justify talking about a populist discourse. As Laclau himself points out, 'The presence of popular elements in a discourse is not sufficient to transform it into a populist one. Populism starts at the point where popular-democratic elements are presented as an *antagonistic* option against the ideology of the dominant bloc'.[40] To conclude, Laclau's *'thesis is that populism consists in the representation of popular-democratic interpellations as a synthetic antagonistic complex with respect to the dominant ideology'*.[41]

But let's take it one step at a time. My claim in this section is that Laclau provides an approach to populism that is theoretically grounded and sophisticated; an approach that not only can withstand the basic criticisms that have been addressed against it, but also can be – and has been – developed further to the benefit of contemporary political analysis.

Although a large part of Laclau's 1977 text is devoted to the importance of class, it is obvious that the kernel of his approach is located beyond such a limited – albeit important – scope. It is of course legitimate to analyse or criticise this class dimension of Laclau's argument,[42] but it seems quite pedantic to stick to an analysis or critique of this class component, avoiding the most important part: his approach to populism *as a discourse*. This is especially so since Laclau has distanced himself from the strict class problematic not only in a variety of subsequent texts,[43] but also (already) in his 1980 text on 'Populist Rupture and Discourse'.[44] It is also true that 'although Laclau's recent work does not deal specifically with populism, it does offer useful insights for a new conceptualisation of populism, which complements his previous analysis ... and may provide a more inclusive definition of populism'.[45]

What remains so refreshing in Laclau's discursive theory of populism? First of all, although Laclau's scope is a theoretical one (we will return to this in a moment), he successfully links theoretical analysis with political practice: 'Laclau's theory is anti-descriptivist in that it does not seek to "define" populism [at least not in an essentialist, reductive way], but rather to study political movements that have already defined themselves as populist by their common reference to "the people"'.[46] The starting point is not some obscure essence imposed by the classificatory system of the political analyst, but an encounter with the *signifying reality* of political struggle itself.

Is this restricting our approach merely to the level of ideology?[47] Indeed, if the analysis was restricted to the ideological level that would create certain problems, not least the one pointed out by Mouzelis: he claims that Laclau's 'ideological' approach remains 'so general that [it] appl[ies] to almost any modern political movement'.[48] Mouzelis proposes to overcome this difficulty by adding criteria beyond the ideological realm, namely the importance of organisational patterns: 'The organisational structures of such movements have to be taken into account as well, particularly the type of authority relationship between leaders, cadres and followers'.[49] However, by moving from *theory of ideology* to *discourse theory*, by stressing the concept of *discourse* rather than that of *ideology*, Laclau – especially in his subsequent work – provides a way to graft Mouzelis's insightful comments within a discursive framework for the analysis of populism. As he was to make clear in *Hegemony and Socialist Strategy*, co-authored with Chantal Mouffe, discourse is not identical with language or text; discourse in Laclau's terminology refers to a network of meaning articulating both linguistic and non-linguistic elements.[50] Discourse is not only words, speech or ideas, but also practices directly connected to the discursive logic that formulates them.[51] Furthermore, it is not even necessary to go to *Hegemony and Socialist Strategy* to reach this conclusion. It already marks Laclau's initial texts on populism. In his 1980 text he argues the following with respect to the meaning of discourse:

> By 'discursive' I do not mean that which refers to 'text' narrowly defined, but to the ensemble of the phenomena in and through which social production of meaning takes place, an ensemble which constitutes a society as such. The discursive is not, therefore, being conceived as a level nor even as a dimension of the social, but rather as being co-extensive with the social as such. This means that the discursive does not constitute a superstructure ... or, more precisely, that all social practice constitutes itself as such insofar as it produces meaning.[52]

Mouzelis may be right in stressing that the themes highlighted by Laclau[53] are of a specific kind: 'on the organisational level they conduce to a type of authority structure that is quite distinct from that of other radically oriented popular movements and parties'.[54] However, given the overall development of Laclau's discursive approach, this can be construed as a criticism of Laclau only if we reduce discourse to ideology. If discourse is conceptualised in the way developed by Laclau in the 1980s, then organisational aspects of populist movements should not be studied independently of populist discourse, but as dimensions of the discourses through which these movements and political identities are constituted.[55] In other words, 'The organisation of political movements must be understood as elements of a wider field of discourse incorporating both organisational and linguistic elements'.[56] It is this angle that permits Lyrintzis to point out that populism is neither a particular set of ideological contents nor a given organisational pattern, but rather a discursive logic, a mode of representing social and political space which, no doubt, influences both these realms.[57]

Now if discourse is a network of meaning, meaning can only be created with reference to central signifiers – *points de capiton* in Lacan's psychoanalytic terminology, *nodal points* in Laclau's and Mouffe's vocabulary. Here one can usefully quote the oft-cited sentences from *Hegemony and Socialist Strategy*:

> Any discourse is constituted as an attempt to dominate the field of discursivity, to arrest the flow of difference, to construct a center. We will call the privileged discursive points of this partial fixation, nodal points. (Lacan has insisted on these partial fixations through his concept of *points de capiton*, that is, of privileged signifiers that fix the meaning of a signifying chain).[58]

Well, if populism exists it can only refer to all discourses in which 'the people' functions as a *point de capiton*, discourses that include 'the people' in the set of their master-signifiers.

If, however, the structural location of 'the people' was enough to define populism, then the majority of political discourses in modernity would probably belong to the populist family. Laclau was from the beginning aware of this problem; hence the introduction of his second criterion for distinguishing populism: 'For a popular positionality to exist, a discourse has to divide society between dominant and dominated; that is, the system of equivalences should present itself as articulating the totality of a society around a fundamental antagonism'.[59] Surely what gives 'the people' its political salience and hegemonic appeal within populist discourses is its antagonistic representation. Apart from being corroborated by the most elementary sociological observation, this second criterion is also (as with the location of 'the people' as a nodal point/*point de capiton*) very firmly grounded in discourse theory, psychoanalysis and semiotics. Indeed it is based on the distinction between two logics of organisation to be found in every discursive construction: *difference* and *equivalence*. The logic of difference, which tends to expand what linguists call the syntagmatic pole of language (the axis of metonymy in Lacanian theory of meaning), is dominant in discourses that stress inclusivity: the continuous articulation of more and more elements (political demands, ideological principles, and so on) entering into a relation of combination. The logic of equivalence, associated with the paradigmatic pole of language (the axis of metaphor in Lacan's reappropriation of Jakobson), reduces the number of positions that can be combined in a discourse, leading to a paratactical division of the political space that simplifies political struggle into an antagonism between 'us' and 'them', good and evil.[60] Laclau utilises the theoretical distinction between the two logics in order to conceptualise the generally accepted 'anti-elitism', the antagonistic character of populist discourses. According to this view, the logic that dominates here is that of equivalence: 'Populism is defined by the logic of the simplification and dichotomisation of the social and political space and is thus distinguished from the logic of difference and articulation'.[61] On the other hand discourses of integration aim at replacing antagonism with unity, equivalence with difference. Laclau provides examples of both strategies from the nineteenth century:

The discourse of rupture was founded on the expansion of the system of equivalences, as for example in the discourse of Chartism in England, the discourse of Mazzinism in Italy and the Jacobin tradition in France. The discourse of integration was founded on the articulation of an increasingly complex system of differences, as in the Tory discourse of Disraeli, Bismarck's discourse of the conservative Prussian revolution or that of Giollitti's transformism in Italy. It is this second kind of discourse which has been dominating in Europe over the past hundred years.[62]

To conclude this section, Laclau's discursive theory of populism seems to be the only one that offers theoretical sophistication without succumbing to idealism or to any kind of intellectualist reductionism, one that combines a thorough philosophical grounding with a sensitivity towards the realities of political struggle in a variety of contexts. Furthermore, 'purified' of its excesses (the class focus) and fortified by the subsequent work of Laclau and Mouffe, it can accommodate most of the criticisms to which it has been subjected (most notably the one by Mouzelis), and has been applied in an expanding variety of empirical analyses with satisfactory explanatory results.[63] It should come as no surprise then that this is the approach to populism we will employ in this text. Is the discourse articulated recently by Archbishop Christodoulos and the Church hierarchy a populist discourse? Does it fulfil the two criteria highlighted by Laclau: a central reference to 'the people' and an equivalential, antagonistic discursive logic? Is it, in other words, organised according to a 'populist logic', a 'populist reason', to use the title of a forthcoming book by Ernesto Laclau? These are the questions guiding our argumentation in the following section.[64]

The discourse of the Greek Church: Christodoulos's populism?[65]

Let us initially explore the first question, the status of 'the people' in the archbishop's discourse. Before the identity cards crisis, 'the people' is not assigned such a privileged status in his discourse; signifiers like 'race'(*genos*) and 'nation'(*ethnos*) are largely preferred. It is the current crisis that led to a radicalisation of the archbishop's discourse, and to the necessity to address the people directly. This change of focus is also depicted in the officially published transcripts of his speeches in the rallies and in the Holy Synod, where *laos* – the Greek word for 'the people' – is printed with the first letter in capitals, together with words like 'God', 'Greece', 'Orthodoxy' and 'Church'. It is obvious then that 'the people' is now becoming central, one of the master signifiers at play; it is also a constant reference, which is to be found in abundance in almost every paragraph, if not in every sentence.

In the Athens rally, for example, the message is crystal clear: the Church 'assumes the role of the leader of the faithful People in its desperate attempt to defend its spiritual self-consciousness'.[66] Christodoulos's main concern is that the Church has to fulfil its duty to 'the people of God' and the homeland.[67] It is representing and defend-ing the people against the attack of an atheist government that ignores and opposes an essential Greekness guaranteed by tradition. More signif-icantly, the modernising government is to be resisted on the grounds of its distance from the people. According to the archbishop, contempo-rary Greek modernisers are characterised by living apart from 'the people', isolated from the 'everyday popular ways of life', 'from the soul and the heart of the people'.[68] This is what, within this discursive uni-verse, explains – and *condemns* – their anti-ecclesiastical campaign. This is also what serves to legitimise and justify his own position.

The Church is presented as eminently qualified to perform this task of representation, since there is no division between the clergy and the people: 'Our clergy is part of the People, kneaded with the People, working for the People, coming from the People'.[69] The clergy consists of persons 'devoted to God and its People'.[70] Replying to the criticism that the Church has no right to speak on behalf of the people since it lacks democratic legitimation, he reasserts his right to speak in the name of the people and vows to continue to do so on the grounds that when he speaks about the Greek people he means the faithful of the Orthodox Church, the 'People of God', the 'People of the Church', and not the atheists or the heterodox. There is no doubt that the notion of 'the people' does have certain theological connotations and a history within theological discourse.[71] However, it seems that 'the people' is used by the archbishop in a clearly political way. For example, it is he who stresses the quantitative parameter of this people: since, according to him – and the available statistical data – atheists and the heterodox comprise only 2 to 4 per cent of the Greek population, this is supposed to legitimise his discourse on behalf of the Greek people in general, a people that 'every day judges and confirms its trust in us'.[72] 'Nowhere else in the world are People and Religion so close',[73] and that's why the people expect support from the Church, 'that's why the Church speaks on behalf of this People'.[74] It becomes clear that 'the people of God' is not used in the ecumenical and theological sense, but as a statistical and territorial reference, a rhetorical device designed to mobilise supporters – through the establishment of a particular relation of representation – and terrify opponents. The argument put forward is that *virtually* all Greek citizens, *virtually* the whole of the Greek people, support the Church in its struggle against the government. Such an instrumental, political conception of the people is often retrieved when – and only when – the Church feels threatened and popular mobilisation is required to defend it; this was also the case with the ecclesiastical property crisis of 1987. As soon as crises are over, 'the people' loses its value for the hierarchy and is returned to silence, to the margins of ecclesiastical life.[75]

The profoundly political references to 'the people' by the archbishop raise the issue of the relation between the people and God. By claiming to represent the people, the archbishop knows that he enters a dangerous field: the views of the people can change over time, while his position (presented as the bastion of traditional Orthodoxy, and, ultimately, the word of God) cannot be seen to change. The result is a hybrid discourse. On the one hand, as a religious discourse, contemporary Church discourse is based on a strong foundationalism and a representationalism, both rather uncharacteristic of Orthodox theology (in its apophatic tradition):

The Word of God is beyond negotiation. It is a Word which is authentic
and revelatory, and which comes from our Lord Jesus Christ himself …
The Church thus, when it speaks with the word of God, is not doing it
the way a University Professor does it for his science or a politician for his
ideology. The Church is not speaking a Word of its own. It is transmitting
the Word of God.[76]

Elsewhere, the archbishop states that 'the Church is unmistakable,
because Christ is leading it'.[77] It is hard to see how 'the people', in its profoundly political sense, can function within such a discourse, which claims
God as the first source of its legitimation. As we have seen, though, the
Church operates both on the sacred and the secular level. Any confusions
are resolved first by attributing to the Greek people the quality of the
chosen, the people of God. On the one hand the Greek people are always
the 'blessed people of God'.[78] On the other, a strong link is articulated
between the voice of the people and the voice of God.[79] If these are presented as overlapping then the archbishop can claim to represent both
without any contradictions. Hence, the voice of the people becomes for
Archbishop Christodoulos the voice of God: 'Your voice is also the voice
of God',[80] *vox populi vox dei* being a standard populist theme.[81]

Thus, the archbishop becomes the direct representative of the voice
of the people, and God ultimately acquires the role of the guarantor of
this direct representation, having entrusted this role to the archbishop.
In the archbishop's own words: 'I have received from God this responsibility, to move forward, and for you to follow your shepherd'.[82] Here,
the metaphor of the flock is also revealing of the organisational aspect
of this discourse, a direct relationship between the leader and the led
without mediating mechanisms, with the priests and the Church hierarchy in the roles of mere transmitters (something, by the way, not entirely
consistent with Orthodox patterns of church organisation). In any case
the emphasis is clearly on the leader's charisma – cultivated by intense
media attention and the archbishop's initially positive response to the
challenge of 'mediatisation' – and on the necessity 'for direct, unmediated rapport between the leader and "his people"'.[83]

This stress on direct representation and on a populist style of organisation (to satisfy Mouzelis's criterion, as incorporated in a discursive problematic) explains the attacks of the archbishop on any other mediating mechanisms that would occupy and regulate the space between him and *his* people. Hence the typical populist distrust of law and rights: 'Laws, when the People does not want them, are not applied, they fall into inactivity and are essentially abolished. They are rejected by the consciousness of the nation on what is right and what is not.'[84] In his Athens speech he resorts to examples from ancient Sparta to justify his view that 'laws are not unchangeable'.[85] Although undoubtedly true (since, at an 'ontological' level, constitutional and legal frameworks are social and political constructions), within the half-religious, half-political discourse of the archbishop, this claim clearly functions as an attack on the constitutional basis of liberal democracy. By legitimising his role as the direct and only true representative of the people, it also invests the Orthodox majority with a divine legitimation: 'It is a powerful idea because it plays on the tension in democracy between the power of popular sovereignty and the possibility of a tyranny of the majority.' To the extent that this tyranny of the majority can only be resisted through the introduction of legal and constitutional provisions, populism – and Greek Church populism – becomes 'hostile to a discourse of rights because, by definition, rights are tools of the embattled minority, while populism sees the majority as embattled and blames the excessive deference of the state to right-claims of minorities for this injustice'.[86] The crude majoritarianism of Church discourse, revealed in its mobilisation behind the petition for a referendum, seems to be based on a neglect of the rights of minorities and an impatience towards what are presented as 'legalistic restrictions that may stand in the way of salvation', to use a phrase of Margaret Canovan's.[87] In other words, a populist modality of discourse is crucial for the Church, because it makes it possible to acquire democratic credentials without accepting the democratic politics of representation.[88]

In any case, we can safely assert that 'the people' does constitute a central reference, a *point de caption*, in the politicised discourse of the

Greek Church. In order, however, to ground in a conclusive way the populist character of this discursive hybrid, this 'mixture of metaphysics and populism',[89] it is necessary to examine the discursive logic dominating its organisation and articulation. Is the discourse of the archbishop an antagonistic discourse marked by the dominant operation of the logic of equivalence?

As with the references to the people, it is possible to view the identity cards issue as the crucial moment that signals a clear shift in Church discourse in this area. Describing the attitude of the Church before the crisis, the archbishop himself points out that it was not antagonistic towards the state, since that would harm 'the people', a people that in Greece are both citizens of the state and faithful to the Church.[90] Consequently, after the crisis, we can assume that it must be the same (populist) priority that obliges the Church to adopt an antagonistic attitude. The antagonism is always between the people (and their direct divine representative, the head of the Church), on the one side, and the state, the government and all the social forces supporting its decisions, on the other. The enemy is clearly the secular power that has been 'autonomised from God and People and stop[ped] discussing with the Church the issues that concern the People'.[91] This claim is also historically contextualised: 'History proves that the Church has always been attacked by the powerful of the day but has always emerged victorious. And it was attacked because it did not succumb to the secular power, because it did not "modernise" and did not follow its orders, orders that opposed the Law of God'.[92] It becomes obvious here that it is particular attributes of the government and its social support that are the primary targets of the archbishop, thus entering into a distinct chain of equivalences. Furthermore, this chain is presented in the archbishop's dramatised quasi-eschatological discourse as comprising 'the forces of evil', fighting against 'the Church and the will of God and trying to de-christianise our society ... only because they hate the Church of God and wish to push it to the margins of social life'.[93] Now, generally speaking, what can these forces of evil be – the antagonistic enemy of the Church and the 'people of God'?

Modernisation is clearly one of them: 'Modernisation leads to the downfall of the nation and the ethical values of the land'.[94] Another is often the intellectuals. Consider, for example, the archbishop's polemic against distinguished Greek intellectuals like Constantine Tsoukalas, in his article 'The Western-fed Intelligentsia' and elsewhere.[95] In his Thessaloniki speech this theme returns: 'Unfortunately some of our intellectuals, the intelligentsia as they are called, want persistently to ignore ... the role of the Church in safeguarding our Tradition'.[96] And he concludes:

> To these progressive technocrats, who want at all cost to transform Greece into a country that will not recognise Orthodoxy and will not lean on it, we say clearly: You are losing your time ... The people of God are not following you. You will be left again alone. You do not express the people ... All the other Greek people are resisting your plans.[97]

This anti-intellectualist attitude, coupled with the constant reference to the people, reveals again the populist mode of the archbishop's discourse. It is also the case that this is a typical populist strategy, to the extent that populism in some of its different forms has expressed hostility towards theory and intellectualism.[98]

Even more revealing, from the antagonistic content of this discourse, is its style and, in particular, the war metaphors, which are numerous. An antagonistic climate of war and struggle is dominant here, with the monasteries becoming 'inviolate fortresses'[99] in the struggle between 'Enlighteners' and tradition,[100] and the people being urged not to lower the flags and banners.[101] It is not a coincidence then that the archbishop himself offered the most graphic image of this struggle by holding the flag of the 1821 revolution, a symbolically charged emblem of the struggle against the Ottomans, in the Athens rally. From a semiotic (Barthesian) point of view, the aims of this move are obvious. A new antagonism is grafted onto a system of signification pertaining to a different context and a different period, in order to acquire some of its mobilising power and popular appeal. This is not the only time the archbishop has utilised national myths and symbols in his discourse. In

December 2001 he stated that 'we [the Greeks] are facing a new battle of Marathon, with new Persians' – apparently a metaphor for the government or the forces it is supposed to obey – threatening 'our faith, language and tradition'.[102] Of course, the struggle against the Ottoman Empire or the Persians is not the same as the struggle against the democratically elected Greek government. How is the Church bridging this gap in its antagonistic discourse?

Before the crisis with identity cards, this antagonistic discursive organisation was present in another form: in the form of all the forces conspiring against Hellenism. In fact the archbishop has spoken openly about the 'conspiracies of the enemies' of Hellenism[103] – conspiracy theories being another standard element in populist discourses.[104] The archbishop has continually overstated the dangers of Islamisation for the Balkans and Europe,[105] and the possibility of cultural obliteration and alienation due to membership of the European Union.[106] Pan-Turkism, pan-Slavism and the threat of 'papal expansionism' were other routine references.[107] In order to avoid all these dangers he seemed willing even to consider an alliance between Orthodox countries (an 'Orthodox axis', mainly between Greece, Serbia and Russia), thus accepting a proposal put forward by Milošević and Karadjic.[108] The change occurring with the articulation of the Church's novel, hybrid populism is that a new, powerful, but this time internal enemy – the government – is added to these external threats. The danger here would be for the government and its supporters – who are Greeks and not foreign conspirators – to 'contaminate' the purity of the 'people of God' as represented by the Church. This possibility, however, can be avoided by attributing their actions to the influence of ideologies (Enlightenment, modernisation, secularism) *foreign* to the Hellenic tradition: the agents of these ideologies are not deemed worthy of being Greek, and thus the essential Hellenic identity defended by the Church retains its supposed purity, and the symbols of past liberating struggles can be utilised without contradictions in the new struggle.

There is no doubt then that the discourse of the archbishop is organised according to an antagonistic schema. It distinguishes between 'us', the forces of Go(o)d (the *People* as represented by the *Church* under *God*) and 'them', the forces of Evil (an *atheist*, *modernising*, *intellectualist* and *repressive* government), constructing thus two chains of equivalences at war with each other. In fact, the division introduced is so strong that the archbishop falls short of assuming full responsibility for it. Presenting the mobilisation of the Church as an automatic and justified reaction, he blames the government for the division. When he is accused of dividing the people he replies that, in fact, he is interested in the unity of the people: 'The division is not caused by us, but by those who created the problem. To them one should address the recommendations for the unity of the people'.[109] Those who oppose 'progress' to 'tradition' are the ones to blame for the 'artificial' division of the people and the nation.[110] Yes, a deep social rift is emerging, he acknowledges in his Athens speech,[111] but this can only be due to the actions of 'the atheists and modernisers of every colour, who believed they could easily ... [m]ake Greece a state without God and the Greeks a people without faith'.[112]

Concluding remarks

My main aim in this chapter has been to examine the discourse articulated recently by the Greek Orthodox Church within the context of the identity cards dispute. To conclude, it is clear from this analysis that the 'politicised' discourse articulated by Archbishop Christodoulos and the hierarchy of the Church of Greece does constitute a populist discourse. It fulfils both criteria highlighted by a discursive approach to populism: a central reference to 'the people' and an antagonistic discursive organisation marked by the dominant operation of the logic of equivalence. This conclusion, however, cannot exhaust the analysis of such a multi-faceted phenomenon. Indeed, in this final section I will highlight some other angles and questions that relate to our discussion up to now, and open new avenues of researching this complex topic. I will start by discussing very briefly the crucial issue of the relation between populist and nationalist dimensions of Christodoulos's politico-religious discourse.

This issue is of both analytical and theoretical importance, insofar as certain approaches have implied that the link between populism and nationalism might be an essential link, typical of all populist discourses. Then we will touch on the very important question of the emergence of populist discourses. Again, this is a problem with theoretical and empirical dimensions, and I will try to make an intervention on both fronts.

Populism and nationalism

From the point of view of social and political analysis the archbishop's discourse is most commonly described as nationalist. There is no doubt that, overall, his discourse is marked by an essentialist understanding of Greek national identity: 'Inside us there is a whole treasure, an unspent richness that has not been distorted up to now, that unites all our race [genos]'.[113] Although he is clearly aware of the modern nature of nationalism, he insists on the exceptionalism of the Greek case.[114] The structural elements of 'our' tradition are presented as 'foundational and unchangeable', 'permanent and irreplaceable'; 'its forms change but its essence remains unchanged, and it is at root Hellenism and Orthodoxy'.[115] The archbishop often refers to the 'interrelated pair Nation–Orthodoxy which has been crafted through the lengthy struggles of our race ... and has been often corroborated from amazing experiences of Godly revelations'.[116] Furthermore, the Church is here granted a causal priority over Hellenism: the Church is called 'the mother of our race [genos]'[117] or 'Mother of the nation'.[118] According to this schema, even the founding act of Greek national independence, the revolution of 1821, was declared by the Church,[119] the Church becoming the 'Great Mother' to whom we owe the freedom of the Greek nation.[120] In view of the various threats – coming from Turkey, the Islamic world, the influence of Europe, the politics of the great powers – Greece has to put forward an 'aggressive' vision inclusive of a new 'irredentism', a new 'Great Idea', that will lead to the 'final victory',[121] whatever that may be.

Analysing and evaluating these nationalist claims falls outside the scope of this paper, although the reader must be able by now to reach her or his own conclusions. Setting these claims aside for the time being will give us the opportunity to focus our attention on the relation between this nationalist dimension and populism. It has been observed in the literature on populism that 'the people' is often and crucially related, or at least co-exists, with a conception of 'the heartland'.[122] From the recent Greek literature, this is the central argument of Pantazopoulos.[123] Such a connection also seems to be the case with religious discourse in Greece today. The question is, what is the exact type of relation between the two dimensions? How is nationalism linked to populism, the nation to the people? Is this a relation of articulation, or of a necessary fusion reducing one to the other? Pantazopoulos seems to oscillate between the two positions: in the beginning it seems as if the nation and the people are presented as two distinct signifiers implicated in a very close and active relation.[124] Later on, however, their relation becomes so close and necessary that the nation seems to become the *signified* of 'the people'; the nation, the heartland, becomes the only meaning a 'people' can have. As his argument progresses, articulation is gradually replaced with syncretism,[125] and the conclusion that follows is left rather unclear: on the one hand it is argued that populism can only be 'national-populism',[126] which might imply a type of reductive relation between the two; on the other, a close link with the 'nation' is presented as something enhancing the hegemonic success of populist discourse.[127]

The question thus remains: Is the relation between nationalism and populism one of articulation or that of a necessary, reductive fusion? From the point of view of a discursive approach to populism one can only resist any type of quasi-reductionism – if indeed Pantazopoulos commits himself to such a position, which is not entirely clear and would seem unlikely – and point to some crucial differences between the political uses of the people and the nation. Although both discourses (populism and nationalism) share an equivalential logic, they are, firstly, articulated around different *points de capiton* (the nation and the people, respectively) and secondly, construct a very different enemy as their

antagonistic 'other': in the case of nationalism the enemy to be opposed
is usually another nation, while in the case of populism the enemy is of
an internal type: the power-bloc, the 'privileged' sectors, and so on; in
our case an atheist, modernising government and the intelligentsia that
supports it. Any connection between the two – connections are obviously present in the discourse of Christodoulos, as was clearly the case
with PASOK, the central object of Pantazopoulos's stimulating analysis
– is an unstable construct, a contingent, historically determined articulation, and not an essential attribute of populism. In that sense, from a
theoretical point of view resisting reductionism, although a populist
dimension is often linked with nationalism, the relation between the
two can only be a relation of articulation, and not of an essential or
necessary fusion.

Although further research is definitely needed if the relation between
populism and nationalism is to be adequately theorised and clarified,
such a conclusion seems to be justified not only on the basis of theoretical clarity and coherence, but also on the basis of historical experience;
on the basis, in other words, of the various examples of nationalist
discourses that make no recourse to populism, and vice versa. The case
of China is revealing in this respect. During the last twenty-five years,
official Chinese political discourse has been marked by a shift from stressing 'the people' to stressing 'the nation'. This difference has important
ideological consequences, and, most crucially from our point of view, it
did not take the form of a gradual redefinition of 'the people', with the
nation becoming the signified of 'the people', thus resulting in a new
national-populist fusion – which, in any case, seems to have been largely
absent from the beginning. Rather it was effected through a replacement.
As a result, whenever both terms are used together, what ensues is not
some kind of fusion but rather an irresolvable contradiction.[128] In
Greece, after 1945 and as part of the anti-communist campaign of the
right-wing state, the tension between 'nation' – understood through the
ideology of *ethnikofrosyni* – and 'people' (*laos*) was so radical that Elefantis
speaks of the right-wing state as an 'a-popular' state, a nation 'without
a people'.[129] This tension was also reflected in the legal system and

constitutional discourse.[130] Although the relations between nationalism and populism do call for further exploration and elaboration, my hypothesis is that, in both theoretical and historical terms, the relation between the nation and the people is *context-dependent*, and does not seem to obey any predetermined reductionist or essentialist logic of fusion.

The emergence of populist discourses and the question of a populist desire

Let us now turn to the question of the emergence of populist discourses. From the point of view of discourse theory, the emergence of new discourses and new identities is always related to the *dislocation* or crisis of previously hegemonic discursive orders. It is a certain failure of previous identifications that forces subjects to seek refuge in a new discursive attachment and investment.[131] This is also the case with populist discourses. Populism is a phenomenon which emerges 'in conditions of crisis and change in cultural values and social structures'.[132] In Laclau's words: 'The emergence of populism is historically linked to a crisis of the dominant ideological discourse, which is in turn part of a more general social crisis'.[133] This was, for example, the case with Peronism: 'The invocation of a sense of crisis was key to Perón's rise and also buttressed the importance of leadership'.[134]

As far as our case is concerned, this pattern seems once more to be reproduced. The increasing centrality of the Orthodox Church in the 1990s and the popular response to initiatives like the petition for a referendum on identity cards have to be seen against the background of a variety of external and internal dislocations marking the late 1980s and early 1990s: these include internal political developments (scandals, corruption, and so on) leading to increasing cynicism and political alienation, as well as international events (such as the crisis of 1989 entailing the collapse of the ideological division between socialism and capitalism). All these events helped the development of a religious sentiment, given that the Church's support of the dictatorship was being gradually forgotten.[135] My hypothesis, however, is that what acted as a catalyst in all these ideological fermentations and displacements was the various dislocations and fears produced by Greece's membership of the EEC, and later Greece's full participation in the EU. Indeed, it has been observed that the upturn in church-going in Greece, and the shrinking of the number of those totally alienated from the Church, coincides with the increasing hegemony of the demand for modernisation (around 1996) and the new challenges this involves.[136] Social subjects previously tied to discourses and demands that were marginalised by the new challenges, incapable of adjusting to the new status quo and alienated from the new style of political discourse, may have comprised a reservoir of tentative followers, from which religious populism could draw support. What happened then might have been an interesting reversal, revealing the inherent contradictions of modernity and modernisation. If, in the beginning of the modern era, 'politics provided a functional alternative to religion, or in Marxist terms, the conditions under which hope loses its fantastic guise and gains the clear-eyed unity of scientific theory and political practice',[137] now we may be witnessing the opposite trend. The fact, however, that this resistance to modernisation has taken a populist direction leads us to another hypothesis which may connect this current form of populism to the populist legacy of Greek politics.

For example, there is no doubt that Papandreou's populism of the late 1970s and 1980s exhibited similar characteristics to Christodoulos's populism. PASOK not only addressed 'the people' (very much like Christodoulos, Papandreou proclaimed: 'No institutions, only the people!'), but also attempted to simplify the social topography according to a logic of equivalence, stressing the antagonism between *them* (the dominant sectors, the power-bloc) and *us* (the underdog, the oppressed and dominated sectors).[138] Indeed PASOK's discourse

> presented the social and political space as divided into two opposed fields. The logic of equivalence has from the beginning characterised PASOK's discourse. The social base, identified as the "under-privileged", is mobilised against the enemy, namely the "privileged", while the political space is divided simply into Right and Left.[139]

However, apart from this structural analogy – easily attributed to the fact that, besides their differences, they are both populist discourses – is there a more direct historical link between the two? Is Greek political culture historically more prone to populist interventions than other societies? Is Christodoulos more appealing to people who were previously interpellated by PASOK's populism? Is there, in other words, a *populist desire* initially cultivated by Papandreou and then hijacked by Church discourse after the change of style in PASOK's political rhetoric? These sound like hypotheses and questions worthy of further exploration.

Acknowledgements

It has been pointed out that it is always impolite to argue religion or politics with strangers and dangerous to do so with friends. I am probably doing both in this paper and would never have found the courage to embark on such a task without the support and valuable comments of colleagues who read earlier drafts of this text. In particular, I would like to thank Nicos Demertzis, Jason Glynos, Marcia Ian, Thanos Lipowatz, Nicos Mouzelis and Francisco Panizza. Many thanks are also due to Loukas Tsoukalis for offering his encouragement in the initial and most difficult stages of research.

10

The Discursive Continuities of the Menemist Rupture

SEBASTIÁN BARROS

In 1983, Raúl Alfonsín of the UCR was elected president of Argentina in the first democratic elections after a long period of military rule. In contrast to the country's violent and authoritarian political traditions, the nascent government set up as its paramount objective the restoration of democratic institutions. However, as a decline in political authority, hyperinflation and popular uprisings prematurely forced Alfonsín to resign before the end of his mandate, in July 1989 Carlos Menem, the opposition Justicialista (Peronist) candidate, won the early elections. In spite of Alfonsín's failure, 1989 marked the beginning of a new political era for Argentina. Not only was there a change of government through free and fair elections, but also for the first time in the country's history an opposition party candidate succeeded a democratically elected president. Since this juncture, the country has known the longest uninterrupted period of democratic rule since independence.

The newly elected president, Carlos Menem, was regarded as representing a radical rupture with the democratic discourse that had dominated the period of transition to democracy under Alfonsín, centred on the recovery of democratic freedoms and rights and the institutionalisation of a stable democratic party system. In contrast, Menem was seen as a charismatic leader from the interior of the country, with a discourse 'contaminated' by demagogic promises, coming to power with the support of groups linked to Argentina's authoritarian past. Moreover, it was argued that Menem had also broken with crucial elements of the Peronist's identity, as his policies were in opposition to those carried out by Perón in the 1950s, to the extent that doubts were expressed about the persistence of a Peronist identity subject to radical changes.

This chapter argues that Menemist discourse had more in common with the democratic discourse of the Alfonsín era and with traditional Peronist identity than is often assumed by the literature. For this purpose I will analyse Menemist discourse and compare it with the discourse of democracy articulated by both Alfonsín and a Peronist group called Renovación Peronista (RP). I will also compare Menem's discourse on the economy with the discourse on economic reform present in the political formation since, at least, 1976. First, I will briefly present the notions of dislocation and relative structurality that will be used for the analysis of Menem's discourse and that of his predecessors.[1] I will then compare Menemist discourse with Alfonsín's and RP's discourses on democracy, and with the liberals' discourse on economic reform, in order to show how, far from being a discourse of rupture, Menem's discourse shared significant elements with political and economic discourses already circulating in Argentina's political formation.

Dislocation and relative structurality

What are the conditions for the emergence of a given discourse? Every social demand emerges as a result of a structural dislocation. When existing forms of political representation are destabilised and dislocated, new meanings and identities are required to institute a new sense of order. The notion of dislocation is thus central for political analysis because a dislocation is the instance that creates new political possibilities. A dislocated political order is the ambiguous condition of possibility for new forms of political action.

The effects of a dislocation are traumatic for the actors of the dislocated social order as it fragments and dissolves social identities

that, under normal circumstances, are not problematised. The dislocation of identities means that new forms of identification are needed
that could give coherence and sense to people's experiences. However,
it is important to point out first that this 'new order' has no a priori
content. This means that the re-articulations of the social order made
possible by the dislocation are in principle indeterminate, as the nature
of the new order would be the result of a hegemonic struggle. The
success of a certain discursive position in occupying the commanding
place of the new order depends on its efficacy in making better sense
of the generalised dislocations. However, the new order is never completely new because it takes place in a political space in which there is
always a relative structuration: the dislocation of a structure does not
mean that everything becomes possible or that all existing symbolic
frameworks of meaning melt into the air. Thus, a particular dislocation
might have had a multiplicity of origins and could be more or less
'deep' in its effects, depending on the context in which it emerges.

The novelty and depth of the structural dislocation requires further
elaboration. Novelty is never completely new. There will always remain
traces of the relative structurality of the dislocated order into which the
new demand anchors its commanding pretensions. This is clear even in the
more radical attempts to constitute a new structurality that would completely erase the dislocated chaos. One of these attempts was Hobbes's
Leviathan. He tried to eliminate all traces of the state of nature by reducing the plurality of voices characteristic of the state of nature to one: the
voice of the sovereign. However, he cannot succeed in his attempt without
constantly referring to the traumatic and miserable experience of the war
of all against all. Thus, the acceptance of the absolute sovereignty of the
Leviathan depends on the constant recollection of the miseries of the
state of nature. Therefore, from the moment in which a discourse emerges
as a response to a dislocation of the social order, and its content starts to
work as the solution to the crisis, it will necessarily have to make reference
to the previous structurality and its failure to provide a stable order.

A dislocation of the existing structures of meaning forces the emergence of different demands that will seek to re-signify the political

context by advancing a specific solution to the critical situation provoked by the dislocated structure. Two points need clarification here. In
the first place, it is important to consider that, as a response to the
dislocation, a particular demand can be characterised in two ways. On
the one hand, it will represent a particular solution to the crisis. But on
the other hand, and at the same time, the demand's particular content
will carry with it a promise of fullness, which is a promise for the realisation of the whole community. This promise, which is grounded in
the relative structurality described above, allows the particular demand
to become a surface of inscription for other demands. This means that
every demand can be potentially articulated with a plurality of other
demands.

The notion of articulation is also central, and takes the argument to
the second point. When a political order is dislocated a multiplicity of
discourses will emerge, seeking to make sense of the new situation.
Among these, there is one that will become hegemonic by imposing its
reading of the situation as the only possible reading, articulating other
readings. But articulation changes both the meaning of the articulating
and the articulated discourses, and because of this a discourse cannot
completely hegemonise the field of interpretation.

The success of a given reading of the situation implies that the new
structurality has in its origins a struggle for excluding other demands.
This shows that a society only exists as a political relationship that
excludes some interpretations of the social order and includes others:
society is always a political construction. The logic of hegemony lies precisely in the notion of articulation and in the possibility of a particular
demand imposing its reading of the dislocation, and working as a surface
of inscription for other demands. The fact that a hegemonic success can
be analysed in terms of the 'imposition of a reading' means that we can
ask if any demand has the same chance of becoming hegemonic. The
answer will be affirmative only if we consider it as a logical possibility.
But in political analysis the answer will be negative. If the imposition of
a demand is a matter of power, it is obvious that not every demand will
have the same chance of success. If, on the one hand, there is no pre-given

essence or objectivity that in the abstract denies or permits a particular demand to embody a more extended generality, we should not forget the relevance of the relative structurality of the dislocated context. There will always be potentially more powerful discourses that would be better suited to impose their particular content as universal, and thus hegemon-ically articulate a response to the dislocation. Let us now examine the relative structurality of the Argentine political formation in which Menem's discourse emerged.

Menemism and democracy

The notion of democracy was the nodal point around which all demands were articulated in Argentina after 1984. This was particularly clear in relation to Alfonsín's discourse, which occupied the centre of the polit-ical formation. The Alfonsinista discourse was organised around the rejection of an authoritarian, bureaucratic and corporatist past that came to an end with the failure of the Proceso de Reorganización Nacional (PRN), as the military called their government, and to which the country should never go back. Alfonsín was referring to a recent political past that was still very much present in the memories of Argentine society. From his point of view, once the Argentine people had agreed to and enacted the democratic organisation of society and the guarantee of civic freedoms, all national problems would be solved. Thus, democracy was the sole condition for the rebirth of Argentina's greatness.

The situation of Peronism was rather different. In 1986 the Partido Justicialista (PJ, the official name of the Peronist party) was seeking to recover from a series of crises that started with Perón's death, from the collapse of the Peronist government in 1976, and from the consequences that the PRN had for the party. The electoral defeat of 1983 was often understood at the time as 'the final blow'[2] for the Peronist movement.

Faced with this challenge a group of Peronist leaders argued that Peronism had to change its internal organisation. Renovación Peronista – as this new group was called – proposed the democratisation and insti-tutionalisation of the party. RP argued that the *movimientista* character of

Peronism had to change, and the movement needed to be transformed into a proper political party. However, the suggestion that Peronism should become a political party represented an important shift in the Peronists' imaginary, since one of its main elements was the critique of the so-called *partidocracia liberal* as the cause of most of the country's problems.[3]

In order to achieve its goals RP faced a political dilemma: they had to show that they were the *real* Peronists after the death of Perón. They had to demonstrate that they were not completely breaking with the Peronist tradition, but at the same time that they were changing the party to 'dance to the music of times', which was democracy. The discourse of this new Peronist group was centred on the eradication of the authoritarian practices still present in the party. The main goal that Renovación set itself was to establish distance from the authoritarian bureaucracy in control of the PJ and transform Peronism into a democratic party. But this was very difficult to carry out, considering the historic characteristics of Peronism, an anti-party movement in which decisions were almost exclusively taken by the leader. Moreover, while they sought to change the party, RP had to stay within the Peronist tradition in order to keep the support of PJ voters.

Renovación's discursive strategy was to reclaim Peronism's popular tradition while trying to articulate it into the democratic discourse that hegemonised the transition to democracy. But the common elements between RP's discourse on democracy and the discourse of the UCR meant that the Radical government perceived Renovación as a threat, as both would effectively be competing for the same voters and presenting similar ideas. The government thus called a series of meetings with the official Peronist leaders, excluding Renovación from the talks. The meetings made evident the first public splits within Renovación. RP's leader Antonio Cafiero objected to the government's meeting with the PJ, and showed concern at the public support that Carlos Menem – then a fellow Renovador leader – gave to the meetings between the party's authoritarian leadership and the president.[4]

Menem's discourse on democracy

Thus Carlos Menem became Cafiero's main opponent within Peronism. The difference between them was initially on a tactical issue: while Menem defended the unity of Peronism, including the authoritarian old guard, Cafiero argued that formal unity was worthless. He cited the electoral defeat of 1983 as an example of a type of unity that had not been particularly successful for Peronism.[5] In a development from Menem and Cafiero's tactical disagreements, the dispute became centred on whether RP should present separate candidates from the official PJ list for the 1987 election.

Menem gained the internal support of the Peronist groups excluded from Renovación's successful struggle to control the party. Hence Renovación found itself having to face the re-emergent anti-party and anti-democratic Peronist tradition now headed by one of Renovación's own leaders. As early as July 1986 Menem was proclaimed as the PJ's presidential candidate for the 1989 election by a Peronist group in Córdoba. Another group that expressed its support for Menem was the right-wing faction that controlled the Peronist party in Buenos Aires Province. Its leader, Herminio Iglesias, was the defeated candidate for the provincial government of Buenos Aires in 1983, and was identified as having violent and gangster-like political manners. His support for Menem was attacked by some RP leaders. Eduardo Duhalde, for example, expressed his concern, arguing that 'Menem's legitimate aspirations to the presidency can suffer a serious stumble if he insists on forming an alliance with Peronist groups close to López Rega and Herminio Iglesias'.[6]

Menem's discourse has to be understood as the articulation of the traditional Peronist discourse on populist democracy with the new liberal-democratic discourses of Renovación and the UCR. In a letter published on 24 March 1988, titled *Carta abierta a la esperanza* (Open Letter to Hope), Menem presented himself as the figure that would make sure that both the formal elements of democracy, as represented by the UCR government, and the social critique of formal democracy carried out by Renovación were preserved – and, in a way, brought together. 'I come to tell them [the poor] that a future is possible. That democracy is still worth it. That justice is a good reason to build something bigger and more transcendental'. Menem's discourse thus took democracy as the bedrock upon which to ground its content.[7] Its main characteristic was an ambiguity – which made possible the inclusion of those who felt excluded from the political articulation centred on the notion of democracy as advocated by RP and the UCR.

In order for a given signifier to become the surface of inscription for a plurality of demands, the signifier's particular content tends to become emptier and emptier and to be opened to different meanings. It is this emptiness that permits a particular demand to symbolise many different demands. In the case of Menem's discourse the 'emptiness' was given by its ambiguity, which made it different from both traditional Peronist discourse and that of RP.[8] Menem's use of ambiguity was evident for instance in his abandonment of the traditional categories used to identify Perón's supporters. Thus, he no longer identified his addressees as 'workers' or *compañeros peronistas*, appealing instead to more ambiguous identities such as 'brothers and sisters from my motherland', 'Argentines', or to sociological categories that were emptied of their previous political meaning: 'I want to talk with you all face to face to express my intimate convictions. With you, workers; with you, professionals; with the youngsters, the women and the elderly of this blessed land of all.'[9]

The appeal to the 'workers' was typical of Peronist discourse, but the fact that this appeal was combined with appeals to 'professionals', 'women' and 'the elderly', transformed the category 'workers' into a mere sociological notion, partially empty of its political significance in the Argentine context. But the emptying of the signifier 'workers' was only partial because, at the same time, the term could still be read as a traditional Peronist category. At other times, the ambiguity of Menem's discourse was represented by elements that seemed charged with a moral content. In the *Carta abierta*, for example, the mediocrity of the Argentine condition was the trait to overcome.

> I summon you to take imagination to power and to follow a path that
> really makes sense. We have to overcome mediocrity. Because the
> mediocre person does not invent anything. The mediocre person specu-
> lates, gives up, feels like a passive spectator of the times he has to live in.
> And this time, precisely, is not for mediocre people.

In other cases, the appeal to the people was formulated as a message
of hope, where hope was defined as 'the realisation of our best dreams',
or as evidence that a better 'future is possible'. This appeal to hope was
even more evident during the presidential campaign of 1989. The main
motto of Menem's campaign was '*Síganme, no los voy a defraudar*' (Follow
Me, I Won't Let You Down).

> I take up this challenge in the face of a life or death alternative. I have two
> banners to confidently look at the horizon and calmly wait for the future
> [electoral] decision [of the people]. One banner is from God: faith. The
> other banner is from the people: hope.[10]

Menem's discourse took distance from RP, in a move that allowed him
to put RP and the government at the same discursive level. Cafiero's
reaction parallelled the denunciation of the military-union pact that
marked the emergence of the Alfonsinist discourse.[11] It stressed
Menem's 'caudillista' attitude and presented it as a return to the worst
characteristics of Peronism. Cafiero criticised Menem's supporters by
claiming that he was surrounded by 'figures from the Montoneros,
López Rega collaborators and other *compañeros* who we can only associ-
ate with the dark days of the electoral defeat'.[12] Cafiero's reference to a
violent political past was almost a carbon-copy of Alfonsín's discourse
in 1983. In Cafiero's discourse Menem represented the return of the so-
called 'marshals of defeat', now reunited around Menem to 'recover the
privileges that the Peronist people took away from them'.[13] Menem's
discourse was thus a critique of the exclusion of certain Peronist
groups from Renovación's project of party renewal, and a reassertion of
the anti-party characteristics of Peronism. This strategy proved to be

successful against the party machine then in the hands of the Renovación candidates: on 9 July 1988 Carlos Menem and Eduardo Duhalde won the PJ primary presidential election with 53.4 per cent of the votes.

It can be argued that Menemist discourse did not represent a radical rupture with the discourse of democracy that dominated Argentina's return to constitutional order. Rather, his discourse shared certain elements with the notion of democracy that characterised the transition, but its contents were re-signified, as the ambiguity of Menemist discourse allowed him to articulate discursive elements so different as to appeal to the followers of both Herminio Iglesias and the Montoneros alike.[14] In this way the notion of democracy in Menemist discourse became the floating signifier of the political formation, and, at the same time, transformed the concept of democracy into an empty signifier that could be clothed with different meanings.[15]

Menem and the Peronist tradition

A good part of the literature about Menemism compares and contrasts it to the 'original' Peronism of 1945. Most authors highlight the policy differences between the two governments while, at the same time, stressing the way in which Menem partly retrieved the Peronist tradition. It was said that Menem had the ability to 'make his mere presence evoke a series of political contexts and messages associated in one way or another with the Peronist identity'.[16] Even when these 'contexts and messages' were never properly defined in the literature, it was clear that the particular style of Menem's discourse allowed a link to be established between the Menemist and Peronist traditions.

It has been argued that Menem presented himself and was perceived by his followers as the heir of the *justicialista* dream; that he was elected 'by the inertia of tradition only to subordinate the Argentine economy to the dominant classes of the international capitalist system, and, in particular, to the financial capital and its "guard dogs" the IMF and the World Bank'.[17] Another writer, Manuel Mora y Araujo, points out that

Menem's success was due to the fact that Peronism had to change after its defeat in 1983. Thus the renovation of the party took place, particularly in the ideas and political style of the PJ.[18] Style was also the term used by José Nun to refer to the changes in the patterns of political representation that made possible the emergence of Menemism. With his particular style 'Menem appealed to the traditional [political] recipes of Peronism in order to be President'. Nun argues that after his election Menem rejected most Peronist policies, but 'retained some that nowadays are related to a kind of peripheral postmodermism'.[19] The contrast between Perón's and Menem's political programmes was also stressed by Juan Carlos Portantiero. But when examining the success of Menemism he also refers to a 'problem of style', and a similarity between the two leaders that 'alludes to deeper zones of the collective sensitivity'. From his point of view, Menem 'established a symbolic relationship with the deep sensitivity of Peronism' different from the 'modernist rationalism' of the 'republican mood' hegemonic in the mid-1980s.[20] According to Ricardo Sidicaro, the Menemist 'anti-elite' character emerged against this 'republican mood' represented by Alfonsín and Cafiero. Menem could become the leader of this reaction 'because of his attachment to the old Peronist style, that appealed to the support of the poorest sectors of society by promising greater social equality and better wages, at the same time that he raised nationalist issues and criticised the world's hegemonic centres'.[21]

Menem's discourse had a particular constitution. It was mainly defined by its closeness to the electorate, by the changes in the patterns of political mobilisation, and by his presentation as a quasi-religious saviour. All these in a moment in which the political word was discredited, political mobilisation and participation were almost non-existent, and a feeling of scepticism and pessimism was widespread. This discursive framework was one of the elements that helped Menem's success in the PJ's primaries of 1988. He entered the political scene with a strategy that was different from those of his opponents. For several years, he visited towns and cities throughout the country where he showed a great ability to establish direct contact with the people based on affect and empathy.[22] Gabriela Cerruti describes Menem's political strategy in her biography of the Peronist leader. She notes how Menem travelled through Argentina, spending two days of the week in La Rioja (his home province), two in Buenos Aires, and three travelling around all over the country meeting the minister of the economy, the president of the Banco Hipotecario and the secretary of sport. In a single week he would appear on several television shows and in some show-business magazines.[23]

At the same time, as Marcelo Cavarozzi and Oscar Landi have explained, 'His closeness to the electorate contrasted with the growing distancing that affected both the actions of a large part of the political class and the technical justifications for the condition of the economy'.[24] Menem's close and direct contact with people was reinforced by changes in the forms of political mobilisation. There were no large mobilisations of people, as was usually the case under Peronism, because this required a significant organisational effort and the collaboration of other sectors within the party – unions, local leaders, and so on. Instead, Menem would go to neighbourhoods and small towns participating in *caravanas* around the country.[25] He would arrive in a town and smile and wave at the people gathered to watch him. He would kiss children and women, constantly repeating blessings and messages of love – 'I bless you', 'I love you all'. When asked about his plans if he won the election, Menem said that he did not want 'to talk about government plans but about a complete change of structures and a rebuilding of the essential national character' of a people that 'have lost all faith'. Menem would 'firmly' try to maintain the religious message and 'the eternal message from God', because 'things that are not made with love, are useless'.[26] This religious appeal was combined with his portrayal as the saviour of the country. When contemplating the possibility of defeat, he would argue that his election as president was the last chance to change things around, because 'if I lose – and I say this with total humbleness – we lose the last chance to recover Argentina and the opportunity to build a great country'.[27]

Menemism appealed, as RP had done before, to the social content that only Peronism could traditionally attach to state policies. His explicit promises were a *salariazo* (slang for a large wage increase), and a *revolución productiva* (a productive revolution) which would mean an increase in jobs. But even the social elements of his political discourse were presented in an ambiguous way:

> First of all, the Productive Revolution is a human accomplishment, a collective epic deed, an arduous and transcendental achievement. It is a challenge that starts in the head and the heart of every Argentine, before starting with the necessary transformation of the social structures. Without this intimate and decisive change, no revolution is possible. No future is possible. There is no possible progress.[28]

By appropriating the discourse of democracy and appealing to ambiguous and more generic or fragmented identities, Menem's discourse achieved two goals. First, it 'peronised' the notion of democracy, without becoming open to the charge of being the government's ally – as had happened to RP. Simultaneously, it could claim that it represented a democratic Peronism even when the most authoritarian groups within the party supported him. Second, the appeal to generic identities allowed Menem's discourse to achieve something that Peronism had failed to do during the transition to democracy. As was argued before, after the death of Perón, Peronist candidates had struggled, firstly, to convince their own partisans that they were true Peronists, and secondly to be regarded as representing something more than just the PJ's core constituency – as Alfonsín did vis-à-vis the UCR. Both discursive achievements were crucial for Menem's electoral win in the PJ's 1988 primary election – and later in the 1989 national election. Menem's success was due to his use of discursive ambiguity to articulate a heterogeneous set of demands around signifiers that had been emptied of their traditional content.

Menemism and economic reform

An important aspect of Menem's presidency was his alleged change of economic policy immediately after ascending to the presidency. It has been alleged that Menem won the election with a traditional Peronist economic discourse, but that once he took office he radically changed course and implemented a series of policies openly opposed to those of Peronism (selling state companies, opening the economy to the world market, reducing the size of the state apparatus, and ending 'state interference' in the economic arena). In this section I will show that the economic reforms that he carried out in the early 1990s were grounded in an economic discourse that was already in circulation in the Argentine political formation before Menem adopted it.

According to the discourse of economic reform circulating in Argentina in the late 1980s, the solution to the country's economic problems required structural changes in the economy through the adoption of liberal economic policies. This diagnosis was not new. Liberal economic ideas were constitutive of one of the poles of political antagonism that had divided the Argentine political scene since 1955. They represented a critique of the model of development identified with Peronism.[29] Economic liberals advocated an economy open to the world market and the reduction of the state's activity in the economy. Controlling inflation was interpreted as the condition for restoring healthy economic growth. The key measures to be adopted were restricting the money supply, holding down wages, and balancing the government's budget by reducing public spending and raising revenue.

In their critique of the economic condition of the country, the liberals highlighted two main issues: on the one hand, the growing state regulation of the economy; on the other, the development of a closed economy isolated from world markets. According to the liberal discourse, state participation in the economy had led to long-term budget deficits financed by monetary emission, the main cause of inflation since 1946.[30] Thus, inflation was characterised as the main problem of the economy, and its solution required important structural changes. The military government that took power in 1976 accepted the liberal diagnosis of the Argentine economy: if the economic crisis is to be overcome, inflation has to be defeated; required for this would be an open economy and the withdrawal of the state from economic activity.

However, liberal economic reform found itself in a predicament during the transition to democracy, as liberal economic ideas became associated with the PRN – not exactly a prestigious association. But while these ideas lost importance in the transition to democracy, this does not mean that the discourse of economic liberalism disappeared from the political formation. On the contrary, economic liberalism was constantly present as the 'other' of the economic discourse of the UCR government from 1984 to 1987. It was the strength of the discourse of democracy that relegated the discourse of economic reform to the background. Economic problems were not absent from the agenda of the 1983 electoral campaign, but the candidates did not address them in detail. After the failure of the military government's economic policies, epitomised in the liberal orthodoxy of the economy minister José A. Martínez de Hoz, the main parties shared the perception that the economic recovery of the country was not a matter of economic reform but only of 'reopening the doors of factories'. This alone would finish with poverty and malnutrition, unemployment and low wages. Economic problems were thus pushed into the background. They were, for example, reduced to the judgment of human rights abuses committed by the military, or the preservation of democratic institutions. But the reduction of economic issues did not equate to the disappearance of the discourse of economic reform, as is evident from an analysis of the discourse structuring Alfonsín's government between 1984 and 1987.

During the first years of Alfonsín's government, economic reform was constantly linked to Argentina's authoritarian past. The main criticism of economic liberalism was that liberal economic policies would harm certain sectors of society to the extent that its alleged objectives were totally incompatible with the idea of democracy. If democracy was going to 'cure, educate, and feed the people' (as Alfonsín claimed), the economic policies associated with the authoritarian past could not be sustained. Thus, the discourse of economic reform was present as an undesirable possibility. Even the incipient reform attempts of the Austral Plan represented this undesirability. In 1985 the economic crisis was put at the centre of the political debate by the president's appeal to

a 'war economy'. But this appeal did not represent an attempt to reform
the economy. Rather, it was presented as an effort to control inflation
and appease social conflict – especially regarding the unions. A strong
discourse of democracy thus precipitated the subordination of economic
reform to other issues.

This situation started to shift in 1987, when the perception of the
economic crisis changed dramatically. By January it was clear that the
heterodox Austral Plan was not working. In July an important change
took place when the minister of the economy, Juan V. Sourrouille,
announced a new plan. The minister pledged to go beyond monetary
stabilisation and carry out structural economic reforms. The minister's
pledge signified a shift in the limits of economic discourse in Argentina.
While the discourse of democracy attributed responsibility for the
country's economic problems to the liberal economic policies enacted by
the military dictatorship, after July 1987 the blame for Argentina's economic situation was placed on the crisis of a dirigiste economic model
that resisted 'the transformations demanded by Argentine society'.[31] The
new economic plan was 'against the populist and facile model' that was
'slowing down the development of the [economic] potential of the
country'.[32]

The objectives of the new economic plan were almost a restatement
of the neoliberal principles of the discourse of the military regime. First,
it was argued that the state had become a major obstacle to economic
restructuring, so the deregulation of markets and the privatisation of
public companies were recommended. Second, it was stated that financial markets provided an opportunity for speculation, so they also had to
be reformed. Finally, a third major objective was to open Argentina's
economy and to integrate it more closely into world markets. The
government's plan of structural reform meant that the liberal discourse
of economic reform regained the place it had lost during the first years
of transition to democracy. And this shift was implemented by the hegemonic discourse that had articulated the transition – Alfonsinismo.

How was it that a discourse that was constituted around the notion of
democracy could change and embrace the discourse of liberal economic

reform which had been regarded as antithetic to democracy? It has to be remembered that 1987 was a critical year for the UCR government. The economic policy represented by the Austral Plan was not successful. Politically, things were no better. On 6 September the PJ won the provincial and legislative elections in twenty out of twenty-two electoral districts. From the point of view of the government, the UCR had lost the elections as a consequence of the poor performance of the economy.

The most visible manifestation of the economic crisis was high inflation. The hegemonic discourse was shifting as a consequence of this dislocation, and it reacted as a critique to it: 'This is precisely the goal of the set of measures we have announced: to dismantle the inflationary bomb.'[33] To overcome the dislocation of the social order brought by high inflation there was only one option: to reform the country's economy. A new order would be achieved by restructuring first the relationship of the Argentine economy with foreign capital, then the role of private economic initiatives, and finally the state's participation in the economy.[34] From this point on, the Alfonsín government repeated the arguments of its predecessor, the PRN: the state had to be reformed and the economy had to be integrated into the world market. The difference from the military regime was that the call to carry out the structural reforms was issued with a warning regarding its social costs. The reform process needed the participation and social responsibility of all sectors of society: 'the collective enterprise of the Argentines implies change and progress with justice and solidarity'.[35]

Alfonsín presented the transformation of the economy as a necessity, and did not leave space for many options. The reform of the economy, as intended, was the only alternative left to the country. The government was not only doing the *right* thing, but the *only* thing that was possible. This required the integration of Argentina into the world market, the reform of the state to make it more efficient, and the spreading of the costs of the economic adjustment to the whole society, and not only the poorest sectors. Thus, if in 1983 democracy was considered a sufficient condition to improve the economic situation of the country, and if in

1985 this had started to change with the Austral Plan, in 1987 the reform of the economy became the necessary condition for the survival of Argentina. The discourse of economic reform ceased to be an undesirable possibility, and was transformed into a necessity.

As was noted earlier, when a particular discourse starts working as a surface of inscription for other demands it functions as a promise of fullness. Faced with the failure of representation provoked by a dislocation, the new demands will present themselves as the representation of plenitude. In the case of the re-articulation of the discourse of economic reform by the Alfonsín government, there was the promise of a 'new society'. The terms of the original equation, democracy = plenitude, radically changed when the control of inflation came to represent the condition of possibility for the establishment of new mechanisms of socio-political negotiation.

Thus, Alfonsín's discourse changed its core priorities. The economic plan was meant to stop inflation in order to achieve democratic stability. High inflation had to be eliminated if democratic negotiations between political parties were to be possible. 'Because, obviously, if we do not deactivate the [inflationary] bomb, no negotiation is possible.' At the same time, the relative structurality of the previous articulation is evident in Alfonsín's speech opening the legislative sessions that year. The president presented the social pact as a negotiating mechanism that was going to erase 'corporatist hindrances' and their authoritarian origins. But, after this reference to the notion of democracy as formulated in the first stage of the transition, a new signifier emerged to replace democracy. The reform of the economy would provide 'certainty, peace, and welfare to the men and women of our country'. In other words, it would 'provide the certainty' that inflation seemed to be taking away from 'our everyday life'.[36]

This process of discursive change was not limited to Alfonsinism. On the contrary, it is possible to trace the dissemination of the discourse of economic reform to almost all political groups. The need for reforming the economic structure of the country was only rejected by left-wing parties and certain sectors of the union movement. From the second half of 1987 onwards, the discussion was not about whether the economy had to be reformed or not, but about the social costs of the reforms, and how they would be distributed among the population. Antonio Cafiero stated that 'the economic adjustment has to be done, but the way in which its costs will be spread has to be examined'.[37] In the case of the unions, there was a split in their attitude towards economic reform. On one hand, there was a group within the CGT that rejected it because it was a proposal that implied 'the handing over of the national patrimony [to foreign interests]'.[38] But on the other, there was a group that was seeking to negotiate the economic adjustment. As union leader Jorge Triaca put it, Peronism had to redefine its 'historic role because the principle of redistribution of wealth is not in accordance with the current economic situation of the country'.[39] Even the leaders of the two main parties, Eduardo Angeloz (Radical) and Carlos Menem (Peronist), were part of the process of dissemination of the discourse of economic reform during the campaign for the presidential election in May 1989. This was more evident in the case of the Radical candidate, Angeloz. He was constantly presented as a good administrator arguing for a change in the model of economic development of Argentina. Menem presented an economic plan called 'We Have to Change, it is the Only Alternative'. The plan proposed 'to subordinate public expenditure to new criteria of morality and austerity' and 'a serious privatisation policy with parliamentary consensus'.[40]

The end of Alfonsín's government was traumatic. After the failure of the Austral Plan the most important attempt to dominate inflation was the Plan Primavera (Spring Plan) of August 1988. In February 1989 the plan could not resist the market coup (*golpe de mercado*) that implied the political destabilisation of the government by different economic groups through currency speculation and reckless price increases. Following the *golpe*, inflation in March stood at 17 per cent, in April 33.4 per cent, and in May at 78.5 per cent. At the same time, political problems were multiplying. In December, another military rebellion took place, and in January a left-wing group attacked the *La Tablada* military barracks causing a violent confrontation with military and police forces.

What followed can only be described as chaos. In May there were food riots and attacks on supermarkets in poor neighbourhoods of the main cities. Fears of a massive popular insurrection provoked the declaration of a state of siege. Inflation was now hyper-inflation, with price increases of 114.5 per cent in June and 196.6 per cent in July. The generalised perception was that of a government with no economic policy, no monopoly on coercion, and no political initiative – especially after its defeat on 14 May when C. Menem and E. Duhalde won the presidential election with 49.3 per cent of the vote, against 37.1 per cent for the UCR candidates.

Menemism and economic stability

Once in power, the position that had become the articulatory demand during 1988 and 1989, thanks to the particular way in which it was constituted and the ambiguity of its content, started to change. Menem's discourse provided a new reading of the dislocatory effects of the crisis, representing it as a terminal crisis that had placed the country in a state of emergency and in danger of dissolution. The critical effects of this reading implied a new positivity, articulated around the idea of national unity. This implied, firstly, the reconciliation of the people, who had suffered artificial divisions as a consequence of the 1989 crisis. Secondly, national unity worked as a justification for the alliance of the government with right-wing political groups. This was particularly important in the PJ, where these groups were understood to be the best representatives of the 'anti-popular front'. Finally, national unity came to represent the restoration of the authority of the state lost in the terminal crisis. This also implied that the diagnosis and prescriptions of the faction occupying the state at the time – Menemism – had to be accepted without any sort of nuances.

Menemism was thus starting to make sense of what was happening in the Argentina of the early 1990s. In other words, the 'political vacuum' of the end of the Radical government had passed, and now there was a discourse that was starting to give coherence to the people's experience.

But the suturing of the dislocated space and the creation of a stable sense of order was not free of problems.

The series of dislocations that took place in 1989 and 1990 were intimately related to those faced by the Radical government. They were a mixture of economic and political problems that tested the reactive capacity of the new government. In this respect, Menem's government had the advantage of the UCR experience – from which some lessons had been learned. And the first lesson was that if the government projected an image of weakness regarding decisions to attack problems, it would not last long. The weakness of Menem's government was related to the credibility of its appropriation of the discourse of economic reform. As has already been said, the discourse of economic reform had gone through a process of expansion since 1987 that meant that it was the central discourse available at the time of the galloping crisis. But it was also said that no other available discourse putting itself forward as an alternative could make sense of the dislocatory effects. Menemism faced this problem. No subject position was going to be credible simply because of its appropriation of the discourse of economic reform.

In March 1991, a month in which Menem had stated that he was 'the best disciple of Perón', and the PJ had called a congress for its doctrinaire updating, the government committed itself to another anti-inflationary shock: the Argentine currency would be freely convertible into US dollars. Congress passed a bill fixing the exchange rate for the dollar and prohibiting the Central Bank from printing money to cover budget deficits unless new emissions were fully backed by gold or foreign currency. The fixing of the price of the dollar was crucial to reverse expectations of inflation, and the results were music to the government's ears: inflation rates in July, August and September were 2.6 per cent, 1.3 per cent, and 1.8 per cent respectively. Inflation in December stood at under 1 per cent for the second month in a row, and the lowest since 1974. Interest rates also plummeted from a 3 per cent daily rate to 3 per cent per month. Real wages improved, and commercial credit was available again. The Buenos Aires stock market experienced a true explosion: 'Operators in the *porteño*[41] financial district joyously welcomed the beginning of the "Argentine miracle'".[42] This euphoria was not exclusive to business. The quick success of the Convertibility or Cavallo Plan, as it was called, moved Menem to say that 'the Plan Cavallo will last for ever [*de por vida*] or at least for the duration of my administration'.[43]

After a year and a half of economic plans and recurrent inflationary crisis, the Peronist government of Carlos Menem had been able to stabilise the situation. The Convertibility Plan created not only economic stability and growth, but, more importantly, gave the country a collective feeling of order that it had lacked for decades. The implementation and success of the plan was explained mainly in economic terms: they were based on the importance of expectations regarding the anti-inflationary shock.[44] Palermo and Novaro's account of the 'political success' of the Convertibility Plan also pointed in this direction. They tried to show that the most important aspect of the plan was the fact that the government was abandoning certain regulatory powers in order to gain credibility.[45] The Convertibility Law not only fixed the exchange rate, but also restricted the powers of the government in the management of monetary policy – thus achieving a 'maximum compromise' regarding exchange rates.[46] The government would not be able to modify the exchange rate to give in to political interests or to party or entrepreneurial pressures. Palermo and Novaro's conclusion is that this politico-institutional arrangement gave the plan the necessary credibility to be successful.

But from the point of view presented here, this explanation might be correct only for the initial success of the plan. Given the poor credibility of institutional arrangements in Argentine politics, it is untenable that a simple law could transmit credibility and help with the expansion of a specific discourse. In 1991 there was no reason to think that after six months of low inflation the government would not pass a different law, surrendering to union pressure for the September elections. Thus, the reason for the change in decisions and expectations has to be sought elsewhere. In this account, it was not until the government could bring inflation down that the political formation, in crisis since 1987, could be stabilised. It was not until a particular position could fulfil the positivity of the discourse of economic reform that the political space could be re-articulated.

After the Convertibility Law, the idea of stability started to play the role that democracy had played during Alfonsín's presidency. Thus, for example, when faced with the resistance of certain groups, mainly unions, to measures that implied redundancies or lower wages, government officials would claim that the opposition were the representatives of a past to which nobody wanted to return. Jorge Triaca, for example, after a period as minister of labour, was designated director of a state-owned steel company in order to close it down. Confronted with the opposition of unions and workers defending their jobs, he claimed that they were 'agitators who want to damage the Convertibility Plan'.[47] As Alfonsín had done during his government, Menem presented any sort of political opposition as an attempt to wipe out the public policy that had 'stopped the country from falling into the abyss towards which it was heading'.[48]

The idea of stability presented by the government was thus the element that articulated, on the one hand, the discourse of economic reform, and, on the other, the policies carried out since 1989. Stability was presented as a consequence of the Convertibility Plan – described by Menem as the 'most important social revolution in the history of Latin America'.[49] At the same time, the idea of stability contained all the elements present in the discourse of economic reform. From the point of view of Menemism, the proposed transformation of Argentina's economic structure implied 'a scenario where private initiative was the driving force, at the same time that the state retired from the scene eliminating all sorts of regulations'.[50] The 'idea of self-sufficiency and absolute autarchy' implied in the old development model were described as 'adventurism' or as 'suicidal' adventurous tendencies.[51] Against these tendencies was the government's project, which had provided 'order and stability' from the chaos of 1989.

Conclusions

I began by stressing the importance of considering the relative structurality of a given discursive context when examining the emergence of a new discourse. If a crisis situation is the origin of new and unfulfilled demands, the particular crisis will mark the contents and meanings of the new structurality. No discourse emerges in a political vacuum. The critical dislocation of the structures of meaning will provoke the emergence of a series of demands claiming to be the solution to the crisis. One of these demands will be able to present itself as the best reading of the situation (i.e. as hegemonic). And this success will crucially depend on the demand's references to the dislocation and relative structurality of the context. It is in relation to these references that the power of a demand to exclude other possible readings lies. In the case of Menemism, this is clear in relation to the discursive articulations that marked the transition to democracy, as I hope to have shown in this chapter.

When the continuities of Menemist discourse with contemporary discourses about politics and the economy are appreciated, Menem's presidency should not be regarded as a radical rupture with the way in which politics and the economy were understood in Argentina. Menemism repeated the arguments of two discursive articulations that were present in the Argentine political formation well before Menemism. Menem's discourse of democracy, which had dominated the transition from the military regime, did not represent a radical break with the Alfonsinist discourse on democracy, which was partially shared by Renovación Peronista. Menem presented himself as part of the new democratic Argentina. He did so by ambiguously emptying certain ideological categories of the new discourse on democracy, while simultaneously presenting his notion of democracy as compatible with traditional Peronist discourse. In the case of the discourse of economic reform, Menemism occupied a discursive place that had already, since 1987, been going through a process of dissemination.

NOTES

INTRODUCTION: FRANCISCO PANIZZA

I want to thank Benjamín Arditi for his comments on this paper and Juliet Martínez for her help in editing the manuscript.

1 See, for instance, M. Mackinnon and M. A. Petrone, eds, *Populismo y Neopopulismo en América Latina: El problema de la Cenicienta*, Buenos Aires 1998; Alan Knight, 'Populism and Neo-Populism in Latin America, especially Mexico', *Journal of Latin American Studies*, vol. 30, no. 2, 1998, pp. 223–48; and Kenneth Roberts, 'Neoliberalism and the Transformation of Populism in Latin America: The Peruvian Case', *World Politics*, vol. 48, no. 1, 1996, pp. 82–116.

2 The term 'populist' was originally used with reference to the People's Party in the US in the mid-1890s but since then hardly any movement or leader has acknowledged being 'populist'. In common political speak the term has a negative connotation, closely associated to terms such as demagogy and economic profligacy, indicating economic or political irresponsibility.

3 Peter Wiles, 'A Syndrome Not a Doctrine', in Ghita Ionescu and Ernest Gellner, eds, *Populism: Its Meaning and National Characteristics*, London 1969, pp. 166–79.

4 The following characterisation of Latin American populism is typical of this empirical-descriptive approach:

'Populism was an expansive style of election campaigning by colourful and engaging politicians who could draw masses of new voters into their movements and hold their loyalty indefinitely, even after their deaths. They inspired a sense of nationalism and cultural pride in their followers, and they promised to give them a better life as well'.

Michael Conniff, 'Introduction' in Michael Conniff, ed., *Populism in Latin America*, Tuscaloosa and London 1999, p. 4.

5 Peter Worsley, 'The Concept of Populism', in Ionescu and Gellner, eds, 1969, p. 243.

6 So, for instance, Paul Drake's claim that Latin America's populism has exhibited three interconnected features:

'First, it has been dominated by paternalistic, personalistic, often charismatic leadership and mobilization from the top down. Second, it has involved multi-class incorporation of the masses, especially urban workers but also middle sectors. Third, populists have emphasised integrationist, reformist, nationalist development programmes for the state to promote simultaneously redistributive measures for populist supporters and, in most cases, import-substitution-industrialization.'

Paul Drake, 'Chile's Populism Reconsidered, 1920s–1990s', in Michael Conniff, ed., *Populism in Latin America*, p. 63.

7 I am borrowing the term 'symptomatic' from the chapter by Stavrakakis in this book, to signify a non-essentialist approach based on a formal conceptualisation of populism that identifies its subject – the people – through the constitutive process of naming.

8 This definition follows Ernesto Laclau's seminal work on populism 'Towards a Theory of Populism', in Ernesto Laclau, *Politics and Ideology in Marxist Theory*, London 1997. For his notion of antagonism see his *New Reflections on the Revolution of Our Time*, London 1990, pp. 5–41. See also his contribution to this volume.

9 Taken from Imelda Vega Centeno, *Aprismo Popular: mito, cultura e historia*, Lima 1986, p. 80.

10 This is a modified version of Michael Kazin's definition of populism as a 'mode of persuasion' in Michael Kazin, *The Populist Persuasion*, Ithaca and London, 1995.

11 The quote from Perot is from Dennis Westlind, *The Politics of Popular Identity: Understanding Recent Populist Movements in Sweden and the United States*, Lund 1996, p. 175. The quote from Chávez is from Luis Ricardo Davila, 'The Rise and Fall and Rise of Populism in Venezuela', *Bulletin of Latin American Research*, vol. 19, no. 2, 2000, p. 236.

12 Edward Shils, *The Torment of Secrecy: The Background and Consequences of American Security Policies*, London 1956, pp. 98–104.

13 Worsley, 1969, p. 242.

14 Margaret Canovan, 'Trust the People! Populism and the Two Faces of Democracy', *Political Studies*, vol. XLVII, 1999, pp. 2–16.

15 I concur with Dave Lewis that it is impossible to provide any set of positive criteria, no matter how minimal, which would remain the same in all counterfactual circumstances in the definition of identity groups. Therefore the only adequate definition for such a group is that they are those individuals and groups that have either identified themselves, or have been identified by others, as constituting such a group. Dave Lewis, 'Fantasy and Identity – the case of New Age Travellers', paper prepared for the conference *Identification and Politics Workshop II*, May 23–24 2002, University of Essex, Colchester, UK.

16 Worsley, 1969, p. 242.

17 Taken from President Bush's State of the Union address, 29 January 2002.

18 Bush presented the September 11 attack as an attack on freedom in several speeches. For instance, in his State of the Union address he said: 'History has called America and our allies to action, and it is both our responsibility and our privilege to fight freedom's fight.'

19 Although shared and disputed by both the American left and the right, the appeal to liberty and freedom against government interference is particularly prominent in right-wing populism. See Joseph Lowndes chapter in this volume and H. Kazin's *The Populist Persuasion*.

20 Kazin, 1995, pp. 2–3.

21 Worsley, 1969, p. 217.

22 So, for instance, the following excerpt from Bush's 2002 State of the Union address: 'The American people have responded magnificently, with courage and compassion, strength and resolve. As I have met the heroes, hugged the families, and looked into the tired faces of rescuers, I have stood in awe of the American people.'

23 This notion can be exemplified by the story of a woman who said that she felt that she had a number of different problems at work and at home, but that she didn't know what these problems signified until the feminist movement named (identified) them as matters of gender.

24 Alejandro Groppo, 'Representation and Subjectivity in Populist Identification. Some Remarks from a Discourse Analysis Perspective', paper

submitted to the *Conference of the European Consortium for Political Research*, 6–8 September 2001, Kent University, Canterbury, p. 8.

25 Howard Gardner, *Leading Minds. An Anatomy of Leadership*, London 1966, p. 17.

26 Steve Stein, 'The Paths to Populism in Peru', in Conniff, ed., 1999, p. 104.

27 This is a modified version of Marcos Novaro's analysis of crises of representation. Marcos Novaro, *Pilotos de Tormentas: Crisis de representación y personalización de la política en Argentina (1989–1993)*, Buenos Aires 1994.

28 Francisco Panizza, 'Neopopulism and its limits in Collor's Brazil', *Bulletin of Latin American Research*, vol. 19, no. 2, 2000, p. 184.

29 John Crabtree, 'Populisms Old and New: The Peruvian Case', *Bulletin of Latin American Research*, vol. 19, no. 2, 2000, pp. 163–76.

30 Kurt Weyland, 'Neopopulism and Neoliberalism in Latin America: Unexpected Affinities', *Studies in Comparative International Development*, vol. 31, no. 3, 1996, pp. 3–31.

31 Guillermo Rochabrún, 'Deciphering the Enigmas of Alberto Fujimori' *NACLA Report on the Americas*, vol. xxx, no. 1, July/August 1996.

32 Spanish journals *El Progreso*, 31 December 1897 and *El Intransigente*, 7 April 1907, cited in José Alvarez Junco, *El Emperador del Paralelo*, Madrid 1990, p. 409.

33 This shouldn't be taken as precluding the possibility of authoritarian or military populisms, or even a populist renewal of political institutions.

34 Crabtree, 2000, p. 165.

35 François-Xavier Guerra, *Modernidad e Independencias*, Bilbao 1992.

36 Cited in J. Alvarez Junco, 'Magia y ética en la retórica política', in *Populismo, caudillaje y discurso demagógico*, Madrid 1987, p. 251.

37 Kazin, 1995, pp. 1–2.

38 Gino Germani, *Política y sociedad en una época de transición*, Buenos Aires 1969.

39 Quoted in Steve Stein, 'The Path to Populism in Peru', in Conniff, ed., 1999, p. 98.

40 The recent history of Argentina is an example of the different outcomes. When Argentina returned to democracy in 1983 the historical dichotomy between Peronism (as representing the people) and its left-wing, liberal and conservative adversaries gave way to a more plural political system. In 1989 Carlos Menem achieved a partial reconstitution of Peronist identity by redefining the political frontier between Peronism and its 'other' along

different lines than those of historical Peronism. However, the failure of Menem and of his successor, the Radical Party's De la Rua, to prevent the collapse of the Argentine economy in December 2001 led to the dissolution of political identities and opened up the possibility for new forms of political identification.

41 Venezuela's president Col Hugo Chávez, cited in Davila, 2000, p. 236.

42 Juan Pablo Lichtmajer, 'Taming the Desert: Nation and Heterogeneity in Nineteenth-Century Argentina', paper prepared for the *Identification and Politics Workshop II*, 23–24 May 2002.

43 Quoted in Carlos de la Torre, *Populist Seduction in Latin America: The Ecuadorian Experience*, Athens, Ohio, 2000, pp. 56–7.

44 Fifty years after the Liberal manifesto, another populist leader, Abdalá Bucaram, was also perceived by modernising intellectuals and conservative politicians as a dangerous demagogue so impervious to the rule of reason that Congress impeached him for reasons of insanity.

45 Jason Glynos, 'Sexual Identity, Identification and Difference', *Philosophy and Social Criticism*, vol. 26, no. 6, 2000, pp. 85–108.

46 Cited in Frederick B. Pike, *The Politics of the Miraculous in Peru: Haya de la Torre and the Spiritualist Tradition*, Lincoln and London 1986, p. 163 .

47 Gardner, 1996.

48 Quoted in Francisco Panizza, *Uruguay, Batllismo y después*, Montevideo 1990, pp. 143–45 (emphasis added).

49 D. Westlind, *The Politics of Popular Identity: Understanding Recent Populist Movements in Sweden and the United States*, Lund 1996, p. 194.

50 De la Torre, 2000.

51 Westlind, 1996, p. 177.

52 De la Torre, 2000, p. 59.

53 Pike, 1986, p. 167.

54 Gardner, p. 14.

55 Journalist Francisco Febres Cordero, 2000, p. 89.

56 De la Torre, 2000, p. 144.

57 Stein, 1999, pp. 99–100.

58 Centeno, 1986, p. 21.

59 Jorge Ferreira, *Trabalhadores do Brasil: O imaginario popular*, Rio de Janeiro 1997, p. 49.

60 Ximena Sosa Buchholz, 'The Strange Career of Populism in Ecuador', in M. Conniff, ed., 1999, p. 145.

61 Slavoj Žižek, *The Sublime Object of Ideology*, London 1989, pp. 105–6.

62 De la Torre, 2000, p. 92.

63 Oscar Reyes, 'Leaders' Personalities and Identification', paper prepared for the *Identification and Politics Workshop II*, 23–24 May 2002.

64 George Shulman, 'The Pathos of Identification and Politics', paper presented for the *Identification and Politics Workshop II*, 23–24 May 2002, The University of Essex, Colchester, UK.

65 Crabtree, 2000, p. 164.

66 Canovan, 1981, p. 9.

67 Claude Lefort, *The Political Forms of Modern Society: Bureaucracy, Democacy, Totalitarianism*, London 1986, p. 279.

68 Quoted in Shulman, 'The Pathos of Idenfitication and Politics'.

69 Worsley, 1969, p. 247.

1 ERNESTO LACLAU

1 'Why Do Empty Signifiers Matter to Politics?' in *Emancipation(s)*, London 1996.

2 CHANTAL MOUFFE

I want to thank Marcus Klein, my research assistant of several years, for his invaluable help in collecting very extensive documentation about the rise of right-wing populism in Europe.

1 Charles Larmore, 'Political Liberalism', in *Political Theory*, vol. 18, no. 3, August 1990, p. 359.

2 C. B. MacPherson, *The Life and Times of Liberal Democracy*, Oxford 1977.

3 For a critique of the 'Third Way' from such a perspective see Chantal Mouffe, *The Democratic Paradox*, London 2000, Chapter 5.

4 I have elaborated on this distinction between 'antagonism' and 'agonism' in *The Democratic Paradox*, Chapter 4.

5 For a useful overall discussion, see *The Haider Phenomenon in Austria*, in Ruth Wodak and Anton Pelinka, eds, New Brunswick and London 2002.

6 One can find a comprehensive presentation of the FPÖ in Kurt Richard Luther, 'Die Freiheitlichen (F)' in *Handbuch des politischen Systems in Österreich: Die Zweite Republik*, Herbert Dachs et al., Wien 1997.

7 A good analysis of this period is provided by Anton Pelinka in *Die Kleine Koalition*, Vienna 1993.

8 For an analysis of Haider's early populist discourse, see Michael Morass and Helmut Reischenböck, 'Parteien und Populismus in Osterreich', in Anton Pelinka, ed., *Populismus in Osterreich*, Vienna 1987.

9 This period is examined in G. Bischof, A. Pelinka and F. Karlhofer, eds, *The Vranitzky Era in Austria*, New Brunswick and London 1999.

10 For a good discussion of this strategy see Sebastian Reinfeldt, *Nicht-wir und Die-da: Studiem zum rechten Populismus*, Wien 2000.

11 Jörg Haider, *The Freedom I Mean*, 1995, p. 16.

12 Ibid., p. 34.

13 See for instance Brigitte Bailer-Galanda and Wolfgang Neugebauer, *Haider und die 'Freiheitlichen' in Osterreich*, Berlin 1997.

14 Haider's background is examined by Christa Zöchling in *Haider – Licht und Schatten einer Karriere*, Wien 1999.

15 See in this connection the article by Richard Mitten, 'Jörg Haider, the Anti-immigrant Petition and Immigration Policy in Austria', in *Patterns of Prejudice*, vol. 28, no. 2, 1994.

16 The French press saw itself as the vanguard of this 'moral crusade', and serious journals like *Libération* and *Le Monde* were full of ill-informed, hysterical pieces attacking Austria in a way that in other circumstances would have been considered 'racist'.

17 For a detailed analysis of this episode, including the judgment of the wise men, see Margaretha Kopeinig and Christoph Kotanko, *Eine europäische Affäre: Der Weisen-Bericht und die Sanktionen gegen Osterreich*, Wien 2000.

18 A very good analysis of the reasons for the success of the VB is provided by Patrick De Vos in his article, 'The Sacralisation of Consensus and the Rise of Authoritarian Populism: the Case of the Vlaams Blok', *Studies in Social and Political Thought* 7, September 2002.

19 This anti-EU component is well analysed in the Danish case by Torben Bech Dyrberg, in 'Racist, Nationalist and Populist Trends in Recent Danish Politics', Research Paper 19/01, Roskilde University, Denmark.

3 BENJAMIN ARDITI

This chapter is a modified version of an article published originally as 'Populism, or, Politics at the Edges of Democracy' in *Contemporary Politics*, vol. 9, no. 1, 2003, pp. 17–31. Margaret Canovan, Juan Martín Sánchez, Francisco Panizza, Nora Rabotnikof, and José Carlos Rodríguez scrutinised earlier versions. I thank them all for their comments.

1   Gino Germani, *Política y sociedad en una época de transición*, Buenos Aires 1969.

2   Torcuato di Tella, 'Populism and Reform in Latin America', in Claudio Véliz, ed., *Obstacles to Change in Latin America*, Oxford 1965, pp. 49–50.

3   Christopher Lasch, *The Revolt of the Elites and the Betrayal of Democracy*, London and New York, 1995; Ernesto Laclau, 'Towards a Theory of Populism', in *Politics and Ideology in Marxist Theory*, London 1977, pp. 143–98; Paul Cammack, 'The Resurgence of Populism in Latin America', *Bulletin of Latin American Research*, vol. 19, no. 2, 2000, pp. 149–61.

4   Peter Worsley, 'The Concept of Populism', in Ghita Ionescu and Ernst Gellner, eds, *Populism: Its Meanings and National Characteristics*, London 1969, pp. 242–3.

5   Peter Wiles, 'A Syndrome, not a Doctrine: Some Elementary Theses on Populism', in Ionescu and Gellner, 1969, p. 166.

6   Michael Kazin, *The Populist Persuasion*, Ithaca, NY 1995, p. 13; Alan Knight, 'Populism and Neo-populism in Latin America, Especially Mexico', *Journal of Latin American Studies*, vol. 30, no. 2, 1999, p. 226; David Marquand, 'Populism or Pluralism? New Labour and the Constitution', Mishcon Lecture, The Constitution Unit, School of Public Policy, University College London, 1999, p. 9.

7   Kurt Weyland, 'Neopopulism and Neoliberalism in Latin America: Unexpected Affinities', *Studies in Comparative International Development*, vol. 31, no. 3, 1996, pp. 3–31; see also Knight, 'Populism and Neo-populism', pp. 246–7.

8   Michael Oakeshott, *The Politics of Faith and the Politics of Scepticism*, edited and introduced by Timothy Fuller, New Haven and London 1996.

9   Gilles Deleuze and Felix Guattari, *A Thousand Plateaus*, London 1988, p. 367.

10 Worsley, 1969, p. 219.

11 Jack Hayward, 'The Populist Challenge to Elitist Democracy in Europe', in J. Hayward, ed., *Elitism, Populism, and European Politics*, Oxford 1996, pp. 10–32; Margaret Canovan, 'Trust the People! Populism and the Two Faces of Democracy', *Political Studies*, vol. XLVII, no. 1, 1999, pp. 2–16.

12 Ernesto Laclau, 'Populism: What's in a Name?', in this volume.

13 C. B. Macpherson, *The Real World of Democracy*, Toronto 1965, p. 11; see also *The Life and Times of Liberal Democracy*, Oxford 1977.

14 Knight, 1998, pp. 223–8, esp. 240.

15 Ibid., p. 225.

16   Oakeshott, 1996, pp. 18, 118.

17   Canovan, 1999, p. 5.

18   Kazin, 1995, p. 3.

19   Ibid., pp. 12–17, 251ff.

20   Carl Schmitt, *The Concept of the Political* [1932], translation and introduction by George Schwab and a foreword by Tracy Strong, Chicago 1996.

21   Jacques Derrida, *Politics of Friendship*, London 1997, pp. 131–2, 139.

22   Francisco Panizza, 'Neopopulism and its Limits in Collor's Brazil', *Bulletin of Latin American Research*, vol. 19, no. 2, 2000, p. 190.

23   Jacques Derrida, 'Sending: On Representation', *Social Research*, vol. 49, no. 2, 1982, pp. 307–9; Hanna Pitkin, *The Concept of Representation*, Berkley and Los Angeles 1967, pp. 237–8.

24   Derrida, 1982, p. 308.

25   Jacques Derrida, 'Signature Event Context' [1971], in *Limited Inc.*, Evanston, Illinois 1988, pp. 1–23.

26   Emilio de Ipola, *Ideología y discurso populista*, Mexico City 1982, p. 113.

27   Roland Barthes, *Mythologies* [1957], London 1973, p. 123.

28   Pitkin, 1967, pp. 30–1.

29   Ibid., p. 91ff.

30   Bernard Manin, *The Principles of Representative Government*, Cambridge 1997, pp. 196–7.

31   Hans Kelsen, *Vom Wesen und Wert der Demokratie* [1929], Aalen 1981.

32   Manin, 1997, pp. 218–26.

33   Quoted by Margaret Carlson in 'The Trouble with Pleasing Everyone', *Time*, 21 June 1999.

34   Manin, 1997, pp. 227–8.

35   Ibid., p. 220.

36   Ibid., p. 221.

37   Ibid., p. 226.

38   Karen Tumulty, 'Five Meanings of Arnold', *Time*, 20 October 2003, p. 38.

39   Julia Flores, quoted in M. Rivera and M. Cuéllar, 'Las razones del cambio', in *La Jornada* (Mexico City), 9 October 2000.

40   Ernesto Laclau, 'Why do Empty Signifiers Matter to Politics?', in J. Weeks, ed., *The Lesser Evil and the Greater Good*, London 1994, pp. 167–78.

41   Sigmund Freud, *Introductory Lectures on Psychoanalysis*, vol. XVI (1916–17) of The Standard Edition of the Complete Psychological Works of Sigmund

Freud, James Strachey, ed., London 1963, pp. 257–302, 358–77; 'Inhibitions, Symptoms and Anxiety', in *An Autobiographical Study, Inhibitions, Symptoms and Anxiety, The Question of Analysis and Other Works*, vol. XX (1925–26) of The Standard Edition of the Complete Psychological Works of Sigmund Freud, pp. 144–5; 'The Return of the Repressed', in *Moses and Monotheism*, vol. XXIII (1937–39) of The Standard Edition of the Complete Psychological Works of Sigmund Freud, edited by James Strachey, The Hogarth Press, London 1964, pp. 124–6.

42 Sigmund Freud, 'The Dissection of the Psychical Personality', in *New Introductory Lectures on Psychoanalysis*, vol. XXII (1932–36) of The Standard Edition of the Complete Psychological Works of Sigmund Freud, p. 57.

43 Slavoj Žižek, *The Sublime Object of Ideology*, London 1989, p. 21.

44 Ibid., p. 21.

45 Ibid., p. 22.

46 Ibid., p. 22.

47 Ibid., p. 23.

48 Jacques Rancière, *Disagreement: Politics and Philosophy*, Minneapolis 1998, pp. 13–15; also his 'The Thinking of Dissensus: Politics and Aesthetics', a paper presented at the conference *Fidelity to the Disagreement: Jacques Rancière and the Political*, Goldsmiths College, London, 16–17 September 2003.

49 Claude Lefort, *Democracy and Political Theory*, Cambridge 1988, pp. 217–19.

50 Slavoj Žižek, *For They Know Not What They Do*, London 1991, pp. 194–5.

51 Michel Foucault, *Il faut défendre la société: Cours au Collège de France, 1976*, Paris 1997.

52 Rancière, 1998, pp. 13–15; 2003.

53 Alain Badiou, 'Highly Speculative Reasoning on the Concept of Democracy', *The Symptom* 2, www.lacan.com/conceptsymf.htm, 2002.

54 Canovan, 1999, pp. 9–10.

55 Lefort, 1988, pp. 19–20.

56 Ibid., p. 20.

57 Claude Lefort, 'Démocratie et représentation', in Daniel Pecaut and Bernardo Sorj, eds, *Metamorphoses de la représentation politique*, Paris 1991, p. 230.

58 Oakeshott, 1996, pp. 28–9.

59 See Robert R. Barr, 'The Persistence of Neopopulism in Peru? From Fujimori to Toledo', *Third World Quarterly*, vol. 24, no. 6 (2003), pp. 1,161–78; Kirk Hawkins, 'Populism in Venezuela: The Rise of Chavismo', *Third World Quarterly*, vol. 24, no. 6, 2003, pp. 1,137–60; Kurt Weyland,

'Neopopulism and Neoliberalism in Latin America: How Much Affinity?', *Third World Quarterly*, vol. 24, no. 6, 2003, pp. 1,095–115.

60 Claude Lefort, 'La representación no agota a la democracia', in Fernando Calderón and Mario dos Santos, eds, *¿Qué queda de la representación política?*, Caracas 1992, pp. 141–2.

61 Ibid.

4 OSCAR REYES

1 Stuart Hall, *The Hard Road to Renewal*, London 1988, p. 10.

2 Daniel Collings and Anthony Seldon, 'Conservatives in Opposition', in Pippa Norris, ed., *Britain Votes 2001*, Oxford 2001, p. 64.

3 The phrase 'skinhead Conservatism' was coined by Michael Brown, an *Independent* columnist and former Conservative MP.

4 Ernesto Laclau and Chantal Mouffe, *Hegemony and Socialist Strategy*, London 1985, p. 112.

5 Collings and Seldon, 2001, p. 64.

6 David Marquand, 'The Blair Paradox', *Prospect*, May 1998, p. 19.

7 Ivor Crewe, 'Has the Electorate Become Thatcherite?' in Robert Skidelsky, ed., *Thatcherism*, London 1988, p. 37. Anna Marie Smith has deftly identified the methodological flaws of Crewe's model – the fact that it takes for granted the fixed meaning of highly contested political terms, and its blindness to the genealogical precedents of Thatcherite discourse. See her *New Right Discourses on Race and Sexuality*, Cambridge 1994.

8 Ernesto Laclau, *Politics and Ideology in Marxist Theory*, London 1977, p. 176.

9 Hall, 1998, p. 71.

10 Section 28 was a symbolic ban on the 'promotion of homosexuality'. It was eventually repealed in September 2003.

11 Peregrine Worsthorne, cited in Crewe, 'Has the Electorate Become Thatcherite?', in *Thatcherism*, p. 32.

12 An initial refinement requires that we temporarily banish 'authoritarianism' from our political vocabulary. Hall uses this term to describe the predominant strain within Thatcherism, which took Britain in the direction of intensive state control but represented itself as the advance of the private citizen against the anonymous, bureaucratic state. I go on to argue that authoritarianism runs to the heart of contemporary disputes about the ideological legacy of Thatcherism, and in this sense it continues to have a bearing on

Conservatism's populist aspect. Nevertheless, if we take it as a starting point we risk overlooking contemporary Conservatism's distinctly populist orientation by reducing it to an authoritarian ideological content – and this trap is already overflowing with accounts of Hague's party.

13 P.-A. Taguieff, 'Political science confronts populism', *Telos* 103, 1995, pp. 9–43.

14 Pollard, cited in Michael C. McGee, 'In search of "the people"', in John Lucaites, Celeste Condit and Sally Caudill, eds., *Contemporary Rhetorical Theory: A Reader*, New York 1999, p. 343; Laclau, 1997, p. 165.

15 Peter Wiles, 'A Syndrome, Not a Doctrine: Some Elementary Theses on Populism', in Ghita Ionescu and Ernest Gellner, eds., *Populism: Its Meanings and National Characteristics*, London 1969; Margaret Canovan, *Populism*, London 1981.

16 Unless we share Taggart's highly questionable, and perfectly arbitrary, assumption that nationalism is 'inclusive' in a way that populism is not. Paul Taggart, *Populism*, Buckingham 2000, pp. 96–7.

17 Canovan, 1981, p. 298; Taggart, 2000, p. 21.

18 Laclau, 1977, pp. 174, 195.

19 Ibid., pp. 172–4.

20 Ernesto Laclau, 'Populist Rupture and Discourse', *Screen Education*, Spring 1981, p. 89.

21 Laclau and Mouffe, 1985, pp. 122–7.

22 Ernesto Laclau, 'Why do Empty Signifiers Matter to Politics?', in *Emancipation(s)*, London 1996, pp. 36–47.

23 Ernesto Laclau, 'Identity and Hegemony', in Judith Butler, Ernesto Laclau and Slavoj Žižek, *Contingency, Hegemony, Universality*, London 2000, p. 56.

24 Ernesto Laclau and Lillian Zac, 'Minding the Gap: the Subject of Politics', in Ernesto Laclau, ed., *The Making of Political Identities*, London 1994.

25 'Decontestation' is the name given to any operation that limits the scope of political disputes by normalising and generalising a particular arrangement of meanings and concepts. See Michael Freeden, *Ideologies and Political Theory*, Oxford 1996, pp. 76, 82.

26 William Hague, *Speaking with Conviction*, London 1998, pp. 8–9.

27 Peter Lilley, 'The Free Market Has Only a Limited Role in Improving Public Services', *Guardian*, 20 April 1999.

28 John Bartle, 'Whatever Happened to the Tories?', Department of Government PhD Colloquium, 17 January 2002.

29 Andrew Cooper, 'The Conservative Campaign', in John Bartle, Simon Atkinson and Roger Mortimore, eds., *Political Communications: The General Election Campaign of 2001*, London 2002.

30 At this point it is worth recalling that the language of compassionate Conservatism was borrowed from George W. Bush – whose 'compassion' has never extended to tolerance and inclusiveness in the liberal sense. In relation to this, the Conservatives' drift to the right from 1999 onwards is not an abandonment of compassionate Conservatism but a closer alignment with it. The developing Conservative discourse might then seem more like a shift in emphasis rather than a decisive break.

31 Hague, 1998, pp. 19–20; Conservative Party, *Believing in Britain*, London 2000, p. 6.

32 Hague, 1998, pp. 60–2.

33 This is a narrow definition of tolerance since it has nothing to say about a legislative promotion of *hetero*sexuality that is undoubtedly damaging to the promotion of full equality.

34 Ann Widdecombe, 'The Role of the State in the Promotion of Private Morality', *The Salisbury Review*, vol.18, no.1, pp. 10–11.

35 William Hague, *HC Debs*, 9 February 2000, column 240; Conservative Party, 2000, p. 15; Hague, 1998, p. 56.

36 Smith, *New Right Discourses on Race and Sexuality*, pp. 19–20. In the case of Section 28 the basic move was to normalise 'thresholds of tolerance', which overzealous gay radicals were said to transgress. Homophobia was recast as a 'backlash', and its perpetrators were not perceived to be at fault insofar as their response was an 'entirely natural' reaction by a majority community that felt threatened.

37 Hague, 1998, p. 20; Conservative Party, *Listening to Britain*, London 1999, p. 3; BBC News Online, 'Tory Way is the British Way', 8 October 1998; BBC News Online, 'Hague: Compassion Key to Tory Revival', 12 February 1999.

38 Norman Fairclough, *New Labour, New Language?*, London 2000, p. 163. Overwording is especially pronounced when it extends across different policy fields, as is the case here.

39 All of these descriptions appear in the *Listening to Britain* document. Some of the fairly banal assumptions are nevertheless significant in terms of their antonyms. Britishness, for example, is opposed to the EU (and Whitehall). In the case of the taxpayer (formerly 'rate-payer'), the Thatcherite precedent is to see this as a code for a certain kind of normalised citizen.

40 Political discourse theory would challenge this argument on the grounds that both linguistic and non-linguistic elements are internal to the totality of Conservative discourse. See Ernesto Laclau and Chantal Mouffe, 'Postmarxism without Apologies', in Ernesto Laclau, *New Reflections on the Revolution of our Time*, London 1990, p. 100.

41 Philip Cowley and Stuart Quayle, 'The Conservatives: Running on the Spot' in Andrew Geddes and Jonathan Tonge, eds, *Labour's Second Landslide*, Manchester 2002, pp. 47–64.

42 William Hague, 'Change and Renewal are Always Difficult' *Guardian*, 28 April 1999.

43 The ontological is the terrain of presuppositions, and opens to question the fundamental bases of politics. The ontic refers to the particular set of practices that is available within any given horizon. See Stephen Mulhall, *Heidegger and 'Being and Time'*, London 1996, p. 4.

44 Laclau and Mouffe, 1985, pp. 105–14.

45 Jean Laplanche and J.-B. Pontalis, *The Language of Pyschoanalysis*, London 1973, pp. 82–3. Nodal points are literally 'privileged condensations of meaning'. David Howarth, *Discourse*, Buckingham 2000, p. 110.

46 It may well be, as Butler and Kavanagh suggest, that Conservative Party spin doctors made the connection between the 'foreign land' and asylum while briefing journalists. But this in no way detracts from my point, because the very plausibility of this spin, and hence its widespread acceptance, suggests that these issues have already been successfully articulated. David Butler and Dennis Kavanagh, *The British General Election of 2001*, Basingstoke 2001, p. 62.

47 Joel Dor, *Introduction to the Reading of Lacan*, New York 1998, pp. 45–50.

48 Laclau and Mouffe, 1985, p. 139.

49 Fairclough, *New Labour, New Language?*, p. 34.

50 Anthony Barnett, 'Corporate control', *Prospect*, February 1999, p. 28. In this respect, Labour continues in the same vein as the Major Government's Citizens' Charter.

51 Jeremy Gilbert, 'Towards a Democratic Populism', *Signs of the Times*, September 2000, www.signsofthetimes.org.uk/dp1.html.

52 Marquand, 'The Blair Paradox', p. 19.

53 Cited in Simon Walters, *Tory Wars: Conservatives in Crisis*, London 2001, pp. 56, 107.

54 *Times*, 6 July 1998.

55 Ivan Massow, 'The Tory Party Has Become Nasty and Intolerant', *Independent*, 2 August 2000; Andrew Grice, 'In Perfect Harmony: the Enforcer and the Defector', *Independent*, 3 August 2000.

56 BBC News Online, 'The Bald Truth about Politics?', 19 June 2001.

57 Michael Foley, *The British Presidency*, Manchester 2000, p. 237.

58 Philip Norton, 'The Conservative Party: Is There Anyone Out There?', in Anthony King, ed., *Britain at the Polls*, Chatham 2001, p. 68: 'The Conservative Party lost the 2001 general election nearly nine years before it took place.'

59 David Sanders et al., 'The Economy and Voting', *Parliamentary Affairs*, 2001, pp. 789–90.

5 GLENN BOWMAN

Research in the Israeli-Occupied Territories was largely funded by the Wenner Gren Foundation for Anthropological Research, while fieldwork in Former Yugoslavia was made possible by a grant from the Economic and Social Research Council. Preparation of this text was generously supported by the Harry Frank Guggenheim Foundation.

1 Anderson, *Imagined Communities: Reflections on the Origins and Spread of Nationalism*, London 1991.

2 Laclau and Mouffe 1985, pp. 93ff.

3 Both the genesis and the structure of nationalist identity are uncannily paralleled in what Sigmund Freud describes as the formation of infantile ego. Freud contends that the infant is forced to make a primary distinction between itself and an outside it initially, narcissistically sees as continuous with itself, because it senses, in the way the source of its sustenance (breast or bottle) is 'taken' from it against its will, an external violence which hurts and deprives it (Freud 1963a, pp. 66–9, 416).

A further incentive to a disengagement of the ego from the general mass of sensations – that is, to the recognition of an 'outside', an external world – is provided by the frequent, manifold and unavoidable sensations of pain and unpleasure ... A tendency arises to separate from the ego everything that can become a source of such unpleasure, to throw it outside and to create a pure pleasure-ego which is confronted by a strange and threatening 'outside' (Freud, 1963b, p. 67).

I have elsewhere used psychoanalytic categories in approaching questions of xenophobic hatred in Yugoslavia (Bowman, 1994b, especially pp. 160–5).

4 M. Taussig, *Shamanism, Colonialism and the Wild Man: A Study in Terror and Healing*, Chicago 1987, pp. 3–36; and Kapferer, *Legends of People/Myths of State: Violence, Intolerance and Political Culture in Sri Lanka and Australia*, Washington, D. C., 1988, pp. 1–26.

5 J. Peters, *From Time Immemorial: The Origins of the Arab-Jewish Conflict over Palestine*, 1984. In 1922 the total population of Palestine (excluding the occupying British forces) was 752,048, of which 589,177 persons were indigenous Muslims (including 103,000 Bedouin), 71,464 indigenous Christians and 83,790 resident Jews, both indigenous and immigrant (Palestine 1946: 141). The remaining 7,617 persons were foreign nationals residing in Christian monasteries and institutions. Peters' thesis, which in effect elaborates Golda Meir's famous assertion that Palestine is a land without a people for a people without a land, has been contested by scholars in the UK, US and Israel (see Finkelstein, 1988, pp. 61–3 for an account of the critical scholarship).

6 See Asali, 1989, p. 206; Abu-Jaber, 1967; Cohen and Lewis, 1978.

7 Betts, 1975, p. 112.

8 See Tamari, 1982, pp. 181–5; Hourani, 1991, p. 30; Lapidus, 1988, p. 363.

9 See Muslih, 1988, pp. 47–54, 58–68; Lesch, 1979, pp. 23–74; Antonius, 1938, pp. 79–148; Hourani, 1991, pp. 258–62.

10 Aaronsohn, 1983, Abu-Lughod, 1971; Ruedy, 1971.

11 Zionist insistence on *avodah ivrit* (Hebrew labour) meant that Jewish land could not be worked by non-Jews. As a result 'settlers refused to let neighbouring villagers and bedouin tribes continue to have customary pasture rights on their lands' (Lesch, 1979; p. 28). As early as 1886 the villagers of al-Yahudiyya, after a dispute over grazing rights, attacked the Jewish colony at Petah Tikva (Muslih, 1988; pp. 71–2) and other armed clashes occurred between peasants and settlers in Tiberias (1901–02) and 'Affula (1911) when local Arabs discovered the land they lived on had been sold from under their feet (Ibid, p. 72).

12 Ruedy, 1971, p. 131.

13 See Lesch, 1979, p. 206.

14 Scholch, 1989, pp. 243–5.

15 Lesch, 1979, p. 99; see also Porath, 1974, p. 241ff.

16 Johnson, 1982, p. 57; see also Tamari, 1982.

17 1971.

18 1971.
19 Ibrahim Abu-Lughod, cited in Waines, 1971, p. 220.
20 Government of Palestine 1946, pp. 19, 34–58; see also Waines, 1971, p. 234.
21 See Hilal, 1992.
22 Morris, 1987, pp. 297–8.
23 Waines, 1971, p. 207.
24 Sayigh, 1979, p. 107.
25 See Tamari, 1982, p. 180; Lustick, 1980, p. 48; Brand, 1988, pp. 1–21.
26 Lustick, 1980.
27 *cf.* Lustick, 1989; Cohen, 1965; Asad, 1975; Morris 1987.
28 Bowman, 1994a.
29 Brand, 1988, p. 28.
30 Brand, 1988, p. 26; see also Cobban, 1984 and Gresh, 1985, on the origins of the PLO.
31 *cf.* Laclau and Mouffe, 1985; pp. 129–130; Bauman, 1989, pp. 26–7.
32 Bowman, 1993a, 1993b, and 1994a.
33 See Cobban, 1984: p. 26.
34 Said, 1993, p. 5.
35 Usher, 1995, pp. 61–83; Bowman, 1999, pp. 73–5.
36 John Allcock's recent *Explaining Yugoslavia* (Allcock, 2000) provides an excellent overview of the development of Yugoslavia, integrating economic, social and cultural determinants and characteristics in a comprehensive and convincing manner. Pavlowitch's work focuses a similar scope and objectivity on the narrower field of Serbia (see Pavlowitch, 1998 and 2002).
37 The salient issue then, as now, was the *Krajina*, a region of present-day Eastern Croatia which had been the frontier line between the Austro-Hungarian and Turkish empires and had been populated not only by Serbs fleeing the Turks but also by Serbs who were recruited into the area by the Austro-Hungarians after 1689 to serve as a defensive shield against the Ottomans along that borderline (Hammel 1993a: 37, see also Hammel 1993b).
38 Pavlowitch, 1988, pp. 2–4.
39 Slovenia and the Dalmatian coast were ceded to Italy, which promoted fascism as an explicit ideology rather than Slovene nationalism *per se* (Clissold, 1968, 209), but in the 'Independent State of Croatia' the German administration fomented the viciously anti-Serb and anti-Jewish Croatian nationalism of Ante Pavelic and his *Ustaše* while in Serbia the Nazis

promoted a loose confederation of Serbian nationalists led by Milan Nedić and Dimitrije Ljotić, which was frequently backed by nominally anti-Nazi yet fiercely nationalist and anti-Muslim *četnici* led by Draña Mihajlović.

40 Banać, 1992, p. 18.
41 Garde, 1992.
42 Pavlowitch, 1988, p. 14.
43 Clissold, 1966, p. 216.
44 Godina, 1998.
45 Auty, 1966, p. 247.
46 Pavlowitch, 1988, pp. 22–25.
47 See Derrida, 1974, pp. 39–44; Staten, 1985, pp. 16–19.
48 Ramet, 1992, 55.
49 See Simmie, 1991 on self-management.
50 See Allcock, 1992, pp. 278, 282–3.
51 Shoup, 1992, p. 52.
52 Pavlowitch, 1988, p. 27.
53 See Pavlowitch 1988, p. 31 and Mencinger, 1991, pp. 76–9.
54 Mastnak, 1991.
55 Pavlowitch, 1988, p. 22.
56 Cottrell, 1990.
57 Meier, 1999, pp. 38–43 and pp. 71–84.
58 Salecl, 1993, pp. 79–81.
59 Rape was used by Bosnian Serbs as a means of terrorizing their Bosnian foes after the war had spread to Bosnia in 1991. The logic of expropriation of the bodies of the enemy, already evident in anti-Kosovan propaganda, was there turned against non-Serbs. Women were mass raped until they became pregnant, after which they were kept in captivity until they bore the rapists' children. Not only was the Serb theft of their enemies' women thus monumentalised, but the Serbs were also thus able to reenact an ancient tactic celebrated in the Serbian epics which chronicled their ancient struggle against the Ottomans. In the BBC2 *Bookmark* programme entitled 'Serbian Epics', Radovan Karadñic, leader of the Bosnian Serbs, sings to the accompaniment of the *guzla* (a single-stringed bowed instrument) the lines 'beautiful Turkish woman, your child will be baptised by a priest'.
60 Ramet, 1992, p. 230.
61 The embodiment of this anti-Serb cabal was, of course, Tito himself, who was both a communist and a Croat (both Comintern and Vatican) and had

occupied the position – dictator of the Yugoslav state – which Milošević intended to usurp (see Ramet, 1992, 226).

62   Norris, 1993, pp. 271–7.

63   Darby, 1966, pp. 96–102.

64   Speech given by Milošević on 19 November 1988, quoted in Ramet, 1992, p. 230.

65   *cf.* Žižek, 1990, on 'nation theft'.

66   See Aspeslagh, 1992; Canak, 1993; Cegorovic, 1993; Poulton 1991, pp. 39–56.

67   See Eric Gordy, *The Culture of Power in Serbia: Nationalism and the Destruction of Alternatives*, University Park 1999, for an extended cataloguing of the ways in which Serbian nationalism in the 1990s came to articulate – and subsume – all aspirations.

68   Godina, 1998.

69   Pavlowitch, 1988, p. 25.

70   Ballinger, 2003.

71   Tudjman quoted in Denich, 1994, p. 377.

72   The wealth of bones in post-war Yugoslavia was providential. As Bloch indicates in his work on Madagascar funerary practices (Bloch, 1982 and 1989, p. 170), bones emblematize undifferentiated community because they are what remains after individuating characteristics have rotted away.

73   Denich, 1991, p. 11.

74   Bowman, 1994b.

75   See Anderson, 1991, pp. 35–6 and, for a critique, Bowman, 1994a.

76   See Althusser, 1971, pp. 152–65.

77   Whether these signs be markers and agencies of individuality such as the eyes, noses and genitals which were carved from the bodies of the enemies or of a cultural presence like the houses, churches and mosques which were desecrated and then destroyed and built over (see Bowman 1994b).

78   An idiom in which the nation remains unrealised, as distinct from a pure designative indication of an existing site.

79   Lacan, 1977, p. 303.

80   See Bowman, 2001.

81   Figures on support for bombings from a *Jerusalem Media and Communications Centre* survey carried out in June 2002; figures on support for negotiations and a peace settlement from a survey carried out at the same time by Birzeit University's *Department of Development Studies* (both sets of statistics supplied

by the Information Office of the Centre for the Advancement of Arab-British Understanding, London). Interesting, and in a bleak way encouraging, is the fact that similar percentiles of the Israeli population support the expulsion of all Palestinians from the West Bank, Gaza and Israel proper *and* the completion of a peace process entailing the creation of a Palestinian state. It is clear, in both the Palestinian and Israeli cases, that a not insubstantial number of people are voting for all options.

6 JOE LOWNDES

1 On populism's shift from left to right, see Michael Kazin, *The Populist Persuasion: An American History*, New York 1995. On conventional American views of the right in the mid-1960s, see Jerome Himmelstein, *To the Right: The Transformation of American Conservatism*, Berkeley 1992; and Daniel Bell, ed., *The Radical Right*, third edition, New York 2001.

2 See in particular Dan T. Carter, *From George Wallace to Newt Gingrich: Race in the Conservative Counterrevolution 1963–1994*, Baton Rouge 1996; *The Politics of Rage: George Wallace, the Origins of the New Conservatism, and the Transformation of American Politics*, New York 1996; Kazin, *Populist Persuasion*, pp. 221–44.

3 On the racial structure of the New Deal, see Michael K. Brown, 'Race in the American Welfare State: The Ambiguities of Universalistic Social Policy Since the New Deal', and Dennis R. Judd, 'Symbolic Politics and Urban Policies: Why African Americans Got So Little from the Democrats', in Adolph Reed, ed., *Without Justice For All: The New Liberalism and Our Retreat from Racial Equality*, Boulder 1999; George Lipsitz, *The Possessive Investment in Whiteness*, Berkeley 1998; Douglass S. Massey and Nancy Denton, *American Apartheid: Segregation and the Making of the Underclass*, Cambridge, 1993; Jill Quadagno, *The Color of Welfare: How Racism Undermined the War on Poverty*, New York 1994.

4 This observation about foundational violence was made best perhaps by Niccolo Machiavelli. See *The Prince*, trans. George Bull, New York 1981, pp. 77, 99; and *The Discourses*, trans. Peter Bondanella and Mark Musa, New York 1970, pp. 132, 134.

5 Ernesto Laclau and Chantal Mouffe, *Hegemony and Socialist Strategy: Toward a Radical Democratic Politics*, London 1985, pp. 65–71.

6 Ibid., pp. 105–14.

7 Laclau, *Emancipation(s)*, London 1996, pp. 43.

8 Ibid., pp. 36–46.

9   In Kazin's words, 'As a metaphor, Middle America evoked, simultaneously, three compelling meanings: the unstylish, traditionalist expanse that lay between the two coasts; an egalitarian social status most citizens either claimed or desired; and a widespread feeling of being squeezed between penthouse and ghetto – between a condescending elite above and scruffy demonstrators below.' (*Populist Persuasion*, p. 253).

10 On politics and the friend/enemy distinction, see Carl Schmitt, *The Concept of the Political*, Chicago 1996; also Chantal Mouffe, *The Return of the Political*, London 1993, pp. 117–34.

11 Machiavelli asserts in the *Discourses* that violence has great capacity to found and shape, as well as shatter and dissolve, political identifications (p. 134). For Freud, the trauma of violence can create new identities, both because new identifications are forged out of the subject's attempt to manage traumatic loss, and because the process of identification itself involves violence. Freud, 'Mourning and Melancholia', from *General Psychological Theory*, New York 1963, p.170; *Civilization and its Discontents*, New York 1963a; and *Group Psychology and the Analysis of the Ego*, New York 1985, p. 46–53. Fanon explicitly links the forging of political identity to violence through contingent, critical events. See Fanon, *The Wretched of the Earth*, New York 1963. Such violence, both material and symbolic, has particular significance in the American context, where the cultural meanings assigned to violence have defined and redefined the identity of the nation itself at critical moments. See Richard Slotkin, *Regeneration Through Violence: The Mythology of the American Frontier, 1600–1860*, Middletown 1973; and *Gunfighter Nation*, New York 1992. See also Anne Norton, *Reflections on Political Identity*, Baltimore 1993, pp. 143–84.

12 On violence and forgetting, see Friedrich Nietzsche, *The Genealogy of Morals*, trans. Walter Kaufmann, New York 1967, second essay, section 2; Benedict Anderson, *Imagined Communities*, London 1994, p. 6; Jacques Derrida, 'Force of Law: The "Mystical Foundation of Authority"', *Cardozo Law Review* 919, 1990.

13 On this notion of readability, see Slavoj Žižek, *The Ticklish Subject*, New York 1999, pp. 179–80.

14 This position was put forth in a number of texts, among them Seymour Lipset, *Political Man*, New York 1963, pp. 119–23; Charles W. Grigg, 'Fundamental Principles of Democracy', *Journal of Politics*, vol. 22, Spring 1960, pp. 276–94; G.H. Smith, 'Liberalism and Level of Information', *Journal of Educational Psychology*, vol. 39, 1948: pp. 65–82.

15 Gunnar Myrdal, *An American Dilemma, Volume I: The Negro Problem and Modern Democracy*, New Brunswick 1996 [1944].

16 On the formation and historical role of whiteness in the US, see David R. Roediger, *The Wages of Whiteness: Race and the Making of the American Working Class*, New York 1991; Toni Morrison, *Playing in the Dark: Whiteness and the Literary Imagination*, New York 1990.

17 Describing this same phenomenon in different language, Edward Carmines and James Stimson see race as an ideological position that has replaced the traditional liberal/conservative divide. See Edward G. Carmines and James A. Stimson, *Race and the Transformation of American Politics*, Princeton 1989, pp. 115–37.

18 Dan T. Carter, *From George Wallace to Newt Gingrich: Race in the Conservative Counterrevolution, 1963–1994*, Louisiana 1999, p. 109.

19 'Speech of Governor George C. Wallace at University of Alabama, January 14, 1963', Microfilm, Governor's Papers, Alabama Department of Archives and History.

20 A few days before his inauguration, Wallace told a group of state senators, 'I'm gonna make race the basis of politics in this state, and I'm gonna make it the basis of politics in this country.' Marshal Frady, *Wallace*, New York 1968, p. 143.

21 Wallace Inaugural Speech, 14 January 1963.

22 Ibid., p. 5.

23 As his Connecticut campaign chairman would say in 1968, 'Alabama is part of the United States and soon the United States will become part of Alabama.' Carol Miller, *The Day*, New London, CT, June 29, 1968.

24 Interview with Former Alabama Attorney General Richmond Flowers in the PBS documentary film 'Settin' the Woods on Fire', 2000.

25 *Meet the Press*, 2 June 1963, Microfilm, Governor's Papers, Alabama Department of Archives and History.

26 'Speech of Governor George C. Wallace at University of Alabama, June 11, 1963', Microfilm, Governor's Papers, Alabama Department of Archives and History.

27 Carter, 1999, p. 154.

28 'Speech Prepared for Delivery by George C. Wallace, Governor of Alabama, Organization Against Communism, Cleveland Ohio, June 11, 1964', Microfilm, Governor's Papers, Alabama Department of Archives and History, p. 2.

29 Stephen Lesher, *George Wallace: American Populist*, Reading, MA, 1995, p. 273.

30 Ibid., p. 280.

31 Carter, 1999, p. 213.

32 Ibid.

33 On the complex relationship of race and ethnicity in twentieth-century American politics, and particularly of Southern and Eastern Europeans from the second great wave of immigration, see Victoria Hattam, *Shadows of Pluralism: The Racial Politics of American Ethnicity*, esp. Chapter 3, 'Constitutive Exclusions: Fixing Race, Constructing Ethnicity', manuscript, 2001. For a very different account, see Matthew Frye Jacobson, *Whiteness of a Different Color: European Immigrants and the Alchemy of Race*, Cambridge, MA, 1999.

34 Lesher, *George Wallace*, p. 200. See also Jody Carlson, *George C. Wallace and the Politics of Powerlessness*, New York 1981, p. 35.

35 As the southern intellectual and Dixiecrat leader Charles Wallace Collins said, 'The white Southerner has been able to preserve his Anglo-Saxon heritage to a remarkable degree.' *Whither Solid South*, New Orleans 1947, p. 4.

36 Bill Jones, *The Wallace Story*, Northport, AL, 1966, p. 188.

37 Lesher, *George Wallace*, p. 300.

38 Seymour Martin Lipset, 'Beyond the Backlash,' *Encounter*, vol. 23, November 1964, p. 1.

39 Lipset, *Political Man*, pp. 119–23; Charles W. Gregg, 'Fundamental Principles of Democracy', *Journal of Politics*, vol. 22, Spring 1960, pp. 276–94; G.H. Smith, 'Liberalism and Level of Information', pp. 65–82.

40 Michael Rogin, 'Wallace and the Middle Class: The White Backlash in Wisconsin', *Public Opinion Quarterly* 30, Spring 1966, pp. 98–108.

41 See Hazel Erskine, 'The Polls: Demonstrations and Race Riots', *Public Opinion Quarterly* 31, Winter 1967–68.

42 Jules Witcover, *The Year the Dream Died: Revisiting 1968 in America*, New York 1997, p. 78.

43 Carlson, *George C. Wallace and the Politics of Powerlessness*, p. 129.

44 Ibid.

45 Cited in 'The Extreme Right Invasion of the 1968 Campaign', Anti-Defamation League of B'nai B'rith, 1968, p. 478.

46 *Boston Herald Traveler*, 9 October 1968, p. 3.

47 Carter, 1999, p. 346.

48 'Third Parties: Collision Course', *Newsweek*, 18 March 1968, p. 48.

49 'The Extreme Right Invasion of the 1968 Campaign', B'nai B'rith, p. 479.

50 The 1964 primary campaign in Indiana, for instance, was organised by two Alabama Klan members, Wallace speechwriter Asa Carter and Grand Dragon Robert Shelton, out of the service-station payphone of a local Indiana Klansman. See Jones, *The Wallace Story*.

51 Or as he once said on *Meet the Press*, 'I am an anti-Nazi. I fought Nazism in World War II, and I think it was one of the worst philosophies ever engendered in the world. I repudiate the support of anyone who says he wants to return to Nazism.' *Meet The Press*, NBC-TV, 23 April 1967.

52 Tom Wicker, *Harper's*, April 1967, cited in 'The Extreme Right Invasion of the 1968 Campaign', B'nai B'rith, 1968, p. 477.

53 'Statement of Governor George C. Wallace, Montgomery, Alabama, June 5, 1968', Ewing Papers, box 3, folder 2, Alabama Department of Archives and History.

54 'Governor's Statement on Killing of Martin Luther King', Ewing Papers, box 3, folder 2, Alabama Department of Archives and History. Reporter Jules Witcover describes a conversation with Wallace about the riots that followed King's assassination that captures the thin line between principle and opportunism on which Wallace walked in relation to bloodshed. 'I don't think about it in terms of how it helps or hurts politics', he said. 'I just hope they catch the one who did it. I wish we could stop all this shooting.' He flicked cigar ashes into a wastebasket, then went on. 'Of course, any break-down in law and order is going to support the position of anybody like me who is against a breakdown in law and order.' He paused, then added, 'Now I don't want to be helped that way. I don't want to see any headlines that say Wallace is helped by the riots. All I say is they seem to be getting worse and nobody wants to try to stop it. And that's all I want to say about that particular subject.' Witcover, *The Year the Dream Died*, p. 162.

55 Quoted in Kazin, *Populist Persuasion*, p. 222.

56 'The Extreme Right Invasion of the 1968 Campaign', B'nai B'rith, p. 480.

57 Nelson Lichtenstein, *The Most Dangerous Man in Detroit: Walter Reuther and the Fate of American Labor*, New York 1995, p. 428.

58 'A Voter's Lexicon of "Wallacisms"', *New York Times*, 25 August 1968.

59 In his study of culturally liminal figures, Victor Turner highlights the role of the jester as a privileged arbiter of a kind of communitas against the reigning stratifications of a given social and political structure. Turner, *The Ritual Process: Structure and Anti-structure*, Chicago 1969, p. 110.

60 Kevin Phillips, *The Emerging Republican Majority*, New Rochelle, 1969.

61 Ibid., p. 471.

62 Carter, 1999, p. 117.

63 William C. Berman, *America's Right Turn From Nixon to Clinton*, Baltimore 1998, p. 13–14.

64 'Speech by George C. Wallace, Governor of Alabama, to National Press Club', Washington, DC, 6 December 1971, Microfilm, Governor's Papers, Alabama Department of Archives and History.

65 *Meet the Press*, transcript of telecast, 22 August, vol. 15, no. 33, NBC News, Washington, DC, 1971.

66 Ibid., p. 417.

67 Ibid., p. 200.

68 Jules Witcover, *Marathon: The Pursuit of the Presidency 1972–1976*, New York 1976, p. 169.

69 'Wallace Defeats Carter Three-To-One in Mississippi Test', *New York Times*, 21 January 1976, p. 1.

70 Kazin, 1995, p. 5.

71 See for instance Thomas Byrne and Mary Edsall, *Chain Reaction: The Impact of Race, Rights, and Taxes on American Politics*, New York 1992; Jim Sleeper, *The Closest of Strangers*, New York 1990; Todd Gitlin, *The Twilight of Common Dreams: Why America is Wracked by the Culture Wars*, New York 1995; Ruy Teixeira and Joel Rogers, *Why the White Working Class Still Matters: America's Forgotten Majority*, New York 2000.

72 I draw this Lacanian insight on political formation from Peter Stallybrass, 'Marx and Heterogeneity: Thinking the Lumpenproletariat', *Representations* 31, Summer 1990.

7 DAVID LAYCOCK

1 Ernesto Laclau, *Politics and Ideology in Marxist Theory*, London 1977, Ch. 4.

2 David Laycock, *Populism and Democratic Thought in the Canadian Prairies, 1910–45*, Toronto 1990.

3 See Margaret Canovan, 'Trust the People! Populism and the Two Faces of Democracy', *Political Studies* vol. XLVII, 1999, 4.

4 For a good brief introduction, see Alain-G. Gagnon, ed., *Québec Politics and Society*, 2nd ed., Toronto 1993.

5 This is so partly because many Reform politicians portrayed Québec's provincial and federal politicians as a major reason for western Canadian maltreatment within the federal polity, partly because Reform's new-right

agenda was unattractive in Québec's more social democratic political culture, and partly because Québec voters have never supported third parties with non-Québec origins.

6   See Laycock, 1990, Ch. 1 and 2.

7   Vernon Fowke, *The National Policy and the Wheat Economy*, Toronto 1957.

8   See Laycock, 1990.

9   Ibid, ch. 2. The term 'crypto-Liberalism' originates with W. L. Morton, *The Progressive Party in Canada*, Toronto: University of Toronto Press, 1950.

10 Laycock, *Populism and Democratic Thought*, Ch. 3.

11 C.B. Macpherson offered a perceptive account of Aberhart's theories, appeal and governance style in his, *Democracy in Alberta*, Toronto 1954.

12 See David Laycock, 'Making Sense of Reform as a Western party', Ch. 8 in Laycock, *The New Right and Democracy in Canada: Understanding Reform and the Canadian Alliance*, Toronto 2001.

13 Ernest and Preston Manning, *Political Re-Alignment: A Challenge to Thoughtful Canadians*, Toronto 1967.

14 See Tom Flanagan, *Waiting for the Wave: The Reform Party and Preston Manning*, Toronto 1995.

15 More details regarding Reform Party policy can be found in Laycock, *The New Right and Democracy in Canada*, especially Chs. 4 and 8.

16 According to a Canadian Labour Congress survey, the NDP in 2000 attracted only 12 per cent of the trade union vote, compared to 41 per cent by the Liberals, and 27 per cent by the Alliance Party. And among private sector trade unionists, the Alliance Party out-polled the NDP 37 per cent to 13 per cent. The Alliance Party also tied the Liberals in attracting 30 per cent of the low-income vote ($20,000 or lower), well ahead of the NDP at 12 per cent. Cited in Jeffrey Simpson, 'Which Way Now for the Friendless NDP?' *The Globe and Mail*, 28 February 2001, A13.

17 See Elisabeth Gidengil, André Blais, Neil Nevitte and Richard Nadeau, 'The Correlates and Consequences of Anti-Partyism in the 1997 Canadian Election', *Party Politics*, vol. 7, no. 4, 2001, pp. 491–513.

18 See James Bickerton, Alain-G. Gagnon, and Patrick J. Smith, *Ties That Bind: Parties and Voters in Canada*, Toronto 1999, Ch. 4.

19 Hanspeter Kriesi, 'Movements of the Left, Movements of the Right: Putting the Mobilisation of Two New Types of Social Movements into Political Context', in Herbert Kitschelt, Peter Lange, Gary Marks and John D. Stephens, eds., *Continuity and Change in Contemporary Capitalism*, New York

1999, pp. 398–423.

20 See Lisa Young, 'Value Clash: Parliament and Citizens after 150 Years of Responsible Government', in F. Leslie Seidle and Louis Massicotte, eds., *Taking Stock of 150 Years of Responsible Government in Canada*, Ottawa: Canadian Study of Parliament Group, 1999.

For a discussion of the blending of Christian fundamentalism and American right-wing populism, see Amy E. Ansell, ed., *Unraveling the Right: The New Conservatism in American Thought and Politics*, Boulder 1998, and Chip Berlet and Matthew Lyons, *Right-Wing Populism in America*, New York 2000, Ch. 10–12. On the Canadian case, see Bruce Foster, 'New Right, Old Canada: An Analysis of the Political Thought and Activities of Selected Contemporary Right-Wing Organisations', PhD Dissertation, Department of Political Science, University of British Columbia, 2000.

21 Regarding reasons for Reform Party support or membership, see Harold Clarke, A. Kornberg, F. G. Ellis, and J. Rapkin, 'Not for Fame or Fortune: A Note on Membership and Activity in the Canadian Reform Party', *Party Politics*, vol. 6, no.1, 2000, pp. 75–93, and Keith Archer and Faron Ellis, 'Opinion Structure of Party Activists: The Reform Party of Canada', *Canadian Journal of Political Science*, vol. 27, no. 2, 1994, pp. 277–308.

22 Gidengil et al., 'The Correlates and Consequences of Anti-Partyism'.

23 Ibid.

24 1997 Reform Party supporters were more than twice as likely as other party supporters to call for less spending on aboriginals. See André Blais, Elisabeth Gidengil, Richard Nadeau and Neil Nevitte, *Unsteady State: The 1997 Canadian General Election*, Toronto 1999, p. 100.

25 For relevant background, see the Reform Party's 1996 *Task Force Report on Aboriginal Affairs*.

26 See especially Hans-Georg Betz, *Radical Right-Wing Populism in Western Europe*, London 1994, and Herbert Kitschelt, *The Radical Right in Western Europe*, Ann Arbor 1996.

For more detail in this regard, see Laycock, *The New Right and Democracy in Canada*, Ch. 3, and Darin D. Barney, 'Push-button Populism: The Reform Party and the Real World of Teledemocracy', *Canadian Journal of Communication*, vol. 21, no. 3, 1996, pp. 381–413.

27 Preston Manning, *The New Canada*, Toronto 1990, p. 321. 'Family Compacts' refers to the self-appointed elite that dominated politics and

society in Ontario in the first half of the nineteenth century, before representative government was granted to the Canadian colonies. In this sense, Manning is making effective use of what Laclau refers to as a 'popular democratic interpellation,' with which populists can remind 'the people' about previous struggles against elites, thereby collecting additional democratic bona fides.

28   For the Australian case, see the chapters by Marian Sawer and Carol Johnson in Marian Sawer and Barry Hindess, eds, *Us and Them: Anti-Elitism in Australia*, Perth: API Press, 2004.

29   For the argument that conservative ideologies are typified by such 'mirror-imaging' discursive strategies, see Michael Freeden, *Ideologies and Political Theory*, Oxford 1996, pp. 336–43.

30   For an account of this battleground in interwar Canadian prairie politics, see Laycock, 1990, Chs. 4–6.

31   See Michael Kazin, *The Populist Persuasion: An American History*, revised edition, Ithaca 1995, especially Introduction, Ch. 10 and 11, and Conclusion.

32   This was a favourite expression of Preston Manning in *The New Canada* and many of his public speeches. See Steve Patten, 'Preston Manning's Populism: Constructing the Common Sense of the Common People', *Studies in Political Economy*, vol. 50, 1996, pp. 95–132.

33   The most notable European new-right party achievements in this regard belong to Jorge Haider's Freedom Party in Austria.

34   Darin Barney and David Laycock, 'Right-populists and Plebiscitary Politics in Canada,' *Party Politics*, vol. 5, no. 3, 1999, pp. 317–39.

35   The Reform Party may have picked up the idea of 'electronic town halls' from Ross Perot's promotion of this anti-party mechanism. See Dennis Westlind, *The Politics of Popular Identity: Understanding Recent Populist Movements in Sweden and the United States*, Lund 1996, pp. 181–82.

36   See Darin D. Barney, 'Push-button Populism', and Barney 'The Recline of Party: Armchair Democracy and the Reform Party of Canada', *American Review of Canadian Studies*, Winter 1996, pp. 577–605.

37   See Barney and Laycock (1999), and Laycock, *The New Right and Democracy in Canada*, Ch. 5 and 6.

38   Following Harris's resignation as Premier of Ontario, Toronto's *Globe and Mail* newspaper – a regular source of media support for Harris-style economic and social policy – commented editorially that Harris has consistently 'treated critics as malevolent obstacles in the path of his

right-thinking crusade.' See *The Globe and Mail*, 'Ontario's Next Leader', 22 October 2001, A14.

39 This was the title given to the 1995 Ontario Progressive Conservative manifesto, a name that they proudly attached to their two terms in office. They lost power in an October 2003 election.

40 In http://www.conservative.ca/english/documents/agreement.pdf, searched 7 January 2004.

41 The NDP held provincial power in Ontario from 1990 to 1995, and in British Columbia from 1991–2001. As of January 2004, in Ontario, the NDP is a distant third in a three-party race, while in BC, the NDP now holds only 2 seats to the right-wing Liberal party's 77 in a 79-seat legislature.

42 See Laycock (2001), Ch. 5 and 6.

43 See http://www.newpolitics.ca for this proposal.

44 For a good account of the formation and dynamics of this coalition in the 1980s, see Jeffrey Ayers, *Defying Conventional Wisdom: Political Movements and Popular Contention against North American Free Trade*, Toronto 1998. An update on the themes and dynamics in the looser, post-1988 coalition can be most easily obtained by a visit to the website of the Council of Canadians, at http://www.canadians.org

45 See Lynda Erickson and David Laycock, 'Post-Materialism vs. the Welfare State? Opinion among English Canadian Social Democrats,' *Party Politics*, vol. 8, no. 3, 2002, pp. 301–326.

46 A classic example of this was the 1993 federal Liberal election campaign promise to dramatically amend the North American Free Trade Agreement, followed by inaction once elected. In the 1988 'free trade election,' the Liberal opposition party had presented itself as the champion of Canadian culture and social programs against the 'continentalizing' agenda of the incumbent Conservative government.

47 For a good example of this, see http://www.rabble.ca

48 Berlet and Lyons, *Right-Wing Populism in America*, focus on the militant, 'World government' conspiracy wing of right-wing populism, not on the mainstream right-populism discussed by Kazin in *The Populist Persuasion*. The former group is a tiny fraction of Canada's right-populist spectrum.

49 In this sense, right-populism employs a historically powerful 'producer ethic', highlighted by both Kazin, in *The Populist Persuasion*, and Berlet and Lyons, in *Right-Wing Populism in America*.

50 Kazin, 1995, p. 289.

8 DAVID HOWARTH

1 The Ossewabrandwag (Ox wagon Sentinel), an Afrikaner nationalist
   movement active in the late 1930s and early 1940s, has also been described
   and analysed in populist terms. See 'The "Ossewabrandwag" as a Mass
   Movement, 1939–1941', *Journal of South African Studies*, 20 (2), Marx, 1994.

2 G. Maré and G. Hamilton, *An Appetite for Power*, Johannesburg 1987, p. 6.

3 R.M, Levine, 'Class Struggle, Popular Democratic Struggle and the South
   African State', *Review of African Politcal Economy*, 40, 1987; T. Lodge,
   'Rebellion: The Turning of the Tide', in T. Lodge and B. Nasson, eds, *All,
   Here and Now! Black Politics in South Africa in the 1980s*, London 1991;
   J. Seekings, *The UDF: A History of the United Democratic Front in South Africa,
   1983–1991*, Ohio 2000; I. van Kessel, *'Beyond our Wildest Dreams': The
   United Democratic Front and the Transformation of South Africa*, Charlottesville
   and London 2000.

4 The basic contours of the approach are put forward in Howarth, 2000a,
   Laclau and Mouffe 1985 and Laclau 1990; 1996.

5 Canovan, 1981; Taggart, 2000.

6 This notion of a picture of populism resonates with Weber's concept of
   ideal types in the sense that it is principally a heuristic device that highlights
   certain features of a phenomenon, and then seeks to account for particular discrepancies and divergences between it and the 'real world'. See
   Weber, 1949, p. 43.

7 Freeden, 1996, p. 76.

8 Laclau, 1977.

9 Laclau and Mouffe, 1985.

10 Lodge, 1992, p. 47.

11 Transvaal Anti-South African Indian Council Committee, Congress 1983:
   Speeches and Papers Delivered at the Congress, Johannesburg 1983.

12 See Barrell, 1984; de le Harpe and Mason, 1983.

13 UDF, 'UDF Working Principles: United Democratic Front Launch
   Document', Witwatersrand 1983.

14 Matiwane and Walters, 1986.

15 See Cape Times, 8 September 1984; Lawrence et al., 1984.

16 City Press, 5 November 1983; *Rand Daily Mail*, 31 October 1983; UDF,
   1985.

17 *Grassroots*, 5 (2), March 1984; *SASPU National*, October 1984, pp. 10–11.
   It should be noted that the UDF fell woefully short of its desired aim of a

million signatures. In total, it is estimated that about 270,000 signatures were collected. See Seekings, 2000, p. 104.

18 Luxemburg, 1981.

19 Seekings, 2000, pp. 21–4.

20 See Marx, 1992, pp. 147–88; Murray, 1987.

21 Sutcliffe, 1986.

22 UDF, 1985.

23 Lodge, 1991, pp. 58–77.

24 Seekings, 1986; 1987; McCarthy and Smit, 1985.

25 Lodge, 1991, pp. 75–76.

26 Boraine, 1988.

27 See National Education Crisis Committee, *Report on National Consultative Conference on the Crisis in Education,* Soweto Parents Crisis Committee, Witwatersrand 1986; Sisulu, 1986, pp. 96–117.

28 Marais, 1998, p. 54; Marx, 1992; Seekings, 2000, pp. 285–324; van Kessel, 2000, pp. 302–3.

29 Baskin, 1991, pp. 18–33; Friedman, 1987b, p. 184. Running parallel to the dominant non-racial and democratic Federation of South African Trade Unions (FOSATU) were those unions with Black Consciousness sympathies and a commitment to black exclusivism, which were gathered together in the Council of South African Trade Unions (CUSA). There were also the so-called community-based trade unions, such as the South African Allied Workers Union (SAAWU), which were to display increasing support for the more popular-democratic forms of political opposition conducted by the UDF and its allies (Davies et al, 1984, pp. 332–346). Emerging in the repressive conditions of the 1970s, the ideology and strategy of FOSATU focused heavily on the creation of factory and industry-based unions with strong democratic accountability and 'worker leadership'.

30 MacShane et al., 1984, pp. 64–66.

31 Foster, 1982, p. 78.

32 Erwin, 1985: 56–69

33 Erwin, 1985; see also Howarth and Norval, 1990, pp. 4–6.

34 See Howarth, 2000b, p. 180; Saul and Gelb, 1986, pp. 16–26; 229–42.

35 The workerist critique was articulated in a number of articles, chapters and position papers. Major interventions include Erwin, 1985; Foster, 1983; Friedman, 1987a; Innes, 1986; Innes, 1987; Silver and Sfarnas, 1983. The terms 'workerism' and 'workerist' cover over differences

between a number of divergent positions – syndicalists, social democrats, labourists, and so forth. I use the terms, firstly, in an ethnographic sense to capture the self-descriptions of the protagonists themselves and, secondly, as a useful means of drawing out the similarities between the different positions.

36 Jay Naidoo cited in Saul, 1986, p. 17.

37 The Charterist response includes Cronin, 1986, pp. 73–79; Karon and Ozinsky, 1986; McLean, 1986, pp. 8–20; Rafel, 1990; Suttner, 1983; Suttner and Cronin, 1986, pp. 127–143. As with the notions of 'workerism' and 'workerist', the term Charterist refers to different positions. Indeed, as Lodge argues, the term refers to at least three positions: those who viewed the demands and programme of the Freedom Charter in nationalist terms, those who might be viewed as national democrats, and those who stressed its socialist content. Again, I employ the term both for its ethnographic import and because of its usefulness as a means of stressing the overriding commonalities amongst Charterists. See Lodge, 1991, pp. 129–35.

38 I take this idea of projecting ontopolitical interpretations into an object of study so as to reveal unacknowledged presuppositions and to dislodge sedimented understandings from William Connolly's synthesis of Nietzsche and Foucault. See Connolly, 1995.

39 The idea of the impossibility of any ultimate democratic or socialist resolution closely parallels Jacques Derrida's concept of 'democracy to come'. Derrida, 1997, p. 306.

40 See Price, 1991, p. 279.

41 Adler and Webster, 1995.

42 Glaser, 2001, pp. 222–3. In a similar vein, despite criticisms about its inability to deliver retributive justice to the victims of human rights abuses, the 'Truth and Reconciliation Commission' has gone a little way in exposing the truth about gross injustices and human rights violations, as well as providing a means of healing the wounds of those who suffered under apartheid rule. See Norval, 1999.

43 See Diamond, 1994.

44 One potentially worrying development is the current ANC government's ambivalent stance towards developments in Zimbabwe.

45 RDP, *White Paper on Reconstruction and Development*, Cape Town 1994, pp. 7–10.

46 Marais, 1988, p. 162.

47   *Guardian*, 30 August 2001.

48   Another symptom of the ANC's failure to pursue a more egalitarian and radical agenda is their policy towards AIDS. Apart from President Mbeki's state of denial about the causes and effects of the AIDS epidemic, worrying in its own terms, there are the ethical and moral consequences of a policy that puts at risk large swathes of the South African population.

49   A fact that has had ongoing political repercussions, as former UDF activists and readers are regularly accused of plotting against the existing ANC government. See *Mail* and *Guardian*, 17 June 2002.

50   *Guardian*, 23 October 2001. My emphasis. Moreover, recent events in Zimbabwe demonstrate the way in which a popular-democratic national liberation movement can easily turn itself into a conservative authoritarian populism pitting itself against a UDF-style opposition. The possibility of an embattled ANC government resorting to a similar style and content of politics is not beyond our imagining.

9   YANNIS STAVRAKAKIS

This paper is part of a broader project examining both the general relation between religion and politics in our late modern age and, in particular, the history and implications of the 'politicisation' of Church discourse in contemporary Greece. A more detailed analysis of certain historical and theoretical aspects only briefly discussed here can be found in Yennis Stavrakakis, *Religion and Populism: Reflections on the 'Politicised' Discourse of the Greek Church*, Discussion Paper no. 7, The Hellenic Observatory, The European Institute, London School of Economics and Political Science, 2002.

1   This was the third in a row for his party, the centre-left PASOK, since 1993.

2   A self-proclaimed 'moderniser', critical of traditionalism and the populist discourse characteristic of Andreas Papandreou's PASOK of the 1980s.

3   *Ethnos*, 6 May 2000.

4   *Eleftherotypia*, 9 May 2000.

5   Appointed as head of the Orthodox Church of Greece only a few years before (1998), and an emerging media star.

6   Christodoulos 2000c, p. 321.

7   According to the last census (2001) the population of Greece is 10,939,605, but the electorate (which excludes foreigners and children) in the last general elections (2000) was 8,976,135.

8 *Kathimerini*, 30 August 2001.

9 Christodoulos, *From Earth and Water*, Athens 1999, p. 145.

10 Ibid., p. 69.

11 Ibid., p. 100.

12 In translating *genos* as 'race' – admittedly not an entirely satisfactory translation – I am taking my lead from Zakythinos 1976, p. 188.

13 Christodoulos, 1999, p. 13.

14 Ibid., p. 15.

15 Ibid., p. 219.

16 Ibid., p. 116.

17 Christodoulos, 2000a, p. 66; my emphasis.

18 Christodoulos, 2001a, p. 17.

19 Christodoulos, 1999, pp. 222–3.

20 S. Agouridis, 'The Church as an Agent of Power', in Karagiorgas Foundation, *Structures and Relations of Power in Contemporary Greece*, vol. 7, 2000, p. 360.

21 Martin, 1978, p. 272.

22 Kitromilides, 1989, p. 166.

23 It has been argued that, in fact, the Church has been acting as an 'ideological state apparatus', in the Althusserian sense of the term (Chiotakis 2000, p. 312). See also Althusser, 1990, pp. 67–121.

24 For example, the course followed by the archbishop has been criticised by a few bishops as leading to the formation of an ideology of 'para-religious populism' (Theoklitos, 2001). Furthermore, he has often been described as 'charismatic and populist' (Pollis, 1999, p. 195), as the bearer of a 'neo-rightist populism' (Pappas, 2001, p. 57), as someone who speaks 'in the name of *the people*' (Manitakis, 2000, p. 140, my emphasis), thus articulating an 'ecclesiastical' (Dimitrakos, 2000) or 'religious populism' (Sotirelis, 2001).

25 Löwy, 1996, pp. 77–8.

26 Lancaster, 1988.

27 The differences are usually due either to the differing disciplinary lens – leading to ideological, comparative and historical approaches – or to the differing theoretical frameworks used, leading to functionalist, Marxist and post-Marxist approaches, and so on.

28 Canovan, 1981, p. 3.

29 Ibid., p. 5.

30 Laclau, 1977, p. 143.

31 Taggart, 2000, p. 2.

32 Canovan, 1981, p. 3.

33 Ibid., p. 7.

34 Ibid., p. 301. For a critique of Canovan along these lines, see Westlind 1996, pp. 43–6. It should be noted at this point that in her more recent work Canovan has shifted her position in a more productive direction (see note 53).

35 This is not as simple as it sounds. Notice for example the inability of Taggart to understand the role of signifiers and signification in politics, and especially in populism. At first he considers the reference to 'the people' as of little importance, since the signifier 'the people' can have different meanings in different populisms, thus choosing to highlight the level of the signified and almost disregard that of the signifier (Taggart, 2000, p. 3). Then he seems unable to distinguish between those who take seriously the location of the signifier 'the people' and those who take populists at their own word. Referring to Westlind's analysis, he claims that 'some commentators have taken populists at their own word and define populism as a movement that represents "the people"' (Taggart, 2000, p. 92). Obviously Taggart subscribes to the curious idea that it is not possible to define a discourse with reference to a central claim without accepting that claim as true. Besides, even if the claim is false – a mere rhetorical strategy – its location still has to be important, not least because it is bound to produce effects beyond the intentionality of its source.

36 Laclau, 1977.

37 Laclau, 1980.

38 Almost half of his 1977 text is devoted to the issue of class politics and its relation to populism in an attempt to avoid Marxist reductionism and stress the articulatory character of links between class and popular interpellations.

39 Laclau, 1977, p. 165.

40 Ibid., p. 173; my emphasis.

41 Ibid., pp. 172–3; emphasis in the original.

42 For a balanced and, more or less, justified critique, see Westlind, 1996, pp. 88–90.

43 Laclau and Mouffe, 1985.

44 Laclau, 1980.

45 Lyrintzis, 1987, p. 685.

46 Westlind, 1996, p. 60.

47 This is the case, for example, with Donald MacRae's contribution, in which ideology is understood as pertaining to an ideational, almost philosophical level (MacRae, 1969, pp. 153–65).

48 Mouzelis 1985, p. 330; 1989, p. 24.

49 Mouzelis, 1985, p. 330; 1989, p. 24.

50 Laclau and Mouffe, 1985.

51 Lyrintzis, 1990, p. 51.

52 Laclau, 1980, p. 86. To go back to the question of economism, Laclau argues here that 'economic practice itself should thus be considered as discourse' (Laclau, 1980, p. 86). On this issue, see also Daly, 1991.

53 In his reading the same themes are also stressed by Canovan (Mouzelis, 1985, p. 330), a link also pointed out by others (Taguieff in Pantazopoulos 2001, p. 47; Lyrintzis, 1987, p. 685). This is mostly based on Canovan's statement that 'all forms of populism without exception involve some kind of exaltation of and appeal to "the people" and all are in one sense or another anti-elitist' (Canovan, 1981, p. 294). In reality, this serves to show that Canovan essentially accepts Laclau's central criteria – phrased in her own way – although in her work they are not given any theoretical grounding or operational sophistication. The result is that for her they remain 'vague and ambiguous' and thus not very helpful in developing a coherent account of populism (Canovan, 1981, pp. 294–5, 298). It is thus somewhat misleading to group Laclau and Canovan together in terms of their acceptance of the two criteria in question; their attitude towards them is very different. In fact only in Laclau are they acknowledged as forming the kernel of a theoretical account of populism with important analytical consequences. Only very recently Canovan's position – developed at the 'structural' level – seems to have overcome her reservations and embraced these criteria as central, thus approaching substantially closer to Laclau's initial position (Canovan, 1999, p. 3).

54 Mouzelis, 1985, p. 341.

55 Sofos, 1994, p. 140–1.

56 Westlind, 1996, p. 91. Westlind almost compromises this insight when he attempts to link organisational patterns with the level of *ideology* and not *discourse* (ibid., p 56).

57 Lyrintzis, 1990, pp. 47–8. In an earlier text Lyrintzis puts it in the following way: 'It is not specific ideas or a specific set of policies that characterise populism, but its internal logic, its way of representing and organising the

social and political space' (Lyrintzis, 1987, p. 669). See also Lyrintzis and
Spourdalakis, 1993, p. 141.

58 Laclau and Mouffe, 1985, p. 112.

59 Laclau, 1980, p. 91.

60 Laclau and Mouffe, 1985, p. 130; Stavrakakis, 1999, p. 76.

61 Lyrintzis, 1990, p. 49.

62 Laclau, 1980, p. 92. The distinction between difference and equivalence, its
theoretical grounding and political applicability, is further elaborated with reference to a variety of empirical examples in Stavrakakis, 1999, pp. 57–9, 76–8.

63 Lyrintzis, 1987, 1990; Sofos, 1994; Westlind, 1996; Barros and Castagnola,
2000; Panizza, 2000 – to name just a few.

64 Although the whole rationale of this exploration is based on Laclau's
discursive approach to populism, I will try to incorporate in my argumentation elements and additional criteria from other approaches (including
those of Canovan, Mouzelis and Taggart), insofar as they can be grafted
into a discursive problematic.

65 Given that the hegemony of Christodoulos's discourse on the official
Church hierarchy has been almost total during this period (with a few
notable exceptions), for analytical purposes we take Church discourse to be
overlapping with his own.

66 Christodoulos, 2000c, p. 309.

67 Christodoulos, 2000a, p. 72.

68 Ibid., 52–3.

69 Christodoulos, 2000c, p. 311.

70 Ibid., p. 322.

71 See special issue (no. 48) of the theological journal *Synaxi*: 'People, Nation,
Church' (1993), and Pinakoulas, 2001, p. 44.

72 Christodoulos, 2000a, p. 64; 2000b, p. 303.

73 Christodoulos, 2000b, p. 292.

74 Ibid., 303.

75 Thermos, 1993, p. 44.

76 Christodoulos, Interview, p. 54.

77 Christodoulos, *Church and Nation*, p. 9.

78 Christodoulos, 2000b, p. 290.

79 The crucial role of voice here should not escape the attention of deconstructionists and Derrideans.

80 Christodoulos, 2000c, p. 327.

81 Canovan, 1999, p. 10.
82 *Kathimerini*, 1 July 2000.
83 Mouzelis, 1985, p. 334.
84 Christodoulos, 2000b, p. 298.
85 Christodoulos, 2000c, p. 322.
86 Taggart, 2000, p. 116.
87 Canovan, 1999, p. 7–8.
88 Taggart, 2000, p. 98.
89 Tsatsos, 2000.
90 Christodoulos, 2000a, p. 35.
91 Christodoulos, 2000b, p. 299.
92 Christodoulos, 2001b, p. 8.
93 *Eleftherotypia*, 26 June 2000.
94 *Eleftherotypia*, 8 October 2001.
95 Christodoulos, 1999, p. 186.
96 Christodoulos, 2000b, p. 296.
97 Ibid., p. 298.
98 Taggart, 2000, p. 50.
99 Christodoulos, 2000b, p. 291.
100 Christodoulos, 2000a, p. 59.
101 Christodoulos, 2000b, p. 308.
102 *Flash.gr*, 2 December 2001.
103 Christodoulos, 1999, p. 54.
104 Taggart, 2000, p. 105.
105 Christodoulos, 1999, pp. 28–32.
106 Ibid., p. 35.
107 Ibid., pp. 51, 108.
108 Ibid., p. 102.
109 Christodoulos, 2000a, p. 70.
110 Christodoulos, 2000c, p. 313.
111 Ibid., p. 324.
112 Christodoulos, 2000a, p. 38.
113 Christodoulos, 2000b, p. 294.
114 Christodoulos, 2001c.
115 Christodoulos, 2000c, p. 314.
116 Christodoulos, 1999, p. 145.
117 Christodoulos, *Church and Nation*, p. 27.

118 Christodoulos, 2000a, p. 38.
119 Christodoulos, *The Role* ..., p. 11.
120 Christodoulos, *Church and Nation*, p. 29.
121 Christodoulos, 1999, pp. 52–3.
122 Taggart, 2000.
123 Pantazopoulos, 2001.
124 Ibid., pp. 35, 54.
125 Ibid., p. 59.
126 Ibid., p. 62.
127 Ibid., p. 63.
128 Jenner, 2001, p. 77.
129 Elefantis, 1991.
130 Alivizatos, 1983.
131 Laclau, 1990, p. 39; Howarth and Stavrakakis, 2000, p. 13.
132 Lyrintzis, 1990, p. 54.
133 Laclau, 1977, p. 175.
134 Taggart, 2000, p. 66.
135 Chiotakis, 2000, p. 315.
136 Georgiadou and Nikolakopoulos, 2000, pp. 177–80.
137 Martin, 1978, pp. 61–2.
138 Lyrintzis, 1990, p. 57.
139 Lyrintzis, 1987, p. 671.

10 SEBASTIÁN BARROS

The author wishes to thank Seth Hague and Mercedes Barros for their help.

1 This chapter draws on the work of Ernesto Laclau and Chantal Mouffe. For empirical analysis using this framework see David Howarth, Aletta Norval and Yannis Stavrakakis, eds, *Discourse Theory and Political Analysis*, Manchester 2000; Ernesto Laclau, ed., *The Making of Political Identities*, London 1994.

2 Vicente Palermo and Marcos Novaro, *Política y poder en el gobierno de Menem*, Buenos Aires 1996, p. 186. See also Manuel Mora y Araujo, 'De Perón a Menem: Una historia del peronismo', in Atilio Borón et al., *Peronismo y menemismo: Avatares del populismo en la Argentina*, Buenos Aires 1995, p. 61.

3 Silvia Sigal and Eliseo Verón, *Perón o muerte. Los fundamentos discursivos del fenómeno peronista*, Buenos Aires 1988. *Partidocracia* is a pejorative way of

referring to the oligarchic government of political parties, something like *party-cracy*.

4 In 1986 Menem was the governor of a poor province in northern Argentina, La Rioja. He gained political prominence when he was one of the few Peronists to support Alfonsín's government's peace treaty with Chile in 1985. He had an active participation in the emergence of Renovación.

5 Antonio Cafiero, 'En qué nos equivocamos', in Unamuno et al., *El peronismo de la derrota*, Buenos Aires 1984, p. 150.

6 *El Bimestre*, no. 38, p. 39. However, later on Duhalde changed his position and accompanied Menem as Vice-President in 1989. Rega and Iglesias were clearly associated with a violent and authoritarian past. López Rega was a policeman who was later Perón's personal assistant, and Minister of Social Welfare between 1973 and 1974. He was the founder of the *Triple A* (AAA), Argentine Anticommunist Alliance, a right-wing paramilitary organisation.

7 The apparent contradiction implied by being a member of Renovación and joining forces with the authoritarian sectors of the party was easily solved by Menem. He could reassert his democratic credentials by playing with the fact that he had been close to Alfonsín and the UCR government in the first period of the transition, and that he had been one of the founders of Renovación.

8 However, it should be clear that the emptiness of the signifier is not necessarily given by the kind of ambiguity attached to Menem's discourse. Alfonsín's discourse is a case in point, in which the content of the discourse was less ambiguous and yet could still work as a surface of inscription for other demands. It should be clear that emptiness is not related to a lack of content – if there is no content, there is no discourse – but to the possibility of understanding this content in different ways.

9 Carlos Menem, 'Carta abierta a la esperanza', *Clarín*, 24 March 1988.

10 Ibid.

11 For a description of this denunciation and its political relevance see Sebastián Barros, 'Derrumbe, crisis y nueva articulación: La Argentina de la transición', *Política y Gestión*, no. 2, November 2001.

12 *El Bimestre*, no. 38, p. 39.

13 *El Bimestre*, no. 39, pp. 18–19.

14 Montoneros was the most important guerrilla group of the Peronist left in the 1970s.

15 For a distinction between nodal and floating signifiers, see Laclau's article in this book.

16 Marcelo Cavarozzi and María Grossi, 'Argentine Parties under Alfonsín: From Democratic Reinvention to Political Decline and Hyperinflation', in Edward Epstein, *The New Argentine Democracy: The Search for a Successful Formula*, Westport 1992, p. 195.

17 Atilio Borón, 'El experimento neoliberal de Carlos Saúl Menem', in Borón et al., *Peronismo y menemismo: Avatares del populismo en la Argentina*, Buenos Aires 1995.

18 Mora y Araujo, 1995, p. 62.

19 José Nun, 'Populismo, representación y menemismo', in Borón, et al., 1995, p. 84.

20 Juan Carlos Portantiero, 'Menemismo y peronismo: continuidad y ruptura', in Borón et al., *Peronismo y menemismo*, p. 106.

21 Ricardo Sidicaro, 'Poder político, liberalismo económico y sectores populares en la Argentina 1989–1995", in Borón, et al., 1995, pp. 128–9.

22 See Cerruti, *El Jefe: Vida y obra de Carlos Saúl Menem*, Buenos Aires 1993; Palermo and Novaro, 1996, pp. 202–14; Cavarozzi and Grossi, 1992, under 'Alfonsín'.

23 Cerruti, 1993, p. 178.

24 Marcelo Cavarozzi and Oscar Landi, 'Political Parties under Alfonsín and Menem: The Effects of State Shrinking and the Devaluation of Democratic Politics', in Epstein, 1992, p. 214.

25 Palermo and Novaro, 1996, p. 206. *Caravana* is a long convoy of vehicles mobilised in support of something or somebody.

26 *El Bimestre*, no. 38, p. 39.

27 *El Bimestre*, no. 37, p. 42.

28 Carlos Menem y Eduardo Duhalde, *La Revolución Productiva*, Buenos Aires 1989, p. 8.

29 For an analysis of this polarised antagonism see Sebastián Barros, *Orden, democracia y estabilidad: Discurso y política en la Argentina entre 1976 y 1991*, Córdoba 2002.

30 José A. Martínez de Hoz, 1981, *Bases para una Argentina Moderna*, Buenos Aires, pp. 21–22.

31 Juan V. Sourrouille, *Mensajes del Ministro de Economía Dr Juan V. Sourrouille*, Buenos Aires 1989.

32 *El Bimestre*, no. 34, pp. 36–7.

33 Raúl Alfonsín, *Discursos presidenciales*, Subsecretaría de Comunicación Social, Dirección General de Difusión, 14 October 1987.

34 Ibid.

35 Raúl Alfonsín, *Discursos presidenciales*, 19 September 1987.

36 Ibid.

37 Ibid., pp. 45–6.

38 *El Bimestre*, no. 36, p. 21.

39 *El Bimestre*, no. 35, p. 48.

40 *El Bimestre*, no. 38, p. 46.

41 A *Porteño* is someone from the city of Buenos Aires.

42 W. Smith (1992) 'Hyperinflation, macroeconomic instability, and neoliberal restructuring in democratic Argentina', in E. Epstein, ed., *The New Argentine Democracy. The Search for a Successful Formula*, Westport, p. 51.

43 *Cronología 1991*, April, pp. 2–3.

44 Roberto Frenkel, 'Las políticas antiinflacionarias en América Latina', *Agora*, 5, 1996, pp. 198–202.

45 Palermo and Novaro, 1996, pp. 288–301.

46 Roberto Frenkel, 1996, p. 200.

47 *Cronología 1991*, October, p. 2.

48 Mario Baizán, *Desde el poder: Carlos Menem responde*, Buenos Aires 1994, p. 41.

49 Ibid., p. 44.

50 Ibid., p. 40.

51 Ibid., p. 51.

BIBLIOGRAPHY

Aaronsohn, R., 1983, 'Building the Land: Stages in the First Aliya Colonization (1882–1904)', in L. Levine, ed., *Jerusalem Cathedra: Studies in the History, Archaeology, Geography and Ethnography of the Land of Israel*, Jerusalem, pp. 236–79.

Abu-Jaber, K., 1967, 'The Millet System in the Nineteenth Century Ottoman Empire', *The Muslim World*, vol. LVII, no. 3, pp. 213–23.

Abu-Lughod, J., 1971, 'Demographic Transformation of Palestine', in I. Abu-Lughod, ed., *The Transformation of Palestine: Essays on the Origin and Development of the Arab-Israeli Conflict*, Evanston, pp. 139–63.

Adler, G., and E. Webster, 1995, 'Challenging Transition Theory: The Labor Movement, Radical Reform, and Transition to Democracy in South Africa', *Politics and Society*, vol. 23, no. 1, pp. 75–106.

Agouridis, S., 2000, 'The Church as an Agent of Power', in Karagiorgas Foundation, *Structures and Relations of Power in Contemporary Greece*, vol. 7.

Alfonsín, R., 1978, *Discursos presidenciales*, Buenos Aires.

—— 1980, *La cuestión argentina*, Buenos Aires.

Alivizatos, N., 1983, '"Nation" against "the People" after 1940', in D. Tsaousis, ed., *Hellenism-Greekness*, Athens.

Allcock, J., 1992, 'Rhetorics of Nationalism in Yugoslav Politics', in J. Allcock, J. Horton and M. Milivojevic, eds, *Yugoslavia in Transition*, London, pp. 276–96.

—— 2000, *Explaining Yugoslavia*, London.

Althusser, L., 1971, 'Ideology and Ideological State Apparatuses (Notes towards an Investigation)', *Lenin and Philosophy and Other Essays*, London, pp. 121–73.

— 1990, *Positions*, Athens.

Alvarez Junco, J., 1987, 'Magia y ética en la retórica política', in *Populismo, caudillaje y discurso demagógico*, Madrid.

— 1990, *El Emperador del Paralelo*, Madrid.

Anderson, B. 1991. *Imagined Communities: Reflections on the Origins and Spread of Nationalism*, revised edition, London.

Andrianopoulos, A., 2001, *Hellenism and Orthodoxy*, Athens.

Ansell, A. E., 1998, ed., *Unravelling the Right: The New Conservatism in American Thought and Politics*, Boulder.

Anti-Defamation League of B'nai B'rith, 1968, 'The Extreme Right Invasion of the 1968 Campaign', New York.

Antonius, G., 1938, *The Arab Awakening: the Story of the Arab National Movement*, London.

Archer, K. and F. Ellis, 1994, 'Opinion Structure of Party Activists: The Reform Party of Canada', *Canadian Journal of Political Science*, vol. 27, no. 2, pp. 277–308.

Arditi, B., and J. Valentine, 1999, *Polemicization: The Contingency of the Commonplace*, Edinburgh and New York.

Asad, T., 1975, 'Anthropological Texts and Ideological Problems: an Analysis of Cohen on Arab Villages in Israel', *Review of Middle East Studies*, vol. I, pp. 1–40.

Asali, K. J., 1989, 'Jerusalem under the Ottomans (1516–1831 AD)', in K. J. Asali, ed., *Jerusalem in History*, London, pp. 200–27.

Aspeslagh, R., 1992, 'Trianon Dissolved: the Status of Vojvodina Reconsidered?' in M. van den Heuvel and J. Siccama, eds, *The Disintegration of Yugoslavia* (Yearbook of European Studies 5), Amsterdam.

Auty, P., 1966, *'The Post-war Period': A Short History of Yugoslavia from Early Times to 1966*, S. Clissold, ed., Cambridge, pp. 236–66.

Ayers, J., 1998, *Defying Conventional Wisdom: Political Movements and Popular Contention against North American Free Trade*, Toronto.

Badiou, A., 2002, 'Highly Speculative Reasoning on the Concept of Democracy', *The Symptom* 2, http://www.lacan.com/conceptsymf.htm.

Bailer-Galandra, B. and Neugebauer, W., 1997, *Haider und die 'Freiheitichen' in Österreich*, Berlin.

Baizán, M., 1994, *Desde el poder: Carlos Menem responde*, Buenos Aires.

Ballinger, P., 'The Politics of Submersion: History, Collective Memory, and Ethnic Group Boundaries in Trieste', unpublished manuscript.

Banać, I., 1992. 'The Origins and Development of the Concept of Yugoslavia (to 1945)', in *The Disintegration of Yugoslavia*, M. van den Heuvel and

J. G. Siccama, eds, Amsterdam, pp. 1–22.

Bárbaro, Julio, 1984, 'Hablemos en serio del peronismo', in Unamuno, ed., *El peronismo de la derrota*, Buenos Aires.

— 1984a, 'No se puede convivir con los enemigos de la vida', in Unamuno, ed., *El peronismo de la derrota*, Buenos Aires.

— 1984b, 'Reportaje a Julio Bárbaro', in M. Unamuno, et al., *El peronismo de la derrota*, Buenos Aires.

Barnett, A., 1999, 'Corporate control', *Prospect* , February, pp. 24–29

Barney, D., 1996a, 'Push-button Populism: The Reform Party and the Real World of Teledemocracy', *Canadian Journal of Communication*, vol. 21, no.3, 1996, pp. 381–413.

— 1996b, 'The Recline of Party: Armchair Democracy and the Reform Party of Canada', *American Review of Canadian Studies*, Winter, pp. 577–605.

Barney, D. and D. Laycock, 1999, 'Right-populists and plebiscitary politics in Canada', *Party Politics*, vol. 5, no. 3, pp. 317–39.

Barr, R., 2003, 'The Persistence of Neopopulism in Peru? From Fujimori to Toledo', *Third World Quarterly*, vol. 24, no. 6, pp. 1161–78.

Barrell, H., 1984, 'The United Democratic Front and National Forum: Their Emergence, Composition and Trends', in *South African Research Services, South African Review Two*, Johannesburg, pp. 6–20.

Barros, S., and G. G. Castagnola, 2000, 'The Political Frontiers of the Social: Argentine Politics after the Emergence of Peronist Populism (1955–1973)', in David Howarth, Aletta Norval and Yannis Stavrakakis, eds., *Discourse Theory and Political Analysis*, Manchester and New York, pp. 53–74.

Barros, S., 2001, 'Derrumbe, crisis y nueva articulación: La Argentina de la transición', *Política y Gestión*, no. 2, November, pp. 53–74.

— 2002, *Orden, democracia y estabilidad. Discurso y política en la Argentina entre 1976 y 1991*, Córdoba.

Barthes, R., 1973, *Mythologies*, London.

Bartle, J., 2002, 'Whatever Happened to the Tories?', Department of Government , PhD Colloquium, University of Essex, 17 January.

Baskin, J., 1991, *Striking Back: A History of COSATU*, London.

Bauman, Z., 1989, *Modernity and the Holocaust*, Cambridge.

Bech Dyrberg, T., 'Racist, nationalist and populist trends in recent Danish politics', *Research Paper* 19/01, Roskilde University, Denmark.

Beck, H.-G., 2000, *The Byzantine Millennium*, third edition, Athens.

Bell, D., 2001, ed., *The Radical Right*, New York.

Berlet, C. and M. Lyons, 2000, *Right Wing Populism in America*, New York.

Berman, W. C., 1998, *American Right Turn from Nixon to Clinton*, Baltimore.

Betz, H. G., 1994, *Radical Right-Wing Populism in Western Europe*, London.

Bischof, G., A. Pelinka and F. Karlhofer, 1999, eds, *The Vranitzky Era in Austria*, New Brunswick and London.

Blais, A., E. Gidengil, R. Nadeau and N. Nevitte, 1999, *Unsteady State: The 1997 Canadian Election*, Toronto.

Bloch, M., 1982, 'Death, Women and Power', in M. Bloch and J. Parry, eds, *Death and the Regeneration of Life*, Cambridge, pp. 211–30.

— 1989, 'Almost Eating the Ancestors', in *Ritual, History and Power: Selected Papers in Anthropology*, London, pp. 166–86.

Boraine, 1988, 'The Canon of Mamelodi: People's Power in an African Township', *South African Institute of Race Relations Paper*, Johannesburg.

Borón, A., et al., 1995, *Peronismo y menemismo: Avatares del populismo en la Argentina*, Buenos Aires.

Bowman, G., 1993a, 'Nationalizing the Sacred: Shrines and Shifting Identities in the Israeli-Occupied Territories', *Man: The Journal of the Royal Anthropological Institute*, vol. XXVIII, no. 3, pp. 431–60.

— 1993b, 'Tales of the Lost Land: Palestinian Identity and the Formation of Nationalist Consciousness', in E. Carter, J. Donald and J. Squires, eds, *Space and Place: Theories of Identity and Location*, London, pp. 73–100.

— 1994a, '"A Country of Words": Conceiving the Palestinian Nation from the Position of Exile', in E. Laclau, ed., *The Making of Political Identities*, London, pp. 138–70.

— 1994b, 'Xenophobia, Fantasy and the Nation: the Logic of Ethnic Violence in Former Yugoslavia', in V. Goddard, J. Llobera and C. Shore, eds, *Anthropology of Europe: Identity and Boundaries in Conflict*, London, pp. 143–71.

— 1999, 'The Exilic Imagination: The Construction of the Landscape of Palestine from Its Outside', in I. Abu-Lughod, R. Heacock and K. Nashef, eds, *The Landscape of Palestine: Equivocal Poetry*, Birzeit, pp. 53–78.

— 2001, 'The Two Deaths of Basem Rishmawi: Identity Constructions and Reconstructions in a Muslim-Christian Palestinian Community', *Identities: Global Studies in Culture and Power*, vol. VIII, no. 1, pp. 1–35.

Brand, L., 1988, *Palestinians in the Arab World: Institution Building and the Search for State*, New York.

Brown, M. K., 1999, 'Race in the American Welfare State: The Ambiguities of Universalistic Social Policy since the New Deal', in A. Reed, ed., *Without Justice For All: The New Liberalism and Our Retreat from Racial Equality*, Boulder.

Butler, D. and D. Kavanagh, 2001, *The British General Election of 2001*, Basingstoke.

Byrne, T. and M. Edsall, 1992, *Chain Reaction: The Impact of Race, Rights, and Taxes in American Politics*, New York.

Cafiero, A., 1984, 'En qué nos equivocamos', in M. Unamuno, ed., *El peronismo de la derrota*, Buenos Aires.

Cammack, P., 2000, 'The Resurgence of Populism in Latin America', *Bulletin of Latin American Research*, vol. 19, no. 2, pp. 149–61.

Canak, N., 1993, 'National Identity in a Multi-cultural Context', in G. Bowman, ed., *Antagonism and Identity in Former Yugoslavia – Journal of Area Studies*, vol. 3, pp. 137–43.

Canovan, M., 1981, *Populism*, London: Junction Books.

— 1999, 'Trust the People! Populism and the Two Faces of Democracy', *Political Studies*, vol. XLVII, no. 1, pp. 2–16.

Carlson, J., 1981, *George Wallace and the Politics of Powerlessness*, New York.

Carlson, M., 1999, 'The Trouble with Pleasing Everyone', *Time* magazine, 21 June.

Carmines, E. and J. A. Stimson, 1989, *Race and the Transformation of American Politics*, Princeton.

Carter, D.T., 1996a, *From George Wallace to Newt Gingrich: Race in the Conservative Contrarevolution 1963–1994*, Baton Rouge.

— 1996b, *The Politics of Rage: George Wallace, the Origins of the New Conservatism, and the Transformation of American Politics*, New York.

— 1999, *From George Wallace to Newt Gingrich: Race in the Conservative Counterrevolution, 1963–1994*, Louisiana.

Cavarozzi, M., and M. Grossi, 1992, 'Argentine Parties under Alfonsín: from Democratic Reinvention to Political Decline and Hyperinflation', in E. Epstein, *The New Argentine Democracy: The Search for a Successful Formula*, Westport, pp. 173–202.

Cavarozzi, M., and O. Landi, 1992, 'Political Parties under Alfonsín and Menem: the Effects of State Shrinking and the Devaluation of Democratic Politics', in E. Epstein, ed., *The New Argentine Democracy: The Search for a Successful Formula*, Westport, pp. 203–27.

Cegorović, N., 1993. 'Montenegrin Identity: Past, Present and Future', in G. Bowman, ed., *Antagonism and Identity in Former Yugoslavia – Journal of Area Studies*, vol. 3, pp. 129–38.

Centeno, I.V., 1986, *Aprismo Popular: mito, cultura and historia*, Lima.

Cerruti, G., 1993, *El Jefe: Vida y obra de Carlos Saúl Menem*, Buenos Aires.

Charalambis, D., 1989, *Clientelist Relations and Populism: The Extra-institutional Consensus in the Greek Political System*, Athens.

Chiotakis, S., 2000, 'Aspects of the "Neo-Orthodox" Reproduction of

"Community" (GEMEINSCHAFT)', in Karagiorgas Foundation, *Structures and Relations of Power in Contemporary Greece*, vol. 7.

Christodoulos, Archbishop (Paraskevaidis, Ch., bishop of Dimitrias) (no date) *Church and Nation*, Athens.

Christodoulos, Archbishop (Paraskevaidis, Ch., bishop of Dimitrias) (no date) *The Role of the Church in 1821*, Athens.

Christodoulos, Archbishop (no date), *Interview*, Athens.

Christodoulos, Archbishop, 1999, *From Earth and Water*, Athens.

— 2000a, 'Foreword to the Second Edition' (Address to the Holy Synod of the Church of Greece, 11 October 2000), in Holy Synod of the Church of Greece, *The Church and Identity Cards*, Athens.

— 2000b, 'Speech of his Beautitude the Archbishop of Athens and All Greece Christodoulos in the rally of Thessaloniki – 14 June 2000', in Holy Synod of the Church of Greece, *The Church and Identity Cards*, Athens.

— 2000c, 'Speech of his Beautitude the Archbishop of Athens and All Greece Christodoulos in the rally of Athens – 21 June 2000', in Holy Synod of the Church of Greece, *The Church and Identity Cards*.

— 2001a, Interview with Th. Lalas, *Vimagasino, To Vima*, 11 February 2001.

— 2001b, Interview with G. Papathanasopoulos, *Identity*, 16 March.

— 2001c, 'Church and People: An Unbreakable Relation', Speech at the Piraeus Maritime Club, available at www.ecclesia.gr/Archbishop/Speeches/19-6-2001.html.

Clarke, H., A. Kornberg, F. G. Ellis and J. Rapkin, 2000, 'Not for Fame or Fortune: A Note on Membership and Activity in the Canadian Reform Party', *Party Politics*, vol. 6, no. 1, 2000.

Cobban, H., 1984, *The Palestinian Liberation Organization: People, Power and Politics*, Cambridge.

Cohen, A., 1965, *Arab Border-Villages in Israel: A Study of Continuity and Change in Social Organization*, Manchester.

Cohen, A, and B. Lewis, 1978, *Population and Revenue in the Towns of Palestine in the Sixteenth Century*, Princeton.

Collins, Ch. W., 1947, *Whiter Solid South*, New Orleans.

Collings, D. and Seldon, A. (2001) 'Conservatives in Opposition', in Norris, P., ed., *Britain Votes 2001*, Oxford.

Conniff, M., ed, 1999, *Populism in Latin America*, Tuscaloosa and London.

— 1999, 'Introduction', in M. Conniff, ed., *Populism in Latin America*, Tuscaloosa and London, pp. 1–21.

Connolly, W. E., 1995, *The Ethos of Pluralization*, Minneapolis.

Conservative Party, 1999, *Listening to Britain*, London.

— 2000, *Believing in Britain*, London.

Cooper, A., 2002, 'The Conservative Campaign', in J. Bartle, S. Atkinson, and R. Mortimore, eds., *Political Communications: The General Election Campaign of 2001*, London.

Cottrell, A., 1990, 'Cross-national Marriages: a Review of the Literature', *Journal of Comparative Family Studies*, vol. XXI, no. 2, pp. 151–65.

Cowley, P. and S. Quayle, 2002, 'The Conservatives: running on the spot' in A. Geddes, and J. Tonge, eds, *Labour's Second Landslide*, Manchester, pp. 47–64.

Crabtree, J., 2000, 'Populisms Old and New: The Peruvian Case', *Bulletin of Latin American Research*, vol. 19, no. 2, pp. 163–76.

Crewe, I.,1988, 'Has the Electorate Become Thatcherite?', in R. Skidelsky, ed., *Thatcherism*, London, pp. 25–49.

Cronin, J., 1986, 'National Democratic Struggle and the Question of Transformation', *Transformation*, 2, pp. 73–8.

Cronología 1983, CISEA-Buenos Aires.

Daly, G., 1991, 'The Discursive Construction of Economic Space', *Economy and Society*, vol. 20, no. 1, pp. 79–102.

Darby, H. C., 1966, 'Serbia', in S. Clissold, ed., *A Short History of Yugoslavia from Early Times to 1966*, Cambridge, pp. 87–134.

Davies, R., D. O'Meara and S. Dlamini, 1984, *The Struggle for South Africa: A Reference Guide to Movements, Organisations and Institutions*, London.

Davila, L. R., 2000, 'The Rise and Fall and Rise of Populism in Venezuela', *Bulletin of Latin American Research*, vol. 19, no. 2, pp. 223–38.

De Castro Gomes and A. De Castro, 1982, 'A construção do homen novo', in A. de Castro Gomes et al., *Estado Novo: ideologia e poder*, Rio de Janeiro.

De Ipola, E., 1982, *Ideología y discurso populista*, Mexico.

De la Torre, C., 2000, *Populist Seduction in Latin America: The Ecuadorian Experience*, Athens, Ohio.

De la Harpe, J., and A. Manson, 1983, 'The UDF and the Development of Resistance in South Africa', *Africa Perspective*, 23, pp. 3–45.

Deleuze, G. and F. Guattari, 1988, *A Thousand Plateaus*, London.

Derrida, J., 1974, *Of Grammatology*, G. Spivak, trans., Baltimore.

— 1982, 'Sending: On Representation', *Social Research*, vol. 49, no. 2, pp. 294–326.

— 1988, 'Signature Event Context' [1971], in *Limited Inc.*, Evanston, Illinois, pp. 1–23.

— 1990, 'Force of Law: The "Mystical Foundation of Authority"', *Cardozo Law Review*, 919 pp. 920–1045.

— 1997, *Politics of Friendship*, London.

De Vos, P., 2002, 'The sacralisation of consensus and the rise of authoritarian populism: the case of Vlaams Blok', *Studies in Social and Political Thought*, vol. 7, September.

Diamandouros, N., 1983, 'Hellenism and Greekness', in D. Tsaousis, ed., *Hellenism-Greekness*, Athens.

Diamond, L., 1994, 'Civil Society and Democratic Consolidation: Building a Culture of Democracy in South Africa', in H. Giliomee, L. Schlemmer and S. Hauptfleisch, eds, *The Bold Experiment: South Africa's New Democracy*, South Africa.

Dimitrakos, D., 2000, 'How the Umbilical Cord Between State and Church Will be Cut', *To Vima*, 4 June.

Di Tella, T.S., 1965, 'Populism and Reform in Latin America', in Claudio Véliz, ed., *Obstacles to Change in Latin America*, Oxford, pp. 47–74.

Dor, J., 1998, *Introduction to the Reading of Lacan*, New York.

Drake, P. W., 1999, 'Chile's Populism Reconsidered, 1920s–1990s', in M. Conniff, ed., *Populism in Latin America*, Tuscaloosa and London, pp. 63–74.

Dyrberg, T. B., 2001, 'Racist, nationalist and populist trends in recent Danish politics', *Research Paper* 19/01, Roskilde University, Denmark.

Elefantis, A., 1991, *In the Constellation of Populism*, Athens.

Epstein, E., 1992, *The New Argentine Democracy: The Search for a Successful Formula*, Westport.

Erickson, L. and D. Laycock, 2002, 'Post-Materialism vs. the Welfare State? Opinion among English Canadian Social Democrats,' *Party Politics*, vol. 8, no. 3, pp. 301–26.

Erskine, H., 1967–68, 'The Polls: Demonstrations and Race Riots', *Public Opinion Quarterly*, vol. 31, Winter, pp. 655–777.

Erwin, A., 1985, 'A Question of Unity in the Struggle', *South African Labour Bulletin*, vol. 11, no. 1, pp. 50–69.

Fairclough, N., 2000, *New Labour, New Language?*, London.

Fanon, F., 1963, *The Wretched of the Earth*, New York.

Ferreira, J., 1997, *Trabalhadores do Brasil: O imaginario popular*, Rio de Janeiro.

Finkelstein, N., 1988, 'Disinformation and the Palestine Question: the Not-So-Strange Case of Joan Peters's *From Time Immemorial*', in E. Said and C. Hitchens, eds, *Blaming the Victims: Spurious Scholarship and the Palestine Question*, London, pp. 33–69.

Flanagan, T., 1995, *Waiting for the Wave: The Reform Party and Preston Manning*, Toronto.

Foley, M., 2002, *The British Presidency*, Manchester.

Ford, G., 1999, quoted in Margaret Carlson, 'The Trouble with Pleasing Everyone', *Time* magazine, 21 June.

Foster, B., 2000, 'New Right, Old Canada: An Analysis of the Political Thought and Activities of Selected Contemporary Right-Wing Organisations', PhD Dissertation, Department of Political Science, University of British Columbia.

Foster, J., 1982, 'The Workers' Struggle: Where Does FOSATU Stand?', *South African Labour Bulletin*, vol. 7, no. 8, pp. 68–79.

Foucault, M., 1997, *Il faut défendre la société – Cours au Collège de France, 1976*, Paris.

Frady, M., 1968, *Wallace*, New York.

Freeden, M., 1996, *Ideologies and Political Theory: A Conceptual Approach*, Oxford.

Frenkel, R., 1996, 'Las políticas antiinflacionarias en América Latina', *Agora*, no. 5, pp. 288–301.

Freud, S., 1959, 'Inhibitions, Symptoms and Anxiety', in *An Autobiographical Study, Inhibitions, Symptoms and Anxiety, The Question of Analysis and Other Works*, vol. XX (1925–1926) of The Standard Edition of the Complete Psychological Works of Sigmund Freud, edited by James Strachey, London, pp. 77–175.

— 1963a, 'Civilization and its discontents', in The Standard Edition of the Complete Psychological Works of Sigmund Freud, J. Strachey, ed., London, pp. 57–145.

— 1963b, 'Introductory lectures on psychoanalysis', in The Standard Edition of the Complete Psychological Works of Sigmund Freud, pp. 9–476.

— 1963c, 'Mourning and Melancholia', in *General Psychological Theory*, New York.

— 1964a, 'The Dissection of the Psychical Personality', in *New Introductory Lectures on Psychoanalysis*, vol. XXII (1932–1936) of The Standard Edition of the Complete Psychological Works of Sigmund Freud, edited by James Strachey, London, pp. 57–80.

— 1964b, 'The Return of the Repressed', in *Moses and Monotheism*, vol. XXIII (1937–1939) of The Standard Edition of the Complete Psychological Works of Sigmund Freud, edited by James Strachey, London, pp. 124–6.

— 1985, *Group Psychology and the Analysis of the Ego*, New York.

Friedman, S., 1987a, 'The Struggle within the Struggle: South African Resistance Strategies', *Transformation*, 3, pp. 58–70.

— 1987b, *Building Tomorrow Today: African Workers in Trade Unions, 1970–1984*, Johannesburg.

Fryre Jacobson, M., 1999, *Whiteness of a Different Color: European Immigrants and the Alchemy of Race*, Cambridge, MA.

Garde, P., 1992, *Vie et mort de la Yougoslavie*, Paris.

Gardner, H., 1996, *Leading Minds: An anatomy of leadership*, London.

Geddes, B., 1996, 'Las políticas de liberalización económica', *Agora*, 5.

Georgiadou, V., 1995, 'Greek Orthodoxy and the Politics of Nationalism', *International Journal of Politics, Culture and Society*, vol. 9, no. 2, pp. 295–316.

Georgiadou, V. and I. Nikolakopoulos, 2000, 'The People of the Church', in C. Vernardakis, ed., *V-PRC Institute: Public Opinion in Greece, Research and Surveys, 2001*, Athens.

Germani, G., 1969, *Política y sociedad en una época de transición*, Buenos Aires.

Gidengil, E., A. Blais, N. Nevitte and R. Nadeau, 2001, 'The Correlates and Consequences of Anti-Partysm in the 1997 Canadian Election', *Party Politics*, vol. 7, no. 4, A13.

Gilbert, J., 2000, 'Towards a Democratic Populism', http://www.signsoft-hetimes.org.uk/dp1.html.

Gitlin, T., 1995, *The Twilight of Common Dreams: Why America is Wracked by the Culture Wars*, New York.

Glaser, D., 2001, *Politics and Society in South Africa: A Critical Introduction*, London.

Glynos, J. 2000, 'Sexual identity, identification and difference', *Philosophy and Social Criticism*, vol. 26, no. 6, pp. 85–108.

Godina, V., 1998, 'The Outbreak of Nationalism on Former Yugoslav Territories: An Historical Perspective on the Problem of Supra-National Identities', *Nations and Nationalisms*, vol. IV, no. 3, pp. 409–22.

Gordy, E., 1999, *The Culture of Power in Serbia: Nationalism and the Destruction of Alternatives*, University Park, Pennsylvania.

Government of Palestine, 1946, *A Survey of Palestine*, vol. I, London.

Gregg, Ch. W., 1960, 'Fundamental Principles of Democracy', *Journal of Politics*, vol. 22, Spring, pp. 276–94.

Gresh, A., 1985, *The PLO: The Struggle Within for an Independent Palestinian State*, London.

Groppo, A., 2001, 'Representation and Subjectivity in Populist Identification: Some Remarks from a Discourse Analysis Perspective', *Paper submitted to the Conference of the European Consortium for Political Research*, 6–8 September, Kent University, Canterbury, UK.

Guerra, F.-X., 1992, *Modernidad e Independencias*, Bilbao.

Hague, W., 1998, *Speaking with Conviction*, London.

— 1999, 'Change and renewal are always difficult', *Guardian*, 28 April.

Haider, J., 1995, *The Freedom I Mean*, Pine Plains.

Hall, S., 1988, *The Hard Road to Renewal*, London.

Hammel, E. A., 1993a, 'The Yugoslav Labyrinth', *The Anthropology of East Europe Review*, vol. XI, nos 1–2, pp. 35–42.

— 1993b, 'Demography and the Origins of the Yugoslav Civil War', *Anthropology Today*, vol. IX, no. 1, pp. 4–9.

Hattan, V., 2001, *Ethnic Shadows: The Racial Politics of American Pluralism*, manuscript.

Hawkins, K., 2003, 'Populism in Venezuela: The Rise of Chavismo', *Third World Quarterly*, vol. 24, no. 6, pp. 1137–60.

Hayward, J., 1996, 'The Populist Challenge to Elitist Democracy in Europe', in J. Hayward, ed., *Elitism, Populism, and European Politics*, Oxford, pp. 10–32.

Hilal, J., 1992, 'West Bank and Gaza Strip Social Formation under Jordanian and Egyptian Rule (1948–1967)', in G. Bowman, ed., *Israel/Palestine: Fields for Identity (Review of Middle East Studies*, vol. V), London, pp. 33–73.

Himmelstein, J., 1992, *To the Right: The Transformation of American Conservatism*, Berkeley.

Holy Synod of the Church of Greece, 2000, *The Church and Identity Cards*, Athens.

Hourani, A., 1991, *A History of the Arab Peoples*, London.

Howarth, D., A. Norval and Y. Stavrakakis, eds, 2000, *Discourse Theory and Political Analysis*, Manchester and New York.

Howarth, D., 2000a, *Discourse*, Buckingham.

— 2000b, 'The Difficult Emergence of a Democratic Imaginary: Black Consciousness and Non-Racial Democracy in South Africa', in D. Howarth, A. Norval and Y. Stavrakakis, eds, *Discourse Theory and Political Analysis*.

Howarth, D., and A. Norval, 1990, 'Strategy and Subjectivity in South African Resistance Politics: Prospects for a New Imaginary', *Essex Papers in Politics and Government*, no. 85.

Innes, D., 1986, 'Unity and the Freedom Charter: Worker Politics and Popular Movement', *Work in Progress*, 41, pp. 11–16.

— 1987, 'The Case for a Worker's Programme', *Work in Progress*, 50, pp. 23–32.

Ionescu, Ghita G., and E. Gellner, eds, 1969, *Populism: Its Meaning and National Characteristics*, London.

Jenner, W. J. F., 2001, 'Race and History in China', *New Left Review*, no. 11, pp. 55–77.

Johnson, N., 1982, *Islam and the Politics of Meaning in Palestinian Nationalism*, London.

Jones, B., 1996, *The Wallace Story*, Northport, Al.

Journal of Latin American Studies, vol. 30, no. 2, 1998.

Judd, D. R., 1999, 'Symbolic Politics and Urban Politics: Why African Americans Got So Little from the Democrats', in A. Reed, ed., *Without Justice for All: The New Liberalism and Our Retreat from Racial Equality*, Boulder.

Kalkas, B., 1971, 'The Revolt of 1936: a Chronicle of Events', in I. Abu-Lughod, ed., *The Transformation of Palestine: Essays on the Origin and Development of the Arab-Israeli Conflict*, Evanston, pp. 237–74.

Kapferer, B., 1988, *Legends of People/Myths of State: Violence, Intolerance, and Political Culture in Sri Lanka and Australia*, Washington, D.C.

Karayannis, G., 1997, *Church and State, 1833–1997*, Athens.

Karon, T., and M. Ozinsky, 1986, 'The Working Class in National Democratic Struggle', *Work in Progress*, 42, pp. 31–6.

Kazin, M., 1995, *The Populist Persuasion: An American History*, New York and London.

Kelsen, H., 1981, *Vom Wessen und Wert der Demokratie* [1929], Aalen.

Kitromilides, P., 1989, '"Imagined Communities" and the Origins of the National Question in the Balkans', *European History Quarterly*, vol. 19, no. 2, pp. 149–92.

Kitschelt, H., 1996, *The Radical Right in Western Europe*, Ann Arbor.

Knight, A., 1998, 'Populism and Neo-populism in Latin America, Especially Mexico', *Journal of Latin American Studies*, vol. 30, no. 2, pp. 223–48.

Kopeinig, M. and Ch. Kotanko, 2000, *Eine Europäische Affäire: Der Weisen-Bericht und die Sanktionen gegen Osterreich*, 2000.

Kriesi, H., 1999, 'Movements of the Left, Movements of the Right: Putting the Mobilisation of Two New Types of Social Movements into Political Context', in H. Kitschelt, P. Lange, G. Marks and J. D. Stephens, eds, *Continuity and Change in Contemporary Capitalism*, New York, pp. 398–423.

Laclau, E., 1977, *Politics and Ideology in Marxist Theory*, London.

— 1997, 'Towards a Theory of Populism', in E. Laclau, *Politics and Ideology in Marxist Theory*, London.

— 1980, 'Populist Rupture and Discourse', in *Screen Education*, no. 34, pp. 87–93.

— 1990, *New Reflections on the Revolution of Our Time*, London.

— 1990, 'Post-marxism without apologies', in E. Laclau, *New Reflections on the Revolution of our Time*, London, pp. 97–132.

— 1994b, 'Why do Empty Signifiers Matter to Politics?', in J. Weeks, ed., *The Lesser Evil and the Greater Good*, London, pp. 167–78.

— 2000, 'Identity and Hegemony', in J. Butler, E. Laclau, and S. Žižek, *Contingency, Hegemony, Universality*, London, pp. 44–89.

Laclau, E., and C. Mouffe, 1985, *Hegemony and Socialist Strategy: Towards a Radical Democratic Politics*, London.

Laclau, E. and L. Zac, (1994) 'Minding the Gap: the subject of politics' in E. Laclau, ed., *The Making of Political Identities*, London, pp. 11–39.

Lancaster, R., 1988, *Thanks to God and the Revolution*, New York.

Lapidus, I., 1988, *A History of Islamic Societies*, Cambridge.

Laplanche, J. and J.-B. Pontalis, 1973, *The Language of Pyschoanalysis*, London.

Larmore, Ch., 1990, 'Political Liberalism', *Political Theory*, vol. 18, no. 3, August.

Lasch, C., 1995, *The Revolt of the Elites and the Betrayal of Democracy*, London and New York.

Lawrence, R., 1984, 'An Analysis of the 1984 Elections', *Paper Presented to Southern African Studies Seminar*, University of Natal, Pietermaritzburg.

Laycock, D., 1990, *Populism and Democratic Thought in the Canadian Prairies 1910–45*, Toronto.

Laycock, D., 2001, *The New Right and Democracy in Canada: Understanding Reform and the Canadian Alliance*, Toronto.

Lefort, C., 1986, *The Political Forms of Modern Society: Bureaucracy, Democracy, Totalitarianism*, London.

— 1988, *Democracy and Political Theory*, Cambridge.

— 1991, 'Démocratie et représentation', in D. Pecaut and B. Sorj, eds, *Metamorphoses de la représentation politique*, Paris, pp. 223–232.

— 1992, 'La representación no agota a la democracia', in F. Calderón and M. R. dos Santos, eds., *¿Qué queda de la representación política?*, Caracas, pp. 139–45.

Lesch, A. M., 1979, *Arab Politics in Palestine, 1917–1939: The Frustration of a Nationalist Movement*, Ithaca.

Lesher, S., 1994, *George Wallace: American Populist*, Reading, MA.

Levin, R. M., 1987, 'Class Struggle, Popular Democratic Struggle and the South African State', *Review of African Political Economy*, 40, pp. 7–31.

Lewis, D., 2002, 'Fantasy and Identity – the case of New Age Travellers', paper prepared for the conference *Identification and Politics Workshop II*, May 23–24, The University of Essex, Colchester, UK.

Liakos, A., 1989, 'On Populism', in *Ta Istorika*, vol. 6, no. 10, pp. 13–28.

Lichtenstein, N., 1955, *The Most Dangerous Man in Detroit: Walter Reuther and the Fate of American Labor*, New York.

Lilley, P., 1999, 'The free market has only a limited role in improving public services', *Guardian*, 20 April.

Lipset, S. M., 1963, *Political Man*, New York.

— 1964, 'Beyond the Backlash', *Encounter*, vol. 23, November, pp. 11–24.

Lipsitz, G., 1998, *The Possessive Investment in Whiteness*, Berkeley.

Litchmajer, J. P., 2002, 'Taming the Dessert: Nation and Heterogeneity in Nineteenth-century Argentina', paper prepared for the *Identification and Politics Workshop II*, May 23–24, The University of Essex, Colchester, UK.

Lodge, T., 1991, 'Rebellion: The Turning of the Tide', in T. Lodge and B. Nasson, eds, *All, Here and Now! Black Politics in South Africa in the 1980s*, London, pp. 23–204.

Löwy, M., 1996, *The War of Gods: Religion and Politics in Latin America*, London.

Lustick, I., 1980, *Arabs in the Jewish State: Israel's Control of a National Minority*, Austin, Texas.

Luther, K. R., 1997, 'Die Freiheitlichen (F)', in H. Dachs et al, eds, *Handbuch des Politischen Systems in Österreich: Die Zweite Republik*, Wien.

Luxemburg, R., 1991, *The Mass Strike, The Political Parties and the Trade Unions*, New York.

Lyrintzis, C., 1987, 'The Power of Populism: The Greek Case', in *European Journal of Political Research*, no. 15, pp. 667–86.

—— 1990, 'Populism: The Concept and the Practices', in C. Lyrintzis and E. Nikolakopoulos, eds, *Elections and Parties in the '80s*, Athens.

Lyrintzis, C., and M. Spourdalakis, 1993, 'On Populism: A Synthesis *à propos* of the Greek Bibliography', in *Greek Political Science Review*, no. 1, pp. 133–62.

McGee, M., 1999, 'In search of "the people"' in J. Lucaites, C. Condit, and S. Caudill, eds., *Contemporary Rhetorical Theory: A Reader*, New York, pp. 341–56.

Machiavelli, N., 1981, *The Prince*, trans. G. Bull, New York.

—— 1970, *Discourses*, trans. P. Bondanella and M. Mussa, New York.

Mackinnon, M., and M. Petrone, eds, 1998, *Populismo y Neopopulismo en América Latina: El problema de la Cenicienta*, Buenos Aires.

McLean, H., 1986, 'Socialism and the Freedom Charter', *South African Labour Bulletin*, vol. 11, no. 6, pp. 8–20.

Macpherson, C. B., 1954, *Democracy in Alberta*, Toronto.

—— 1965, *The Real World of Democracy*, The Massey Lectures, Toronto.

—— 1977, *The Life and Times of Liberal Democracy*, Oxford.

MacRae, D., 1969, 'Populism as an Ideology', in G. Ionescu and E. Gellner, *Populism: Its Meanings and National Characteristics*, London.

MacShane, D., M. Plaut and D. Ward, 1984, *Power! Black Workers and the Struggle for Freedom in South Africa*, Nottingham.

Makrides, V., 1991, 'Orthodoxy as a Conditio sine qua non: Religion and State/Politics in Modern Greece from a Socio-Historical Perspective', *Oskirchliche Studien*, vol. 40, no. 4.

Mango, C., 1994, *Byzantium: The Empire of New Rome*, London.

Manin, B., 1997, *The Principles of Representative Government*, Cambridge.

Manning E. and P., 1967, *Political Re-Alignment: A Challenge to Thoughtful Canadians*, Toronto.

Manning P., 1990, *The New Canada*, Toronto.

Manitakis, A., 2000, *Relations Between the Church and the Nation-State: In the Shadow of Identity Cards*, Athens.

Marais, H., 1998, *South Africa: Limits to Change*, London.

Maré, G., and G. Hamilton, 1987, *An Appetite for Power: Buthelezi's Inkatha and the Politics of 'Loyal Resistance'*, Johannesburg.

Marquand, D., 1998, 'The Blair Paradox', *Prospect*, May 1998, pp. 19–24.

— 1999, 'Populism or Pluralism? New Labour and the Constitution', *Mishcon Lecture*, The Constitution Unit, School of Public Policy, University College London.

Martin, D., 1969, *The Religious and the Secular*, London.

— 1978, *A General Theory of Secularization*, Oxford.

Martínez de Hoz, J.A., 1981, *Bases para una Argentina Moderna*, Buenos Aires.

Marx, A., 1992, *Lessons of Struggle: South African Internal Opposition, 1960–1990*, Oxford.

Marx, C., 1994, 'The "Ossewabrandwag" as a Mass Movement, 1939–1941', *Journal of Southern African Studies*, vol. 20, no. 2, pp. 195–219.

Massey, D. S., and N. Denton, 1993, *American Apartheid: Segregation and the Making of the Underclass*, Cambridge.

Massow, I., 2000, 'The Tory party has become nasty and intolerant', *The Independent*, 2 August.

Mastnak, T., 1991, 'From the New Social Movements to Political Parties', in J. Simmie and J. Dekleva, eds, *Yugoslavia in Turmoil: After Self-management?*, London, pp. 45–64.

Matiwane, M., and S. Walters, 1986, *The Struggle for Democracy: A Study of Community Organisations in Greater Cape Town from the 1960s to 1985*, Cape Town.

Mayorga, F., 2000, *Neopopulismo y democracia en Bolivia: Compadres y padrinos en la política (1988–1999)*, PhD Thesis, Mexico City: FLACSO.

Meier, V., 1999, *Yugoslavia: A History of Its Demise*, S. Ramet, trans., London.

Mencinger, J., 1991, 'From a Capitalist to a Capitalist Economy?', in J. Simmie and J. Dekleve, eds, *Yugoslavia in Turmoil: After Self-management?*, London, pp. 71–86.

Menem, C. and Eduardo Duhalde, 1989, *La Revolución Productiva*, Buenos Aires.

Menem, C., 1988, 'Carta abierta a la esperanza', *Clarín*, 24 March.

Metallinos, G., 2000, *Church and Polity in the Orthodox Tradition*, Athens.

Miller, C., 1968, *The Day*, New London, CT, June 29.

Mitten, R., 1994, 'Jörg Haider, the Anti-immigrant Petition and Immigration Policy in Austria', in *Patterns of Prejudice*, vol. 28, no. 2.

Morass, M and H. Reischenböck, 1987, 'Parteien und Populismus in Osterreich' in A. Pelinka, ed., *Populismus in Osterreich*, Vienna.

Mora y Araujo, M., 1995, 'De Perón a Menem: Una historia del peronismo', in Atilio Borón et al., *Peronismo y menemismo: Avatares del populismo en la Argentina*, Buenos Aires, pp. 47–66.

Morris, B., 1987, *The Birth of the Palestinian Refugee Problem 1947–1949*, Cambridge.

— 1985, 'On the Concept of Populism: Populist and Clientelist Modes of Incorporation in Semiperipheral Politics', *Politics and Society*, vol. 14, no. 3, pp. 329–47.

— 1989, 'Populism: A new Mode of Incorporation of the Masses into Political Processes?', in N. Mouzelis, T. Lipowatz and M. Spourdalakis, *Populism and Politics*, Athens.

Morrison, T., 1990, *Playing in the Dark: Whiteness and the Literary Imagination*, New York.

Mouffe, Ch., 1993, *The Return of the Political*, London.

— 2000, *The Democratic Paradox*, London.

Mulhall, S., 1996, *Heidegger and Being and Time*, London.

Murray, M., 1987, *South Africa: Time of Agony, Time of Destiny*, London.

Muslih, M., 1988, *The Origins of Palestinian Nationalism*, New York.

Myrdal, G., 1966, *An American Dilemma, Volume I: The Negro Problem and Modern Democracy*, New Brunswick.

National Education Crisis Committee, 1986, *Report on National Consultative Conference on the Crisis in Education, Soweto Parents Crisis Committee*, University of Witwatersrand.

Newspapers, 2000–2001, *Eleftherotypia, Ethnos, Kathimerini, To Vima*.

Newsweek, 1968, 'Third Parties: Collision Course', 18 March, p. 48.

New York Times, 1968, 'A Voter's Lexicon of "Wallacisms"', 25 August.

— 1976, 'Wallace Defeats Carter Three-To-One in Mississippi Test', 21 January.

Nietzsche, F., 1967, *The Genealogy of Morals*, trans. W. Kaufman, New York.

Norris, H., 1993, *Islam in the Balkans: Religion and Society between Europe and the Arab World*, London.

Norton, A., 1993, *Reflections on Political Identity*, Baltimore.

Norton, P., 2001, 'The Conservative Party: Is There Anyone Out There?', in A. King, ed., *Britain at the Polls*, New York, pp. 68–94.

Norval, A. J., 1999, 'Truth and Reconciliation: the Birth of the Present and the Reworking of History', *Journal of Southern African Studies*, vol. 25, no. 3, pp. 499–519.

Novaro, M., 1994, *Pilotos de Tormentas: Crisis de representación y personalización de la política en Argentina (1989–1993)*, Buenos Aires.

Nun, J., 1995, 'Populismo, representación y menemismo', in Borón et al., *Peronismo y menemismo*, Buenos Aires, pp. 67–100.

Oakeshott, M., 1996, *The Politics of Faith and the Politics of Scepticism*, edited and introduced by T. Fuller, New Haven and London.

Palermo, V., and M. Novaro, 1996, *Política y poder en el gobierno de Menem*, Buenos Aires.

Panizza, F., 1990, *Uruguay: Batllismo y después*, Montevideo.

— 2000, 'Neopopulism and its Limits in Collor's Brazil', *Bulletin of Latin American Research*, vol. 19, no. 2, pp. 177–92.

Pantazopoulos, A., 2001, *'For the People and the Nation': The Moment Andreas Papandreou*, Athens.

Pappas, T., 2001, *Orthodox Caesaropapism*, Athens.

Patten, S., 1996, 'Preston Manning's Populism: Constructing the Common Sense of the Common People', *Studies in Political Economy*, vol. 50, 1996, pp. 95–132.

Pavlowitch, S., 1988, *The Improbable Survivor: Yugoslavia and its Problems, 1918–1988*, London.

Pelinka, A., 1993, *Die Kleine Koalition*, Vienna.

Peters, J., 1984, *From Time Immemorial: The Origins of the Arab–Jewish Conflict Over Palestine*, New York.

Philip, G., 1998, 'The New Populism, Presidentialism and Market-Oriented Reform in Spanish South America', *Government and Opposition*, vol. 33, no. 1, pp. 81–97.

Phillips, K., 1969, *The Emerging Republican Majority*, New Rochelle.

Pike, F., 1986, *The Politics of the Miraculous in Peru: Haya de la Torre and the Spiritualist Tradition*, Lincoln and London.

Pinakoulas, A., 2001, 'Church and Hellenism in Modern Greece', *Synaxi*, no. 79, *Church and Nation: Bonds and Bondages*, pp. 36–50.

Pitkin, H. F., 1967, *The Concept of Representation*, Berkeley and Los Angeles.

Pollis, A., 1999, 'Greece a Problematic Secular State', in D. Christopoulos, ed., *Legal Issues of Religious Heterodoxy in Greece*, Athens.

Porath, Y., 1974, *The Emergence of the Palestinian–Arab National Movement 1918–1929*, London.

Portantiero, J. C., 1995, 'Menemismo y peronismo: continuidad y ruptura', in Borón et al., *Peronismo y menemismo*, Buenos Aires, pp. 101–18.

Poulton, H., 1991, *The Balkans: Minorities and States in Conflict*, London.

Price, R. M., 1991, *The Apartheid State in Crisis: Political Transformation in South Africa, 1975–1990*, London.

Quadagno, J., 1994, *The Color of Welfare: How Racism Undermined the War on Poverty*, New York.

Rafel, R., 1990, '"Workers" Charter: Taking it to the streets', *Work in Progress*, 69, pp. 27–30.

RDP, 1994, 'White Paper on Reconstruction and Development', *Republic of South Africa Government Gazette*, Cape Town.

Ramet, S., 1992, *Nationalism and Federalism in Yugoslavia 1962–1991*, second edition, Bloomington, Indiana.

Rancière, J., 1998, *Disagreement: Politics and Philosophy*, Minneapolis.

— 2003, 'The Thinking of Dissensus: Politics and Aesthetics', paper presented at the conference *Fidelity to the Disagreement: Jacques Rancière and the Political*, Goldsmiths College, London, 16–17 September.

Reinfeldt, S., 2000, *Nitcht-wir und Die-da: Studiem zum Rechten Populismus*, Wien.

Reyes, O., 2002, 'Leaders' personalities and identification', paper prepared for the *Identification and Politics Workshop II*, The University of Essex, Colchester, UK.

Rivera, M and M. Cuéllar, 2000, 'Las rezones del cambio', in *La Jornada*, Mexico City, 9 October.

Roberts, K., 1995, 'Neoliberalism and the Transformation of Populism in Latin America: The Peruvian Case', *World Politics*, October.

— 1996, 'Neoliberalism and the Transformation of Populism in Latin America: The Peruvian Case', *World Politics* 48 (1), pp. 82–116.

Rochabrún, G., 1996, 'Deciphering the Enigmas of Alberto Fujimori', *NACLA Report on the Americas*, vol. XXX, no. 1, July/August.

Roediger, D. R., 1991, *The Wages of Whiteness: Race and the Making of the American Working Class*, New York.

Rogin, M., 1966, 'Wallace and the Middle Class: The White Backlash in Wisconsin', *Public Opinion Quarterly*, vol. 30, Spring, pp. 98–108.

Ruedy, J., 1971, 'Dynamics of Land Alienation', in I. Abu-Lughod, ed., *The Transformation of Palestine: Essays on the Origin and Development of the Arab-Israeli Conflict*, Evanston.

Runciman, S., 1968, *The Great Church in Captivity*, Cambridge.

Said, E., 1993, 'The morning after', *The London Review of Books*, vol. XV, nos. 20, 21 October, pp. 3–5.

Salecl, R., 1993, 'Nationalism, Anti-semitism and Anti-feminism in Eastern Europe', *Antagonism and Identity in Former Yugoslavia (Journal of Area Studies* 3), G. Bowman, ed., pp. 78–90.

Saul, J., and S. Gelb, 1986, *The Crisis in South Africa*, London.

Sawer, M. and B. Hindess, 2004, eds, *Us and Them: Anti-Elitism in Australia*, Perth.

Sayigh, R., 1979, *The Palestinians: From Peasants to Revolutionaries*, London.

Schmitt, C., 1996, *The Concept of the Political* [1932], translation and introduction by G. Schwab, foreword by T. Strong, Chicago.

Scholch, A., 1989, 'Jerusalem in the Nineteenth Century (1831–1917 AD)', in K. J. Asali, ed., *Jerusalem in History*, London, pp. 228–48.

Schvarzer, J., 1986, 'Crisis económica argentina: la carencia de modelos para enfrentarla exige una firme determinación política', *El Bimestre*, no. 13, pp. 1–2.

Seekings, J., 2000, *The UDF: A History of the United Democratic Front in South Africa 1983–1991*, James Currey.

Shils, E., 1956, *The Torment of Secrecy: The Background and Consequences of American Security Policies*, London.

Shoup, P., 1992, 'Titoism and the National Question in Yugoslavia: a Reassessment', in M. van den Heuvel and J. Siccama, eds, *The Disintegration of Yugoslavia*, Amsterdam, pp. 47–72.

Shulman, G., 2002, 'The Pathos of Identification and Politics', paper prepared for the *Identification and Politics Workshop II*, The University of Essex, Colchester, UK.

Sidicaro, R., 1995, 'Poder político, liberalismo económico y sectores populares en la Argentina 1989–1995', in A. Borón et al., *Peronismo y menemismo*, Buenos Aires.

Sigal, S. and E. Verón, 1988, *Perón o muerte: Los fundamentos discursivos del fenómeno peronista*, Buenos Aires.

Silver, I., and A. Sfarnas, 1983, 'The UDF: A "Workerist" Response', *South African Labour Bulletin*, vol. 8, nos. 8/9, pp. 96–110.

Simmie, J., 1991, 'Self-management in Yugoslavia', in J. Simmie and J. Dekleve, eds, *Yugoslavia in Turmoil: After Self-Management*, London, pp. 3–9.

Sisulu, Z., 1986, 'People's Education for People's Power', *Transformation*, 1, pp. 96–117.

Slipper, J., 1990, *The Closest of Strangers*, New York.

Slotkin, R., 1973, *Regeneration Through Violence: The Mythology of the American Frontier, 1600–1860*, Middletown.

— 1992, *Gunfighter Nation*, New York.

Smith, A.-M., 1994, *New Right Discourses on Race and Sexuality*, Cambridge.

Smith, G. H., 1948, 'Liberalism and Level of Information', *Journal of Education of Psychology*, vol. 39, pp. 65–82.

Smith, W., 1992, 'Hyperinflation, Macroeconomic Instability, and Neoliberal Restructuring in Democratic Argentina', in Edward Epstein, ed., *The New Argentine Democracy: The Search for a Successful Formula*, Westport, pp. 20–60.

Sofos, S., 1994, 'Popular Identity and Political Culture in Post-dictatorial Greece: Towards a Cultural Approach of the Phenomenon of Populism', in N. Demertzis, ed., *Greek Political Culture Today*, Athens.

Sosa Buchholz, X., 1999, 'The Strange Career of Populism in Ecuador', in M. Conniff, ed., *Populism in Latin America*, Tuscaloosa and London.

Sotirelis, G., 2001, 'Winners and Losers', *Ta Nea*, 4 September.

Sourrouille, J., 1989, *Mensajes del Ministro de Economía Dr Juan V. Sourrouille*, Buenos Aires.

Stallybras, P., 1990, 'Marx and Heterogeneity: Thinking the Lumpenproletariat', *Representations*, vol. 31, Summer, pp. 69–95.

Staten, H., 1985, *Wittgenstein and Derrida*, Oxford.

Stavrakakis, Y., 1999, 'Lacan and History', *Journal for the Psychoanalysis of Culture and Society*, vol. 4, no. 1, pp. 99–118.

Stavrakakis, Y., 1999, *Lacan and the Political*, London.

— 2002, 'Religion and Populism: Reflections on the 'Politicised' Discourse of the Greek Church', *Discussion Paper* no. 7, The Hellenic Observatory, The European Institute, The London School of Economics and Political Science, London.

Stein, S., 1999, 'The Path to Populism in Peru', in M. Conniff, ed., *Populism in Latin America*, Tuscaloosa and London.

Sutcliffe, M., 1986, 'The Crisis in South Africa: Material Conditions and the Reformist Response', paper presented to The Southern African Economy after Apartheid Conference, York University.

Suttner, R., and J. Cronin, 1986, *30 Years of the Freedom Charter*, Johannesburg.

Szusterman, C., 2000, 'Carlos Saúl Menem: Variations on the Theme of Populism', *Bulletin of Latin American Research*, vol. 19, 2, pp. 193–206.

Taggart, P., 2000, *Populism*, Buckingham.

Taguieff, P-A., 1995, 'Political science confronts populism', *Telos* 103, pp. 9–43.

Tamari, S., 1982, 'Factionalism and Class Formation in Recent Palestinian History', in R. Owen, ed., *Studies in the Economic and Social History of Palestine in the Nineteenth and Twentieth Centuries*, London, pp. 177–202.

Taussig, M., 1987, *Shamanism, Colonialism, and the Wild Man: A Study in Terror and Healing*, Chicago.

Theoklitos, Bishop of Ioannina, 2001, Interview to Thomas Tsatsis, *Eleftherotypia*, 2 May.

Thermos, V., 1993, 'When Will the Quotation Marks be Lifted?', *Synaxi*, no. 48, *People, Nation, Church*, pp. 43–5.

Thomas, R., 1999, *Serbia Under Milošević: Politics in the 1990s*, London.

Touraine, A., 1992, 'Comunicación política y crisis de la representatividad', in J.-M. Ferry et al., *El nuevo espacio público*, Barcelona, pp. 47–56.

Transvaal Anti-SAIC Committee, 1983, Congress 1983, *Speeches and Papers Delivered at the Congress*, Johannesburg.

Tsatsos, D., 2000, 'From the Church to the Agora', *Ta Nea*, 26 June.

Tumulty, K., 2003, 'Five Meanings of Arnold', *Time* magazine, 20 October, pp. 37–9.

Turner, V., 1969, *The Ritual Process: Structure and Anti-structure*, Chicago.

UDF, 1983, 'UDF Working Principles: United Democratic Front Launch Document', William Curren Library Collection, University of Witwatersrand, 20 August.

— 1985, 'National General Council Report', *Colin Putney Papers*, William Cullen Library, University of Witwatersrand.

Unamuno, M., 1984, 'El Perón de la lucha, no el de la leyenda', in Unamuno, *El peronismo de la derrota*, Buenos Aires.

Usher, G., 1995, *Palestine in Crisis: the Struggle for Peace and Political Independence after Oslo*, London.

Van den Heuvel, M., and J. G. Siccama, eds., 1992, *The Disintegration of Yugoslavia*, Amsterdam.

Van Kessel, I., 2000, *'Beyond our Wildest Dreams': The United Democratic Front and the Transformation of South Africa*, Charlottesville and London.

Vega Centeno, I., 1986, *Aprismo Popular: mito, cultura e historia*, Lima.

Verón, E., et al., 1987, *El discurso político: Lenguajes y acontecimientos*, Buenos Aires.

Waines, D., 1971, 'The Failure of the Nationalist Resistance', in I. Abu-Lughod, ed., *The Transformation of Palestine: Essays on the Origin and Development of the Arab-Israeli Conflict*, Evanston, Illinois, pp. 207–35.

Walters, S., 2001, *Tory Wars: Conservatives in Crisis*, London.

Weber, M, 1949, *The Methodology of the Social Sciences*, New York.

Weffort, F., 1998, 'El populismo en la política brasilena', in M. M. Mackinnon and M. A. Petrone, eds, *Populismo y Neopopulismo en América Latina: El problema de la cenicienta*, Buenos Aires, pp. 135–52.

Westlind, D., 1996, *The Politics of Popular Identity*, Lund.

Weyland, K., 1996, 'Neopopulism and Neoliberalism in Latin America:

Unexpected Affinities', *Studies in Comparative International Development*, vol. 31, no. 3, pp. 3–31.

— 2003, 'Neopopulism and Neoliberalism in Latin America: How Much Affinity?', *Third World Quarterly*, vol. 24, no. 6, pp. 1095–115.

Widdecombe, A., 1999, 'The Role of the State in the Promotion of Private Morality', *The Salisbury Review*, vol. 18, no. 1, pp. 10–11.

Wiles, P., 1969, 'A Syndrome, not a Doctrine: Some Elementary Theses on Populism', in G. Ionescu and E. Gellner, eds., *Populism: Its Meanings and National Characteristics*, London, pp. 166–79.

Witcover, J., 1997, *The Year the Dream Died: Revisiting 1968 in America*, New York.

Wodak, R. and A. Pelinka, 2002, eds, *The Haider Phenomenon in Austria*, New Brunswick and London.

— 1976, *Marathon: The Pursuit of the Presidency 1972–1976*, New York.

Worsley, P., 1969, 'The Concept of Populism', in G. Ionescu and E. Gellner, eds., *Populism: Its Meanings and National Characteristics*, London, pp. 212–21.

Young, L., 1999, 'Value Clash: Parliament and Citizens after 150 Years of Responsible Government,' in F. L. Seidle and L. Massicotte, eds, *Taking Stock of 150 Years of Responsible Government in Canada*, Ottawa.

Zakythinos, D., 1976, *The Making of Modern Greece*, Oxford.

Žižek, S., 1989, *The Sublime Object of Ideology*, London.

— 1991, *For They Know Not What They Do*, London.

— 1990, 'Eastern Europe's Republics of Gilead', *New Left Review*, p. 183. Sept, pp. 50–62.

— 1999, *The Ticklish Subject*, New York.

Zöching, Ch., 1999, *Haider-Licht und Schatten einer Karriere*, Wien.

LIST OF CONTRIBUTORS

Benjamin Arditi teaches Political Theory at the National University of Mexico (UNAM). He is co-editor of *Taking on the Political*, a book series on Continental thought published by Edinburgh University Press. Recent publications include *Polemicization: The Contingency of the Commonplace* (1999, with J. Valentine), the edited volumes *Fidelity to the Disagreement: Jacques Rancière and Politics* (2005) and *Democracia Post-Liberal?* (2005), and articles in *Parallax*, *Contemporary Political Theory*, *Political Studies*, *New Political Science* and *Contemporary Politics*.

Sebastián Barros is Professor in the School of Law and the Faculty of Humanities and Social Sciences at the Universidad Nacional de la Patagonia San Juan Bosco, Argentina. He is currently working on the constitution of political identities at a local level, and has published several articles on Argentine politics, as well as the book *Orden, democracia y estabilidad. Discurso y política en la Argentina* (2002).

Glenn Bowman teaches in the anthropology department of the University of Kent (Canterbury, U.K.) where he convenes the MA programme in the Anthropology of Ethnicity, Nationalism, and Identity. He is Honorary Editor of the *Journal of the Royal Anthropological Institute* (formerly Man) and is on the editorial board of *Critique of Anthropology*.

David Howarth is a Lecturer in Political Theory in the Department of Government at the University of Essex, where he is currently Director of the Doctoral Programme in Ideology and Discourse Analysis. He has recently published a book entitled *Discourse* (2000) and has co-edited books entitled *South Africa in Transition* (1998), *Discourse Theory and Political Analysis* (2000) and *Discourse Theory in European Politics* (2005). He has published numerous articles and chapters on theories on discourse, post-Marxist political theory and its application to empirical cases, most notably South African politics and new environmental movements.

Ernesto Laclau is Professor of Political Theory in the Department of Government, University of Essex, and in the Department of Comparative Literature, State University of New York at Buffalo. He has lectured in many universities of Western Europe, North America and Latin America and was the founder and Director of the Doctoral Programme in Ideology and Discourse Analysis and The Centre for Theoretical Studies, both at the University of Essex. He is the author, among other works, of *Hegemony and Socialist Strategy* (with Chantal Mouffe), *New Reflections on the Revolution of Our Time*, *Emancipation(s)*, and *Contingency, Hegemony and Universality* (co-authored with Judith Butler and Slavoj Žižek).

David Laycock is Professor, Political Science at Simon Fraser University, Burnaby BC, Canada. He is the Author of *Populism and Democratic Thought in the Canadian Prairies* (1990) and *The New Right and Democracy in Canada* (2001); editor of *Representation and Democratic Theory* (2004); and co-editor of *Studies in Comparative Political Economy and Public Policy*, a research monograph series published by the University of Toronto Press.

Joseph Lowndes is an Assistant Professor of Political Science at the University of Oregon. He is currently completing a book on race and conservatism in the United States.

Chantal Mouffe is Professor of Political Theory at the Centre for the Study of Democracy, University of Westminster. She is the author of, among other works, *Hegemony and Socialist Strategy: Towards a Radical Democratic Politics* (with Ernesto Laclau), *The Return of the Political* and *The Democratic Paradox*. Her most recent book is *On the Political* (2005).

Oscar Reyes is currently completing his PhD in the Department of Government at the University of Essex. He has published articles and chapters on different aspects of British politics.

Yannis Stavrakakis is Visiting Research Fellow at the Department of Government, University of Essex. He is the author of *Lacan and the Political* (1999), and co-editor of *Discourse Theory and Political Analysis* (2000) and *Lacan and Science* (2002).

INDEX

Made in the USA
Monee, IL
27 August 2020